The
NYSTROM
DESK
ATLAS

NYSTROM
DIVISION OF HERFF JONES, INC.

CREDITS

Executive Editor	Charles Novosad
Project Design and Direction	Matthew V. Kania
Project Editor	Joan Pederson
Cartographic Manager	Christine D. Bosacki
Design/Production Manager	Ruth P. Koval
Nystrom Computer Cartography and Graphics	Bonnie Jones, Charlaine Wilkerson
Additional Computer Cartography	Maryland CartoGraphics, Inc.
Additional Nystrom Cartography	Louise Feeney, James Franklin, Phyllis Kawano, Gerald Keefe, Michael Nauert
Map Compilation	Valerie Krejcie, John Chalk, Sharon Knight
Writer	Emily B. Good
Statistical Research	Jennifer Stevens
Photographic Research	Charlotte Goldman
Index	Irene B. Keller, Michael Sweeney
Cover Design	The Quarasan Group, Inc.
Desktop Publishing	Janet Winkler, Jeff Jackson

Photo credits by page 21 *left:* FPG International, *right:* UPI/Bettmann 32 *clockwise from top left:* Joan Pederson, Willard Clay/FPG International, Willard Clay/Tony Stone Images, S.J. Krasemann/Peter Arnold, Inc., David Matherly/Visuals Unlimited, William J. Weber/Visuals Unlimited, Paul Osman 38 *top:* Ron Thomas/FPG International, *bottom:* Stan Osolinski/Tony Stone Images 39 Dave Gleiter/ FPG International 48 *top:* Philip & Karen Smith/Tony Stone Images, *bottom:* Kjell B. Sandved/Visuals Unlimited 51 Greg Stott/Masterfile 74 E. Nagele/FPG International 75 Baron Wolman/Tony Stone Images 77 *left:* R. Laird/FPG International, *right:* Gerald French/FPG International 78 Alex S. MacLean/Peter Arnold, Inc 79 *top:* Science VU – AISI/Visuals Unlimited, *bottom:* Phil Degginger/Tony Stone Images 80 Jim Pickerell/ FPG International 87 Doug Armand/Tony Stone Images 91 Salomon Cytrynowicz/D. Donne Bryant Stock 92 Haroldo & Flavia de Faria Castro/ FPG International 93 David Levy/Tony Stone Images 100 AP/Wide World Photos 102 *left:* Bruce Berg/Visuals Unlimited, *right:* Vladimir Pcholkin/FPG International 109 Freeman Patterson/Masterfile 111 *clockwise from top left:* Guido Alberto Rossi/The Image Bank, Telegraph Colour Library/FPG International, Jeffrey L. Rotman/Peter Arnold, Inc., Telegraph Colour Library/ FPG International 112 Travelpix/FPG International 122 David Sutherland/ Tony Stone Images 123 Travelpix/FPG International 124 Paolo Negri/ Tony Stone Images 125 David Bartruff/FPG International 126 Adrian Masters/Tony Stone Images 132 *left:* Buddy Mays/FPG International, *right:* Mitch Reardon/Tony Stone Images 136 David Hiser/Tony Stone Images 137 AP/Wide World Photos

Copyright © 1994 **NYSTROM**
Division of Herff Jones, Inc.
3333 Elston Avenue
Chicago, Illinois 60618

ISBN: 0-7825-0349-7

For information about ordering this atlas, call toll-free 800-621-8086.

10 9 8 7 6 5 4 3   99 98 97 96 95 94
Printed in U.S.A.   9A94

CONTENTS

Introduction   6–7

Maps and Graphics   6
Continents and Oceans   7
Complete Legend   7

World   8–35

Physical Map   8–9
Political Map   10–11
Thematic Maps and Graphs   12–35

North America   36–39

Physical Map   36
Political Map   37
Thematic Maps and Graphs   38–39

Canada   40–51

Physical Map   40–41
Political Map   42–43
Western Canada   44–45
South Central Canada   46–47
Thematic Maps and Graphs   48–51

United States   52–81

Physical Map   52–53
Political Map   54–55
Alaska and Hawaii   57
Southwestern U.S.   58–59
Northwestern U.S.   60–61
North Central U.S.   62–63
Central U.S.   64–65
South Central U.S.   66–67
Southeastern U.S.   68–69
East Central U.S.   70–71
Northeastern U.S.   72–73
Thematic Maps and Graphs   74–81

Middle America   82–87

Physical Map   82–83
Political Map   84–85
Thematic Maps and Graphs   86–87

South America   88–93

Physical Map   88
Political Map   89
Northern South America   90
Thematic Maps and Graphs   90–93

Europe   94–105

Physical Map   94–95
Political Map   96–97
Western Europe   98
Central Europe   99
Former Soviet Union   100–101
Thematic Maps and Graphs   101–105

Africa   106–113

Physical Map   106
Political Map   107
Western Africa   108
South Africa   109
Eastern Africa   110
Thematic Maps and Graphs   108–113

Mediterranean Basin and Persian Gulf   114–117

Political Map   114–115
Thematic Maps and Graphs   116–117

Asia   118–129

Physical Map   118–119
Political Map   120–121
Southern Asia   122
Southeastern Asia   123
China   124
Eastern Asia   125
Thematic Maps and Graphs   122–129

Australia   130–133

Physical Map   130
Political Map   131
Southeastern Australia   133
Thematic Maps and Graphs   132–133

Pacific Rim   134–135

Political Map   134–135
Thematic Maps and Graphs   134–135

Arctic   136

Physical Map   136
Thematic Map   136

Antarctica   137

Physical Map   137
Thematic Maps   137

Geographic Facts and Index   138–176

Map Projections   138–139
Country Tables   140–147
Glossary   148–149
Abbreviations   149
Index   150–176
Pronunciation Key   inside back cover

THEMATIC MAPS AND GRAPHS

Cross Sections

Antarctica   137
Asia   126–127
South America   92
United States   74–75

Culture and History

Africa's Rise to Independence   110
Changing Boundaries
    Europe in 1914   101
    Europe in 1948   101
    Middle East   117
    Soviet Union   100–101
    World   20
European Imperialism   105
Immigration to the U.S.   20
Latin American Languages   87
Major Languages   28
Major Religions   21
Middle East Religions   116
Slave Trade   108
World Migration   21

Environmental Concerns

Acid Rain   34
Changing Sahara   112
Domestic Water Use (U.S.)   76
Endangered Species (Africa)   111
Ivory Trade   111
Ozone Depletion   35
Safe Drinking Water   34
Threatened Water Supplies (U.S.)   76
Tropical Rain Forests
    South America   91
    World   35
Wetlands (U.S.)   75

Ethnicity and Indigenous Peoples

Canada   49
Latin America   87
North America   38
Oceania   132
South Africa   109
South America   91
United States   76

Land Use

Africa   113
Asia   128
Australia   133
Canada   48
Europe   103
Middle America   87
North America   39
South America   93
United States   76
World   33

Mineral and Energy Resources

Africa   112
Asia   128
Canada   51
Europe   102
Middle East   117
South America   91
United States   78–79
World   30–31

Natural Vegetation

Africa   112
Asia   127
Australia   132
Europe   103
North America   38
South America   92
United States   75
World   32

Physical World

Climates   14–15
Earthquakes and Volcanoes   12–13
Monsoon Asia   122–123
Ocean Depths and Currents   12–13
Temperature and Precipitation   16–17

Population Density

Africa   113
Asia   129
Australia   133
Canada   49
Europe   104
Middle America   86
North America   39
South America   93
United States   77
World   18

Population Growth and Profiles

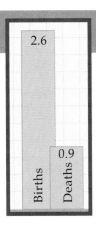

Africa 19
Algeria 110
Brazil 93
Canada 50
China 124
European Community 19
Haiti 86
Iraq 116
New Zealand 132
Nigeria 113
United Kingdom 104
United States 77
Urban Areas 22
World 18–19

Precipitation

Africa 112
Asia 126
Australia 132
Europe 102
North America 38
South America 92
United States 74
World 16

Quality of Life

AIDS 25
Bicycles in China 124
Causes of Death 25
Food
    Availability 22
    Cropland Per Capita 23
    Fisheries 33
    Staple Food Production 23
Leading Automobile Manufacturers 125
Life Expectancy 24
Literacy 29
Persons Per
    Automobile 30
    Newspaper 29
    Physician 24
    Radio 29
    Telephone 29
    Television 29

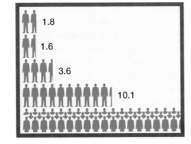

Relative Location and Travel

Arctic Distances 136
Australia's Isolation 133
Canada's Highways and Airports 50
Speed of Travel 29
Time Zones 28
U.S. Air and Rail Transportation 81
U.S. Regions 56

Size Comparisons

Alaska and U.S. 74
Antarctica and U.S. 137
Canada and U.S. 48
China and U.S. 124
Europe and U.S. 102
Indonesia and U.S. 126
Mexico and U.S. 39
Sahara and U.S. 112
South America and U.S. 90

Trade and Economics

Angola 113
Australia 133
Canada 50–51
Chile 93
China 127
Drug Trade (Americas) 90
Europe 105
Greece 104
India 127
Israel 116
Japan 125
Libya 113
Mexico 86
Nicaragua 87
North America 39
OPEC 117
Poland 104
Saudi Arabia 116
South Africa 109
South Korea 125
United States 79–81
Venezuela 92
World 26–27, 134–135

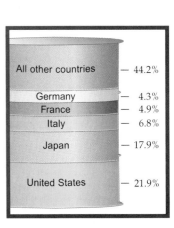

All other countries — 44.2%
Germany — 4.3%
France — 4.9%
Italy — 6.8%
Japan — 17.9%
United States — 21.9%

INTRODUCTION

The Nystrom Desk Atlas includes physical and political maps of large areas, regional maps of smaller areas, thematic maps, graphic presentations of data, and illustrative photographs. Each map, graph, and photo is best suited to providing specific kinds of information.

Physical Maps

Physical maps in this atlas are designed so that the names and relative locations of natural features can be seen at a glance. Colors represent water depths and land elevations. Although the emphasis is on natural features, countries and key cities also are named.

Political Maps

Political maps are colored by state, province, or country, making it as easy as possible to tell where one ends and another begins. The names of capitals and other major cities are quickly found because the maps are carefully edited to keep them uncluttered.

Thematic Maps

Thematic maps focus on single topics or themes, and the subject can be anything that is mappable. Among the thematic maps in this atlas are maps of rainfall, land use, and population. Often the patterns on one thematic map become more meaningful when compared to the patterns on another.

Regional Maps

Regional maps in this atlas offer close-up views of areas on the political maps. Because regional maps enlarge the areas shown, they can name more cities while remaining highly readable. Other details also are added, such as the names of landforms, including some not given on the physical maps.

Legends

Legends are provided for all maps. For most of the thematic maps, the legends are simple keys showing what the map colors stand for. The legends for the physical, political, and regional maps are lengthier. To save space, the complete legend for these maps is given only once, on the facing page.

Graphs

Graphs summarize facts in a visual way, making it easier to see trends and make comparisons. Many different topics are presented in a variety of graphic styles. Some topics are graphed only once, while others form strands that run through the whole book.

Photographs

Photographs can portray the characteristics of a place like nothing else can. The photos in this atlas were carefully chosen to illustrate the natural setting and cultural aspects of places around the world. Photographic realism is the perfect complement to the abstract symbolism of maps.

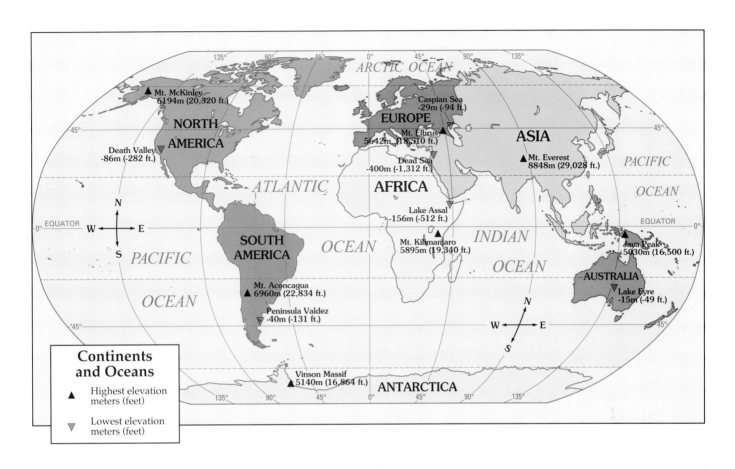

Continents and Oceans

▲ Highest elevation meters (feet)

▽ Lowest elevation meters (feet)

Map labels:
- Mt. McKinley 6194m (20,320 ft.)
- Death Valley -86m (-282 ft.)
- NORTH AMERICA
- Caspian Sea -29m (-94 ft.)
- EUROPE
- Mt. Elbrus 5642m (18,510 ft.)
- ASIA
- Dead Sea -400m (-1,312 ft.)
- Mt. Everest 8848m (29,028 ft.)
- AFRICA
- Lake Assal -156m (-512 ft.)
- Mt. Kilimanjaro 5895m (19,340 ft.)
- Jaya Peak 5030m (16,500 ft.)
- SOUTH AMERICA
- Mt. Aconcagua 6960m (22,834 ft.)
- Peninsula Valdez -40m (-131 ft.)
- AUSTRALIA
- Lake Eyre -15m (-49 ft.)
- Vinson Massif 5140m (16,864 ft.)
- ANTARCTICA
- ARCTIC OCEAN
- ATLANTIC OCEAN
- PACIFIC OCEAN
- INDIAN OCEAN
- EQUATOR

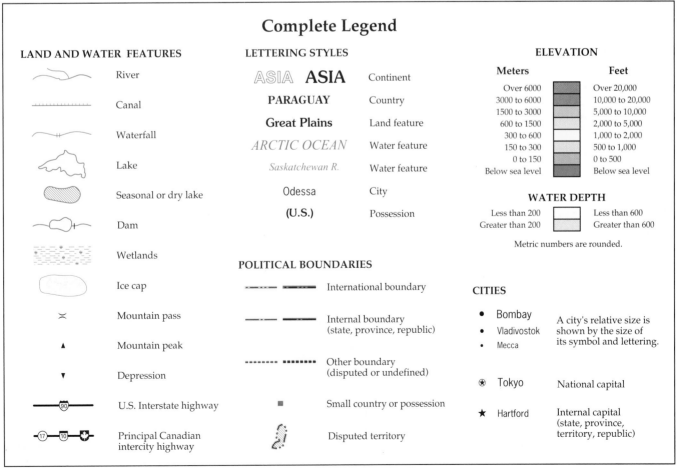

Complete Legend

LAND AND WATER FEATURES

- River
- Canal
- Waterfall
- Lake
- Seasonal or dry lake
- Dam
- Wetlands
- Ice cap
- Mountain pass
- ▲ Mountain peak
- ▼ Depression
- U.S. Interstate highway (90)
- Principal Canadian intercity highway (17) (10)

LETTERING STYLES

ASIA **ASIA**	Continent
PARAGUAY	Country
Great Plains	Land feature
ARCTIC OCEAN	Water feature
Saskatchewan R.	Water feature
Odessa	City
(U.S.)	Possession

POLITICAL BOUNDARIES

- International boundary
- Internal boundary (state, province, republic)
- Other boundary (disputed or undefined)
- ■ Small country or possession
- Disputed territory

ELEVATION

Meters		Feet
Over 6000		Over 20,000
3000 to 6000		10,000 to 20,000
1500 to 3000		5,000 to 10,000
600 to 1500		2,000 to 5,000
300 to 600		1,000 to 2,000
150 to 300		500 to 1,000
0 to 150		0 to 500
Below sea level		Below sea level

WATER DEPTH

Less than 200		Less than 600
Greater than 200		Greater than 600

Metric numbers are rounded.

CITIES

- ● Bombay
- ● Vladivostok
- · Mecca

A city's relative size is shown by the size of its symbol and lettering.

- ⊛ Tokyo — National capital
- ★ Hartford — Internal capital (state, province, territory, republic)

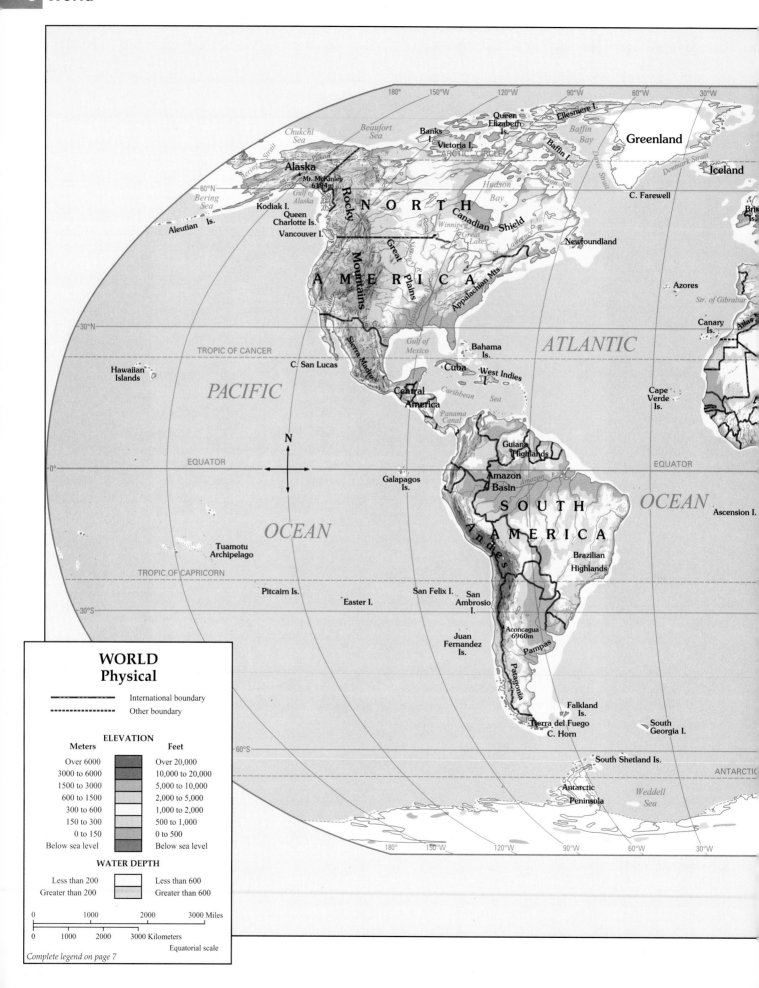

180°   150°W   120°W   90°W   60°W   30°W

Chukchi Sea

Beaufort Sea

Banks I.

Queen Elizabeth Is.

Ellesmere I.

Baffin Bay

Victoria I.

Baffin I.

ARCTIC CIRCLE

Greenland

Denmark Strait

Iceland

Bering Strait

Yukon

Alaska

Mt. McKinley 6194m

Gulf of Alaska

60°N

Bering Sea

N O R T H

Hudson Bay

Hudson Str.

Davis Strait

C. Farewell

Kodiak I.

Queen Charlotte Is.

Vancouver I.

Rocky Mountains

Winnipeg

Canadian Shield

Great Lakes

Lawrence R.

Newfoundland

A M E R I C A

Great Plains

Azores

Appalachian Mts.

30°N

Str. of Gibraltar

Aleutian Is.

Mississippi

TROPIC OF CANCER

Sierra Madre

C. San Lucas

Gulf of Mexico

Canary Is.

Atlas

Hawaiian Islands

Bahama Is.

ATLANTIC

Cuba

PACIFIC

Central America

West Indies

Caribbean Sea

Cape Verde Is.

Panama Canal

N

Guiana Highlands

EQUATOR

Galapagos Is.

Amazon Basin

Amazon R.

EQUATOR

OCEAN

Ascension I.

S O U T H

Tuamotu Archipelago

Andes

A M E R I C A

Brazilian Highlands

OCEAN

TROPIC OF CAPRICORN

Pitcairn Is.

San Felix I.

San Ambrosio I.

Easter I.

30°S

Aconcagua 6960m

Juan Fernandez Is.

Pampas

Patagonia

Falkland Is.

South Georgia I.

Tierra del Fuego
C. Horn

60°S

South Shetland Is.

Antarctic Peninsula

ANTARCTIC

Weddell Sea

180°   150°W   120°W   90°W   60°W   30°W

ARCTIC OCEAN

Svalbard
North Cape
-wegian Sea
Barents Sea
Novaya Zemlya
Kara Sea
Severnaya Zemlya
Laptev Sea
New Siberian Is.
East Siberian Sea
ARCTIC CIRCLE

Scandinavia
Northern European Plain
EUROPE
Alps
Caucasus Mts.
Mt. Elbrus 5642m
Black Sea
Mediterranean Sea
Sicily

Ural Mountains
Volga R.
Ob R.
Yenisey R.
West Siberian Plain
Central Siberian Plateau
Siberia
ASIA
Verkhoyansk Range
Kolyma Range
60°N
Kamchatka Peninsula
Sea of Okhotsk
Sakhalin
Amur R.
Manchurian Plain
Kuril Is.
Hokkaido
Honshu
Sea of Japan
PACIFIC

Aral Sea
L. Balkhash
Caspian Sea
Altai Mts.
Tien Shan
Gobi Desert
Kunlun Mts.
Plateau of Tibet
Hindu Kush
Himalayas
Mt. Everest 8848m
Yunnan Plateau
North China Plain
Huang He
Yellow Sea
East China Sea
Kyushu
Ryukyu Is.
30°N
OCEAN
TROPIC OF CANCER

Iranian Plateau
Arabian Peninsula
Red Sea
Ganges
Deccan Plateau
Bay of Bengal
Taiwan
Philippine Is.
Mariana Is.

-ahara
Ahaggar Mts.
Tibesti Mts.
-RICA
Sahel
Arabian Sea
Sri Lanka
Maldives
South China Sea
Philippine Sea
Caroline Is.

Ethiopian Highlands
Congo R.
Congo Basin
L. Victoria
Mt. Kilimanjaro 5895m
Zanzibar I.
Seychelles
Chagos Archipelago
Sumatra
Borneo
Celebes Sea
Celebes
Java
New Guinea
Solomon Is.
EQUATOR
0°

INDIAN
Comoros
Madagascar
Mozambique Channel
Mauritius
OCEAN
Timor
Timor Sea
Arafura Sea
Fiji Is.
New Caledonia

Bie Plateau
Kalahari Desert
Drakensberg
C. of Good Hope
TROPIC OF CAPRICORN
Great Sandy Desert
AUSTRALIA
Darling
Great Dividing Range
Coral Sea
30°S

Amsterdam I.
St. Paul I.
C. Leeuwin
Mt. Kosciusko 2228m
Tasmania
Bass Strait
Tasman Sea
North I.
New Zealand
South I.
Stewart I.

Kerguelen I.
Auckland I.
60°S

-RCLE
ANTARCTICA

30°E   60°E   90°E   120°E   150°E   180°

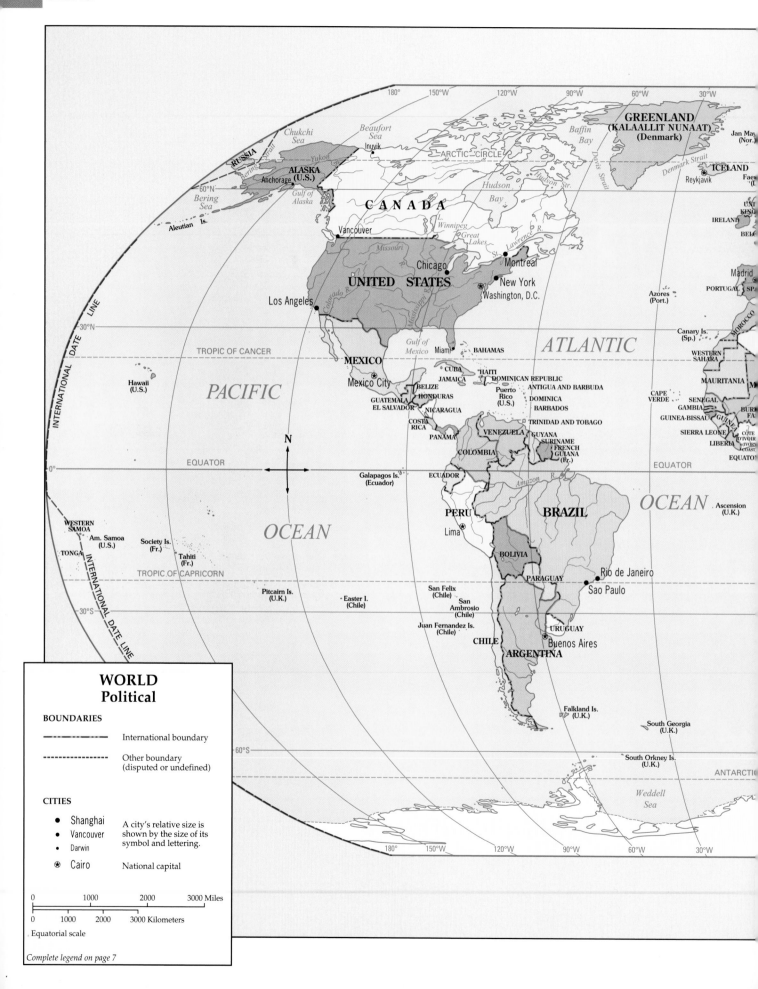

RUSSIA
Chukchi Sea
Bering Strait
Beaufort Sea
Inuvik
Yukon R.
ALASKA (U.S.)
Anchorage
Gulf of Alaska
ARCTIC CIRCLE
Baffin Bay
GREENLAND (KALAALLIT NUNAAT) (Denmark)
Jan May (Nor.)
Denmark Strait
ICELAND
Reykjavik
Faer (D
Bering Sea
60°N
Hudson Str.
Davis Strait
Hudson Bay
Aleutian Is.
CANADA
Vancouver
L. Winnipeg
Great Lakes
St. Lawrence R.
Montreal
UNI KING
IRELAND
BEL
Missouri
UNITED STATES
Chicago
New York
Washington, D.C.
Madrid
PORTUGAL SP
Azores (Port.)
Los Angeles
Colorado R.
Mississippi
30°N
Canary Is. (Sp.)
MOROCCO
TROPIC OF CANCER
Gulf of Mexico
Miami
BAHAMAS
ATLANTIC
WESTERN SAHARA
MAURITANIA
M
MEXICO
CUBA
HAITI
DOMINICAN REPUBLIC
ANTIGUA AND BARBUDA
CAPE VERDE
SENEGAL
Hawaii (U.S.)
Mexico City
JAMAICA
Puerto Rico (U.S.)
DOMINICA
GAMBIA
GUINEA-BISSAU
GUI
BURN FA
PACIFIC
BELIZE
GUATEMALA
EL SALVADOR
HONDURAS
NICARAGUA
BARBADOS
TRINIDAD AND TOBAGO
SIERRA LEONE
CÔTE D'IVOIR (IVORY COAST
LIBERIA
COSTA RICA
PANAMA
VENEZUELA
GUYANA
SURINAME
FRENCH GUIANA (Fr.)
EQUATO
N
COLOMBIA
EQUATOR
Galapagos Is. (Ecuador)
ECUADOR
EQUATOR
Amazon R.
PERU
Lima
BRAZIL
OCEAN
Ascension (U.K.)
WESTERN SAMOA
Am. Samoa (U.S.)
Society Is. (Fr.)
Tahiti (Fr.)
TONGA
BOLIVIA
OCEAN
TROPIC OF CAPRICORN
PARAGUAY
Rio de Janeiro
Sao Paulo
Pitcairn Is. (U.K.)
Easter I. (Chile)
San Felix (Chile)
San Ambrosio (Chile)
30°S
Juan Fernandez Is. (Chile)
URUGUAY
Buenos Aires
CHILE
ARGENTINA
Falkland Is. (U.K.)
South Georgia (U.K.)
60°S
South Orkney Is. (U.K.)
ANTARCTI
Weddell Sea

180° 150°W 120°W 90°W 60°W 30°W

INTERNATIONAL DATE LINE

WORLD
Political

BOUNDARIES

——————— International boundary

- - - - - - - - Other boundary (disputed or undefined)

CITIES

● Shanghai

• Vancouver

· Darwin

A city's relative size is shown by the size of its symbol and lettering.

⊛ Cairo   National capital

| 0 | 1000 | 2000 | 3000 Miles |

| 0 | 1000 | 2000 | 3000 Kilometers |

Equatorial scale

Complete legend on page 7

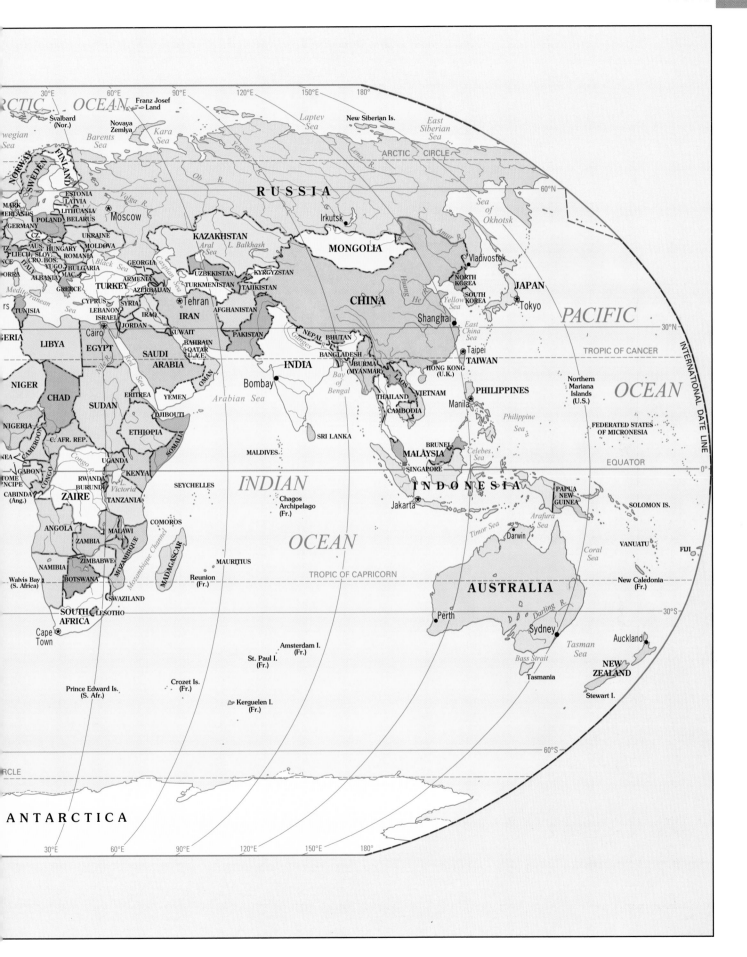

ARCTIC OCEAN
30°E 60°E 90°E 120°E 150°E 180°
Franz Josef Land
Svalbard (Nor.)
Novaya Zemlya
Laptev Sea
New Siberian Is.
East Siberian Sea
Norwegian Sea
Barents Sea
Kara Sea
Yenisey R.
Lena R.
ARCTIC CIRCLE
60°N
NORWAY
SWEDEN
FINLAND
Ob R.
RUSSIA
Sea of Okhotsk
ESTONIA
LATVIA
LITHUANIA
BELARUS
Moscow
Volga R.
Irkutsk
Amur R.
DENMARK
NETHERLANDS
GERMANY
POLAND
KAZAKHSTAN
Aral Sea
L. Balkhash
MONGOLIA
Vladivostok
CZ.
SL.
AUS. HUNGARY
LIECH. SLOV.
FRANCE
ITALY
CRO. BOS.
YUGO.
MAC.
ALBANIA
UKRAINE
MOLDOVA
ROMANIA
BULGARIA
Black Sea
GEORGIA
ARMENIA
AZERBAIJAN
Caspian Sea
UZBEKISTAN
TURKMENISTAN
KYRGYZSTAN
TAJIKISTAN
CHINA
Huang He
NORTH KOREA
SOUTH KOREA
JAPAN
Tokyo
PACIFIC
ANDORRA
GREECE
TURKEY
SYRIA
Tehran
AFGHANISTAN
NEPAL BHUTAN
Ganges R.
Shanghai
Yellow Sea
East China Sea
TAIPEI
30°N
CYPRUS
LEBANON
ISRAEL
JORDAN
IRAQ
KUWAIT
IRAN
PAKISTAN
BANGLADESH
BURMA (MYANMAR)
HONG KONG (U.K.)
TAIWAN
TROPIC OF CANCER
TUNISIA
Mediterranean Sea
Cairo
BAHRAIN
QATAR
U.A.E.
INDIA
LAOS
VIETNAM
PHILIPPINES
Northern Mariana Islands (U.S.)
OCEAN
ALGERIA
LIBYA
EGYPT
Nile R.
SAUDI ARABIA
Red Sea
OMAN
Bombay
Bay of Bengal
THAILAND
CAMBODIA
Manila
Philippine Sea
NIGER
CHAD
SUDAN
ERITREA
YEMEN
Arabian Sea
SRI LANKA
FEDERATED STATES OF MICRONESIA
NIGERIA
C. AFR. REP.
ETHIOPIA
DJIBOUTI
SOMALIA
MALDIVES
BRUNEI
MALAYSIA
Celebes Sea
EQUATOR
GUINEA
CAMEROON
Congo R.
UGANDA
RWANDA
BURUNDI
L. Victoria
KENYA
SEYCHELLES
INDIAN
SINGAPORE
INDONESIA
PAPUA NEW GUINEA
0°
SAO TOME & PRINCIPE
GABON
CONGO
ZAIRE
TANZANIA
Chagos Archipelago (Fr.)
Jakarta
SOLOMON IS.
CABINDA (Ang.)
ANGOLA
ZAMBIA
MALAWI
COMOROS
OCEAN
Arafura Sea
Timor Sea
Darwin
Coral Sea
VANUATU
FIJI
NAMIBIA
ZIMBABWE
BOTSWANA
MOZAMBIQUE
Mozambique Channel
MADAGASCAR
MAURITIUS
TROPIC OF CAPRICORN
New Caledonia (Fr.)
Walvis Bay (S. Africa)
Reunion (Fr.)
AUSTRALIA
30°S
SOUTH AFRICA
SWAZILAND
LESOTHO
Perth
Darling R.
Sydney
Tasman Sea
Auckland
Cape Town
Amsterdam I. (Fr.)
St. Paul I. (Fr.)
Bass Strait
Tasmania
NEW ZEALAND
Crozet Is. (Fr.)
Stewart I.
Prince Edward Is. (S. Afr.)
Kerguelen I. (Fr.)
60°S
CIRCLE
ANTARCTICA
30°E 60°E 90°E 120°E 150°E 180°
INTERNATIONAL DATE LINE

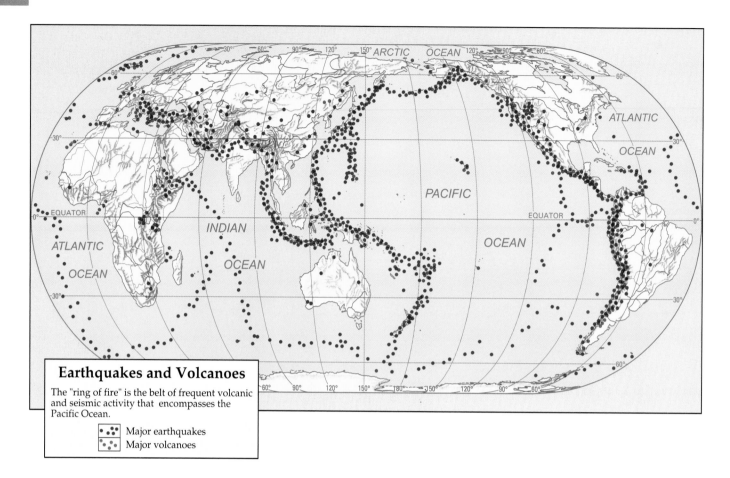

Earthquakes and Volcanoes

The "ring of fire" is the belt of frequent volcanic and seismic activity that encompasses the Pacific Ocean.

- Major earthquakes
- Major volcanoes

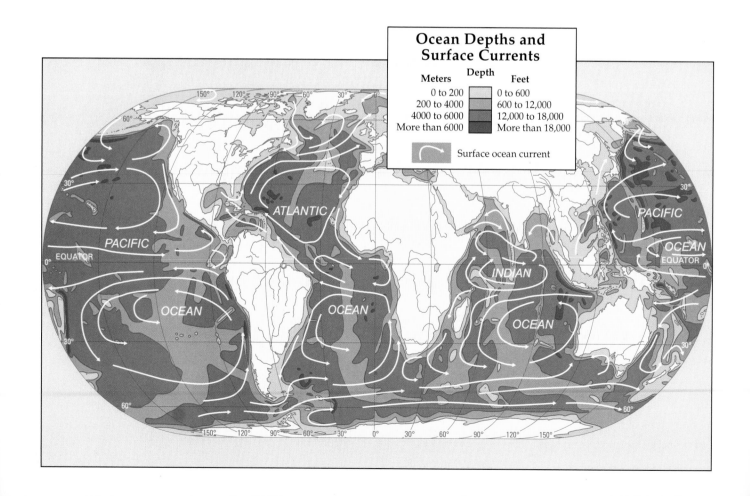

Ocean Depths and Surface Currents

Depth

Meters		Feet
0 to 200		0 to 600
200 to 4000		600 to 12,000
4000 to 6000		12,000 to 18,000
More than 6000		More than 18,000

Surface ocean current

Notable Earthquakes

Earthquake	Date	Magnitude (Richter Scale)	Deaths
Central India	Sept. 30, 1993	6.4	22,000
Northwestern Iran	June 21, 1990	7.7	40,000+
Loma Prieta, CA, U.S.	October 17, 1989	6.9	62
Northwestern Armenia	December 7, 1988	6.8	55,000+
Mexico City, Mexico	Sept. 19-21, 1985	8.1	4,200+
Tangshan, China	July 28, 1976	7.6	242,000
Guatemala	February 4, 1976	7.5	22,778
San Fernando, CA, U.S.	February 9, 1971	6.5	65
Northern Peru	May 31, 1970	7.8	66,794
Kenai Pen., AK, U.S.	March 28, 1964	8.6	131
Nan-Shan, China	May 22, 1927	8.3	200,000
Yokohama, Japan	September 1, 1923	8.3	143,000
Gansu, China	December 16, 1920	8.6	100,000
Messina, Italy	December 28, 1908	7.5	83,000
San Francisco, CA, U.S.	April 18, 1906	8.3	700
New Madrid, MO, U.S.	December 16, 1811- February 7, 1812	8.7	unknown
Calcutta, India	October 11, 1737	---	300,000
Shemaka, Azerbaijan	November 1667	---	80,000
Shaanxi, China	January 24, 1556	---	830,000
Antioch, Syria	May 20, 526	---	250,000

Notable Volcanic Eruptions

Volcano	Place	Year	Deaths
Kilauea	Hawaii, U.S.	1983-present	1
Pinatubo	Philippines	1992	200+
Redoubt	Alaska, U.S.	1989-1990	0
Nevada del Ruiz	Colombia	1985	22,940
Mauna Loa	Hawaii, U.S.	1984	0
El Chicon	Mexico	1982	100+
St. Helens	Washington, U.S.	1980	57
Erebus	Ross I., Antarctica	1970-1980	0
Surtsey	N. Atlantic Ocean	1963-1967	0
Paricutin	Mexico	1943-1952	1,000
Kelud	Java, Indonesia	1919	5,000
Pelee	Martinique	1902	26,000
Krakatoa	Sumatra, Indonesia	1883	36,000
Tambora	Sumbawa, Indonesia	1815	56,000
Unzen	Japan	1792	10,400
Etna	Sicily, Italy	1669	20,000
Kelud	Java, Indonesia	1586	10,000
Etna	Sicily, Italy	1169	15,000
Vesuvius	Italy	79	16,000
Thera (Santorini)	Aegean Sea	1645 B.C.	thousands

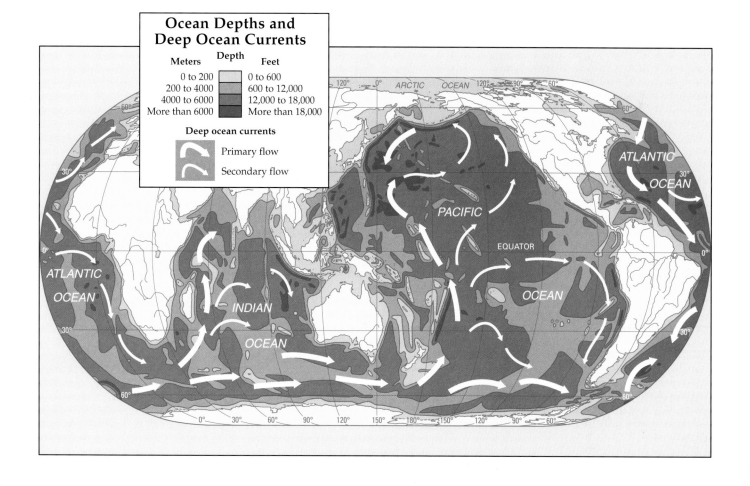

Ocean Depths and Deep Ocean Currents

Depth

Meters		Feet
0 to 200		0 to 600
200 to 4000		600 to 12,000
4000 to 6000		12,000 to 18,000
More than 6000		More than 18,000

Deep ocean currents

Primary flow

Secondary flow

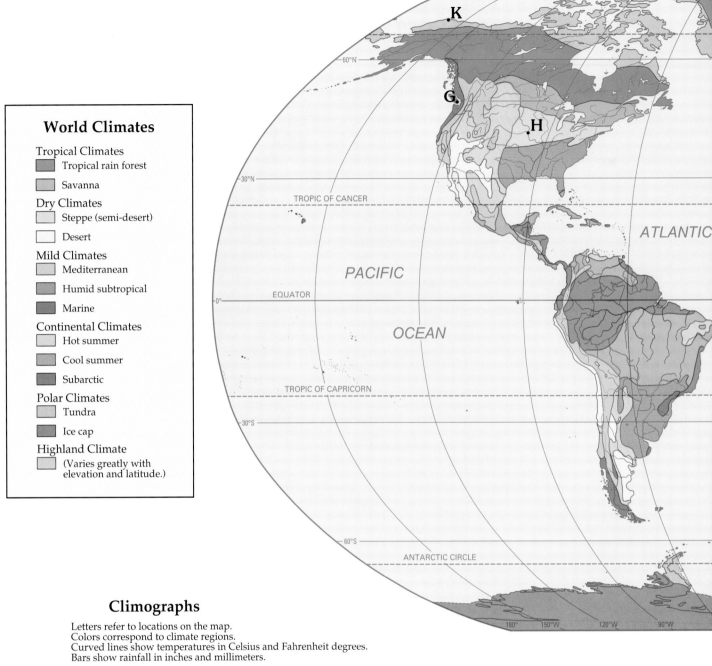

World Climates

Tropical Climates
- Tropical rain forest
- Savanna

Dry Climates
- Steppe (semi-desert)
- Desert

Mild Climates
- Mediterranean
- Humid subtropical
- Marine

Continental Climates
- Hot summer
- Cool summer
- Subarctic

Polar Climates
- Tundra
- Ice cap

Highland Climate
- (Varies greatly with elevation and latitude.)

Climographs

Letters refer to locations on the map.
Colors correspond to climate regions.
Curved lines show temperatures in Celsius and Fahrenheit degrees.
Bars show rainfall in inches and millimeters.

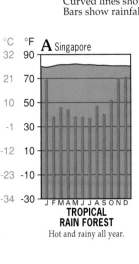

A Singapore

TROPICAL RAIN FOREST

Hot and rainy all year.

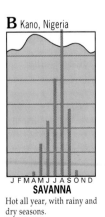

B Kano, Nigeria

SAVANNA

Hot all year, with rainy and dry seasons.

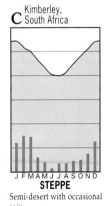

C Kimberley, South Africa

STEPPE

Semi-desert with occasional rain.

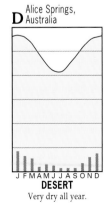

D Alice Springs, Australia

DESERT

Very dry all year.

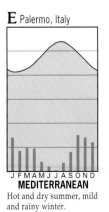

E Palermo, Italy

MEDITERRANEAN

Hot and dry summer, mild and rainy winter.

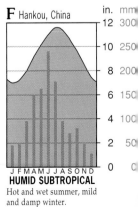

F Hankou, China

HUMID SUBTROPICAL

Hot and wet summer, mild and damp winter.

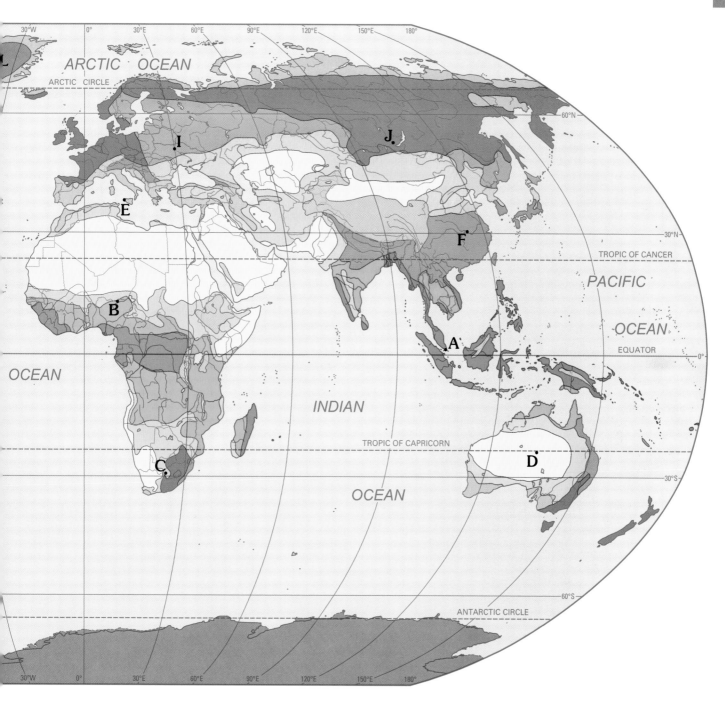

ARCTIC OCEAN
ARCTIC CIRCLE
60°N
30°N
TROPIC OF CANCER
PACIFIC
OCEAN
EQUATOR
0°
INDIAN
OCEAN
TROPIC OF CAPRICORN
30°S
OCEAN
60°S
ANTARCTIC CIRCLE

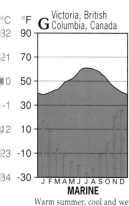

°C °F **G** Victoria, British Columbia, Canada
32 90
21 70
0 50
-1 30
12 10
23 -10
34 -30
J F M A M J J A S O N D
MARINE
Warm summer, cool and wet winter.

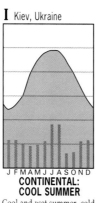

H Omaha, Nebraska, United States
J F M A M J J A S O N D
CONTINENTAL: HOT SUMMER
Hot and wet summer, cold and snowy winter.

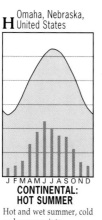

I Kiev, Ukraine
J F M A M J J A S O N D
CONTINENTAL: COOL SUMMER
Cool and wet summer, cold and very snowy winter.

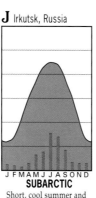

J Irkutsk, Russia
J F M A M J J A S O N D
SUBARCTIC
Short, cool summer and very cold, snowy winter.

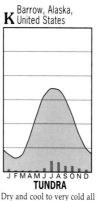

K Barrow, Alaska, United States
J F M A M J J A S O N D
TUNDRA
Dry and cool to very cold all year.

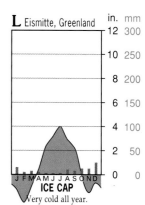

L Eismitte, Greenland
in. mm
12 300
10 250
8 200
6 150
4 100
2 50
0 0
J F M A M J J A S O N D
ICE CAP
Very cold all year.

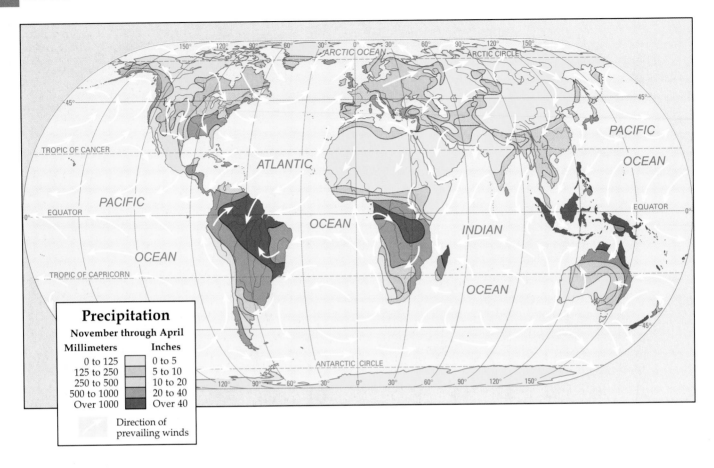

Precipitation

November through April

Millimeters	Inches
0 to 125	0 to 5
125 to 250	5 to 10
250 to 500	10 to 20
500 to 1000	20 to 40
Over 1000	Over 40

Direction of prevailing winds

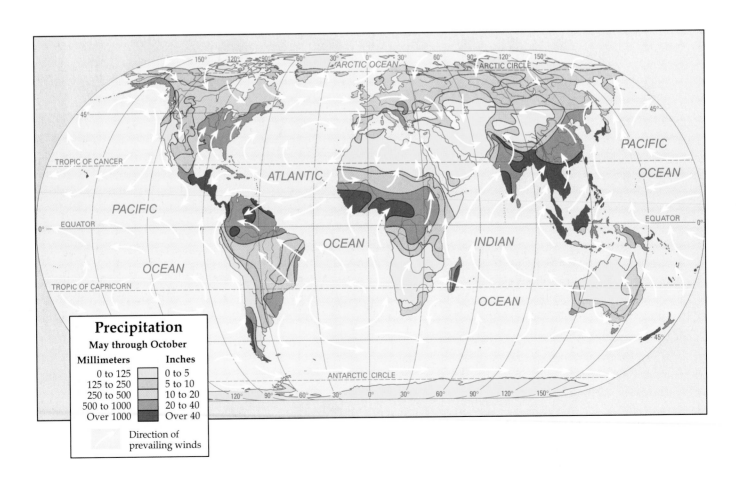

Precipitation

May through October

Millimeters	Inches
0 to 125	0 to 5
125 to 250	5 to 10
250 to 500	10 to 20
500 to 1000	20 to 40
Over 1000	Over 40

Direction of prevailing winds

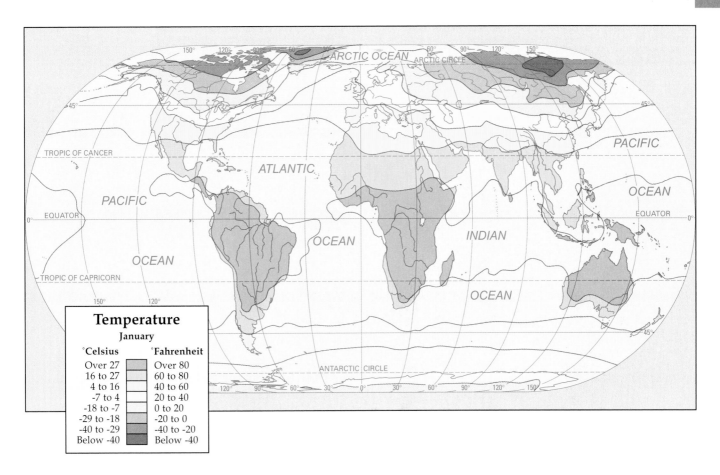

Temperature

January

°Celsius	°Fahrenheit
Over 27	Over 80
16 to 27	60 to 80
4 to 16	40 to 60
-7 to 4	20 to 40
-18 to -7	0 to 20
-29 to -18	-20 to 0
-40 to -29	-40 to -20
Below -40	Below -40

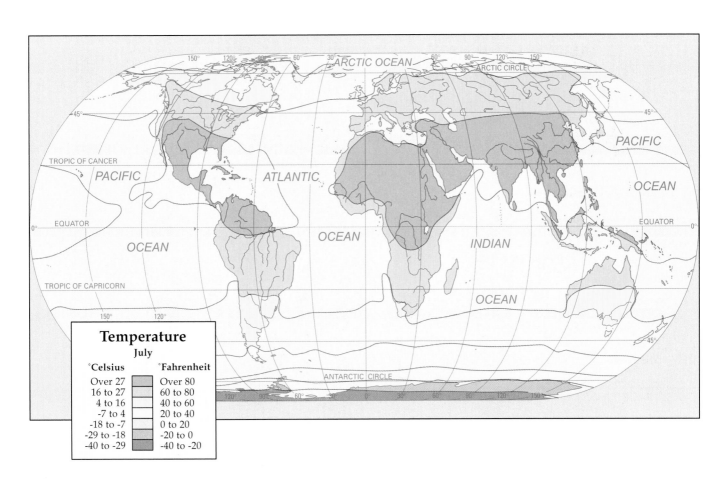

Temperature

July

°Celsius	°Fahrenheit
Over 27	Over 80
16 to 27	60 to 80
4 to 16	40 to 60
-7 to 4	20 to 40
-18 to -7	0 to 20
-29 to -18	-20 to 0
-40 to -29	-40 to -20

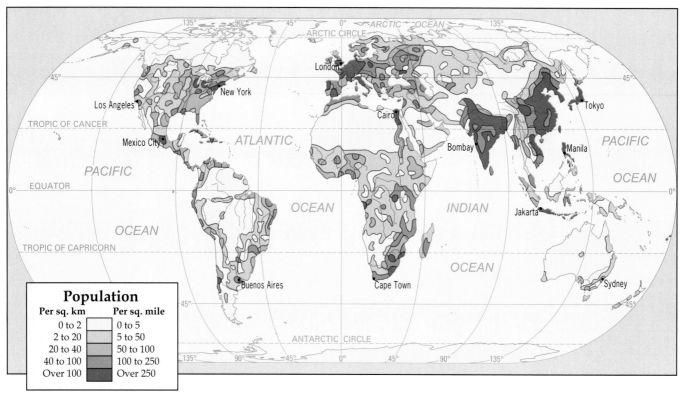

Population

Per sq. km	Per sq. mile
0 to 2	0 to 5
2 to 20	5 to 50
20 to 40	50 to 100
40 to 100	100 to 250
Over 100	Over 250

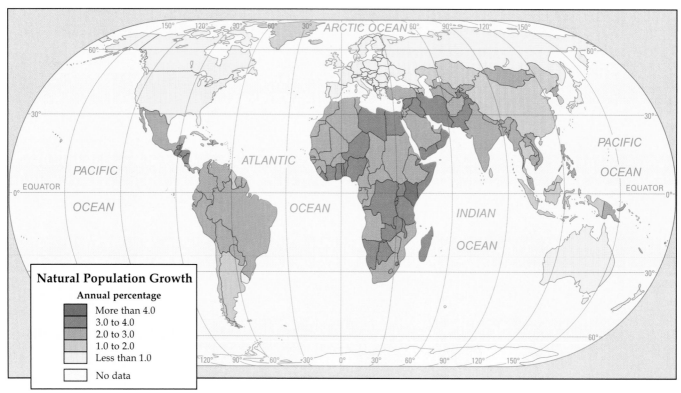

Natural Population Growth

Annual percentage

- More than 4.0
- 3.0 to 4.0
- 2.0 to 3.0
- 1.0 to 2.0
- Less than 1.0
- No data

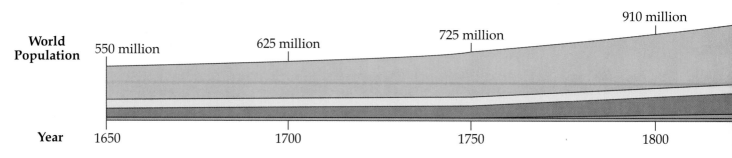

World Population

550 million 625 million 725 million 910 million

Year 1650 1700 1750 1800

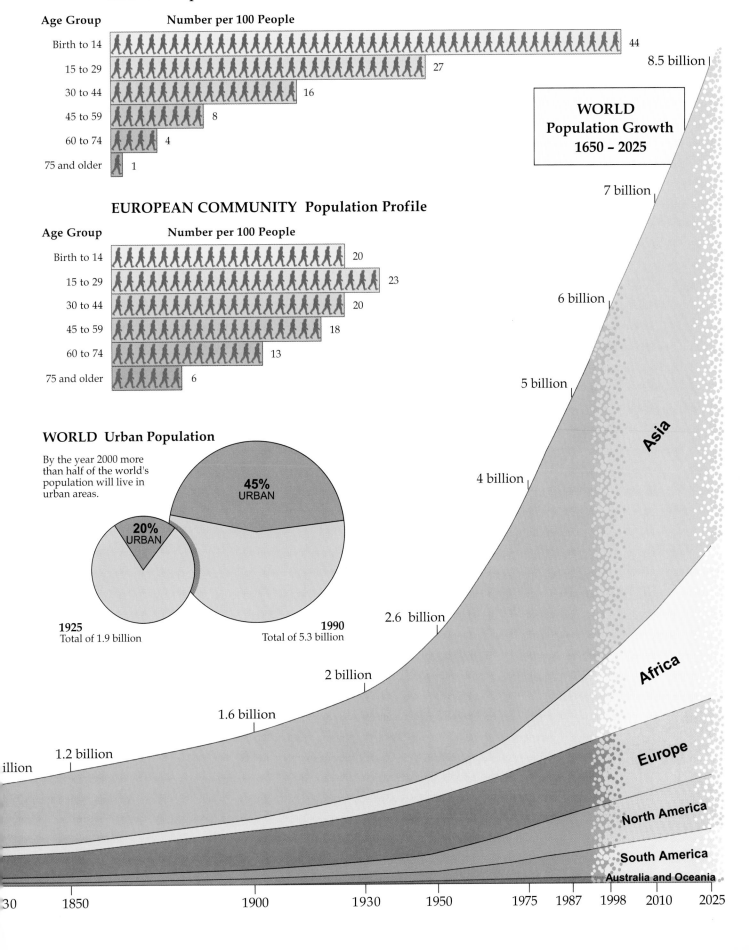

AFRICA Population Profile

Age Group	Number per 100 People	
Birth to 14		44
15 to 29		27
30 to 44		16
45 to 59		8
60 to 74		4
75 and older		1

EUROPEAN COMMUNITY Population Profile

Age Group	Number per 100 People	
Birth to 14		20
15 to 29		23
30 to 44		20
45 to 59		18
60 to 74		13
75 and older		6

WORLD Urban Population

By the year 2000 more than half of the world's population will live in urban areas.

20% URBAN

45% URBAN

1925
Total of 1.9 billion

1990
Total of 5.3 billion

WORLD
Population Growth
1650 – 2025

8.5 billion

7 billion

6 billion

5 billion

4 billion

Asia

2.6 billion

2 billion

1.6 billion

1.2 billion

illion

Africa

Europe

North America

South America

Australia and Oceania

30 1850 1900 1930 1950 1975 1987 1998 2010 2025

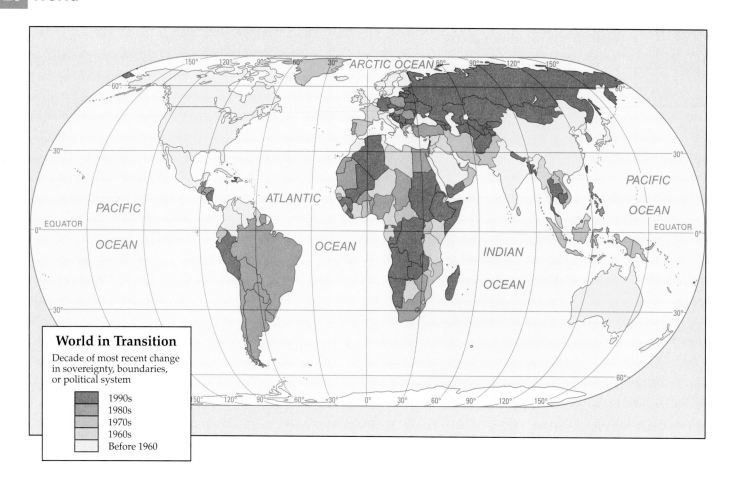

World in Transition

Decade of most recent change in sovereignty, boundaries, or political system

- 1990s
- 1980s
- 1970s
- 1960s
- Before 1960

Worldwide Immigration to the United States

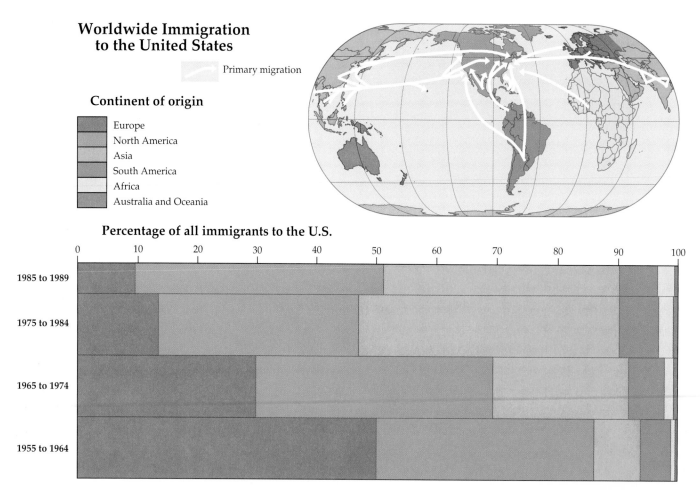

Primary migration

Continent of origin

- Europe
- North America
- Asia
- South America
- Africa
- Australia and Oceania

Percentage of all immigrants to the U.S.

	0	10	20	30	40	50	60	70	80	90	100

1985 to 1989

1975 to 1984

1965 to 1974

1955 to 1964

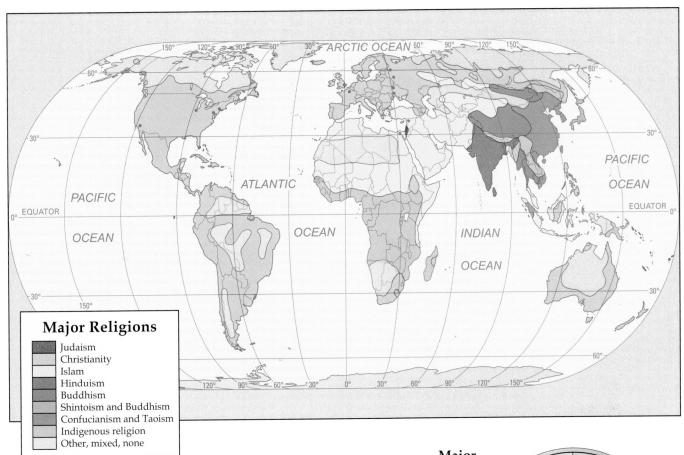

Major Religions

- Judaism
- Christianity
- Islam
- Hinduism
- Buddhism
- Shintoism and Buddhism
- Confucianism and Taoism
- Indigenous religion
- Other, mixed, none

World Migration

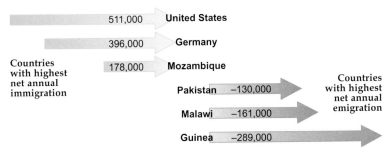

Countries with highest net annual immigration

- 511,000 → **United States**
- 396,000 → **Germany**
- 178,000 → **Mozambique**

Countries with highest net annual emigration

- **Pakistan** −130,000 →
- **Malawi** −161,000 →
- **Guinea** −289,000 →

Major Religions

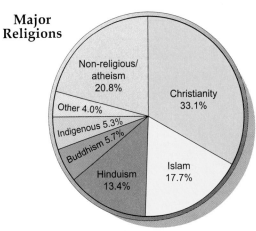

- Christianity 33.1%
- Islam 17.7%
- Hinduism 13.4%
- Buddhism 5.7%
- Indigenous 5.3%
- Other 4.0%
- Non-religious/atheism 20.8%

European immigrants were sworn in as citizens at New York's Ellis Island in the early 1900s. By then, laws restricted the number of aliens admitted into the United States.

Hispanic residents become U.S. citizens in a mass naturalization ceremony at a Miami stadium. Many immigrants are political or economic refugees from countries in turmoil.

World's Fastest Growing Urban Areas

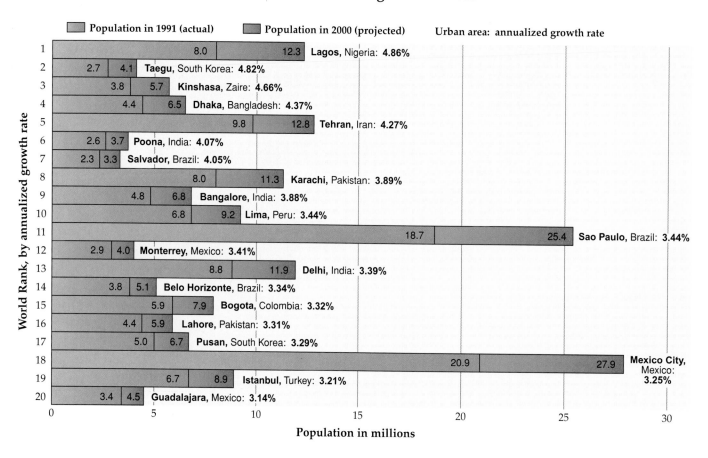

Population in 1991 (actual)   Population in 2000 (projected)   Urban area: annualized growth rate

World Rank, by annualized growth rate

1 — 8.0 | 12.3 — **Lagos**, Nigeria: **4.86%**
2 — 2.7 | 4.1 — **Taegu**, South Korea: **4.82%**
3 — 3.8 | 5.7 — **Kinshasa**, Zaire: **4.66%**
4 — 4.4 | 6.5 — **Dhaka**, Bangladesh: **4.37%**
5 — 9.8 | 12.8 — **Tehran**, Iran: **4.27%**
6 — 2.6 | 3.7 — **Poona**, India: **4.07%**
7 — 2.3 | 3.3 — **Salvador**, Brazil: **4.05%**
8 — 8.0 | 11.3 — **Karachi**, Pakistan: **3.89%**
9 — 4.8 | 6.8 — **Bangalore**, India: **3.88%**
10 — 6.8 | 9.2 — **Lima**, Peru: **3.44%**
11 — 18.7 | 25.4 — **Sao Paulo**, Brazil: **3.44%**
12 — 2.9 | 4.0 — **Monterrey**, Mexico: **3.41%**
13 — 8.8 | 11.9 — **Delhi**, India: **3.39%**
14 — 3.8 | 5.1 — **Belo Horizonte**, Brazil: **3.34%**
15 — 5.9 | 7.9 — **Bogota**, Colombia: **3.32%**
16 — 4.4 | 5.9 — **Lahore**, Pakistan: **3.31%**
17 — 5.0 | 6.7 — **Pusan**, South Korea: **3.29%**
18 — 20.9 | 27.9 — **Mexico City, Mexico: 3.25%**
19 — 6.7 | 8.9 — **Istanbul**, Turkey: **3.21%**
20 — 3.4 | 4.5 — **Guadalajara**, Mexico: **3.14%**

Population in millions

0   5   10   15   20   25   30

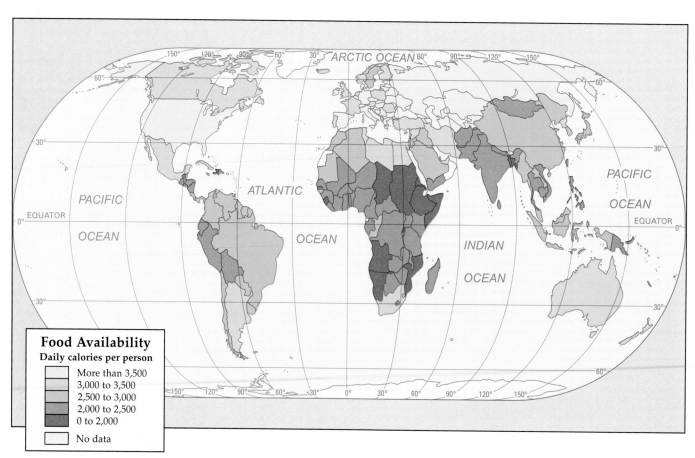

Food Availability
Daily calories per person

- More than 3,500
- 3,000 to 3,500
- 2,500 to 3,000
- 2,000 to 2,500
- 0 to 2,000
- No data

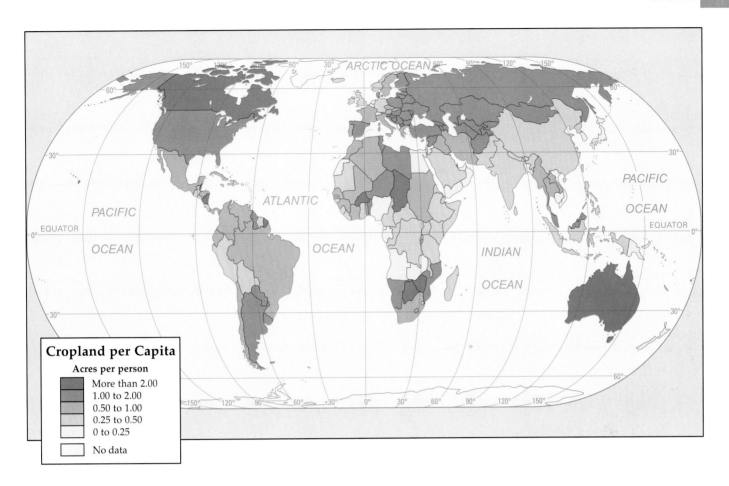

Cropland per Capita

Acres per person

More than 2.00
1.00 to 2.00
0.50 to 1.00
0.25 to 0.50
0 to 0.25

No data

Staple Food Production

Grains are the main source of food for most of the world's population. Many grains are also used in processed foods and livestock feed. Grain producers range from large commercial farms that export their harvest to small farms that grow grains for regional consumption.

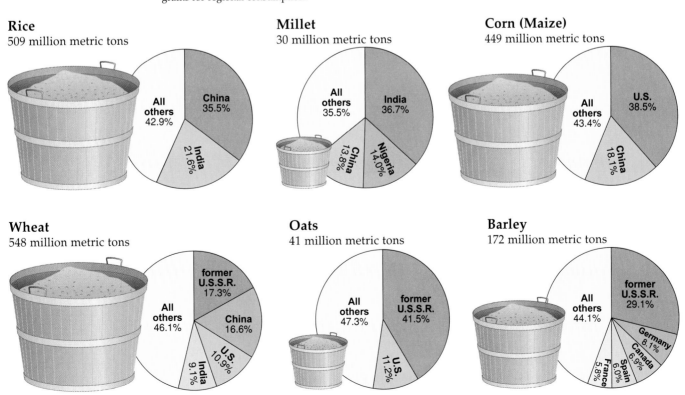

Rice
509 million metric tons

China 35.5%
India 21.6%
All others 42.9%

Millet
30 million metric tons

India 36.7%
Nigeria 14.0%
China 13.8%
All others 35.5%

Corn (Maize)
449 million metric tons

U.S. 38.5%
China 18.1%
All others 43.4%

Wheat
548 million metric tons

former U.S.S.R. 17.3%
China 16.6%
U.S. 10.9%
India 9.1%
All others 46.1%

Oats
41 million metric tons

former U.S.S.R. 41.5%
U.S. 11.2%
All others 47.3%

Barley
172 million metric tons

former U.S.S.R. 29.1%
Germany 8.1%
Canada 6.9%
Spain 6.0%
France 5.8%
All others 44.1%

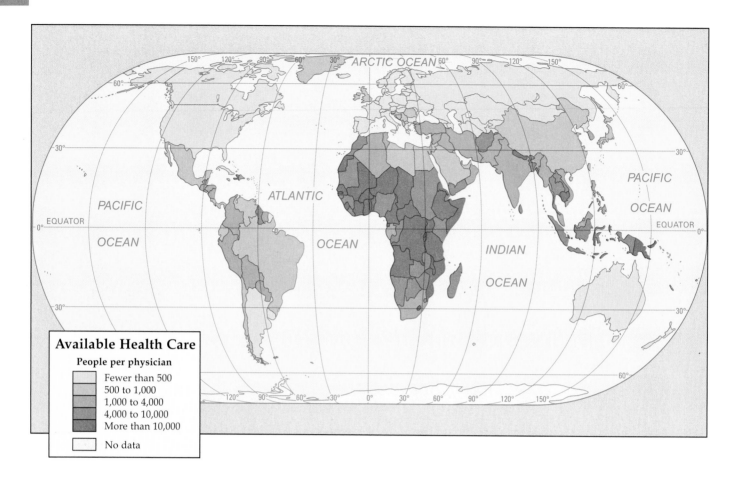

Available Health Care

People per physician

- Fewer than 500
- 500 to 1,000
- 1,000 to 4,000
- 4,000 to 10,000
- More than 10,000
- No data

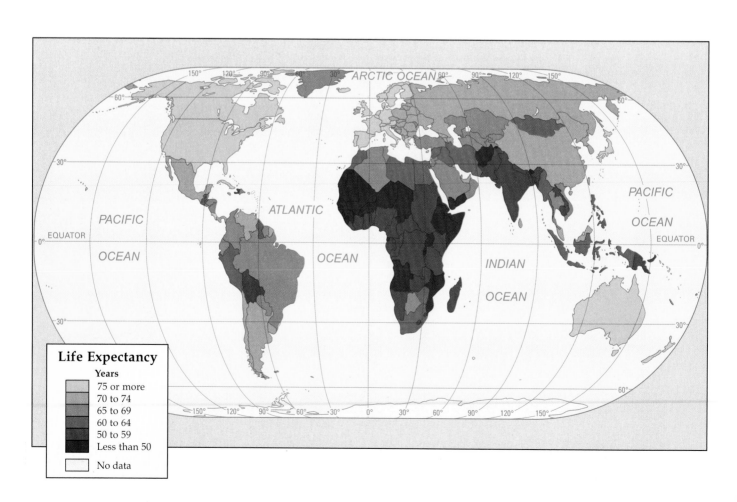

Life Expectancy

Years

- 75 or more
- 70 to 74
- 65 to 69
- 60 to 64
- 50 to 59
- Less than 50
- No data

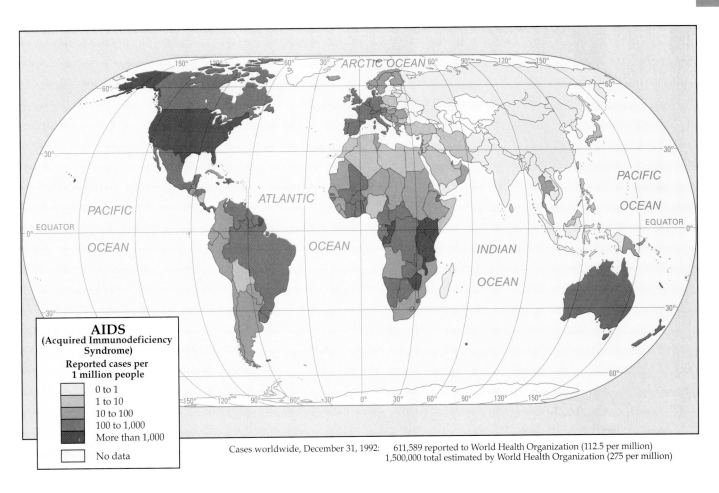

AIDS
(Acquired Immunodeficiency Syndrome)
Reported cases per 1 million people

- 0 to 1
- 1 to 10
- 10 to 100
- 100 to 1,000
- More than 1,000
- No data

Cases worldwide, December 31, 1992: 611,589 reported to World Health Organization (112.5 per million)
1,500,000 total estimated by World Health Organization (275 per million)

Causes of Death

- Infectious and parasitic diseases
- Cancer
- Circulatory system diseases
- Respiratory system diseases
- Accidents, poisonings, and violence
- Other

Percentage of all deaths

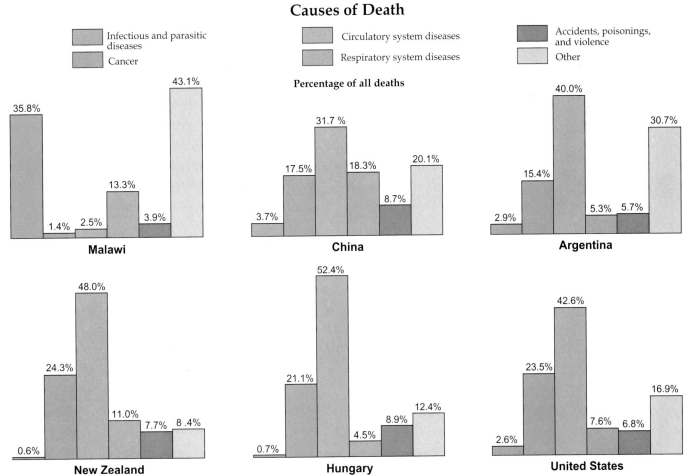

Malawi
35.8% 1.4% 2.5% 13.3% 3.9% 43.1%

China
3.7% 17.5% 31.7% 18.3% 8.7% 20.1%

Argentina
2.9% 15.4% 40.0% 5.3% 5.7% 30.7%

New Zealand
0.6% 24.3% 48.0% 11.0% 7.7% 8.4%

Hungary
0.7% 21.1% 52.4% 4.5% 8.9% 12.4%

United States
2.6% 23.5% 42.6% 7.6% 6.8% 16.9%

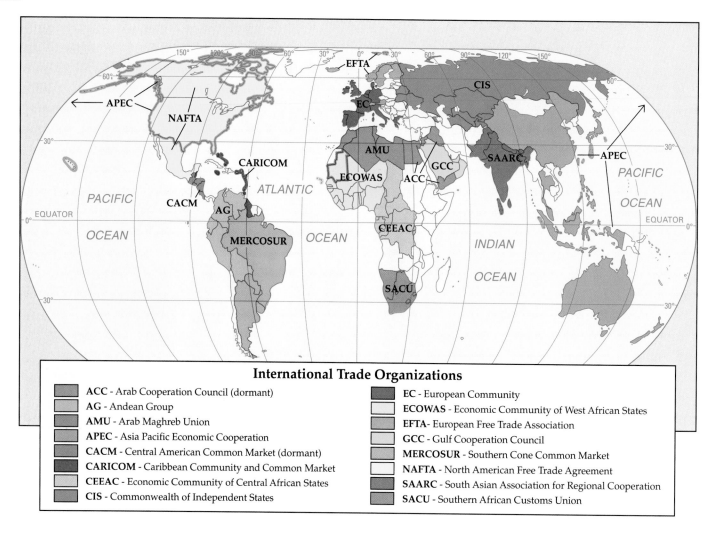

International Trade Organizations

- **ACC** - Arab Cooperation Council (dormant)
- **AG** - Andean Group
- **AMU** - Arab Maghreb Union
- **APEC** - Asia Pacific Economic Cooperation
- **CACM** - Central American Common Market (dormant)
- **CARICOM** - Caribbean Community and Common Market
- **CEEAC** - Economic Community of Central African States
- **CIS** - Commonwealth of Independent States
- **EC** - European Community
- **ECOWAS** - Economic Community of West African States
- **EFTA** - European Free Trade Association
- **GCC** - Gulf Cooperation Council
- **MERCOSUR** - Southern Cone Common Market
- **NAFTA** - North American Free Trade Agreement
- **SAARC** - South Asian Association for Regional Cooperation
- **SACU** - Southern African Customs Union

Single-Commodity Economies

Many countries rely on only one natural resource to support 75% or more of their export economies.

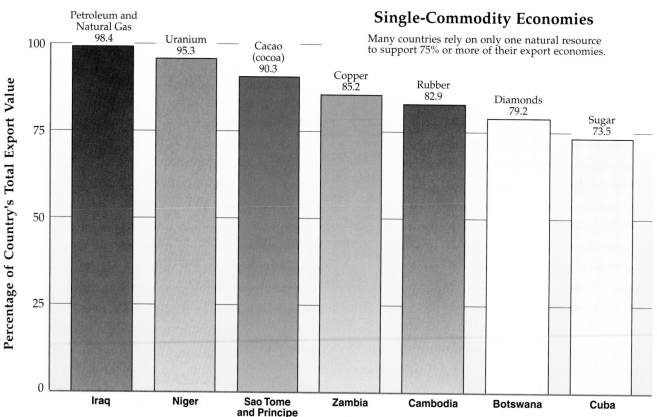

Percentage of Country's Total Export Value

- Petroleum and Natural Gas 98.4 — Iraq
- Uranium 95.3 — Niger
- Cacao (cocoa) 90.3 — Sao Tome and Principe
- Copper 85.2 — Zambia
- Rubber 82.9 — Cambodia
- Diamonds 79.2 — Botswana
- Sugar 73.5 — Cuba

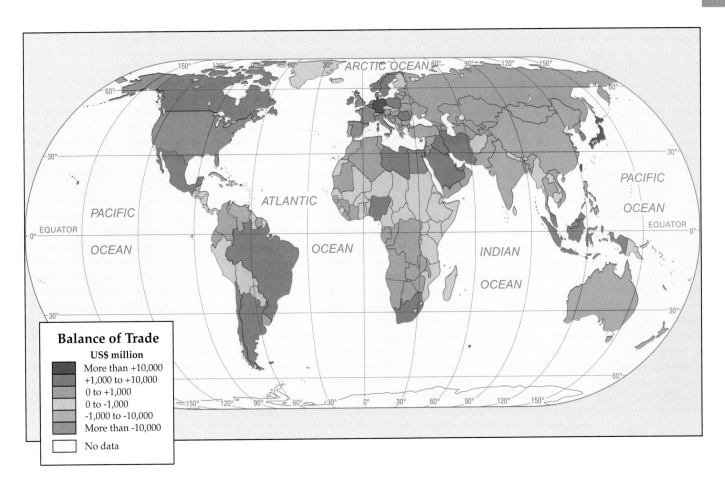

Balance of Trade

US$ million

More than +10,000
+1,000 to +10,000
0 to +1,000
0 to -1,000
-1,000 to -10,000
More than -10,000

No data

Disparity of Income

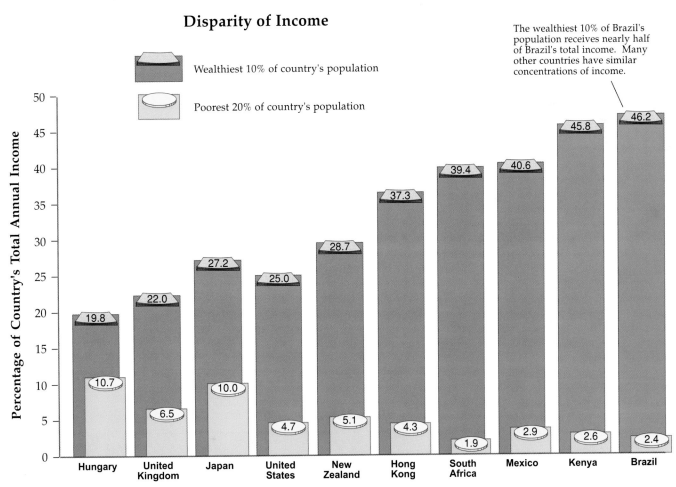

Wealthiest 10% of country's population

Poorest 20% of country's population

The wealthiest 10% of Brazil's population receives nearly half of Brazil's total income. Many other countries have similar concentrations of income.

Percentage of Country's Total Annual Income

Country	Wealthiest 10%	Poorest 20%
Hungary	19.8	10.7
United Kingdom	22.0	6.5
Japan	27.2	10.0
United States	25.0	4.7
New Zealand	28.7	5.1
Hong Kong	37.3	4.3
South Africa	39.4	1.9
Mexico	40.6	2.9
Kenya	45.8	2.6
Brazil	46.2	2.4

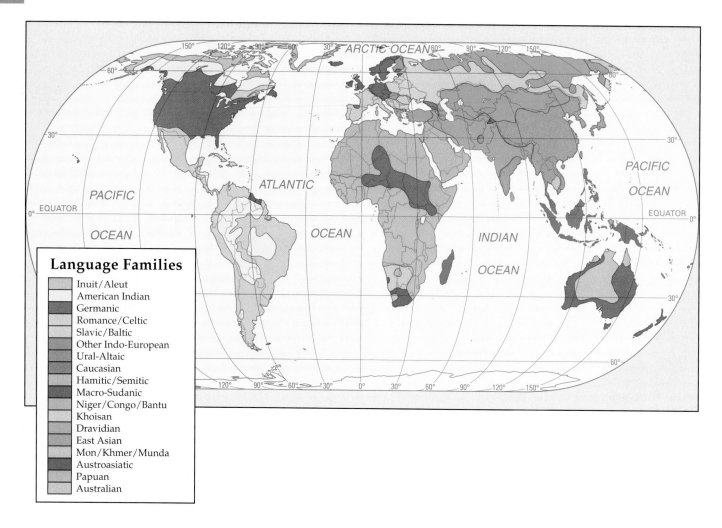

Language Families

- Inuit/Aleut
- American Indian
- Germanic
- Romance/Celtic
- Slavic/Baltic
- Other Indo-European
- Ural-Altaic
- Caucasian
- Hamitic/Semitic
- Macro-Sudanic
- Niger/Congo/Bantu
- Khoisan
- Dravidian
- East Asian
- Mon/Khmer/Munda
- Austroasiatic
- Papuan
- Australian

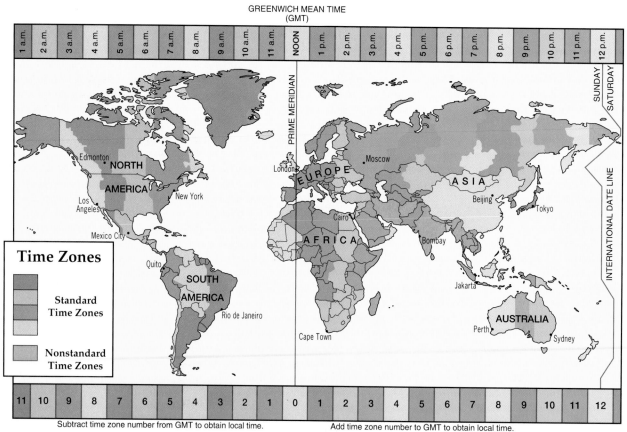

GREENWICH MEAN TIME
(GMT)

| 1 a.m. | 2 a.m. | 3 a.m. | 4 a.m. | 5 a.m. | 6 a.m. | 7 a.m. | 8 a.m. | 9 a.m. | 10 a.m. | 11 a.m. | NOON | 1 p.m. | 2 p.m. | 3 p.m. | 4 p.m. | 5 p.m. | 6 p.m. | 7 p.m. | 8 p.m. | 9 p.m. | 10 p.m. | 11 p.m. | 12 p.m. |

Time Zones

Standard Time Zones

Nonstandard Time Zones

| 11 | 10 | 9 | 8 | 7 | 6 | 5 | 4 | 3 | 2 | 1 | 0 | 1 | 2 | 3 | 4 | 5 | 6 | 7 | 8 | 9 | 10 | 11 | 12 |

Subtract time zone number from GMT to obtain local time.

Add time zone number to GMT to obtain local time.

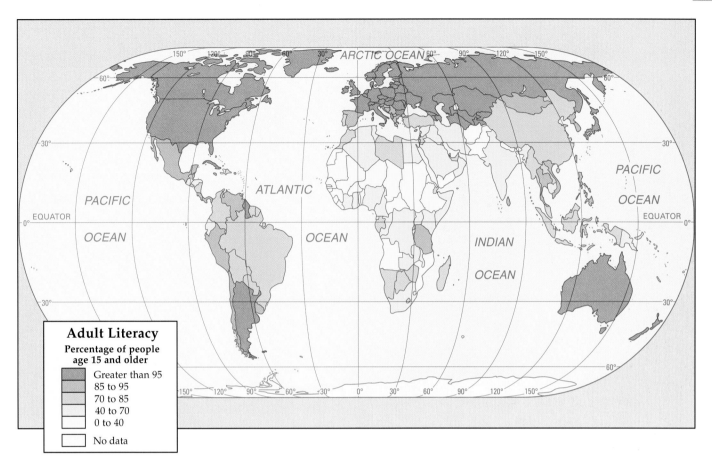

Adult Literacy

Percentage of people age 15 and older

- Greater than 95
- 85 to 95
- 70 to 85
- 40 to 70
- 0 to 40
- No data

Persons per Newspaper

Daily circulation	Country		Persons
25,200,000	United Kingdom		2.5
62,700,000	United States		4.0
11,300,000	Mexico		7.0
16,700,000	India		46.2

Persons per Telephone

Telephones owned	Country		Persons
181,000,000	United States		1.3
14,000,000	Brazil		10
77,000	Angola		123
26,000	Nepal		412

Persons per Radio

Radios owned	Country		Persons
520,000,000	United States		0.5
7,200,000	Australia		1.9
7,000,000	Vietnam		9.5
400,000	Somalia		19

Persons per Television

Televisions owned	Country		Persons
200,000,000	United States		1.2
31,500,000	Japan		2.4
200,000	Nicaragua		18
20,000	Zaire		1,708

Speed of Travel

Route	Year	Means of travel		Length of time
New York to Europe via air	1978	Concorde SST – supersonic jet		3.5 hours
	1950	Intercontinental jet – twin engine jet		10 hours
	1927	*Spirit of St. Louis* – single engine aircraft		33.5 hours
New York to Europe via ocean	1993	*Queen Elizabeth II* – ocean liner		5 days
	1898	*Lucania* – steamer		5.5 days
	1497	John Cabot – sailing vessel		43 days

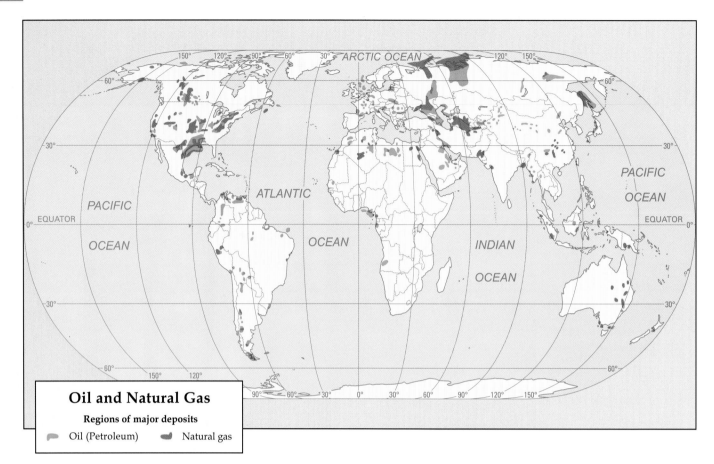

Oil and Natural Gas

Regions of major deposits

Oil (Petroleum)   Natural gas

Oil Production and Consumption

Leaders in World Production

20.1% **former U.S.S.R**
13.1% **United States**
9.3% **Saudi Arabia**
4.6% **Iran**
4.6% **China**
All other countries 48.3%

Leaders in World Consumption

22.2% **United States**
16.1% **former U.S.S.R**
5.9% **Japan**
3.6% **China**
3.2% **Germany**
All other countries 49.0%

Natural Gas Production and Consumption

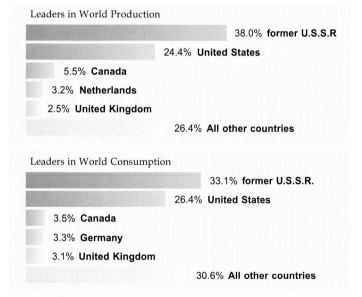

Leaders in World Production

38.0% **former U.S.S.R**
24.4% **United States**
5.5% **Canada**
3.2% **Netherlands**
2.5% **United Kingdom**
26.4% **All other countries**

Leaders in World Consumption

33.1% **former U.S.S.R.**
26.4% **United States**
3.5% **Canada**
3.3% **Germany**
3.1% **United Kingdom**
30.6% **All other countries**

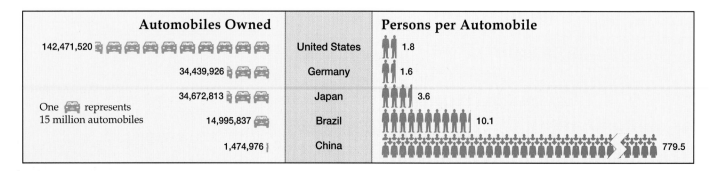

Automobiles Owned		Persons per Automobile
142,471,520	United States	1.8
34,439,926	Germany	1.6
34,672,813	Japan	3.6
14,995,837	Brazil	10.1
1,474,976	China	779.5

One represents
15 million automobiles

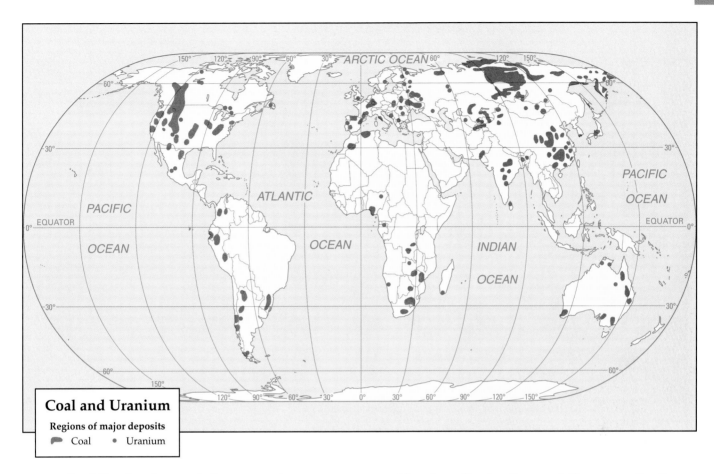

Coal and Uranium

Regions of major deposits

🐾 Coal   • Uranium

Coal Production and Consumption

Leaders in World Production

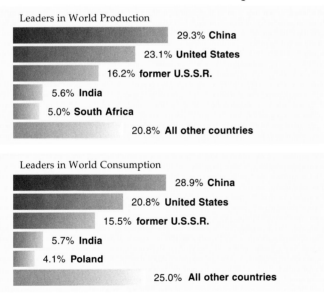

29.3% **China**

23.1% **United States**

16.2% **former U.S.S.R.**

5.6% **India**

5.0% **South Africa**

20.8% **All other countries**

Leaders in World Consumption

28.9% **China**

20.8% **United States**

15.5% **former U.S.S.R.**

5.7% **India**

4.1% **Poland**

25.0% **All other countries**

Uranium Production and Consumption*

Leaders in World Production

30.3% **Canada**

17.9% **South Africa**

12.9% **United States**

10.0% **Australia**

8.9% **France**

20.0% **All other countries**

Leaders in World Consumption

28.9% **United States**

15.7% **France**

9.9% **Japan**

8.4% **Germany**

6.2% **former U.S.S.R.**

30.9% **All other countries**

*Includes only uranium used to generate electricity.

Lifetime of Fossil Fuels	Initial World Supply	Supply Consumed To Date	Remaining Known Reserves	Estimated Unknown Reserves	Estimated Year of Depletion*
Coal	7,600,000 million tons	190,000 million tons	7,410,000 million tons (known and unknown)		**2200 to 5500**
Oil (petroleum)	1,721,000 million barrels	560,320 million barrels	535,380 million barrels	525,300 million barrels	**2035**
Natural gas	255,400,000 million cubic meters	36,400,000 million cubic meters	97,300,000 million cubic meters	121,800,000 million cubic meters	**2050**

*given present rates of use

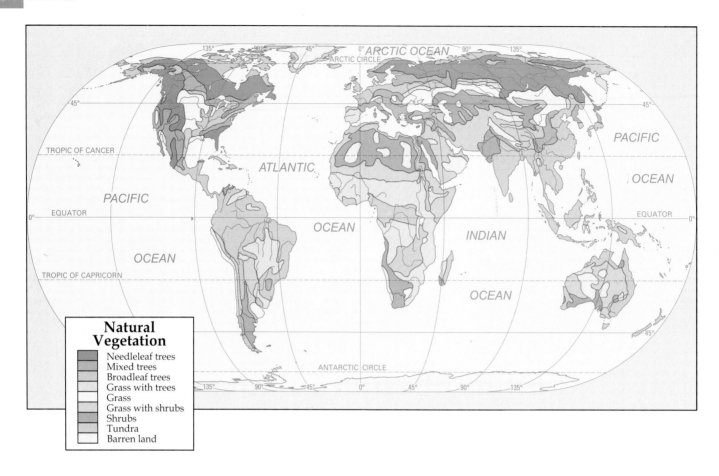

Natural Vegetation

	Needleleaf trees
	Mixed trees
	Broadleaf trees
	Grass with trees
	Grass
	Grass with shrubs
	Shrubs
	Tundra
	Barren land

Natural Vegetation

The world can be divided into zones of natural vegetation. Several categories of vegetation are mapped above.

Most of the categories can be sub-divided. For example, there are several kinds of broadleaf trees: maples, oaks, birches, sycamores, cottonwoods, and so on.

Seven types of vegetation listed in the map key are shown here.

needleleaf trees

mixed trees

broadleaf trees

grass with trees

grass

shrubs

tundra

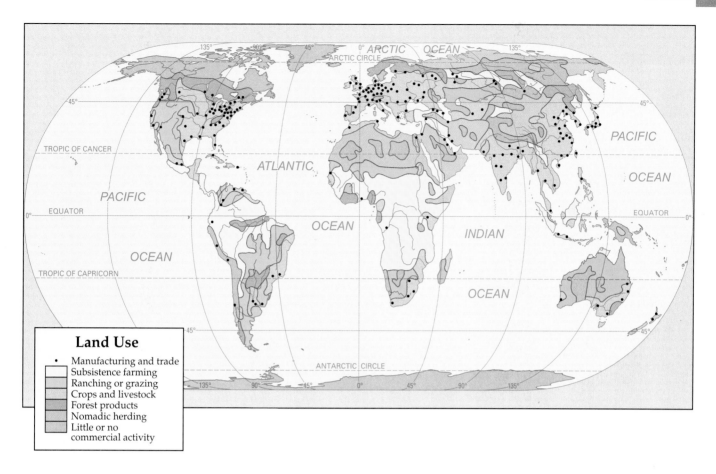

Land Use

- • Manufacturing and trade
- Subsistence farming
- Ranching or grazing
- Crops and livestock
- Forest products
- Nomadic herding
- Little or no commercial activity

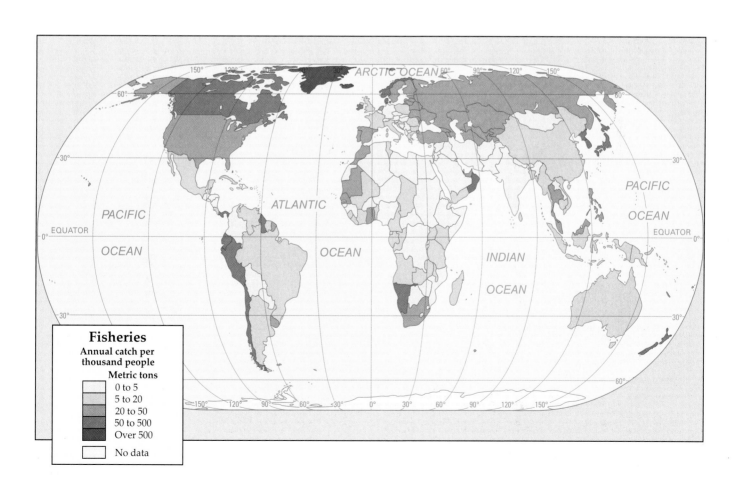

Fisheries

Annual catch per thousand people

Metric tons

- 0 to 5
- 5 to 20
- 20 to 50
- 50 to 500
- Over 500
- No data

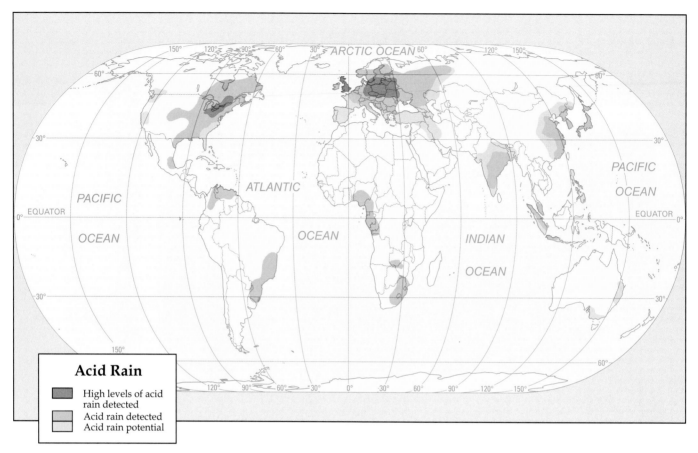

Acid Rain

- High levels of acid rain detected
- Acid rain detected
- Acid rain potential

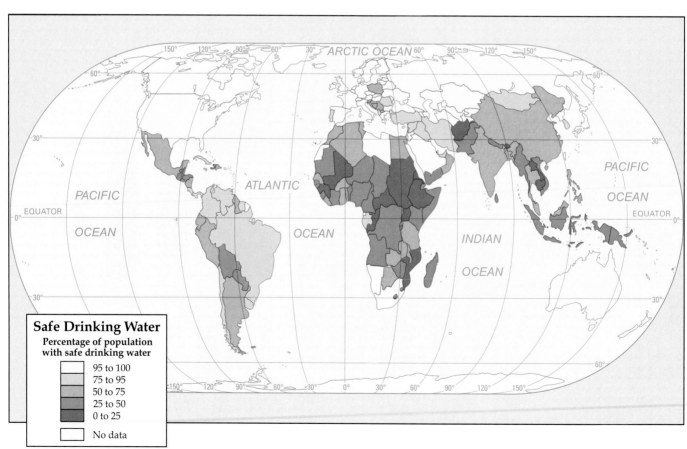

Safe Drinking Water

Percentage of population with safe drinking water

- 95 to 100
- 75 to 95
- 50 to 75
- 25 to 50
- 0 to 25

- No data

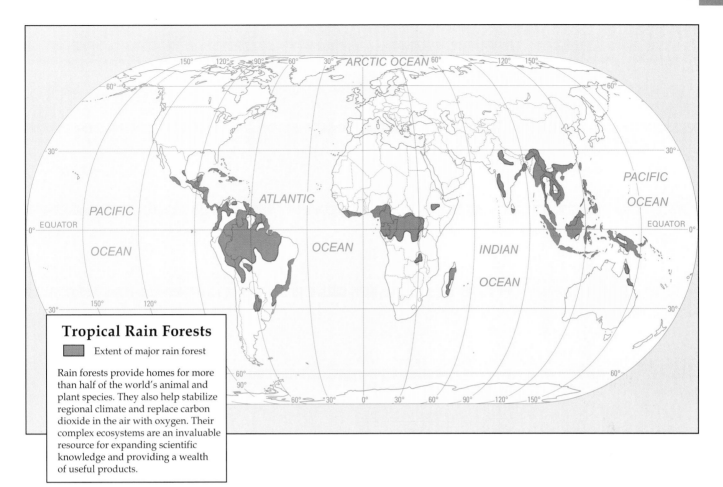

Tropical Rain Forests

Extent of major rain forest

Rain forests provide homes for more than half of the world's animal and plant species. They also help stabilize regional climate and replace carbon dioxide in the air with oxygen. Their complex ecosystems are an invaluable resource for expanding scientific knowledge and providing a wealth of useful products.

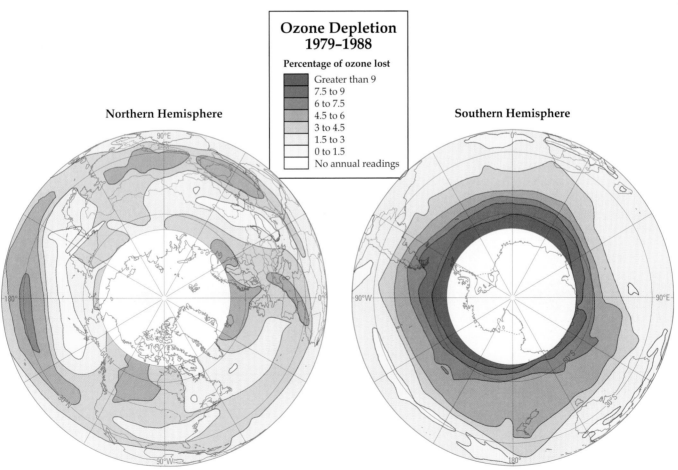

Ozone Depletion 1979–1988

Percentage of ozone lost

Greater than 9
7.5 to 9
6 to 7.5
4.5 to 6
3 to 4.5
1.5 to 3
0 to 1.5
No annual readings

Northern Hemisphere

Southern Hemisphere

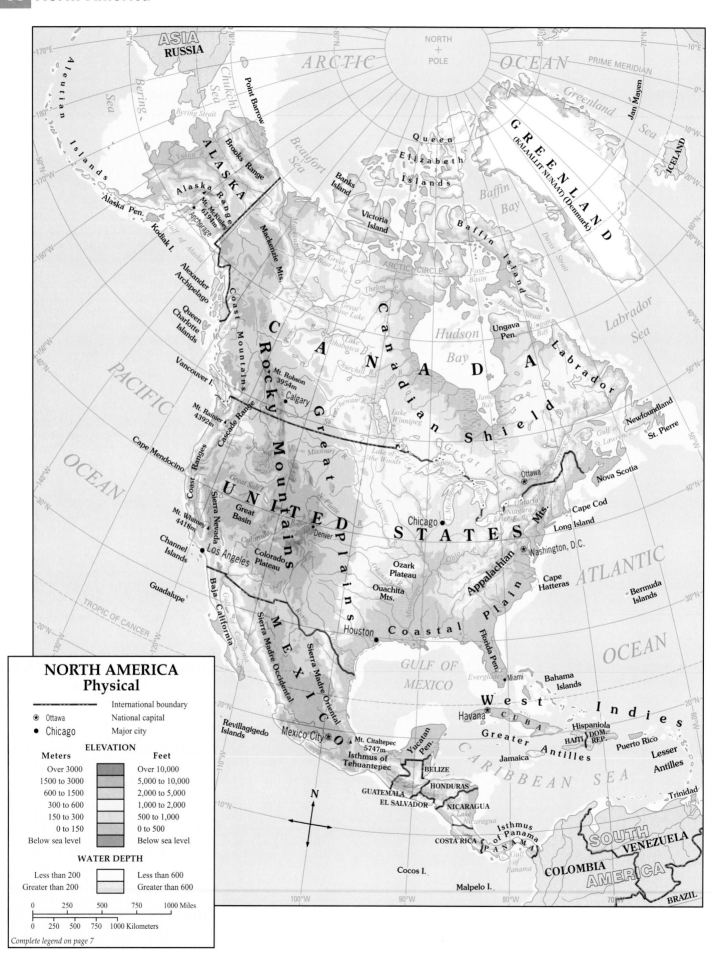

NORTH AMERICA
Physical

———	International boundary
⊛ Ottawa	National capital
● Chicago	Major city

ELEVATION

Meters		Feet
Over 3000		Over 10,000
1500 to 3000		5,000 to 10,000
600 to 1500		2,000 to 5,000
300 to 600		1,000 to 2,000
150 to 300		500 to 1,000
0 to 150		0 to 500
Below sea level		Below sea level

WATER DEPTH

Less than 200		Less than 600
Greater than 200		Greater than 600

0   250   500   750   1000 Miles

0   250   500   750   1000 Kilometers

Complete legend on page 7

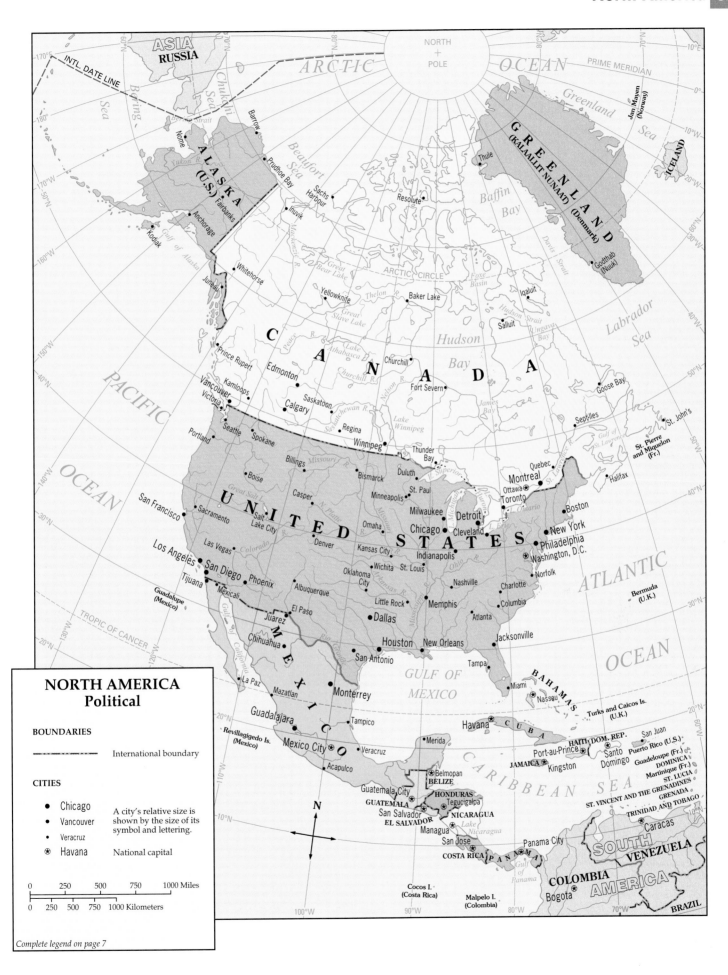

ASIA
RUSSIA
INTL. DATE LINE
ARCTIC OCEAN
NORTH POLE
PRIME MERIDIAN

Bering Strait
Chukchi Sea
Bering Sea
Barrow
Nome
Beaufort Sea
Prudhoe Bay
Sachs Harbour
Inuvik
Resolute
Baffin Bay
GREENLAND (KALAALLIT NUNAAT) (Denmark)
Jan Mayen (Norway)
Greenland Sea
Thule
ICELAND

ALASKA (U.S.)
Fairbanks
Anchorage
Gulf of Alaska
Kodiak
Yukon R.
Whitehorse
Juneau
Mackenzie R.
Great Bear Lake
ARCTIC CIRCLE
Igaluit
Godthab (Nuuk)
Davis Strait
Denmark Sea

PACIFIC OCEAN

Prince Rupert
Peace R.
Edmonton
Yellowknife
Great Slave Lake
Thelon R.
Baker Lake
Foxe Basin
Hudson Strait
Salluit
Ungava Bay
Labrador Sea

CANADA
Lake Athabasca
Churchill
Churchill R.
Fort Severn
Hudson Bay
James Bay
Goose Bay
Sept-Îles
St. John's

Kamloops
Vancouver
Victoria
Calgary
Saskatoon
Saskatchewan R.
Regina
Nelson R.
Lake Winnipeg
Winnipeg
Thunder Bay
Quebec
Montreal
Ottawa
Toronto
Halifax
St. Pierre and Miquelon (Fr.)

Portland
Seattle
Spokane
Billings
Boise
Bismarck
Minneapolis
St. Paul
Duluth
Lake Superior
Lake Michigan
Lake Huron
Lake Ontario
Lake Erie
Milwaukee
Detroit
Cleveland
Boston
New York
Philadelphia
Washington, D.C.

UNITED STATES
San Francisco
Sacramento
Great Salt L.
Salt Lake City
Casper
N. Platte R.
Denver
Omaha
Chicago
Kansas City
Indianapolis
St. Louis
Ohio R.
Nashville
Charlotte
Columbia
Norfolk

Las Vegas
Colorado R.
Los Angeles
San Diego
Tijuana
Phoenix
Albuquerque
Oklahoma City
Wichita
Arkansas R.
Memphis
Atlanta
Little Rock
Mississippi R.
Columbia
Jacksonville
ATLANTIC OCEAN
Bermuda (U.K.)

Guadalupe (Mexico)
Mexicali
El Paso
Juarez
Chihuahua
Dallas
Houston
New Orleans
Tampa
Miami
BAHAMAS
Nassau

TROPIC OF CANCER
Rio Grande
San Antonio
GULF OF MEXICO
Turks and Caicos Is. (U.K.)

MEXICO
La Paz
Gulf of California
Mazatlan
Monterrey
Tampico
Havana
CUBA
HAITI DOM. REP.
Port-au-Prince
Santo Domingo
San Juan
Puerto Rico (U.S.)
Guadeloupe (Fr.)
DOMINICA
Martinique (Fr.)
ST. LUCIA

Revillagigedo Is. (Mexico)
Guadalajara
Mexico City
Veracruz
Merida
JAMAICA
Kingston
ST. VINCENT AND THE GRENADINES
GRENADA
TRINIDAD AND TOBAGO

N

Acapulco
BELIZE
Belmopan
Guatemala City
GUATEMALA
San Salvador
EL SALVADOR
HONDURAS
Tegucigalpa
NICARAGUA
Managua
Lake Nicaragua
CARIBBEAN SEA
Caracas
VENEZUELA

Cocos I. (Costa Rica)
Malpelo I. (Colombia)
San Jose
COSTA RICA
PANAMA
Panama City
Gulf of Panama
SOUTH AMERICA
COLOMBIA
Bogota
BRAZIL

NORTH AMERICA
Political

BOUNDARIES

⎯ ⎯ ⎯ International boundary

CITIES

● Chicago

• Vancouver

· Veracruz   A city's relative size is
                    shown by the size of its
⊛ Havana   symbol and lettering.

                    National capital

0   250   500   750   1000 Miles

0   250 500 750 1000 Kilometers

Complete legend on page 7

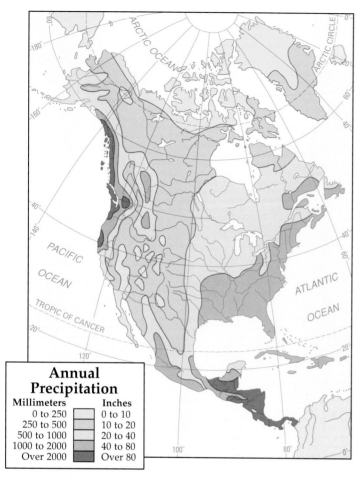

Annual Precipitation

Millimeters	Inches
0 to 250	0 to 10
250 to 500	10 to 20
500 to 1000	20 to 40
1000 to 2000	40 to 80
Over 2000	Over 80

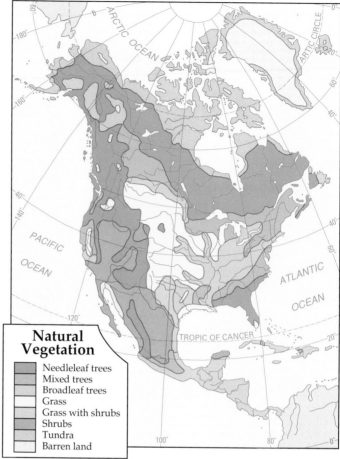

Natural Vegetation

- Needleleaf trees
- Mixed trees
- Broadleaf trees
- Grass
- Grass with shrubs
- Shrubs
- Tundra
- Barren land

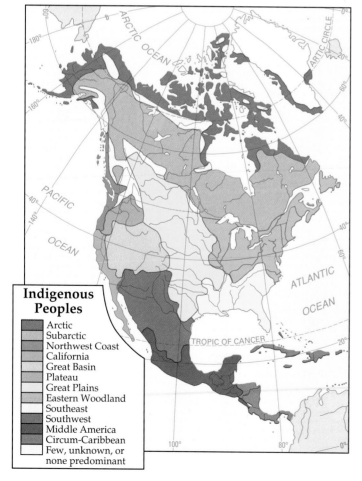

Indigenous Peoples

- Arctic
- Subarctic
- Northwest Coast
- California
- Great Basin
- Plateau
- Great Plains
- Eastern Woodland
- Southeast
- Southwest
- Middle America
- Circum-Caribbean
- Few, unknown, or none predominant

The Canadian Rockies stretch across British Columbia and Alberta. They are part of the Rocky Mountain chain, which extends from New Mexico to northern Alaska.

Yellowstone National Park preserves over 2,000,000 acres (809 400 hectares) of evergreen forests and mountain meadows. Its natural wonders include 3,000 geysers and hot springs.

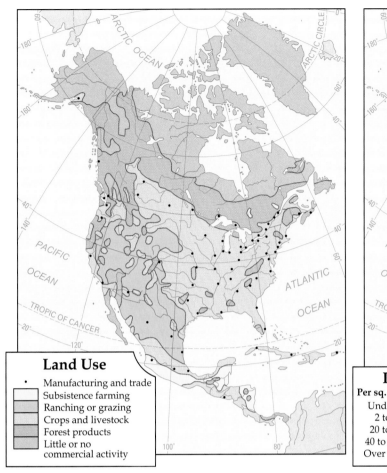

Land Use

- • Manufacturing and trade
- Subsistence farming
- Ranching or grazing
- Crops and livestock
- Forest products
- Little or no commercial activity

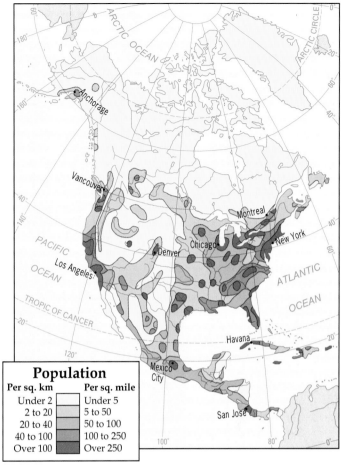

Population

Per sq. km	Per sq. mile
Under 2	Under 5
2 to 20	5 to 50
20 to 40	50 to 100
40 to 100	100 to 250
Over 100	Over 250

MEXICO
Area Comparison

Mexico is about one-fourth the size of the United States. Even though both countries have vast deserts and rugged mountains, Mexico has nearly twice as many people per square mile as the United States.

Mexico	761,604 sq. mi. (1 972 554 sq. km)
Contiguous U.S.	3,021,295 sq. mi. (7 825 112 sq. km)

North American Trade

The United States accounts for at least half of all imports to and/or exports from many North American countries.

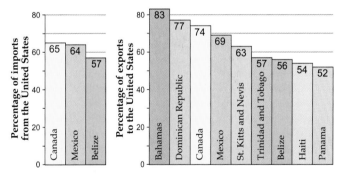

Percentage of imports from the United States: Canada 65, Mexico 64, Belize 57

Percentage of exports to the United States: Bahamas 83, Dominican Republic 77, Canada 74, Mexico 69, St. Kitts and Nevis 63, Trinidad and Tobago 57, Belize 56, Haiti 54, Panama 52

North America--the world's breadbasket--is the leading producer and exporter of wheat.

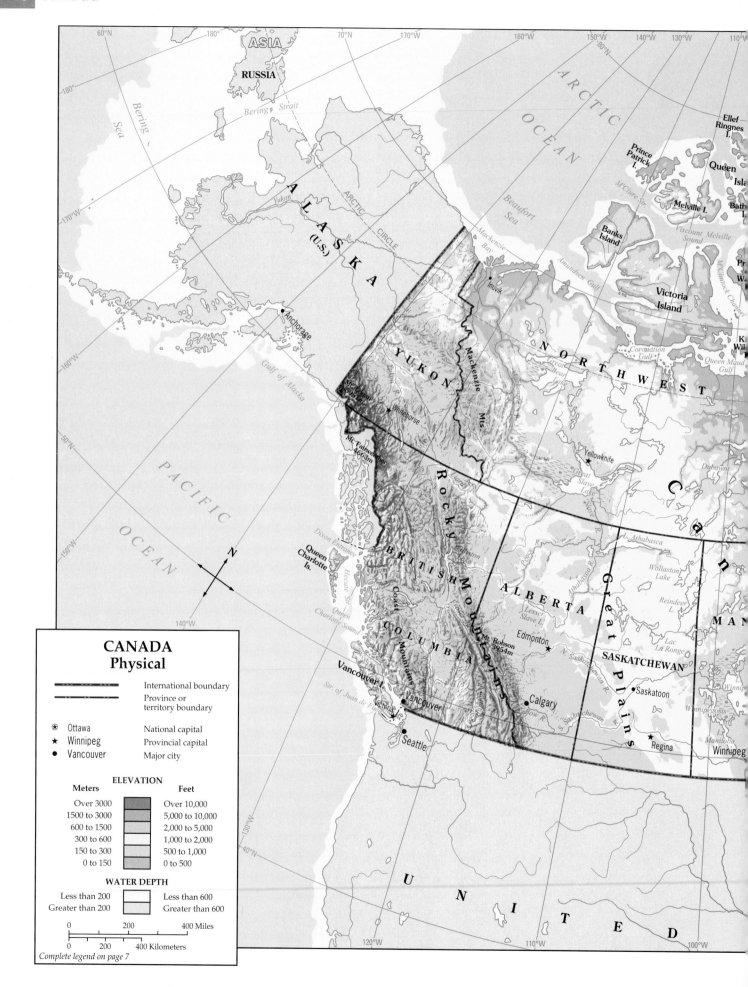

CANADA
Physical

▦▦▦▦▦	International boundary
▬▬▬▬▬	Province or territory boundary
⊛ Ottawa	National capital
★ Winnipeg	Provincial capital
● Vancouver	Major city

ELEVATION

Meters		Feet
Over 3000		Over 10,000
1500 to 3000		5,000 to 10,000
600 to 1500		2,000 to 5,000
300 to 600		1,000 to 2,000
150 to 300		500 to 1,000
0 to 150		0 to 500

WATER DEPTH

Less than 200		Less than 600
Greater than 200		Greater than 600

0   200   400 Miles

0   200   400 Kilometers

Complete legend on page 7

GREENLAND
(KALAALLIT NUNAAT) (Denmark)

ICELAND

ARCTIC CIRCLE

Axel
Heiberg
I.

Ellesmere Island

abeth

Kane
Basin

Devon Island

Lancaster Sound

merset
I.

othia
en.

Gulf of Boothia

Baffin
Bay

Davis
Strait

Denmark
Strait

ATLANTIC

OCEAN

Baffin
Island

Cape Farewell

Melville
Peninsula

Foxe
Basin

Cumberland Sd.

Labrador

TERRITORIES

Foxe Channel

Foxe
Peninsula

Iqaluit

Frobisher Bay

Sea

Southampton
I.

Hudson
Strait

Chesterfield
Inlet

Coats
I.

Cape
Chidley

Mansel
I.

Ungava
Peninsula

Ungava
Bay

Torngat
Mts.

Labrador

OBA

Hudson

Belcher
Is.

Smallwood

Happy Valley-
Goose Bay

i

Bay

James
Bay

Churchill

NEWFOUNDLAND

Newfoundland

St. John's

a

L.
Mistassini

S

h

i

e

l

d

Cape Race

ONTARIO

Albany R.

QUEBEC

Manicouagan
Inlet

Anticosti
I.

Gulf of
St. Lawrence

Miquelon
(Fr.)

St. Pierre
(Fr.)

Lake-of-
the-Woods

Nipigon

Gaspe Pen.

St. Lawrence R.

Strait of Belle Isle

Cape
Breton
Island

Thunder
Bay

L. Superior

Sault Ste.
Marie

Nipissing

Georgian Bay

L.
Simcoe

Quebec

Montreal

Ottawa

PRINCE
EDWARD
ISLAND

NEW
BRUNSWICK

Fredericton

NOVA
SCOTIA

Halifax

Sable I.

Bay of Fundy

L. Huron

L. Michigan

Toronto

L. Ontario

L. Erie

Niagara
Falls

Cape Sable

ATLANTIC

Detroit

Windsor

OCEAN

S

T

A

T

E

S

ASIA
RUSSIA

INTERNATIONAL DATE LINE

60°N
180°
70°N
170°W
160°W
150°W
140°W
130°W
110°
80°N

Bering Strait

Bering Sea

ARCTIC OCEAN

ARCTIC CIRCLE

ALASKA (U.S.)

Yukon R.

Anchorage

Gulf of Alaska

PACIFIC OCEAN

Old Crow

Inuvik

Mackenzie Bay

Beaufort Sea

Amundsen Gulf

Banks I.

Sachs Harbour

M'Clure Str.

Viscount Melville Sound

Prince Patrick I.

Melville I.

Ba

Ellef Ringnes I.

Queen Isl

NORTHWEST

Victoria Island

Cambridge Bay

Coronation Gulf

M'Clintock Channel

Queen Mau Gulf

W

Dawson

YUKON

Pelly Crossing

Yukon R.

Whitehorse

Norman Wells

Great Bear Lake

Mackenzie R.

Juneau

Watson Lake

Fort Simpson

Yellowknife

Great Slave Lake

Hay River

Fort Smith

Dubawnt

L. Athabasca

Liard R.

Fort Nelson

Williston Lake

Dixon Entrance

Prince Rupert

Queen Charlotte Is.

Skeena R.

Hecate Str.

Kitimat

Queen Charlotte Sound

BRITISH COLUMBIA

Dawson Creek

Prince George

Fraser R.

Peace R.

Peace River

Grande Prairie

Lesser Slave L.

ALBERTA

Athabasca R.

Fort McMurray

Buffalo Narrows

Reindeer L.

Wollaston Lake

Lac La Ronge

MA

Thompson

Flin Flon

Edmonton

N. Saskatchewan R.

SASKATCHEWAN

Prince Albert

Saskatoon

N

Vancouver I.

Str. of Juan de Fuca

Victoria

Vancouver

Kamloops

Columbia R.

Red Deer

Calgary

Bow R.

Saskatchewan R.

Winnipe

L. Winnipegosis

L. Manitoba

Seattle

Medicine Hat

Lethbridge

Moose Jaw

Regina

Winnipeg

Brandon

Portland

UNITED

D

40°N

150°W

140°W

130°W

120°W

110°W

100°W

50°N

CANADA
Political

BOUNDARIES

International boundary

Province or territory boundary

CITIES

● Montreal

● Saskatoon

• Resolute

⊛ Ottawa — National capital

★ Winnipeg — Provincial capital

A city's relative size is shown by the size of its symbol and lettering.

0	200	400 Miles
0	200	400 Kilometers

Complete legend on page 7

70°W 60°W 50°W 40°W 30°W 20°W 70°N 10°W 60°N

Axel
Heiberg
I.

Ellesmere Island

Kane
Basin

ARCTIC CIRCLE

ICELAND

10°W

abeth

Devon I.

G R E E N L A N D
(KALAALLIT NUNAAT) (Denmark)

esolute

Lancaster Sound

Baffin

20°W

erset I.

Bay

Gulf of Boothia

Clyde

Baffin
Island

Davis

Strait

Denmark Strait

Pelly Bay

Foxe

Basin

Cumberland Sd.

Godthab

Cape Farewell

30°W

T E R R I T O R I E S

Chesterfield Inlet

Iqaluit

Frobisher Bay

Labrador

Sea

50°N

Southampton
I.

Hudson

Strait

40°W

Coats I.

Salluit

Ungava
Bay

Mansel I.

George R.

Foxe Channel

Churchill

Hudson

Kuujjuaq

Feuilles R.

Happy Valley-
Goose Bay

NEWFOUNDLAND

St. John's

Bay

Belcher
Is.

Kuujjuarapik

Smallwood
Res.

Churchill R.

Strait of Belle Isle

Corner
Brook

Newfoundland

OBA

Fort Severn

James
Bay

Labrador
City

Severn R.

Winisk R.

Manicouagan
Lake

Sept-Îlles

Anticosti
I.

ST. PIERRE AND
MIQUELON
(France)

40°W

Moosonee

L.
Mistassini

Q U E B E C

Gulf of
St. Lawrence

Cape Breton I.

Albany R.

St. Lawrence R.

PRINCE
EDWARD
ISLAND

Charlottetown

Sable I.
(Nova Scotia)

Kenora

O N T A R I O

L.
Nipigon

Val-d'Or

Quebec

St. John R.

NEW
BRUNSWICK
Fredericton

NOVA
SCOTIA

40°N

Lake of
the Woods

Thunder
Bay

Hull

Montreal

Saint John

Halifax

Superior

Sault Ste.
Marie

Sudbury

L.
Nipissing

Ottawa

Bay of Fundy

Yarmouth

L. Superior

Georgian B.

Kingston

ATLANTIC

50°W

Minneapolis

L. Michigan

L. Huron

L.
Simcoe

Toronto

L. Ontario

Boston

Chicago

Detroit

London
Windsor

Hamilton

Buffalo

Niagara
Falls

L. Erie

New York

OCEAN

S T A T E S

90°W 80°W 70°W 60°W

ATLANTIC

OCEAN

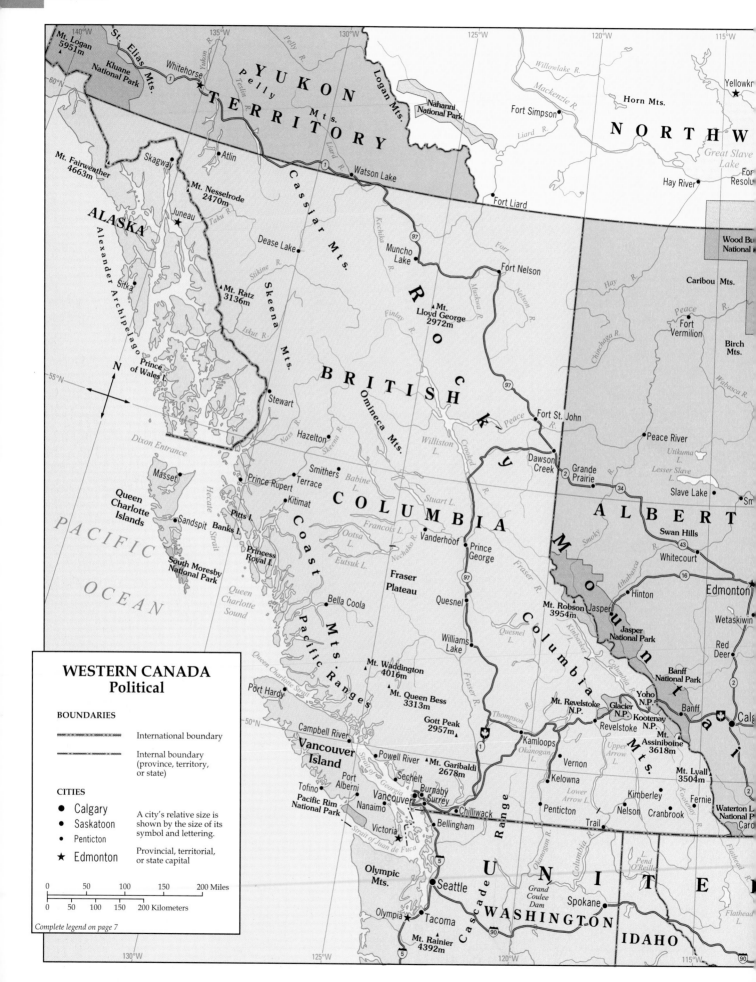

140°W 135°W 130°W 125°W 120°W 115°W

Mt. Logan 5951m
St. Elias Mts.
Kluane National Park
Whitehorse
60°N

YUKON
Pelly R.
Pelly Mts.
TERRITORY
Atlin

Logan Mts.
Nahanni National Park
Liard R.

Willowlake R.
Mackenzie R.
Horn Mts.
Fort Simpson

Yellowkr★
NORTHW

Mt. Fairweather 4663m
Skagway

Mt. Nesselrode 2470m
Taku R.

Cassiar Mts.
Watson Lake

Liard R.
Fort Liard

Liard R.

Hay River

Great Slave Lake
For Resolu

ALASKA
Juneau ★

Alexander Archipelago
Stikine R.

Mt. Ratz 3136m

Skeena Mts.

Dease Lake

Muncho Lake

Kechika R.
Fort Nelson

Fort Nelson R.

Hay R.

Wood Bu National

55°N
Sitka
N

Prince of Wales I.

Iskut R.

Stewart

Nass R.

Finlay R.

Mt. Lloyd George 2972m

R

O

Muskwa R.

Nelson R.

Chinchaga R.

Peace R.

Caribou Mts.

Fort Vermilion

Birch Mts.

Hazelton

B R I T I S H

Omineca Mts.

C

Fort St. John

Dawson Creek

Peace R.

Grande Prairie

Utikuma L.
Lesser Slave L.

Peace River

Slave Lake

Sm

Dixon Entrance

Masset

Queen Charlotte Islands

Hecate Strait

Sandspit

Prince Rupert
Terrace
Kitimat

Pitts I.

Smithers

Babine L.

C O L U M B I A

Stuart L.

Williston L.

Vanderhoof

Francois L.

K

Y

Prince George

Swan Hills

Whitecourt

A L B E R T

Edmonton ★

Wetaskiwin

South Moresby National Park

Banks I.

Princess Royal I.

Ootsa L.

Eutsuk L.

Nechako R.

Fraser R.

Fraser Plateau

Mt. Robson 3954m

Jasper

Hinton

Jasper National Park

Red Deer

PACIFIC

Queen Charlotte Sound

Quesnel

OCEAN

Bella Coola

Coast Mts. Pacific Ranges

Mt. Waddington 4016m

Mt. Queen Bess 3313m

Gott Peak 2957m

Williams Lake

Quesnel L.

Fraser R.

Kinbasket L.

M

o

u

n

Mt. Assiniboine 3618m

Mt. Lyall 3504m

Columbia R.

Banff National Park

Yoho N.P.

Banff

Calg

WESTERN CANADA
Political

BOUNDARIES

——·——·—— International boundary

———————— Internal boundary (province, territory, or state)

CITIES

● Calgary

● Saskatoon

• Penticton

★ Edmonton

A city's relative size is shown by the size of its symbol and lettering.

Provincial, territorial, or state capital

0   50   100   150   200 Miles
0 50 100 150 200 Kilometers

Complete legend on page 7

Port Hardy

Queen Charlotte Strait

Campbell River

50°N

Vancouver Island

Powell River

Mt. Garibaldi 2678m

Sechelt

Port Alberni

Tofino

Nanaimo

Pacific Rim National Park

Strait of Georgia

Vancouver

Burnaby

Surrey

Chilliwack

Bellingham

Victoria ★

Strait of Juan de Fuca

Kamloops

Thompson R.

Okanogan R.

Vernon

Kelowna

Penticton

Upper Arrow L.

Lower Arrow L.

Revelstoke

Mt. Revelstoke N.P.

Glacier N.P.

Kootenay N.P.

Mt. Revelstoke

Kimberley

Nelson

Cranbrook

Fernie

Waterton L National P Card

t

a

i

2

Olympic Mts.

Seattle

5

U N I T E

WASHINGTON

Grand Coulee Dam

Spokane

L. Pend O'Reille

Columbia R.

Trail

Kootenay R.

Flathead R.

Olympia ★

Tacoma

90

Mt. Rainier 4392m

125°W

120°W

IDAHO

115°W

90

130°W

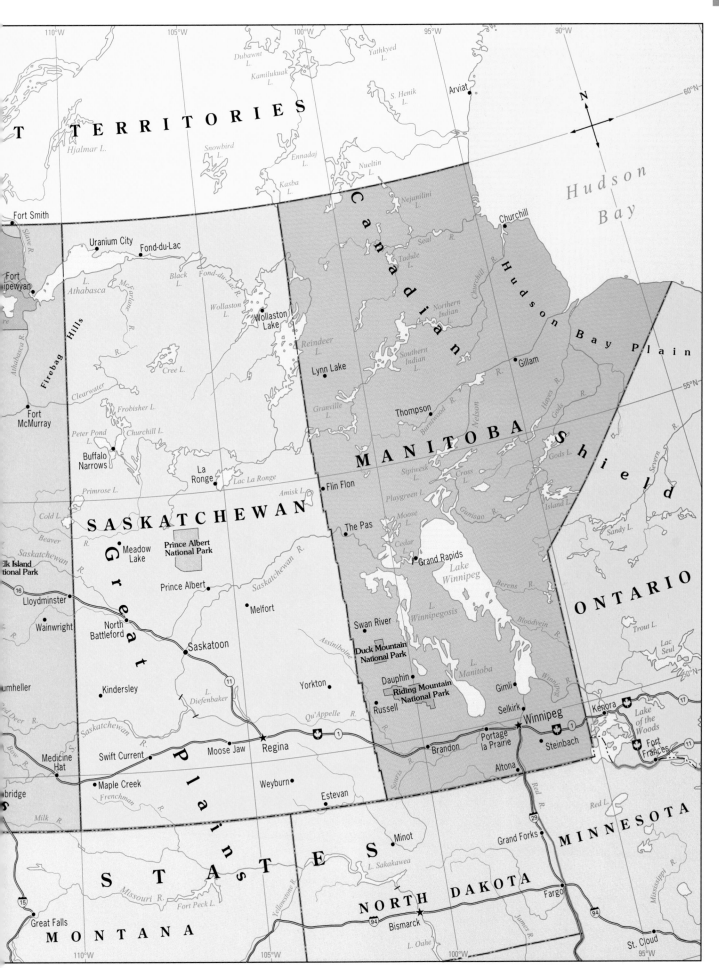

T E R R I T O R I E S

Dubawnt L.

Kamilukuak L.

Yathkyed L.

S. Henik L.

Arviat

60°N

N

Hudson Bay

Hjalmar L.

Snowbird L.

Ennadaj L.

Nueltin L.

Kasba L.

Nejanilini L.

Fort Smith

Uranium City   Fond-du-Lac

Churchill

Fort Chipewyan

L. Athabasca

McFarlane R.

Black L.

Fond-du-Lac R.

Wollaston Lake

Wollaston L.

Seal R.

Tadule L.

Northern Indian L.

Churchill R.

Hudson Bay Plain

Firebag Hills

Clearwater R.

Cree L.

Reindeer L.

Lynn Lake

Southern Indian L.

Gillam

Athabasca R.

Fort McMurray

Peter Pond L.

Frobisher L.

Churchill L.

Buffalo Narrows

Granville L.

Thompson

Burntwood R.

Nelson R.

Hayes R.

Gods R.

55°N

Primrose L.

La Ronge

Lac La Ronge

Amisk L.

Flin Flon

M A N I T O B A

Sipiwesk L.

Cross L.

Gunisao R.

Island L.

Gods L.

Sandy L.

Cold L.

SASKATCHEWAN

The Pas

Playgreen L.

Beaver R.

Great

Meadow Lake

Prince Albert National Park

Moose L.

Cedar L.

Grand Rapids

Lake Winnipeg

Berens R.

Severn R.

Saskatchewan R.

Saskatchewan R.

Elk Island National Park

Lloydminster

16

North Battleford

Prince Albert

Melfort

Swan River

L. Winnipegosis

Bloodvein R.

O N T A R I O

Trout L.

Lac Seul

Wainwright

Kindersley

Saskatoon

11

L. Diefenbaker

Yorkton

Assiniboine R.

Duck Mountain National Park

Dauphin

Russell

Riding Mountain National Park

L. Manitoba

Gimli

Selkirk

Winnipeg R.

Kenora

17

Lake of the Woods

50°N

umheller

Medicine Hat

Swift Current

Moose Jaw

Regina

Qu'Appelle R.

1

Brandon

Portage la Prairie

Steinbach

Winnipeg

1

Fort Frances

11

Bow R.

Red Deer R.

Maple Creek

Saskatchewan R.

Weyburn

Estevan

Souris R.

Altona

Red R.

Red L.

bridge

Frenchman R.

Milk R.

S T A T E S

29

M I N N E S O T A

Mississippi R.

15

Great Falls

Missouri R.

Fort Peck L.

Yellowstone R.

Minot

L. Sakakawea

N O R T H   D A K O T A

Grand Forks

Fargo

94

James R.

Red L.

11

M O N T A N A

105°W

94

Bismarck

L. Oahe

100°W

St. Cloud

95°W

MANITOBA

95°W · 60°N · 90°W · 85°W · Hudson · Bay · 80°W

Hudson Bay Plains

Cape Henrietta Maria

Long I. (N.W.T.)

Kuujjuarapik

Sachigo R.

Severn R.

Island L.

Sachigo L.

Big Trout L.

Fawn R.

Winisk R.

Winisk

Bear I. (N.W.T.)

Pointe Louis-XIV

James Bay

Sandy L.

Sutton L.

Chisasibi

La Grande R.

Ekwan R.

Berens R.

C a n a d i a n

Akimiski I. (N.W.T.)

Wemindji

Trout L.

St. Joseph L.

Central Patricia

Otoskwin R.

Attawapiskat

Kapiskau R.

Kashechewan

Balmertown

L. Seul

Albany R.

Albany R.

Little Current R.

Ogoki Res.

Ogoki R.

ONTARIO

Fort Albany

Charlton I. (N.W.T.)

Eastmain

Moosonee

Moose Factory

Waskaganish

Ruper

Broadbac

50°N

Kenora

Lake of the Woods

Dryden

Armstrong

Nakina

Kenogami R.

L. Nipigon

Longlac

Missinaibi R.

Moose R.

Abitibi R.

Kesagami L.

Nottaway R.

Hurricana R.

17

Fort Frances

Rainy L.

Atikokan

71

Rainy R.

Pigeon R.

Thunder Bay

Nipigon

Schreiber

Aguasabon R.

Marathon

Hearst

11

Oba

Kapuskasing

Cochrane

Kabinakagami R.

Kapuskasing R.

La Sarre

Matagami

Abitibi R.

International Falls

St. Ignace I.

White River

Wawa

Chapleau

Groundhog R.

Mattagami R.

Timmins

Kirkland Lake

L. Abitibi

Rouyn-Noranda

Sennet

66

MINNESOTA

Isle Royale

Pukaskwa National Park

Michipicoten I.

17

Biscotasi L.

Ramsey L.

Mississagi R.

Indian L.

Spanish R.

Cobalt

Val-d'Or

Res. Decelles

Duluth

Superior

Lake Superior

Temagami

L. Kipawa

Simard

35

Marquette

Whitefish Bay

Sault Ste. Marie

Sudbury

11

North Bay

Temiscaming

Ottawa R.

17

WISCONSIN

Upper Peninsula

Sault Ste. Marie

St. Joseph I.

Blind River

North Channel

Temiscaming

L. Nipissing

69

17

MICHIGAN

Cockburn I.

Manitoulin I.

Georgian Bay

Parry Sound

Pembr

45°N

75

Green Bay

Alpena

Bruce Peninsula N.P.

Georgian Bay Islands National Park

Huntsville

Bancroft

11

Madawas

Traverse City

Lake Huron

Owen Sound

Barrie

Simcoe L.

Kawartha Lakes

Peterborough

Bellevi

400

Oshawa

401

SOUTH CENTRAL CANADA
Political

BOUNDARIES

—·—·— International boundary

——— Internal boundary (province or state)

CITIES

● Montreal

● Thunder Bay

· Saint John

A city's relative size is shown by the size of its symbol and lettering.

✪ Ottawa — National capital

★ Halifax — Provincial or state capital

0 50 100 150 200 Miles

0 50 100 150 200 Kilometers

Complete legend on page 7

Lower Peninsula

Saginaw

Goderich

North York

Brampton

Etobicoke

Waterloo

Kitchener

Markham

Scarborough

Toronto

Mississauga

Hamilton

La Onta

Milwaukee

69

London

402

Brantford

St. Catharines

Niagara Falls

Rochester

Racine

43

96

Sarnia

Thames R.

401

NEW

Lake Michigan

UNITED

Lansing

94

75

Detroit

St. Clair

Chatham

Windsor

Welland Canal

Buffalo

Erie

Chicago

80 90

Gary

STATE

Pt. Pelee N.P.

Lake Erie

Erie

90

79

ILLINOIS

57

65

INDIANA

69

75

OHIO

85°W

Toledo

Cleveland

80°W

PENNSYLVANI

90°W

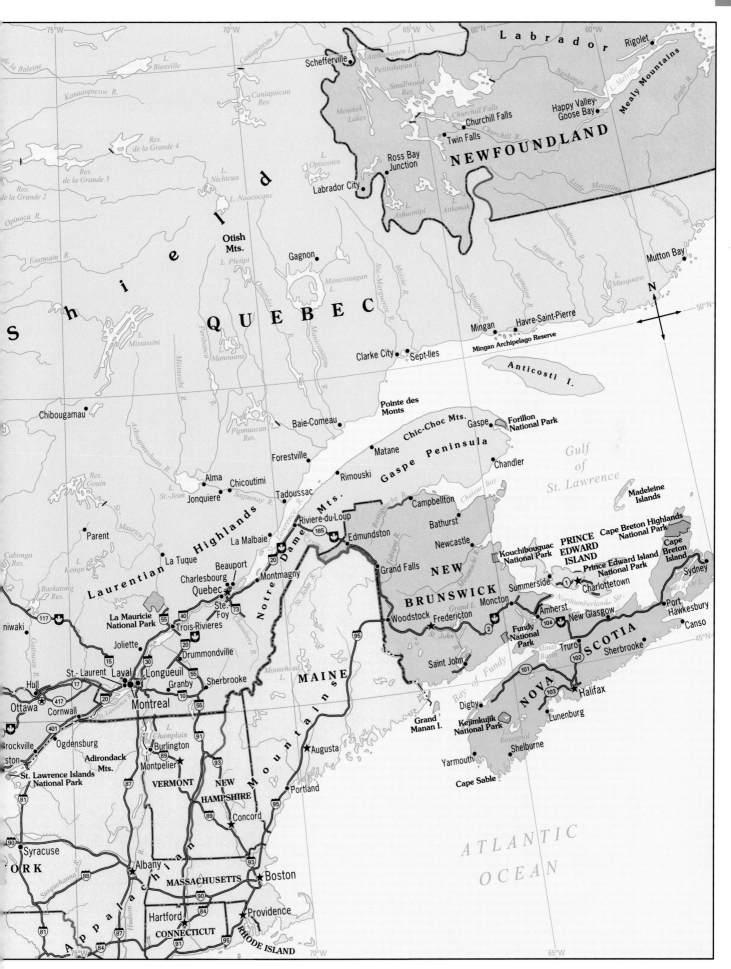

L a b r a d o r

Rigolet

Mealy Mountains

Scheffervile

Attikamagen L.

Petitsikapau L.

Smallwood Res.

Churchill Falls

Happy Valley-Goose Bay

Twin Falls

NEWFOUNDLAND

Ross Bay Junction

Labrador City

L. Opiscoteo

L. Ashuanipi

L. Atikonak

Mutton Bay

Otish Mts.

Gagnon

L. Pletipi

Manicouagan L.

QUEBEC

Mingan

Havre-Saint-Pierre

L. Musquaro

Clarke City

Sept-Iles

Mingan Archipelago Reserve

A n t i c o s t i I.

Chibougamau

Pointe des Monts

Baie-Comeau

Chic-Choc Mts.

Gaspe

Forillon National Park

Gulf of St. Lawrence

Matane

Forestville

G a s p e   P e n i n s u l a

Chandler

Madeleine Islands

Rimouski

Alma

Chicoutimi

Jonquiere

Tadoussac

Campbellton

Chaleur Bay

Cape Breton Highlands National Park

Parent

Riviere-du-Loup

Bathurst

PRINCE EDWARD ISLAND

Cape Breton Island

La Malbaie

Edmundston

Newcastle

Kouchibouguac National Park

Prince Edward Island National Park

Sydney

La Tuque

Beauport

Grand Falls

Summerside

Charlottetown

Port Hawkesbury

Charlesbourg

Quebec

Montmagny

NEW

Moncton

Amherst

New Glasgow

Canso

La Mauricie National Park

Ste. Foy

BRUNSWICK

Grand L.

Northumberland Str.

Trois-Rivieres

Woodstock

Fredericton

Fundy National Park

NOVA SCOTIA

Jolliette

Drummondville

Truro

Sherbrooke

St.-Laurent

Laval

Longueuil

Granby

Sherbrooke

Saint John

MAINE

Minas Basin

Ottawa

Cornwall

Montreal

Bay of Fundy

Digby

Halifax

Brockville

Ogdensburg

L. Champlain

Burlington

Grand Manan I.

Kejimkujik National Park

Lunenburg

St. Lawrence Islands National Park

Adirondack Mts.

Montpelier

Augusta

Shelburne

Syracuse

Albany

VERMONT

NEW HAMPSHIRE

Concord

Portland

Yarmouth

Cape Sable

ATLANTIC

OCEAN

MASSACHUSETTS

Boston

Hartford

Providence

CONNECTICUT

RHODE ISLAND

N

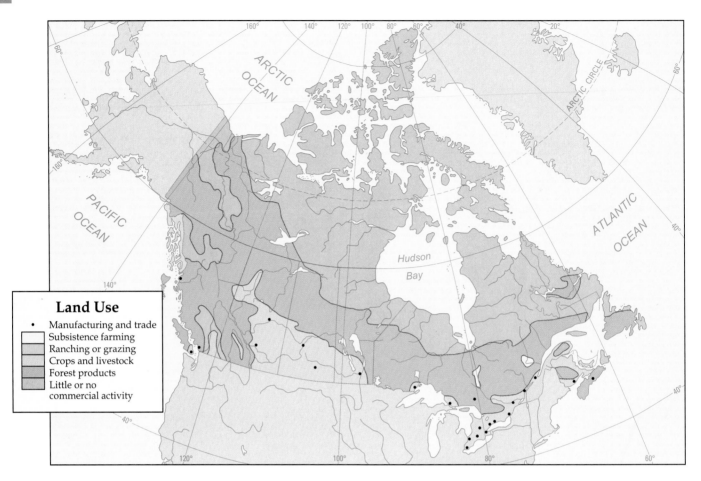

Land Use

- Manufacturing and trade
- Subsistence farming
- Ranching or grazing
- Crops and livestock
- Forest products
- Little or no commercial activity

CANADA
Area Comparison

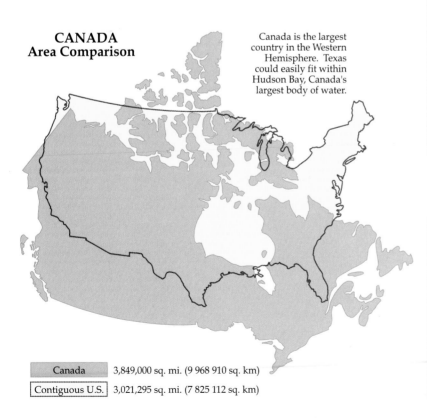

Canada is the largest country in the Western Hemisphere. Texas could easily fit within Hudson Bay, Canada's largest body of water.

Canada	3,849,000 sq. mi. (9 968 910 sq. km)
Contiguous U.S.	3,021,295 sq. mi. (7 825 112 sq. km)

Vancouver, Canada's third-largest metropolitan area, is a major center for commerce and transportation. Known as the Gateway to the Pacific, it has the busiest seaport in Canada.

Fishing has been an important industry in Canada's Maritime Provinces since the late 1400s. The region's picturesque seacoast also attracts many tourists.

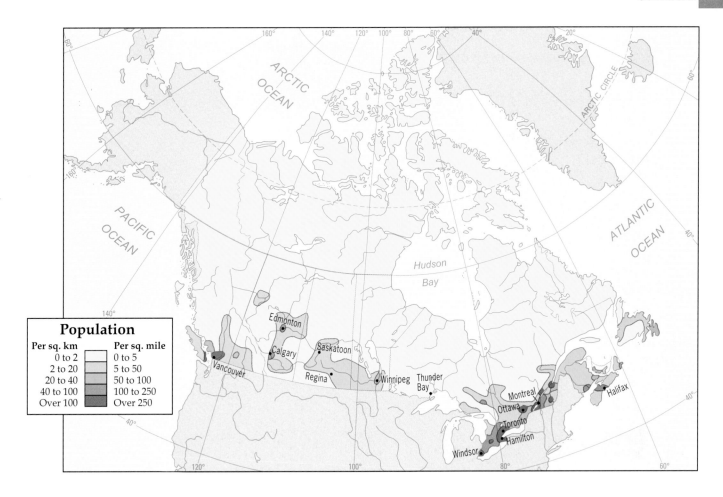

Population

Per sq. km	Per sq. mile
0 to 2	0 to 5
2 to 20	5 to 50
20 to 40	50 to 100
40 to 100	100 to 250
Over 100	Over 250

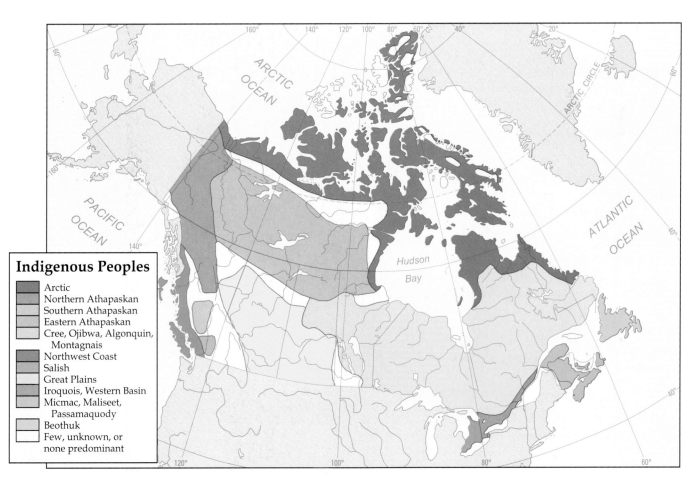

Indigenous Peoples

- Arctic
- Northern Athapaskan
- Southern Athapaskan
- Eastern Athapaskan
- Cree, Ojibwa, Algonquin, Montagnais
- Northwest Coast
- Salish
- Great Plains
- Iroquois, Western Basin
- Micmac, Maliseet, Passamaquody
- Beothuk
- Few, unknown, or none predominant

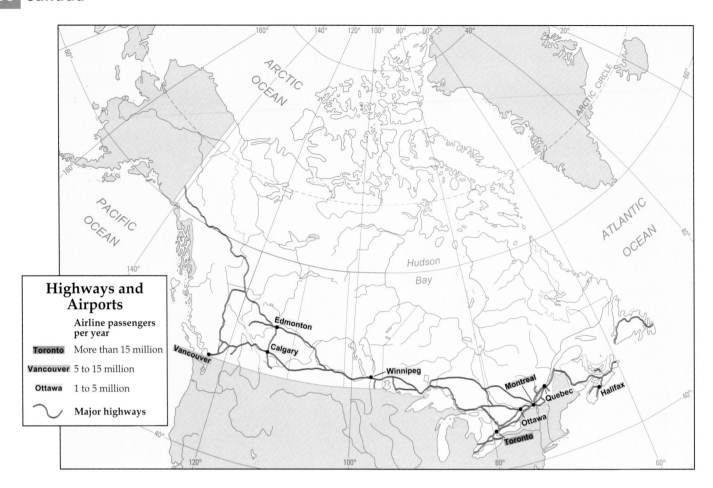

Highways and Airports

Airline passengers per year

Toronto	More than 15 million
Vancouver	5 to 15 million
Ottawa	1 to 5 million
∿	Major highways

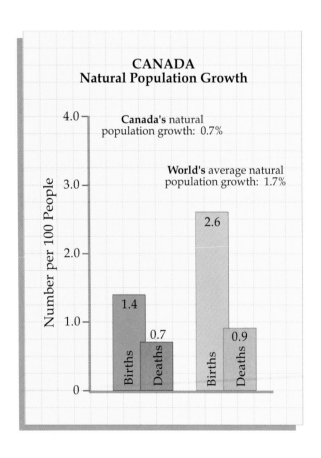

CANADA
Natural Population Growth

Canada's natural population growth: 0.7%

World's average natural population growth: 1.7%

Number per 100 People

Births 1.4
Deaths 0.7
Births 2.6
Deaths 0.9

CANADA
Balance of Trade

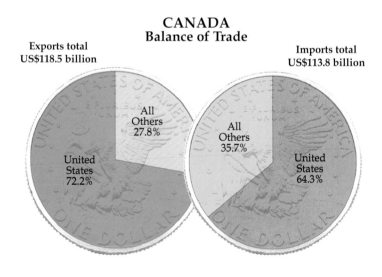

Exports total
US$118.5 billion

All Others 27.8%
United States 72.2%

Imports total
US$113.8 billion

All Others 35.7%
United States 64.3%

Export Destinations		Import Sources	
United States	72.2%	United States	64.3%
Japan	6.2%	Japan	7.1%
United Kingdom	2.4%	United Kingdom	3.4%
China	1.3%	Germany	2.8%
Germany	1.2%	South Korea	1.7%
South Korea	1.0%	Taiwan	1.7%
Netherlands	1.0%	France	1.6%
All others	14.7%	All others	17.4%

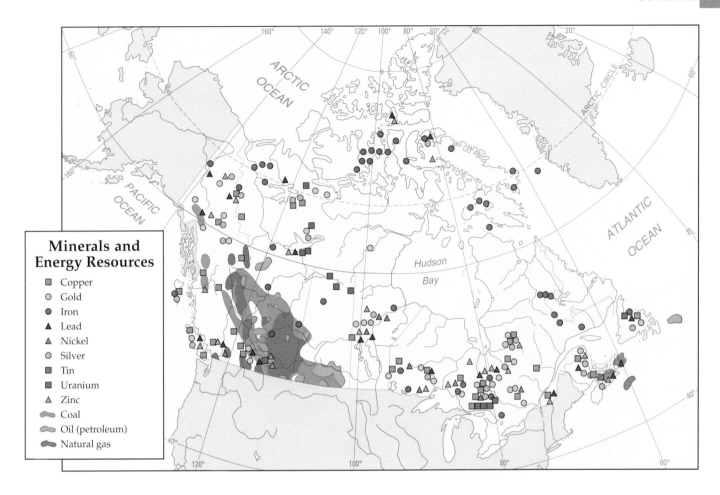

Minerals and Energy Resources

- ■ Copper
- ○ Gold
- ● Iron
- ▲ Lead
- ▲ Nickel
- ○ Silver
- ■ Tin
- ■ Uranium
- ▲ Zinc
- Coal
- Oil (petroleum)
- Natural gas

Forestry Exports

More of Canada's forest products are exported to the United States than to any other country.

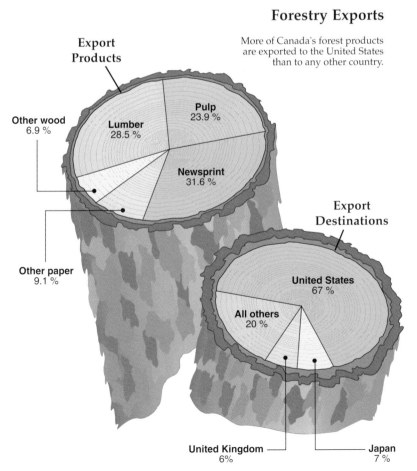

Export Products

Lumber 28.5 %

Pulp 23.9 %

Newsprint 31.6 %

Other wood 6.9 %

Other paper 9.1 %

Export Destinations

United States 67 %

All others 20 %

United Kingdom 6%

Japan 7%

Quebec's growing industrial strength is partly due to its hydro-electric power. High-voltage lines carry electricity from dams in the north to cities near the St. Lawrence River.

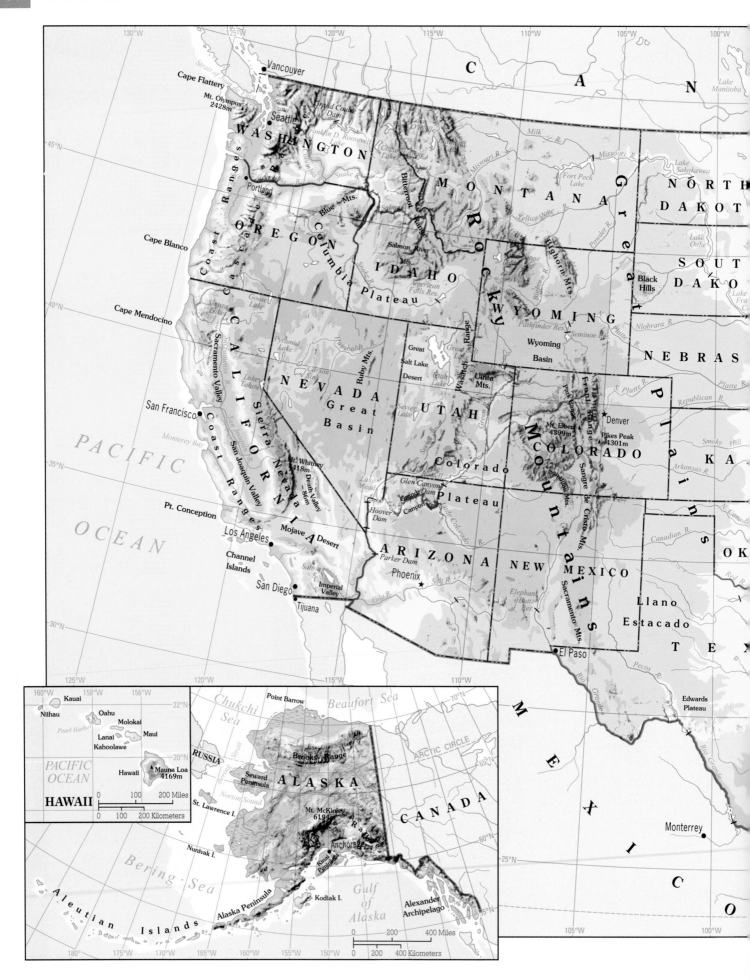

UNITED STATES
Physical

International boundary
State boundary
⊛ Washington, D.C. National capital
★ Atlanta State capital
● Detroit Major city

ELEVATION

Meters		Feet
Over 3000		Over 10,000
1500 to 3000		5,000 to 10,000
600 to 1500		2,000 to 5,000
300 to 600		1,000 to 2,000
150 to 300		500 to 1,000
0 to 150		0 to 500
Below sea level		Below sea level

WATER DEPTH

Less than 200	Less than 600
Greater than 200	Greater than 600

0   100   200   300 Miles
0 100 200 300 Kilometers

Complete legend on page 7

130°W 125°W 120°W 115°W 110°W 105°W 100°W

Calgary

C A N

Vancouver
Bellingham
Strait of Juan de Fuca
Puget Sound
Seattle
Olympia Tacoma
WASHINGTON
45°N
Astoria
Vancouver
Portland
Salem
Eugene
Coos Bay
OREGON
Medford
Klamath Falls
40°N
Eureka
Shasta Lake
Goose Lake

Spokane
Franklin D. Roosevelt Lake
Lake Pend O'Reille
Coeur d'Alene
Moscow
Lewiston
Walla Walla
Pendleton
Baker
Ontario
Snake R.
IDAHO
Boise
American Falls Res.
Idaho Falls
Pocatello
Twin Falls
Salmon R.

Lake Manitoba
Minot
NORTH DAKOTA
Bismarck
Lake Sakakawea

Flathead Lake
Missoula
Great Falls
Milk R.
Fort Peck Lake
Missouri R.
MONTANA
Butte Helena
Yellowstone R.
Billings
Powder R.
Bighorn R.

Lake Oahe
Aberdeen
SOUTH DAKOTA
Rapid City Pierre
Lake Fr.

Yellowstone Lake
Sheridan
WYOMING
Casper
Pathfinder Res.
Pathfinder Res.
Seminoe Res.
N. Platte R.
Niobrara R.

NEBRASKA

PACIFIC
Sacramento R.
CALIFORNIA
Sacramento
San Francisco
Oakland
San Jose
Monterey Bay
Monterey
Fresno
35°N
Bakersfield
Santa Barbara

Winnemucca
Pyramid Lake
Humboldt R.
Elko
Reno
Carson Sink
Lake Tahoe
Carson City
NEVADA

Great Salt Lake
Ogden
Salt Lake City
Utah Lake Provo
Sevier Lake
UTAH
Sevier R.
Green R.
Moab
Lake Powell

Rock Springs
Laramie Cheyenne
Fort Collins
Boulder Greeley
S. Platte R.
Grand Junction Denver
Colorado R.
COLORADO
Colorado Springs
Pueblo
Durango
Trinidad

Grand Is.
North Platte
Platte R.
Republican R.
Goodland
KA
Smoky Hill R.
Arkansas R.
Dodge City

OCEAN
Los Angeles
Pasadena
Long Beach San Bernardino
Riverside
Salton Sea
San Diego
Tijuana
30°N

Las Vegas
Lake Mead
Boulder City
Colorado R.
ARIZONA
Flagstaff
Prescott
Phoenix Salt R.
Gila R.
Yuma
Tucson
Nogales
Nogales
Little Colorado R.
Farmington
Gallup
Santa Fe
Albuquerque
NEW MEXICO
Elephant Butte Res.
Silver City
Roswell
Las Cruces
Carlsbad
Raton
Canadian R.
Amarillo
OK
Lav
Red R.
Wichita Fa
Lubbock
Abilene
TE
Pecos R.

El Paso
Juarez

125°W 120°W 115°W 110°W 105°W 100°W

HAWAII inset:
160°W 158°W 156°W
Lihue 22°N
Honolulu Wailuku
PACIFIC OCEAN
Hilo 20°N
Pahala
HAWAII
0 100 200 Miles
0 100 200 Kilometers

ALASKA inset:
Chukchi Sea
Beaufort Sea
70°N
Prudhoe Bay
RUSSIA
Kotzebue
65°N
ARCTIC CIRCLE
Nome
ALASKA
Fairbanks
Yukon R.
Norton Sound
Kuskokwim R.
CANADA
60°N
Bethel
Anchorage
Valdez
Seward
Juneau
25°N
INTERNATIONAL DATE LINE
Bering Sea
Kodiak
Gulf of Alaska
Sitka
55°N
Dutch Harbor
180° 175°W 170°W 165°W 160°W 155°W 150°W
0 200 400 Miles
0 200 400 Kilometers

M E X I C O
San Antonio
Del Rio
Rio Grande
Laredo
Nuevo Laredo
Monterrey

70°N 65°N 60°N 55°N
105°W 100°W

Winnipeg
Lake Winnipeg
Lake of the Woods
Red Lake
Grand Forks
Red R.

C A N A D A

Gulf of St. Lawrence

Quebec

Moosehead Lake
M A I N E
Bangor
Augusta
Portland

Duluth
Thunder Bay
Lake Superior
Marquette
Sault Ste. Marie
Sault Ste. Marie

MINNESOTA
St. Cloud
St. Paul
Minneapolis
Rochester

WISCONSIN
Superior
Wausau
Green Bay
La Crosse
Madison
Milwaukee
Racine

M I C H I G A N
Alpena
Lake Huron
Traverse City
Saginaw
Grand Rapids
Lansing
Detroit
Ann Arbor
Lake Michigan

Montreal
Lake Champlain
Burlington
VERMONT
Montpelier
NEW HAMPSHIRE
Concord
Manchester
MASSACHUSETTS
Springfield
Boston
Providence
RHODE ISLAND
Hartford
CONNECTICUT

Ottawa
Lake Ontario
Toronto
Georgian Bay
St. Lawrence R.
Ogdensburg
Watertown
Utica
Rochester
Syracuse
Albany
Buffalo
Binghamton
NEW YORK

Sioux City
Mason City
Cedar Rapids
Waterloo
Dubuque
Rockford
I O W A
Davenport
Moline
Rock Island
Des Moines
Burlington
Council Bluffs
Omaha
Lincoln

Chicago
Gary
Hammond
Joliet
South Bend
ILLINOIS
Peoria
Champaign
Springfield
Terre Haute

INDIANA
Fort Wayne
Indianapolis

Toledo
Lima
Dayton
Columbus
Cincinnati
O H I O
Cleveland
Akron
Canton
Youngstown
Lake Erie
Erie
Oil City

PENNSYLVANIA
Scranton
Wilkes-Barre
Allentown
Harrisburg
Pittsburgh
Clarksburg

Newark
New York
Trenton
NEW JERSEY
Philadelphia
Wilmington
Dover
Atlantic City
Delaware Bay

St. Joseph
Hannibal
Kansas City
Independence
Topeka
Lawrence
Kansas City
St. Louis
Jefferson City
Lake of the Ozarks
MISSOURI
Springfield
Joplin
Carbondale
Evansville
Owensboro
Paducah
Bowling Green

Wichita
Pittsburg

KENTUCKY
Louisville
Frankfort
Lexington
Nashville

WEST VIRGINIA
Charleston
Huntington

Arlington
Washington, D.C.
Annapolis
Baltimore
MARYLAND
DELAWARE

Chesapeake Bay
Charlottesville
Richmond
Roanoke
Portsmouth
Norfolk
VIRGINIA

ATLANTIC OCEAN

Albemarle Sound

Clark Hill Lake
Lake O' the Cherokees
Tulsa
Table Rock Lake
Fort Smith
ARKANSAS
Fayetteville
Little Rock
Hot Springs
Pine Bluff
Blytheville
Memphis
TENNESSEE
Knoxville
Chattanooga
Huntsville
Rome

OKLAHOMA
Oklahoma City

Johnson City
Bristol
Winston-Salem
Greensboro
Roanoke
Durham
Raleigh
NORTH CAROLINA
Asheville
Greenville
Charlotte
Wilmington
Pamlico Sound
Pee Dee R.

Columbia
SOUTH CAROLINA
Charleston
Savannah R.
Augusta

Dallas
Fort Worth
Waco
Austin
Texarkana
Shreveport
Monroe
Alexandria
Toledo Bend Res.
Sam Rayburn Res.
LOUISIANA
MISSISSIPPI
Jackson
Vicksburg
Greenville
Meridian
Hattiesburg
ALABAMA
Birmingham
Tuscaloosa
Montgomery
Dothan
GEORGIA
Atlanta
Macon
Columbus
Albany
Valdosta
Savannah

Houston
Beaumont
Lake Charles
Baton Rouge
Biloxi
Mobile
New Orleans
Mobile Bay
Pensacola
Galveston Bay
Galveston
Atchafalaya Bay
Mississippi River Delta

Tallahassee
Apalachee Bay
Jacksonville
Daytona Beach
Orlando
F L O R I D A
Tampa
St. Petersburg
Tampa Bay
Lake Okeechobee
Fort Lauderdale
Miami

Corpus Christi
Brownsville
Matamoros

Gulf of Mexico

N

Key West
Straits of Florida

TROPIC OF CANCER

C U B A

Traditional Regions and Regional Names

Pacific Northwest

Great Plains States

Great Lakes States

NORTHEAST

New England States

PACIFIC

ROCKY MOUNTAIN

MIDWEST

Middle Atlantic States

Arizona and New Mexico are often included in the Rocky Mountain region.

SOUTHWEST

SOUTHEAST

South Atlantic States

Gulf Coast States

PACIFIC

Alaska

Hawaii

States can be grouped into regions in many ways. The map above identifies some traditional regions and regional names and shows that regions often overlap each other. What is more, the same name may be used to describe different groups of states. For example, compare the Southwest in the map above with the Southwest in the locator map below. The locator map shows how states are grouped in the regional maps that follow.

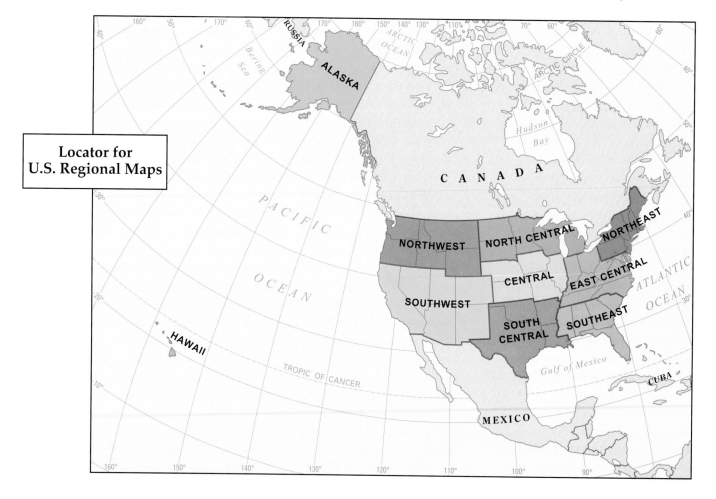

Locator for U.S. Regional Maps

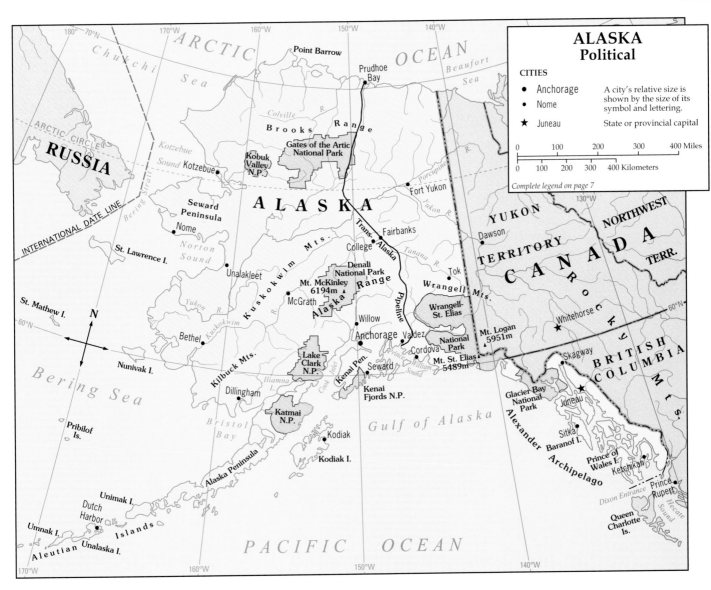

ALASKA
Political

CITIES

● Anchorage

● Nome   A city's relative size is shown by the size of its symbol and lettering.

★ Juneau   State or provincial capital

0   100   200   300   400 Miles
0   100   200   300   400 Kilometers

Complete legend on page 7

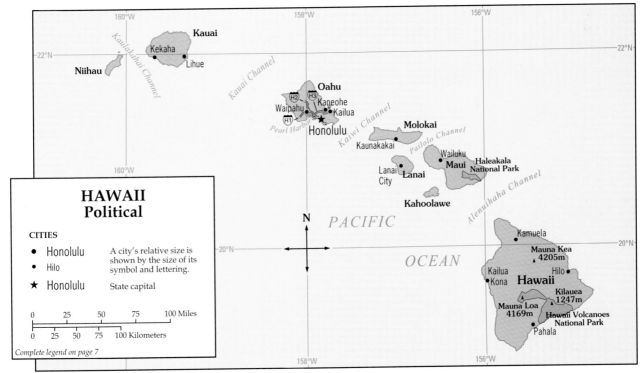

HAWAII
Political

CITIES

● Honolulu

● Hilo   A city's relative size is shown by the size of its symbol and lettering.

★ Honolulu   State capital

0   25   50   75   100 Miles
0   25   50   75   100 Kilometers

Complete legend on page 7

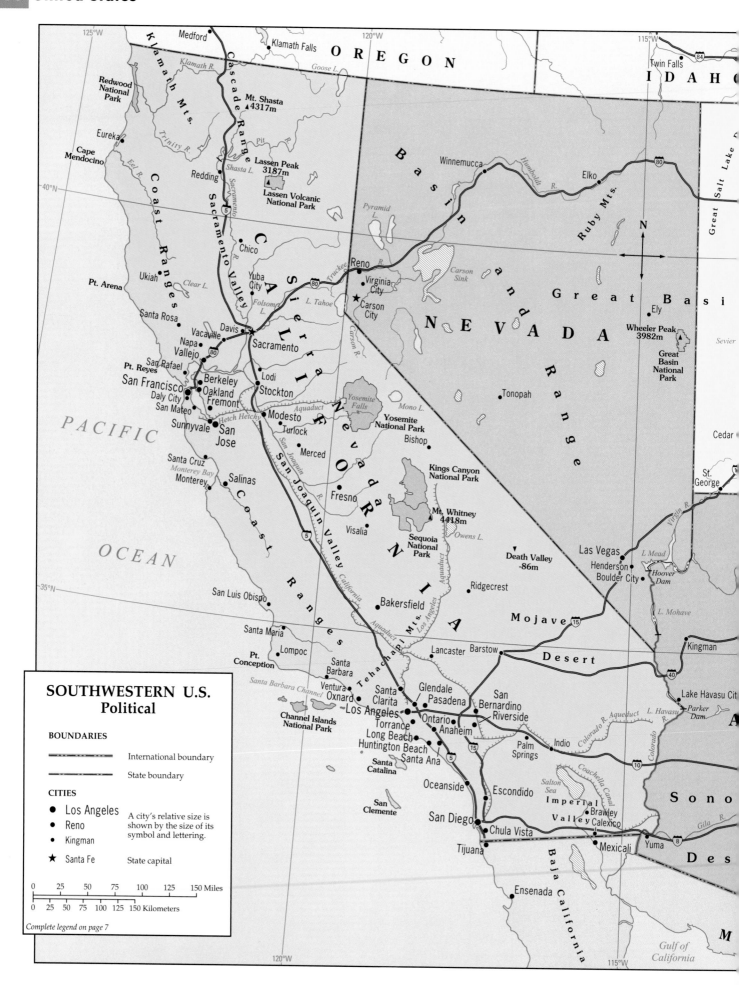

Medford
Klamath Falls
O R E G O N
Goose L.
Twin Falls
I D A H O

Klamath Mts.
Klamath R.
Cascade Range

Redwood National Park
Mt. Shasta 4317m

Eureka
Cape Mendocino
Shasta L.
Redding
Lassen Peak 3187m
Lassen Volcanic National Park

Trinity R.
Pit R.
Sacramento R.

Winnemucca
Humboldt R.
Elko
Great Salt Lake

40°N

Coast Ranges
Sacramento Valley
Chico
Ruby Mts.

B a s i n

N

Ukiah
Clear L.
Yuba City
Folsom L.
Reno
Virginia City
Carson City
Pyramid L.
Carson Sink
G r e a t   B a s i

Pt. Arena
Santa Rosa
Davis
Vacaville
L. Tahoe
Carson R.
N E V A D A
Ely
Wheeler Peak 3982m

Napa
Vallejo
Sacramento
Great Basin National Park

Pt. Reyes
San Rafael
San Francisco
Berkeley
Oakland
Fremont
Lodi
Stockton
Sevier

Daly City
San Mateo
Sunnyvale
Hetch Hetchy
Modesto
Aquaduct
Yosemite Falls
Mono L.
Tonopah

San Jose
Turlock
Yosemite National Park

Santa Cruz
Monterey Bay
Salinas
Merced
Kings Canyon National Park
St. George

Monterey
Fresno
Mt. Whitney 4418m
Sequoia National Park
Owens L.

PACIFIC
San Joaquin R.
Visalia
Las Vegas
L. Mead

OCEAN
Coast
San Joaquin Valley
N
Death Valley -86m
Henderson
Boulder City
Hoover Dam

35°N
San Luis Obispo
Aqueduct
I
A
Ridgecrest
L. Mohave

Ranges
Aqueduct
Los Angeles
Bakersfield
M o j a v e
Kingman

Santa Maria
Lompoc
Tehachapi Mts.
Lancaster
Barstow
D e s e r t

Pt. Conception
Santa Barbara
Ventura
Oxnard
Santa Clarita
Glendale
Pasadena
San Bernardino
Riverside
Lake Havasu Cit
Parker Dam
A

Santa Barbara Channel
Channel Islands National Park
Los Angeles
Torrance
Long Beach
Huntington Beach
Ontario
Anaheim
Santa Ana
Indio
Palm Springs
Colorado R. Aqueduct
L. Havasu
Colorado

Santa Catalina
Oceanside
Escondido
Salton Sea
Coachella Canal
Imperial
Valley
S o n o

San Clemente
San Diego
Chula Vista
Brawley
Calexico
Gila R.
Yuma

Tijuana
Mexicali
Baja California
D e s

Ensenada
Gulf of California
M

SOUTHWESTERN U.S.
Political

BOUNDARIES

International boundary

State boundary

CITIES

● **Los Angeles**

● Reno

• Kingman
A city's relative size is shown by the size of its symbol and lettering.

★ Santa Fe
State capital

| 0 | 25 | 50 | 75 | 100 | 125 | 150 Miles |
| 0 | 25 | 50 | 75 | 100 | 125 | 150 Kilometers |

Complete legend on page 7

125°W
120°W
120°W
115°W
115°W

C A L I F O R N I A
S i e r r a   N e v a d a   R a n g e
California Aqueduct

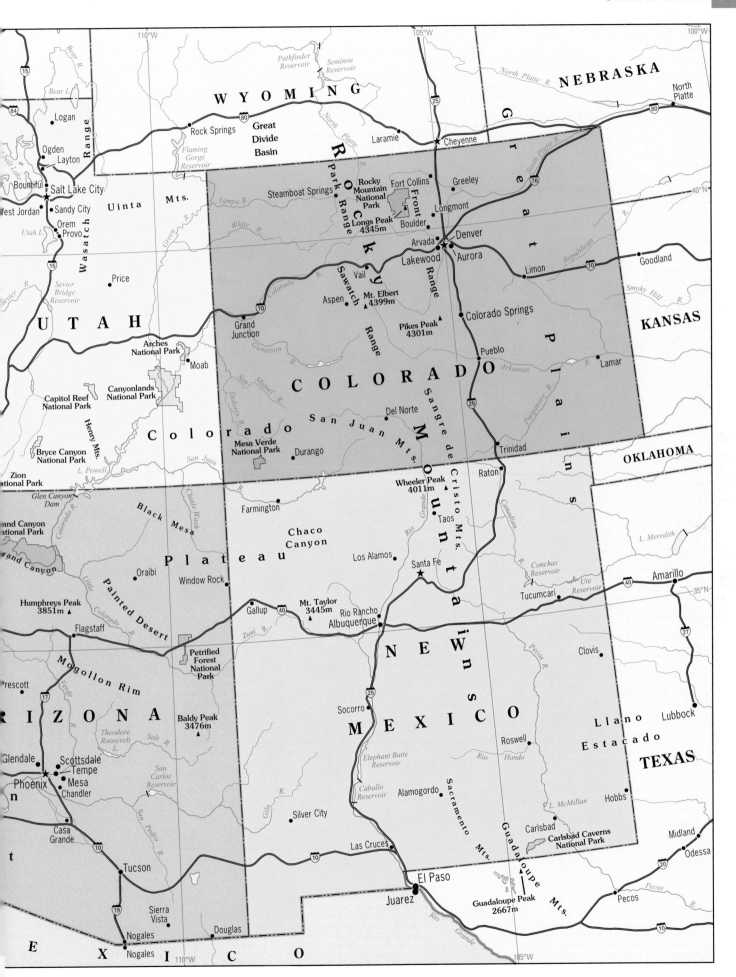

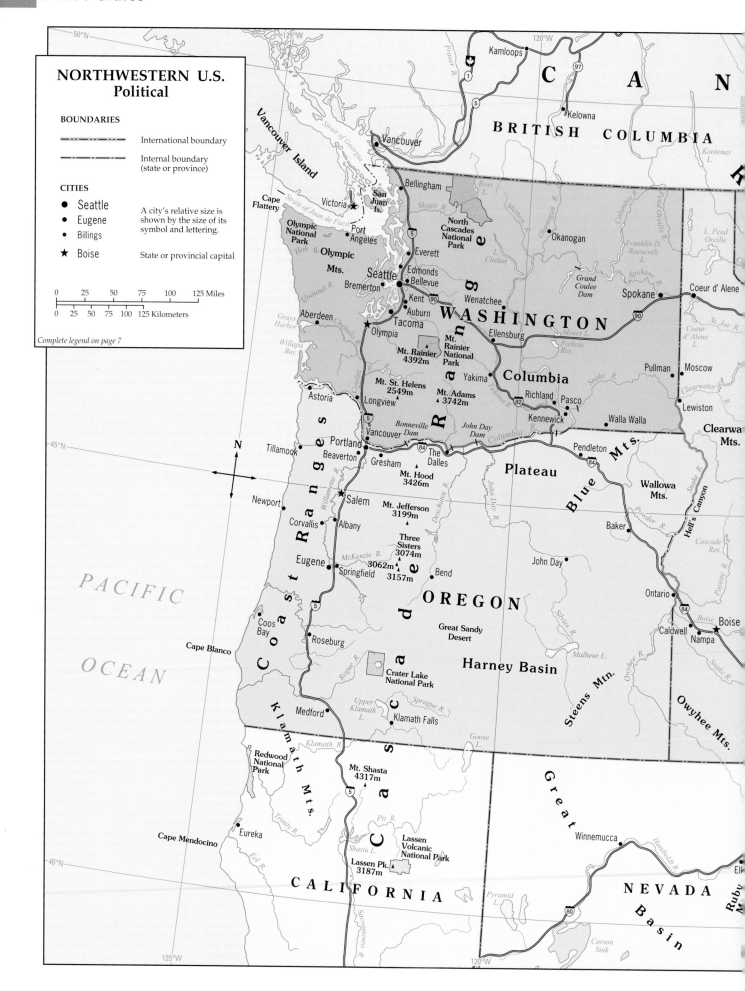

NORTHWESTERN U.S.
Political

BOUNDARIES

International boundary

Internal boundary
(state or province)

CITIES

● Seattle

● Eugene

• Billings

★ Boise

A city's relative size is
shown by the size of its
symbol and lettering.

State or provincial capital

0 25 50 75 100 125 Miles

0 25 50 75 100 125 Kilometers

Complete legend on page 7

CANADA

SASKATCHEWAN

Regina

ALBERTA

Lethbridge

NORTH DAKOTA

Glacier National Park

Kalispell

Flathead L.

Cut Bank Creek

L. Elwell

Marias

Milk R.

Havre

Malta

Fort Peck Dam

Missouri R.

Wolf Point

Fort Peck L.

L. Sakakawea

Theodore Roosevelt National Park

Lewis Range

Missouri R.

Great Falls

Glendive

ROCKY

Blackfoot R.

Missoula

Helena

White Sulphur Springs

Lewistown

Judith R.

MONTANA

Great Plains

Miles City

Little Missouri R.

SOUTH DAKOTA

Bitterroot R.

Clark Fork

Butte

Canyon Ferry L.

Big Belt Mts.

Bozeman

Musselshell R.

Yellowstone R.

Billings

Crow Agency

Powder R.

Bitterroot Range

Salmon R.

Salmon

Jefferson R.

Madison R.

Gallatin R.

MOUNTAINS

Hebgen L.

Yellowstone National Park

Yellowstone L.

Absaroka Range

Clarks Fork

Bighorn L.

Little Bighorn R.

Sheridan

Bighorn R.

Powder R.

Devils Tower 1558m

Bear Lodge Mts.

Black Hills

Harney Pk. 2207m

Rapid City

Salmon River Mts.

Borah Pk. 3859m

Lemhi Range

Big Lost R.

Beaverhead Mts.

Rexburg

Teton Range

Grand Teton National Park

Cody

Bighorn Mts.

Buffalo

Powder River Basin

Gillette

Belle Fourche

Cheyenne R.

Wind Cave N.P.

IDAHO

Snake River Plain

Idaho Falls

Snake R.

Jackson

Thermopolis

Wind R.

Boysen Res.

Riverton

WYOMING

Lander

Casper

Douglas

N. Platte R.

White R.

Niobrara R.

NEBR.

Pocatello

American Falls Res.

Wind River Range

Wyoming Range

Sweetwater R.

Pathfinder Res.

Laramie Mts.

Great Plains

Twin Falls

Raft R.

Salmon Creek Res.

Bear R.

South Pass

Great Divide Basin

Rawlins

Seminoe Res.

Laramie

Cheyenne

Green R.

Rock Springs

Medicine Bow Mts.

Logan

Ogden

Evanston

Flaming Gorge Res.

Bear R.

Great Salt Lake

Uinta Mts.

Green R.

Rocky Mountain National Park

Park Range

Fort Collins

Greeley

S. Platte R.

Boulder

Front Range

Salt Lake City

Wasatch Range

Provo

Utah L.

Great Salt Lake Desert

UTAH

Green R.

Colorado R.

COLORADO

Denver

S. Platte R.

SASKATCHEWAN

Moose Jaw
Regina
105°W 11
100°W
95°W
50°N

Great Plains

MANITOBA

Brandon
Assiniboine R.
Winnipeg
L. Manitoba
L. Winnipeg

Kenora

Pembina
75
Lake of the Woods

MONTANA

Williston
Stanley
Minot
Rugby
Turtle Mts.
Souris R.
Devils L.
Grafton
Red R.
Thief River Falls

International Fall

Rainy R.

Upper Red
Lower Red L.

Theodore Roosevelt National Park

Badlands

94

Garrison Dam
L. Sakakawea
Knife R.
Missouri R.
Grand Forks
29

Bemidji

Red River

L. Itasca

Leech

NORTH DAKOTA

Medora
Dickinson
Mandan Bismarck
Jamestown
Valley City
Fargo Moorhead

MINNESOT

Heart R.
Cannonball R.
James R.
Sheyenne R.
Wahpeton

Brain

Yellowstone

Little Missouri

Missouri R.

94

Fergus Falls

Alexandria

St. C°

Mille Lacs L.

Mississippi R.

Buffalo
Grand R.
Mobridge
Moreau R.
Oahe
Sisseton
L. Traverse
Big Stone L.

Willmar

Minneap

45°N

Belle Fourche

Little R.

SOUTH DAKOTA

Aberdeen

Big *Sioux* R.

Bloomin

Black Hills

90

Harney Pk. 2207m
Rapid City Mt. Rushmore
Wind Cave N.P.
Cheyenne R.
Hot Springs

WYO.

Badlands

Pierre
Oahe Dam
L. Sharpe
Murdo
90
Bad R.
Badlands National Park
Big Bend Dam

Huron
Watertown
Brookings

Marshall

Minnesota

L. Shetak

Mankato

Sands

Wounded Knee
Pine Ridge
White R.

Mitchell

L. Francis Case

Vermillion R.

Sioux Falls
29
90
Worthington

Fairmont

Niobrara R.

Fort Randall Dam

Lewis and Clark L.

Gavin's Point Dam

Yankton
Vermillion

Des Moines R.

NEBRASKA

South Sioux City
Sioux City

N. Platte R.

80

North Platte

Platte R.

Grand Island

Fremont
Omaha
Council Bluffs

COLORADO
76
S. Platte R.
100°W
95°W
80
29
3

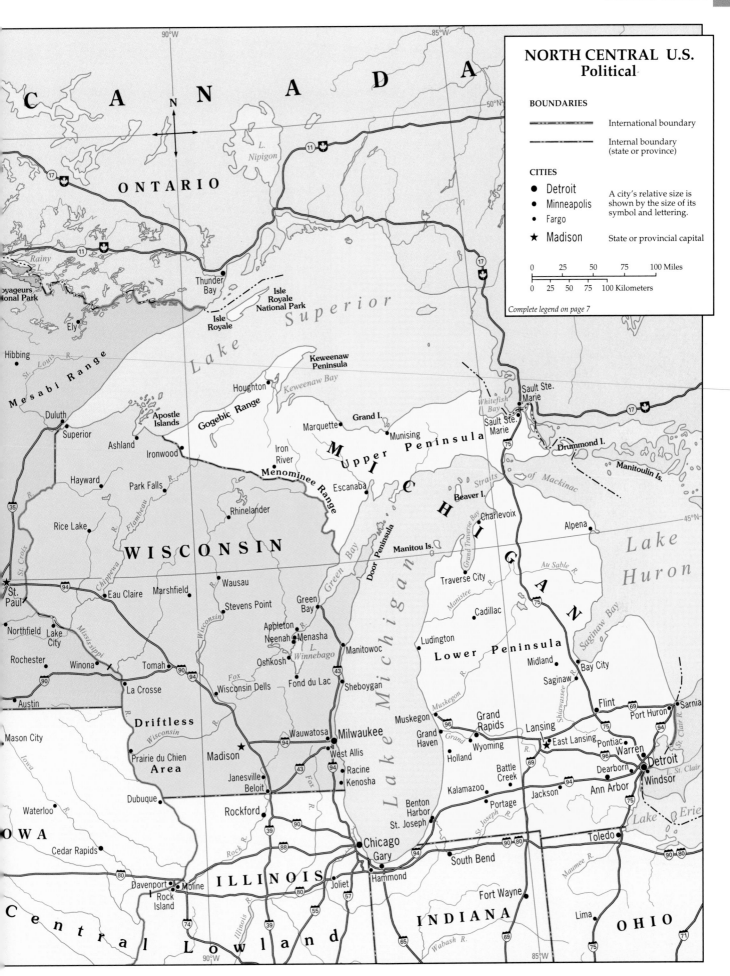

NORTH CENTRAL U.S.
Political

BOUNDARIES

International boundary

Internal boundary
(state or province)

CITIES

● Detroit

● Minneapolis

• Fargo

★ Madison

A city's relative size is
shown by the size of its
symbol and lettering.

State or provincial capital

0   25   50   75   100 Miles

0   25   50   75   100 Kilometers

Complete legend on page 7

CANADA

ONTARIO

L. Nipigon

Voyageurs
National Park

Rainy L.

Ely

Hibbing

Mesabi Range

Duluth

Superior

Ashland

Ironwood

Hayward

Park Falls

Rice Lake

WISCONSIN

Thunder Bay

Isle Royale
National Park

Isle Royale

Lake Superior

Keweenaw
Peninsula

Houghton

Keweenaw Bay

Apostle
Islands

Gogebic Range

Marquette

Grand I.

Munising

Iron River

Menominee Range

Escanaba

Rhinelander

MICHIGAN

Upper Peninsula

Whitefish Bay

Sault Ste. Marie

Sault Ste. Marie

Drummond I.

Manitoulin Is.

Straits of Mackinac

Beaver I.

Charlevoix

Alpena

Lake Huron

Eau Claire

Marshfield

Wausau

Stevens Point

Green Bay

Green Bay

Door Peninsula

Manitou Is.

Grand Traverse Bay

Traverse City

Au Sable R.

Saginaw Bay

St. Paul

Northfield

Lake City

Rochester

Winona

Tomah

La Crosse

Austin

Appleton

Menasha

Neenah

Oshkosh

L. Winnebago

Fond du Lac

Wisconsin Dells

Fox R.

Manitowoc

Sheboygan

Lake Michigan

Cadillac

Ludington

Lower Peninsula

Manistee R.

Midland

Bay City

Saginaw

Muskegon

Flint

Port Huron

Sarnia

Driftless

Wauwatosa

Milwaukee

Muskegon

Grand Rapids

Grand Haven

Wyoming

Lansing

East Lansing

Pontiac

Warren

Mason City

Prairie du Chien
Area

Madison

West Allis

Racine

Kenosha

Holland

Battle Creek

Kalamazoo

Jackson

Dearborn

Ann Arbor

Detroit

Windsor

L. St. Clair

Janesville

Beloit

Portage

Benton Harbor

St. Joseph

St. Joseph R.

Lake Erie

Waterloo

Dubuque

Rockford

Chicago

Gary

South Bend

Fort Wayne

Toledo

IOWA

Cedar Rapids

Davenport

Moline

Rock Island

ILLINOIS

Joliet

Hammond

INDIANA

OHIO

Central Lowland

Maumee R.

Wabash R.

Lima

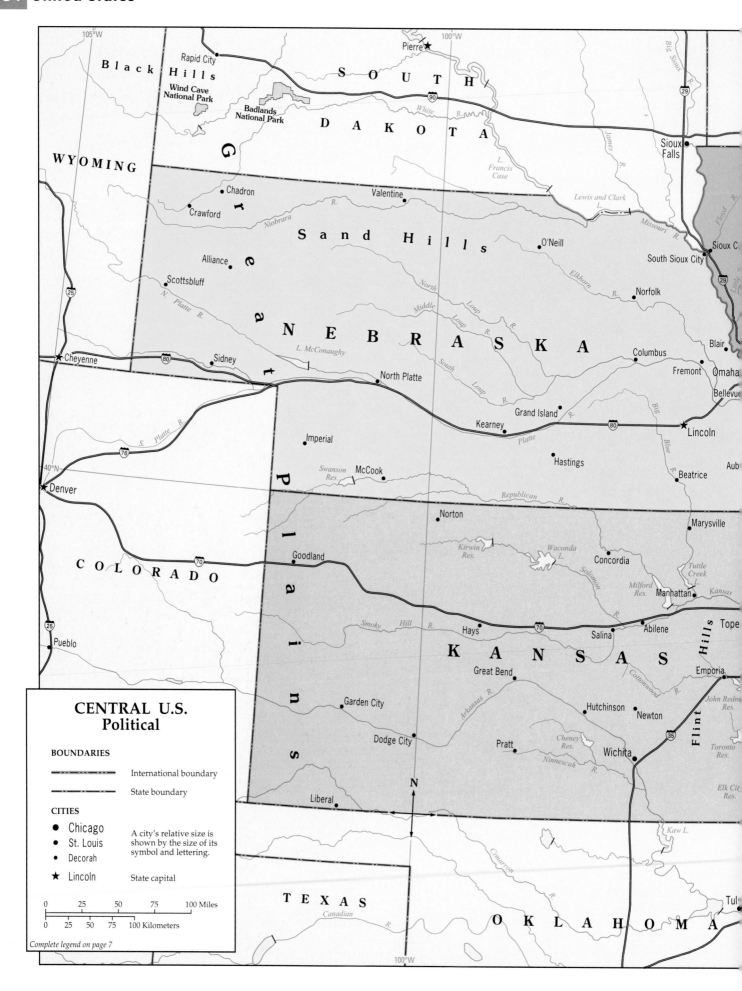

Black Hills

Rapid City

Wind Cave
National Park

Badlands
National Park

WYOMING

SOUTH

DAKOTA

Pierre ★

100°W

105°W

100°W

White R.

L. Francis Case

James R.

Lewis and Clark L.

Missouri R.

Big Sioux R.

Sioux Falls

29

Floyd R.

Sioux C.

Chadron

Crawford

Valentine

Sand Hills

O'Neill

South Sioux City

29

Niobrara R.

Alliance

Scottsbluff

North Loup R.

Middle Loup R.

Norfolk

Elkhorn R.

N. Platte R.

Great

NEBRASKA

South Loup R.

Columbus

Blair

Cheyenne

80

Sidney

L. McConaughy

North Platte

Fremont

Omaha

Bellevue

Big Blue R.

Grand Island

Platte R.

80

Lincoln ★

S. Platte R.

76

Imperial

Kearney

Hastings

Beatrice

Aub

40°N

Denver ★

Swanson Res.

McCook

Republican R.

Blue R.

Norton

Marysville

COLORADO

70

Goodland

Plains

Kirwin Res.

Waconda L.

Concordia

Solomon R.

Milford Res.

Tuttle Creek L.

Manhattan

Kansas R.

25

Pueblo

Smoky Hill R.

Hays

70

Salina

Abilene

Tope

Flint Hills

KANSAS

Garden City

Great Bend

Arkansas R.

Hutchinson

Newton

Cottonwood R.

Emporia

John Redmo Res.

35

Dodge City

Pratt

Cheney Res.

Wichita

Flint

Toronto Res.

Ninnescah R.

N

Elk Cit Res.

Liberal

Kaw L.

TEXAS

Canadian R.

Cimarron R.

100°W

OKLAHOMA

Tul

MINNESOTA

WISCONSIN

MICH.

Rochester

La Crosse

L. Winnebago

Lake Michigan

Milwaukee

Madison

Racine

Wisconsin R.

Forest City

Decorah

Mason City

Fayette

Waukegan

Freeport

Arlington Heights

Evanston

Spencer

Dubuque

Galena

Rockford

De Kalb

Elgin

Elmhurst

Chicago

Storm Lake

Fort Dodge

Cedar Falls

Waterloo

Cedar Rapids

Clinton

Sterling

Aurora

Naperville

Gary

South Bend

Denison

I O W A

Ames

Marshalltown

Grinnell

Bettendorf

Davenport

Moline

Rock Island

La Salle

Joliet

Calumet City

Saylorville Res.

Des Moines

Iowa City

Galesburg

Peoria

Kankakee

Pontiac

Watseka

cil Bluffs

Osceola

Ottumwa

Burlington

Macomb

Normal Bloomington

Champaign

Danville

Keokuk

I L L I N O I S

Rathbun Res.

C e n t r a l

Bethany

Kirksville

Urbana

INDIANA

St. Joseph

Chillicothe

Quincy

Hannibal

Jacksonville

Springfield

Decatur

L. Shelbyville

Mattoon

Charleston

Terre Haute

Holt

Columbia

L o w l a n d

Effingham

eavenworth

Kansas City

Independence

Kansas City

Overland Park

Lee's Summit

Olathe

Alton

St. Peters

Florissant

St. Louis

University City

Kirkwood

East St. Louis

Belleville

Mount Vernon

Carlyle L.

Little Wabash

Wabash R.

Sedalia

Jefferson City

M I S S O U R I

Rend L.

Evansville

Owensboro

Fort Scott

Lake of the Ozarks

Rolla

Ste. Genevieve

Carbondale

Big Muddy R.

KENTUCKY

Pittsburg

Stockton L.

Pomme de Terre Res.

O z a r k   P l a t e a u

Cape Girardeau

Cairo

Paducah

Springfield

West Plains

Poplar Bluff

Wappapello L.

New Madrid

Joplin

Sikeston

offeyville

Table Rock L.

Branson

Bull Shoals L.

Norfolk L.

Lake O' the Cherokees

Fayetteville

A R K A N S A S

Blytheville

Nashville

TENNESSEE

Boston Mts.

Mississippi R.

Iowa R.

Des Moines R.

Skunk R.

Cedar R.

Wapsipinicon R.

Turkey R.

Upper Iowa R.

Rock R.

Fox R.

Illinois R.

Vermilion R.

Kankakee R.

Sangamon R.

Spoon R.

Kaskaskia R.

Embarrass R.

Missouri R.

Gasconade R.

Meramec R.

Osage R.

Niangua R.

Chariton R.

Grand R.

Salt R.

Current R.

Black R.

St. Francis R.

White R.

James R.

Tennessee R.

Cumberland R.

Ohio R.

Coralville Res.

Nodaway R.

Perry L.

Carlyle L.

mona Res.

Colorado

ARIZ.

Gallup

Santa Fe

Albuquerque

35°N

NEW MEXICO

Plateau

Sacramento Mts.

Silver City

Las Cruces

El Paso

Juarez

Wheeler Pk. 4011m

Sangre de Cristo Mts.

Rocky Mts.

Raton

105°W

Canadian R.

Conchas Res.

Rio Grande

Pecos R.

Clovis

Roswell

Carlsbad

Elephant Butte Res.

Guadalupe Mts.

Guadalupe Mts. N.P.

Guadalupe Pk. 2667m

Salt Basin

Rio Bravo del Norte

Rio Grande

MEXICO

Sierra Madre Occidental

30°N

Conchos R.

Davis Mts.

Alpine

Stockton Plateau

Big Bend National Park

Sierra Madre Oriental

KANSAS

Guymon

Woodward

Dalhart

Great

Canadian

L. Meredith

Pampa

Salt

Amarillo

Hereford

Plains

Prairie Dog Town Fork

Wichita Mts.

Lawton

Elk City

Salt

Llano

Double

Lubbock

Mountain

Fork

Fork

Estacado

L. Kemp

Wichita Falls

Brazos

R.

Graha

Possum Kingdom L.

Midland

Odessa

Big Spring

Colorado R.

Abilene

Pecos

San Angelo

Brownwood

Fort Stockton

Pecos R.

TEXAS

Edwards

L. Buchanan

Lyndon B. Johnson

Plateau

Devils R.

Llano R.

Amistad Res.

San Marco

New Braunfels

San Antonio

Del Rio

Eagle Pass

Rio Bravo del Norte

Rio Grande

Nueces R.

Geo We

Laredo

Nuevo Laredo

Falfurria

Falcon Res.

Edinb

McAlle

105°W

100°W

100°W

SOUTH CENTRAL U.S.
Political

BOUNDARIES

International boundary

State boundary

CITIES

● Dallas

● Tulsa

• Monroe

★ Little Rock

A city's relative size is shown by the size of its symbol and lettering.

State capital

0   25   50   75   100   125 Miles

0   25   50   75   100   125 Kilometers

Complete legend on page 7

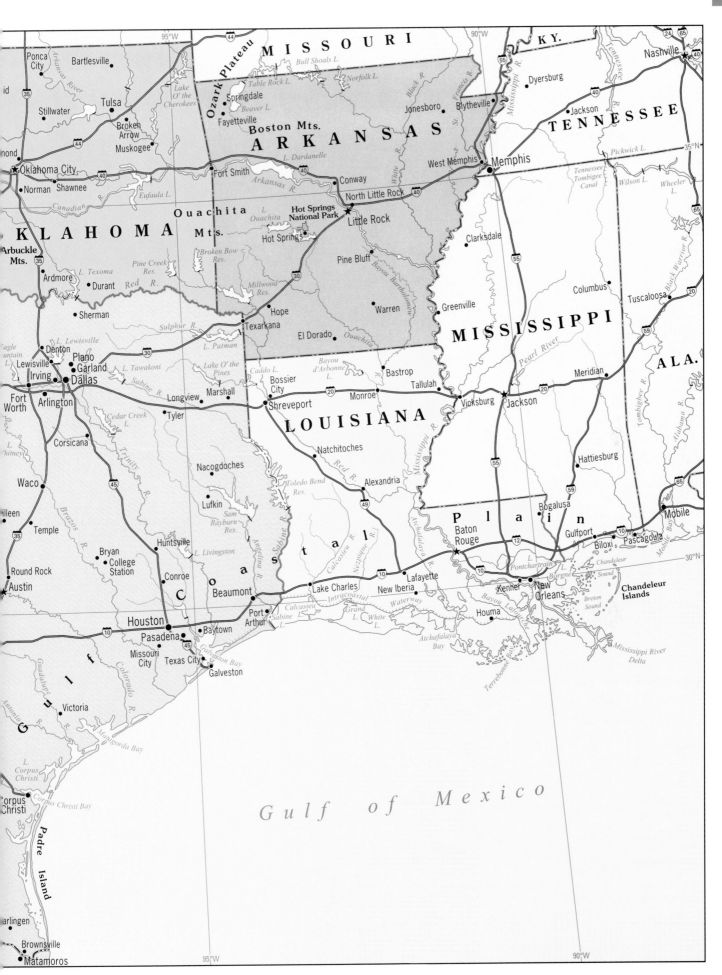

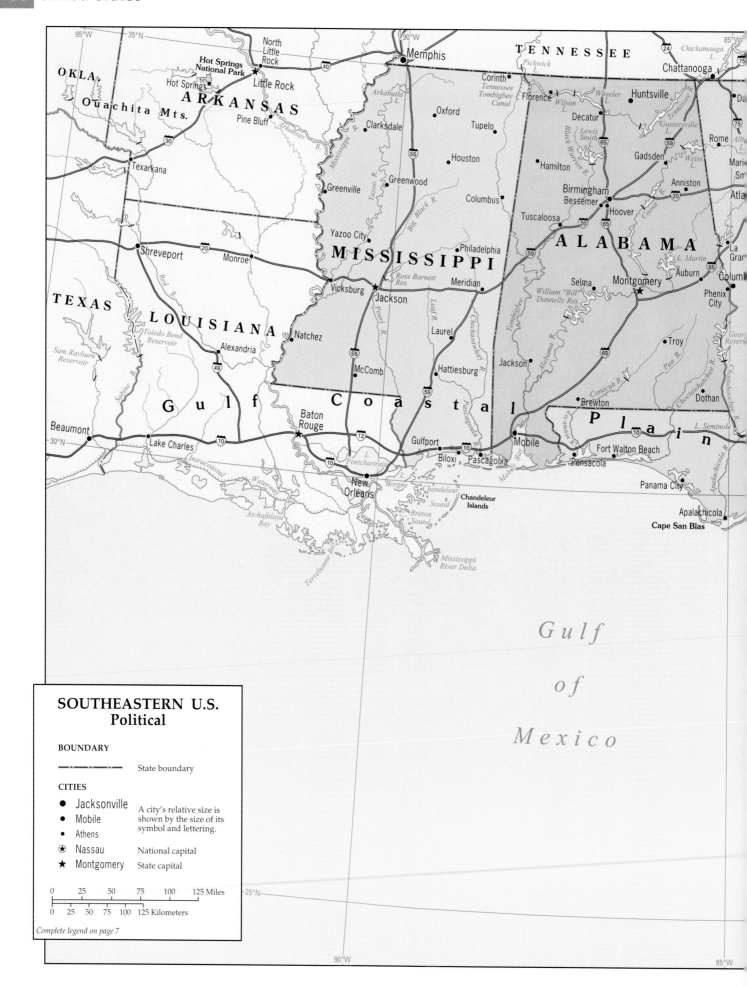

95°W — 35°N

OKLA.
Ouachita Mts.
ARKANSAS
Hot Springs National Park
Hot Springs
North Little Rock
Little Rock
Pine Bluff
Arkansas R.
Texarkana

Memphis
90°W
TENNESSEE
Chickamauga L.
Chattanooga
24
Pickwick L.
Corinth
Tennessee Tombigbee Canal
Florence
Wilson L.
Decatur
Wheeler L.
Huntsville
Rome
75
Mari
Sm
65
59
Guntersville L.
Lewis Smith L.
Black Warrior R.
Gadsden
Weiss L.
Anniston
Atla
20

Arkabutla L.
Oxford
Clarksdale
Tupelo
Houston
Hamilton
Birmingham
Bessemer
Hoover
Tuscaloosa
ALABAMA
L. Martin
La Gra

MISSISSIPPI
Mississippi R.
Yazoo R.
Greenville
Greenwood
Columbus
Big Black R.
Yazoo City
Philadelphia
Meridian
Coosa R.
85
Auburn
Colum
Phenix City

TEXAS
LOUISIANA
Shreveport
Monroe
20
Red R.
Toledo Bend Reservoir
Sam Rayburn Reservoir
Vicksburg
Jackson
Ross Barnett Res.
Pearl R.
Leaf R.
Chickasawhay R.
Tombigbee R.
William "Bill" Dannelly Res.
Selma
Montgomery
Alabama R.
Troy
Pea R.
Geor Reservo

Natchez
55
Laurel
Jackson
Conecuh R.
Choctawhatchee R.
Chattahoochee R.
49
McComb
Hattiesburg
59
Brewton
Dothan
Alexandria

Gulf Coastal Plain
Beaumont
30°N
Lake Charles
10
Baton Rouge
12
55
Pascagoula R.
Gulfport
Biloxi
Pascagoula
Mobile
10
Mobile Bay
Fort Walton Beach
Pensacola
L. Seminole
Apalachicola R.

Intracoastal Waterway
10
L. Pontchartrain
New Orleans
L. Borgne
Chandeleur Sound
Chandeleur Islands
Panama City

Atchafalaya Bay
Breton Sound
Apalachicola
Cape San Blas

Terrebonne Bay
Mississippi River Delta

Gulf
of
Mexico

90°W
25°N
85°W

NORTH CAROLINA

Pamlico Sound

35°N 75°W

Great Smoky Mountains N.P.

Appalachian Mts.

Blue Ridge

Charlotte

Rock Hill

Greenville
Spartanburg

Piedmont Plateau

SOUTH

Anderson

Hartwell L.

L. Lanier

Wateree L.

Wilmington

Athens

Stone Mt. 514m

Decatur

Greenwood

Saluda R.

Columbia

L. Murray

Sumter

Florence

CAROLINA

Cape Fear

Myrtle Beach

oswell

st oint

Augusta

Orangeburg

L. Marion

Moultrie

Santee R.

Long Bay

Atlantic

Coastal

Clark Hill Lake

L. Oconee

Savannah R.

North Charleston

Cooper R.

Charleston
Mount Pleasant

GEORGIA

Macon

Dublin

Ogeechee R.

Ocmulgee R.

Warner Robbins

Flint R.

Americus

Oconee R.

Altamaha R.

Savannah

Sea Islands

Albany

Tifton

Waycross

Brunswick

Thomasville

Valdosta

Okefenokee Swamp

ATLANTIC

30°N

Tallahassee

Jacksonville

N

OCEAN

Apalachee Bay

Branford
Gainesville

St. Johns R.

St. Augustine

F

L

O

Cross City

Palatka

Suwannee R.

R

Ocala

L. George

Ormond Beach
Daytona Beach
Port Orange

I

D

Sanford

Florida

Spring Hill

Altamonte Springs
Orlando
Kissimmee

Titusville

Cape Canaveral

A

Clearwater
Tampa

Lakeland
Winter Haven

L. Kissimmee

Melbourne

Peninsula

St. Petersburg

Tampa Bay

Kissimmee R.

Peace R.

Fort Pierce
Port St. Lucie

Bradenton

Sarasota

Arcadia

L. Istokpoga

Lake Okeechobee

West Palm Beach

Great Abaco I.

Punta Gorda

Fort Myers

Caloosahatchee R.

Belle Glade

Cape Coral

Coral Springs

Boca Raton
Pompano Beach

Grand Bahama I.

Naples

Big Cypress Swamp

Davie
Hialeah
Everglades

Fort Lauderdale
Hollywood
Miami Beach
Miami

Bahama Islands

BAHAMAS

Coral Gables
Homestead

Biscayne National Park

Bimini Is.

Eleuthera I.

Everglades National Park

Cape Sable

Florida Bay

25°N

Nassau

New Providence I.

Andros I.

Dry Tortugas

Key West

Florida Keys

Straits of Florida

Cat I.

80°W

80°W

75°W

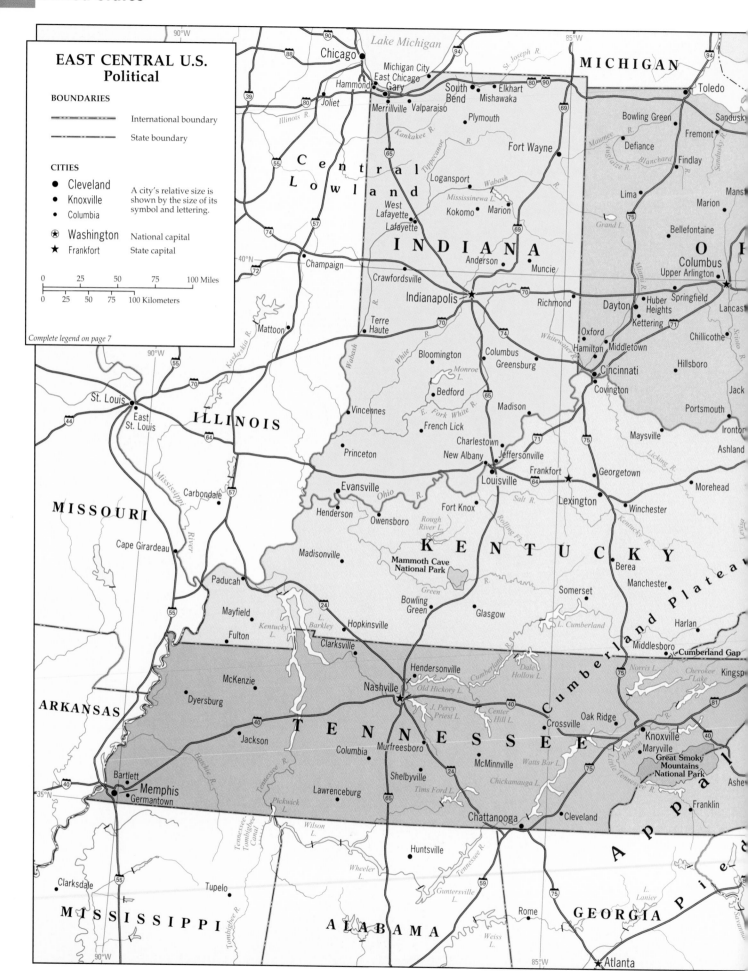

EAST CENTRAL U.S.
Political

BOUNDARIES

International boundary

State boundary

CITIES

● Cleveland

● Knoxville

● Columbia

A city's relative size is shown by the size of its symbol and lettering.

⊛ Washington — National capital

★ Frankfort — State capital

0 25 50 75 100 Miles

0 25 50 75 100 Kilometers

Complete legend on page 7

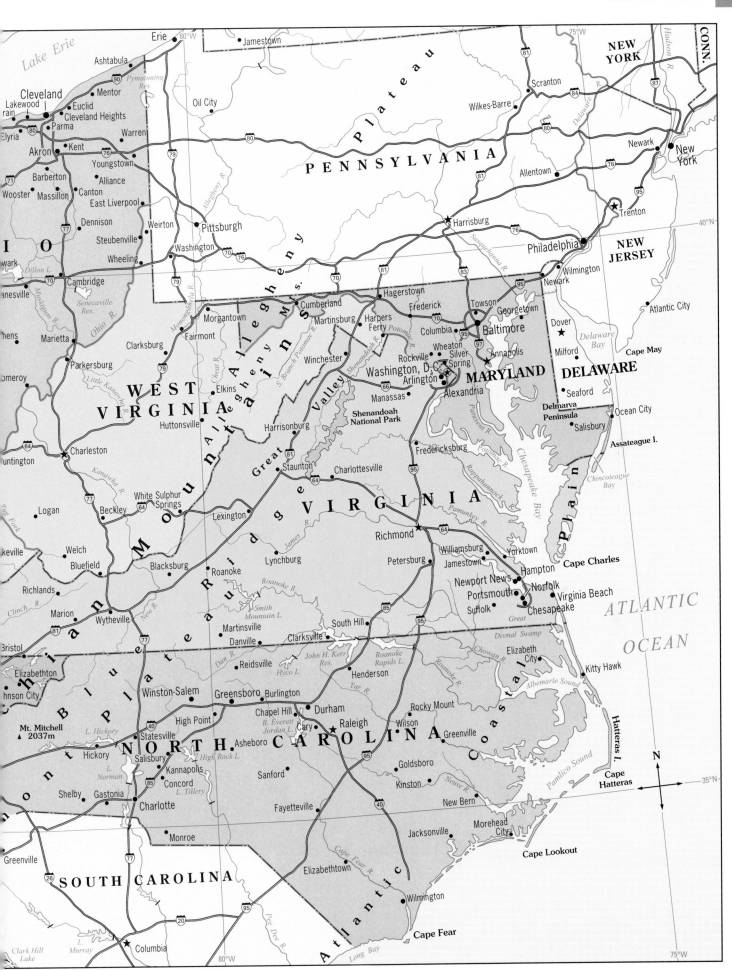

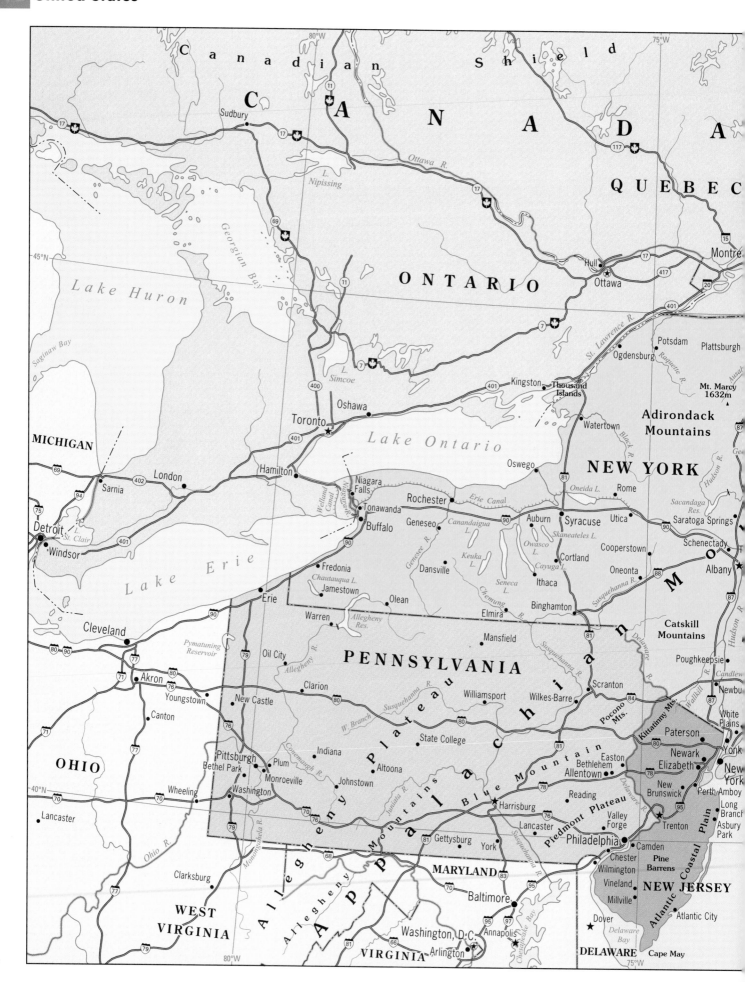

Gulf of
St. Lawrence

St. Lawrence R.

185

Quebec

20

Trois-Rivières

St. Maurice R.

40

73

55

Richelieu R.

20

55

Sherbrooke

10

55

L. Memphremagog

St. Francis R.

St. John R.

Caribou

Presque Isle

NEW BRUNSWICK

PRINCE EDWARD ISLAND

1

16

104

Fredericton

2

2

St. John R.

45°N

Eagle L.

Chamberlain L.

95

Chesuncook L.

Mt. Katahdin 1606m ▲

Aroostook R.

Chiputneticook Lakes

Lincoln

Saint John

Moosehead L.

Pemadumcook L.

MAINE

West Grand L.

Big L.

St. Croix R.

Bay of Fundy

NOVA SCOTIA

101

102

Flagstaff L.

Longfellow Mountains

Eastport

Grand Manan I.

89

Mt. Mansfield 1342m ▲

L. Champlain

St. Johnsbury

91

Berlin

Rangeley L.

Androscoggin R.

Bangor

95

Penobscot R.

Ellsworth

103

Halifax

65°W

Essex

Burlington

Montpelier

VERMONT

Farmington

Waterville

Bar Harbor

Mount Desert I.

Mt. Washington 1917m ▲

White Mts.

Kennebec R.

Augusta

Acadia National Park

Penobscot Bay

93

Auburn

Lewiston

Yarmouth

Green Mts.

Mountains

Sebago L.

Brunswick

Cape Sable

Rutland

Lebanon

L. Winnipesaukee

Westbrook

Portland

Casco Bay

Connecticut R.

Laconia

Sanford

89

Rochester

Biddeford

91

Concord

Dover

NEW HAMPSHIRE

95

Portsmouth

Bennington

Manchester

Derry

Brattleboro

Keene

Nashua

93

Haverhill

Merrimack R.

Lawrence

Cape Ann

Fitchburg

Lowell

Salem

...field

Northampton

Worcester

Cambridge

Lynn

Massachusetts Bay

MASSACHUSETTS

90

Framingham

Boston

ATLANTIC

Holyoke

Quincy

Springfield

Brockton

Enfield

Attleboro

Plymouth

Cape Cod

OCEAN

CONNECTICUT

Pawtucket

Taunton

Hartford

Providence

Fall River

...terbury

Manchester

New Britain

Warwick

Barnstable

84

91

Norwich

New Bedford

Nantucket Sound

...amden

New Haven

Groton

Newport

95

New London

Martha's Vineyard

Nantucket I.

...nbury

Bridgeport

RHODE ISLAND

...rwalk

Stamford

Narragansett Bay

Long Island Sd.

Montauk Point

...mpstead

Long Island

Lindenhurst

N

40°N

70°W

65°W

NORTHEASTERN U.S. Political

BOUNDARIES

——————— International boundary

——————— Internal boundary (state or province)

CITIES

● New York

● Paterson

• Lynn

A city's relative size is shown by the size of its symbol and lettering.

⊛ Washington   National capital

★ Boston   State or provincial capital

| 0 | 25 | 50 | 75 | 100 Miles |

| 0 | 25 | 50 | 75 | 100 Kilometers |

Complete legend on page 7

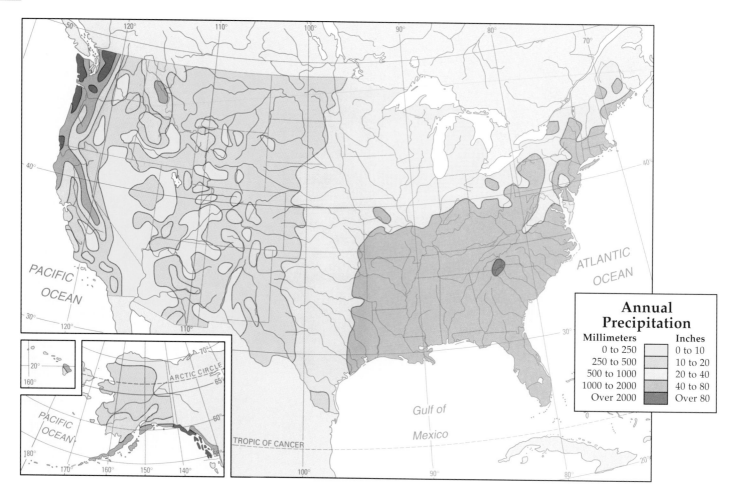

Annual Precipitation

Millimeters	Inches
0 to 250	0 to 10
250 to 500	10 to 20
500 to 1000	20 to 40
1000 to 2000	40 to 80
Over 2000	Over 80

ALASKA
Area Comparison

Alaska is one-fifth the size of the first 48 states combined. It is twice as big as Texas, which is the second-largest state.

Alaska	591,004 sq. mi. (1 530 700 sq. km)
Contiguous U.S.	3,021,295 sq. mi. (7 825 112 sq. km)

Bryce Canyon's rock formations are a spectacular example of the rugged terrain that is found in the desert areas of the Southwest.

ELEVATION

Meters		Feet
Over 3000		Over 10,000
1500 to 3000		5,000 to 10,000
600 to 1500		2,000 to 5,000
300 to 600		1,000 to 2,000
150 to 300		500 to 1,000
0 to 150		0 to 500
Below sea level		Below sea level

Cross Section of the United States

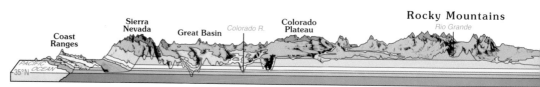

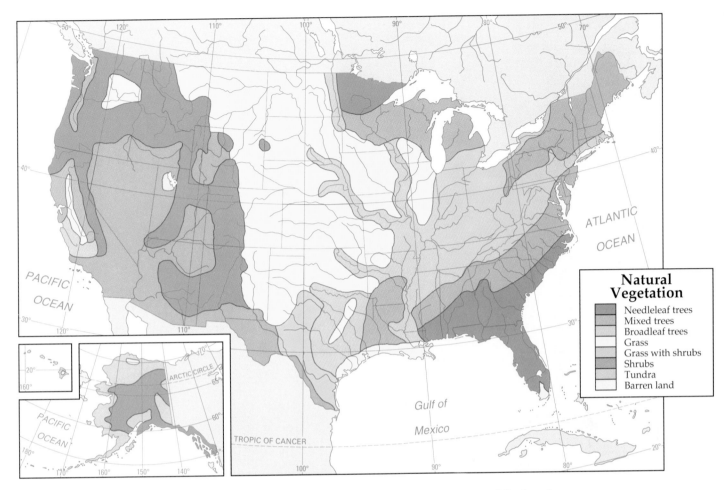

Natural Vegetation
- Needleleaf trees
- Mixed trees
- Broadleaf trees
- Grass
- Grass with shrubs
- Shrubs
- Tundra
- Barren land

Wetlands

Wetlands are an important natural resource that provides habitat for wildlife, controls floods, and produces clean fresh water. During the past 200 years, however, more than half the wetlands in the United States have been drained, filled, or paved to develop agricultural land or to expand urban areas.

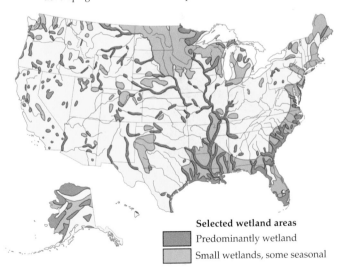

Florida's Everglades is a unique tropical savanna dominated by saltwater marshes and mangrove swamps. These wetlands are home to a great variety of birds and other animals.

Selected wetland areas
- Predominantly wetland
- Small wetlands, some seasonal

Great Plains   Ozark Plateau   Central Lowland   *Mississippi R.*   *Tennessee R.*   Appalachian Mountains   Atlantic Coastal Plain   ATLANTIC OCEAN   35°N

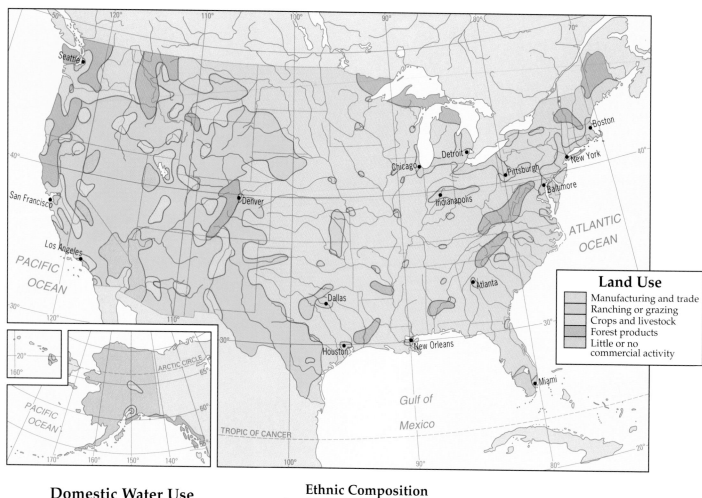

Land Use
- Manufacturing and trade
- Ranching or grazing
- Crops and livestock
- Forest products
- Little or no commercial activity

Domestic Water Use

In the United States, an average family of four uses 240 gallons of water each day. Only ten gallons, or four percent, are used for preparing food or drinking.

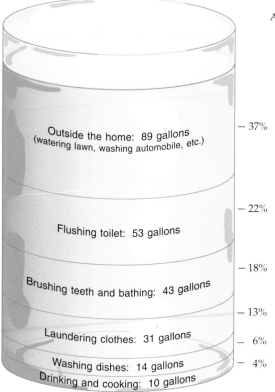

Outside the home: 89 gallons — 37%
(watering lawn, washing automobile, etc.)

Flushing toilet: 53 gallons — 22%

Brushing teeth and bathing: 43 gallons — 18%

Laundering clothes: 31 gallons — 13%

Washing dishes: 14 gallons — 6%

Drinking and cooking: 10 gallons — 4%

Ethnic Composition
(based on responses to 1990 U.S. census)

Population: 248,709,873

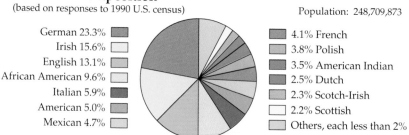

- German 23.3%
- Irish 15.6%
- English 13.1%
- African American 9.6%
- Italian 5.9%
- American 5.0%
- Mexican 4.7%

- 4.1% French
- 3.8% Polish
- 3.5% American Indian
- 2.5% Dutch
- 2.3% Scotch-Irish
- 2.2% Scottish
- Others, each less than 2%

Threatened Water Supplies

Rivers and aquifers in the arid regions of the West and Great Plains are being drained to supply water for farm and ranch irrigation, hydroelectric plants, flood-control dams, and industrial and residential needs.

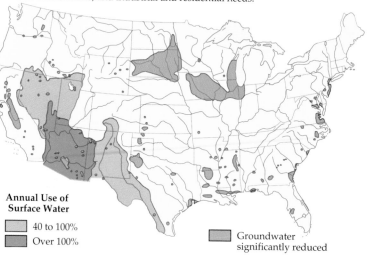

Annual Use of Surface Water
- 40 to 100%
- Over 100%
- Groundwater significantly reduced

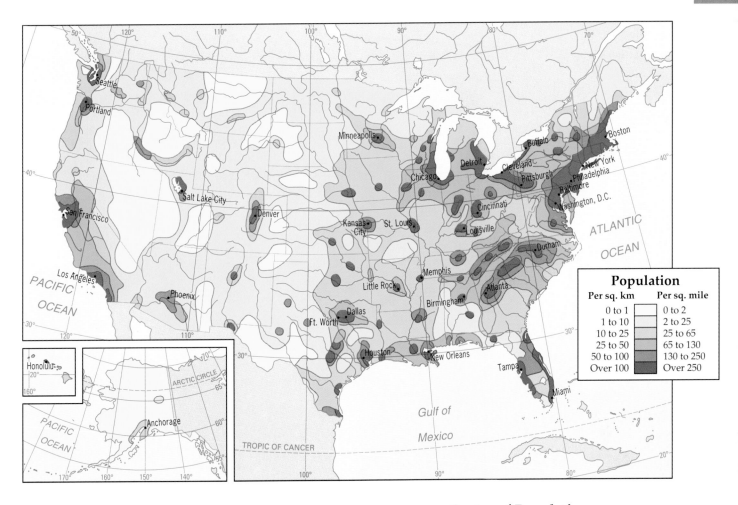

Population

Per sq. km	Per sq. mile
0 to 1	0 to 2
1 to 10	2 to 25
10 to 25	25 to 65
25 to 50	65 to 130
50 to 100	130 to 250
Over 100	Over 250

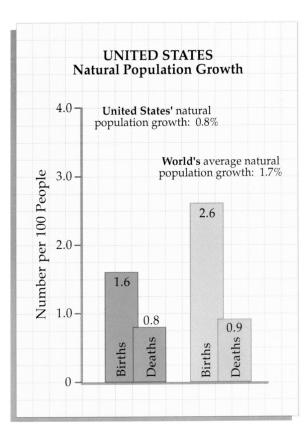

UNITED STATES
Natural Population Growth

United States' natural population growth: 0.8%

World's average natural population growth: 1.7%

Number per 100 People

4.0

3.0

2.6

2.0

1.6

1.0

0.8   0.9

0

Births Deaths   Births Deaths

Center of Population

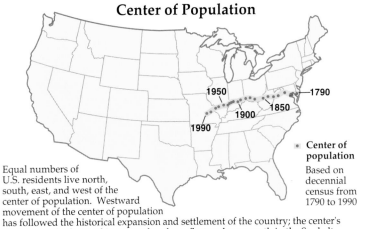

1950   1790
1900 1850
1990

● Center of population

Based on decennial census from 1790 to 1990

Equal numbers of U.S. residents live north, south, east, and west of the center of population. Westward movement of the center of population has followed the historical expansion and settlement of the country; the center's slightly southerly trend in recent decades reflects urban growth in the Sunbelt.

New York, New York

Petaluma, California

Bumper-to-bumper traffic is a way of life in big cities, while small towns face few problems with congestion. Towns, however, may have their economic base eroded by the loss of population to the cities.

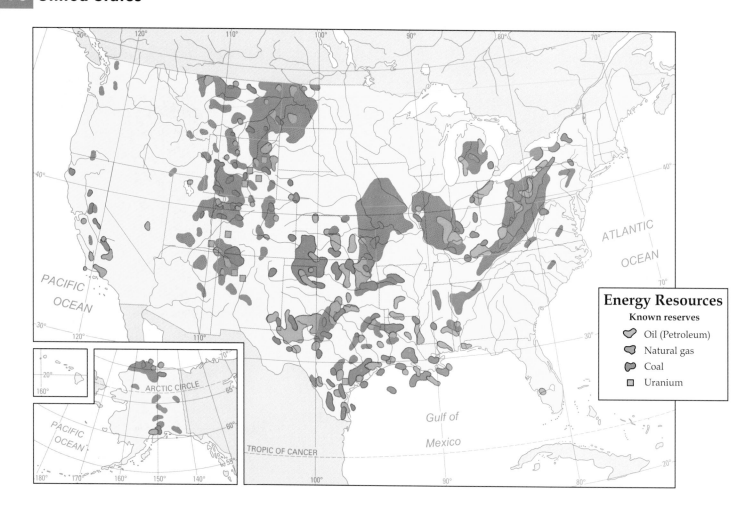

Energy in the United States
1950 and 1990

Coal
41.3%

Natural gas
19.1%

Petroleum
35.2%

Hydroelectric
4.4%

Sources of Consumed Energy: 1950

Other
0.3%

Coal
23.3%

Nuclear 7.0%

Petroleum
42.1%

Natural gas
23.8%

Hydroelectric
3.5%

Sources of Consumed Energy: 1990

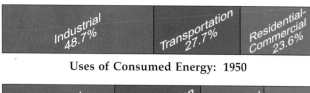

Uses of Consumed Energy: 1950

Uses of Consumed Energy: 1990

Barges offer an inexpensive way to deliver coal to factories along rivers in the Midwest and Northeast.

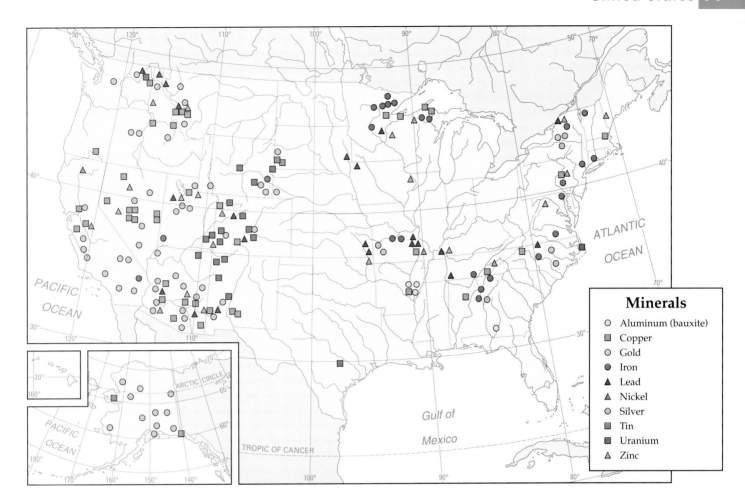

Minerals

- ○ Aluminum (bauxite)
- ▣ Copper
- ○ Gold
- ● Iron
- ▲ Lead
- △ Nickel
- ○ Silver
- ▣ Tin
- ▣ Uranium
- △ Zinc

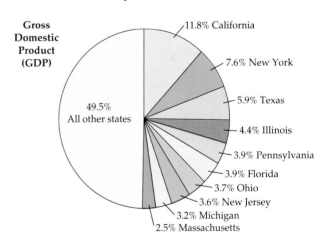

Two-thirds of the steel produced in the United States comes from the Midwest. But competition from other countries has reduced steel production and forced the closing of many plants.

More than half of the aluminum cans used in the United States are recycled into new cans and other metal products.

Productivity in the United States

Gross Domestic Product (GDP)

- 11.8% California
- 7.6% New York
- 5.9% Texas
- 4.4% Illinois
- 3.9% Pennsylvania
- 3.9% Florida
- 3.7% Ohio
- 3.6% New Jersey
- 3.2% Michigan
- 2.5% Massachusetts
- 49.5% All other states

The United States has the highest GDP in the world: US$ 5,439.4 billion. If individual states were compared with other countries, two would rank in the world's top 10, and ten in the world's top 30.

Rank	Country or state	GDP or GNP (US$ billion)
1	Japan	3,154.1
2	Germany	1,398.6
3	France	1,090.2
4	Italy	970.7
5	United Kingdom	911.4
6	**California**	**642.7**
7	Canada	535.6
8	Russia	480.1
9	Spain	426.7
10	**New York**	**415.3**

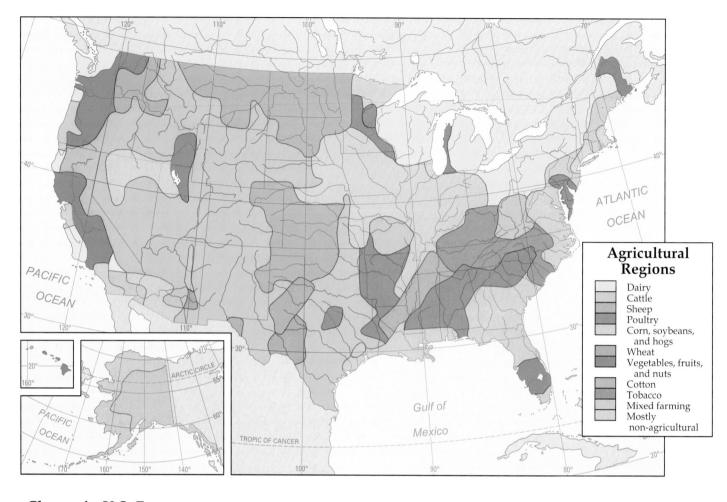

Agricultural Regions

- Dairy
- Cattle
- Sheep
- Poultry
- Corn, soybeans, and hogs
- Wheat
- Vegetables, fruits, and nuts
- Cotton
- Tobacco
- Mixed farming
- Mostly non-agricultural

Change in U.S. Farms

	1910	1930	1950	1970	1990
Number of people engaged in farming = 1 million	32.1 million	30.5 million	23.3 million	9.7 million	4.6 million
Farmers, as a percentage of U.S. population = percentage	34.3%	24.7%	15.5%	4.8%	1.9%
Number of farms = 1 million farms	6.4 million	6.3 million	5.4 million	2.9 million	2.1 million
Average farm size = 100 acres	138 acres	157 acres	215 acres	374 acres	445 acres

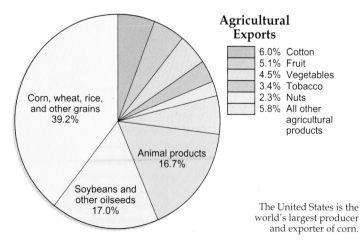

Agricultural Exports

- Corn, wheat, rice, and other grains 39.2%
- Animal products 16.7%
- Soybeans and other oilseeds 17.0%
- 6.0% Cotton
- 5.1% Fruit
- 4.5% Vegetables
- 3.4% Tobacco
- 2.3% Nuts
- 5.8% All other agricultural products

The United States is the world's largest producer and exporter of corn.

UNITED STATES
Balance of Trade

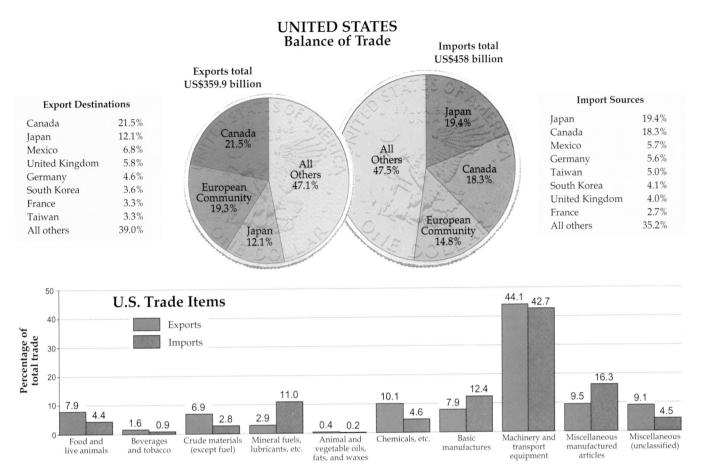

Exports total
US$359.9 billion

Imports total
US$458 billion

Export Destinations

Canada	21.5%
Japan	12.1%
Mexico	6.8%
United Kingdom	5.8%
Germany	4.6%
South Korea	3.6%
France	3.3%
Taiwan	3.3%
All others	39.0%

Import Sources

Japan	19.4%
Canada	18.3%
Mexico	5.7%
Germany	5.6%
Taiwan	5.0%
South Korea	4.1%
United Kingdom	4.0%
France	2.7%
All others	35.2%

Exports pie chart: Canada 21.5%, European Community 19.3%, Japan 12.1%, All Others 47.1%

Imports pie chart: Japan 19.4%, Canada 18.3%, European Community 14.8%, All Others 47.5%

U.S. Trade Items

Percentage of total trade

Legend: Exports, Imports

Item	Exports	Imports
Food and live animals	7.9	4.4
Beverages and tobacco	1.6	0.9
Crude materials (except fuel)	6.9	2.8
Mineral fuels, lubricants, etc.	2.9	11.0
Animal and vegetable oils, fats, and waxes	0.4	0.2
Chemicals, etc.	10.1	4.6
Basic manufactures	7.9	12.4
Machinery and transport equipment	44.1	42.7
Miscellaneous manufactured articles	9.5	16.3
Miscellaneous (unclassified)	9.1	4.5

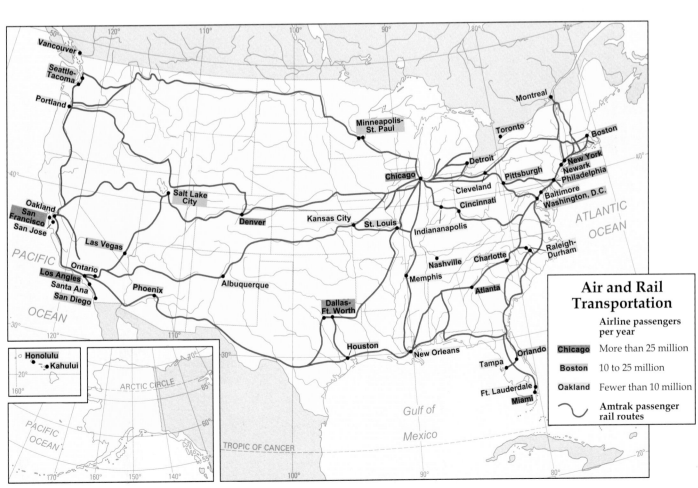

Air and Rail Transportation

Airline passengers per year

Chicago	More than 25 million
Boston	10 to 25 million
Oakland	Fewer than 10 million
∿	Amtrak passenger rail routes

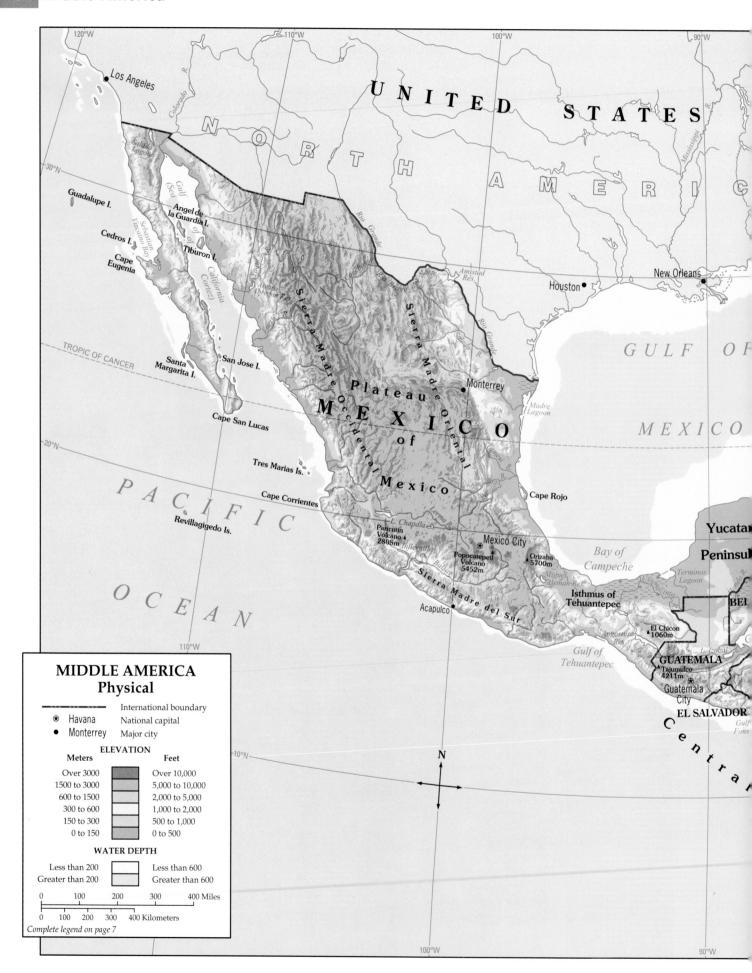

UNITED STATES

NORTH AMERICA

Los Angeles

Guadalupe I.

Angel de
la Guardia I.

Cedros I.

Tiburon I.

Cape
Eugenia

Salada
Lagoon

Gulf
(Sea)

Sebastian
Vizcaino Bay

Gulf
of
California
(Cortez)

Colorado

Rio Grande

Conchos R.

Sierra Madre Occidental

Sierra Madre Oriental

Houston

New Orleans

Amistad
Res.

Rio Grande

Salado R.

GULF OF

MEXICO

Monterrey

Madre
Lagoon

TROPIC OF CANCER

Santa
Margarita I.

San Jose I.

Cape San Lucas

Plateau
MEXICO
of
Mexico

L. Chapala

Paricutin
Volcano
2808m

Infiernillo
Res.

Lerma R.

Balsas R.

Panuco R.

Popocatepetl
Volcano
5452m

Mexico City

Orizaba
5700m

Cape Rojo

Bay of
Campeche

MEXICO

Yucatan

Peninsul

Terminos
Lagoon

Usumacinta R.

Grijalva R.

Tres Marias Is.

Cape Corrientes

PACIFIC

Revillagigedo Is.

OCEAN

Sierra Madre del Sur

Acapulco

Gulf of
Tehuantepec

Isthmus of
Tehuantepec

Miguel
Aleman Res.

El Chicon
1060m

Angostura
Res.

BEL

GUATEMALA
Tajumulco
4211m

Guatemala
City

EL SALVADOR

Gulf
Fons

Central

L. Izabal

N

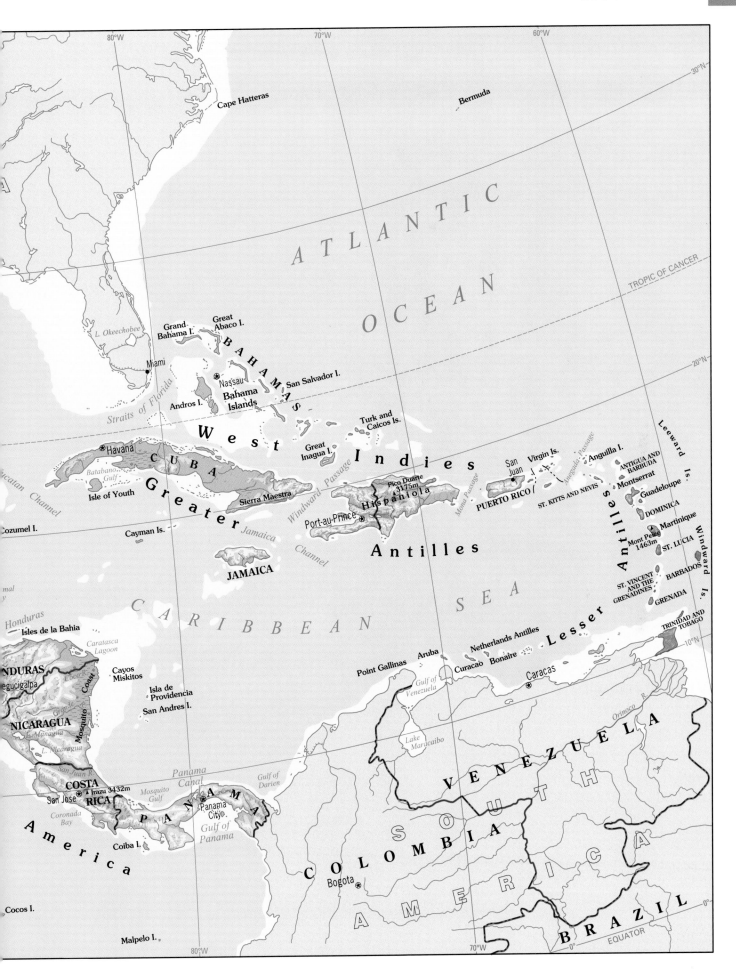

ATLANTIC

OCEAN

Cape Hatteras

Bermuda

TROPIC OF CANCER

30°N

80°W

70°W

60°W

L. Okeechobee

Grand
Bahama I.

Great
Abaco I.

B A H A M A S

Miami

20°N

Nassau

San Salvador I.

Andros I.

Bahama
Islands

Straits of Florida

W
e
s
t

Turk and
Caicos Is.

Havana

I
n
d
i
e
s

Leeward Is.

Yucatan Channel

Batabano
Gulf

C U B A

Great
Inagua I.

San
Juan

Virgin Is.

Anguilla I.

ANTIGUA AND
BARBUDA

Isle of Youth

G
r
e
a
t
e
r

Pico Duarte
3175m

Mona Passage

Anegada Passage

Montserrat

Guadeloupe

Sierra Maestra

Hispaniola

PUERTO RICO

ST. KITTS AND NEVIS

DOMINICA

Cozumel I.

Port-au-Prince

A
n
t
i
l
l
e
s

Mont Pelee
1463m

Martinique

Cayman Is.

Jamaica

Windward Passage

ST. LUCIA

Channel

L
e
s
s
e
r

W
i
n
d
w
a
r
d

I
s
.

JAMAICA

ST. VINCENT
AND THE
GRENADINES

BARBADOS

GRENADA

C A R I B B E A N

S E A

A
n
t
i
l
l
e
s

TRINIDAD AND
TOBAGO

Honduras

Isles de la Bahia

Caratasca
Lagoon

10°N

NDURAS

egucigalpa

Cayos
Miskitos

Coco R.

Mosquito Coast

Point Gallinas

Aruba

Netherlands Antilles

Curacao

Bonaire

Caracas

Gulf of
Venezuela

NICARAGUA

Isla de
Providencia

San Andres I.

Grande

L.
Managua

L. Nicaragua

V
E
N
E
Z
U
E
L
A

Lake
Maracaibo

Orinoco R.

San Juan R.

Panama
Canal

Gulf of
Darien

COSTA

Irazu 3432m

Mosquito
Gulf

P A N A M A

S
O
U
T
H

San Jose

RICA

Panama
City

C
O
L
O
M
B
I
A

A
M
E
R
I
C
A

Coronada
Bay

Gulf of
Panama

A
m
e
r
i
c
a

Coiba I.

Bogota

Cocos I.

B R A Z I L

80°W

70°W

EQUATOR

0°

Malpelo I.

mal

Mosquito

mal

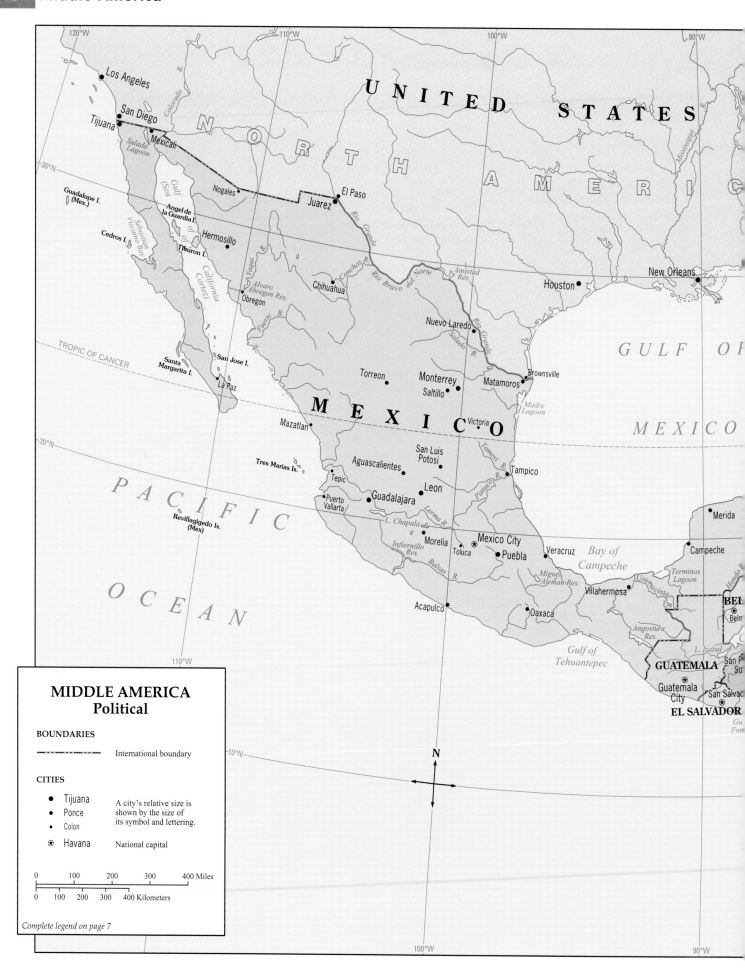

UNITED STATES

NORTH AMERICA

MEXICO

PACIFIC OCEAN

GULF OF MEXICO

Los Angeles
San Diego
Tijuana
Mexicali
Salada Lagoon
Nogales
Juarez
El Paso
Colorado R.
Guadalupe I. (Mex.)
Gulf (Sea of California Cortez)
Angel de la Guardia I.
Cedros I.
Sebastian Vizcaino Bay
Tiburon I.
Hermosillo
Yaqui R.
Alvaro Abregon Res.
Obregon
Chihuahua
Fuerte R.
Conchos R.
Rio Bravo del Norte
Rio Grande
Amistad Res.
Houston
New Orleans
Mississippi
TROPIC OF CANCER
Santa Margarita I.
San Jose I.
La Paz
Torreon
Mazatlan
Tres Marias Is.
Aguascalientes
Tepic
Puerto Vallarta
Guadalajara
Leon
L. Chapala
Lerma R.
Infiernillo Res.
Morelia
Toluca
Nuevo Laredo
Salado R.
Monterrey
Saltillo
Matamoros
Brownsville
Madre Lagoon
Victoria
San Luis Potosi
Tamesi R.
Tampico
Panuco R.
Mexico City
Puebla
Veracruz
Bay of Campeche
Balsas R.
Acapulco
Oaxaca
Miguel Aleman Res.
Villahermosa
Usumacinta R.
Terminos Lagoon
Hondo R.
Merida
Campeche
Angostura Res.
Gulf of Tehuantepec
L. Izabal
BEL
Belm
GUATEMALA
Guatemala City
San P
San Salvad
EL SALVADOR
Gu
Fon

120°W 110°W 100°W 90°W
30°N
20°N
10°N
N

MIDDLE AMERICA
Political

BOUNDARIES

————— International boundary

CITIES

● Tijuana   A city's relative size is
● Ponce   shown by the size of
· Colon   its symbol and lettering.

⊛ Havana   National capital

0   100   200   300   400 Miles
0 100 200 300   400 Kilometers

Complete legend on page 7

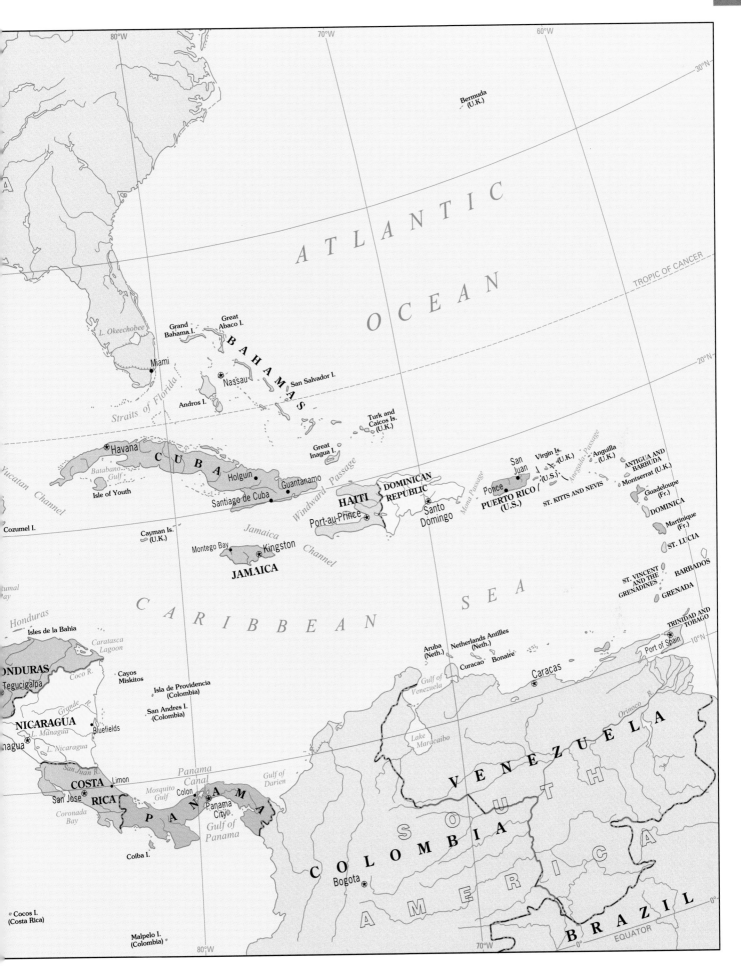

ATLANTIC

OCEAN

TROPIC OF CANCER

30°N

20°N

Bermuda
(U.K.)

L. Okeechobee

Miami

Straits of Florida

Grand
Bahama I.

Great
Abaco I.

B A H A M A S

Nassau

Andros I.

San Salvador I.

Turk and
Caicos Is.
(U.K.)

Great
Inagua I.

Yucatan Channel

Havana

C U B A

Batabano
Gulf

Holguin

Isle of Youth

Santiago de Cuba

Guantanamo

Cozumel I.

Cayman Is.
(U.K.)

Jamaica

Montego Bay

Kingston

JAMAICA

Windward Passage

HAITI

Port-au-Prince

DOMINICAN
REPUBLIC

Santo
Domingo

Mona Passage

San
Juan

Ponce

PUERTO RICO
(U.S.)

Virgin Is.
(U.K.)
(U.S.)

Anegada Passage

Anguilla (U.K.)

ANTIGUA AND
BARBUDA

Montserrat (U.K.)

Guadeloupe
(Fr.)

DOMINICA

Martinique
(Fr.)

ST. LUCIA

ST. KITTS AND NEVIS

C A R I B B E A N

Jamaica
Channel

S E A

ST. VINCENT
AND THE
GRENADINES

BARBADOS

GRENADA

TRINIDAD AND
TOBAGO

Port of Spain

10°N

Honduras

Isles de la Bahia

Caratasca
Lagoon

Coco R.

Cayos
Miskitos

Isla de Providencia
(Colombia)

San Andres I.
(Colombia)

Aruba
(Neth.)

Netherlands Antilles
(Neth.)

Curacao

Bonaire

Caracas

Gulf of
Venezuela

ONDURAS

Tegucigalpa

Grande

NICARAGUA

L. Managua

nagua

Bluefields

L. Nicaragua

San Juan R.

COSTA

San Jose

RICA

Coronada
Bay

Mosquito
Gulf

Limon

Colon

Panama
Canal

P A N A M A

Panama
City

Gulf of
Panama

Gulf of
Darien

Coiba I.

Lake
Maracaibo

V E N E Z U E L A

Orinoco

S
O
U
T
H

C O L O M B I A

A
M
E
R
I
C
A

Bogota

B R A Z I L

EQUATOR

0°

Cocos I.
(Costa Rica)

Malpelo I.
(Colombia)

80°W

70°W

60°W

80°W

70°W

0°

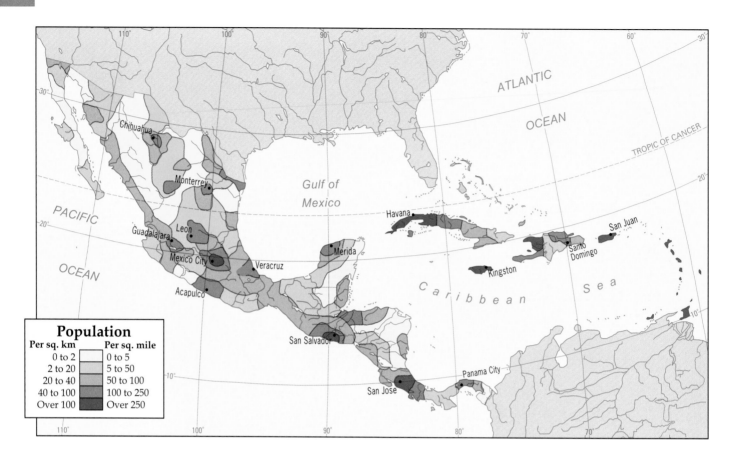

Population

Per sq. km	Per sq. mile
0 to 2	0 to 5
2 to 20	5 to 50
20 to 40	50 to 100
40 to 100	100 to 250
Over 100	Over 250

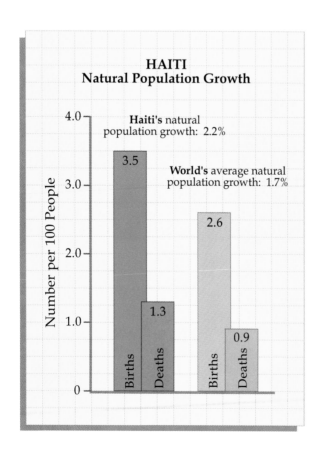

HAITI
Natural Population Growth

Haiti's natural population growth: 2.2%

World's average natural population growth: 1.7%

Number per 100 People

3.5 Births
1.3 Deaths
2.6 Births
0.9 Deaths

MEXICO
Balance of Trade

Exports total US$25.6 billion

United States 63.9%

All Others 36.1%

Imports total US$25 billion

All Others 34.3%

United States 65.7%

Mexico City's Population Growth

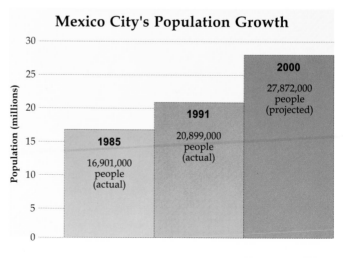

Population (millions)

1985 16,901,000 people (actual)

1991 20,899,000 people (actual)

2000 27,872,000 people (projected)

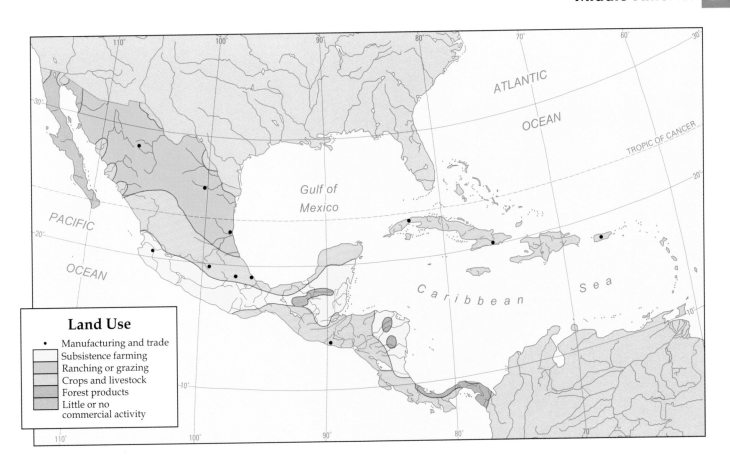

Land Use

- • Manufacturing and trade
-   Subsistence farming
-   Ranching or grazing
-   Crops and livestock
-   Forest products
-   Little or no commercial activity

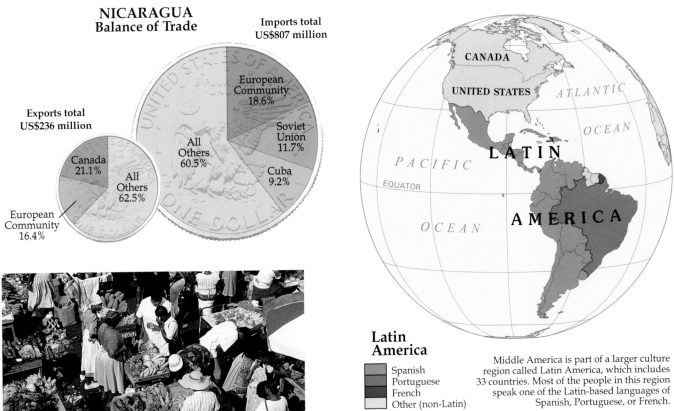

NICARAGUA
Balance of Trade

Imports total
US$807 million

European Community 18.6%

Soviet Union 11.7%

All Others 60.5%

Cuba 9.2%

Exports total
US$236 million

Canada 21.1%

All Others 62.5%

European Community 16.4%

Latin America

-   Spanish
-   Portuguese
-   French
-   Other (non-Latin)

Middle America is part of a larger culture region called Latin America, which includes 33 countries. Most of the people in this region speak one of the Latin-based languages of Spanish, Portuguese, or French.

Caribbean people enjoy daily visits to open-air markets that offer a variety of fresh tropical produce.

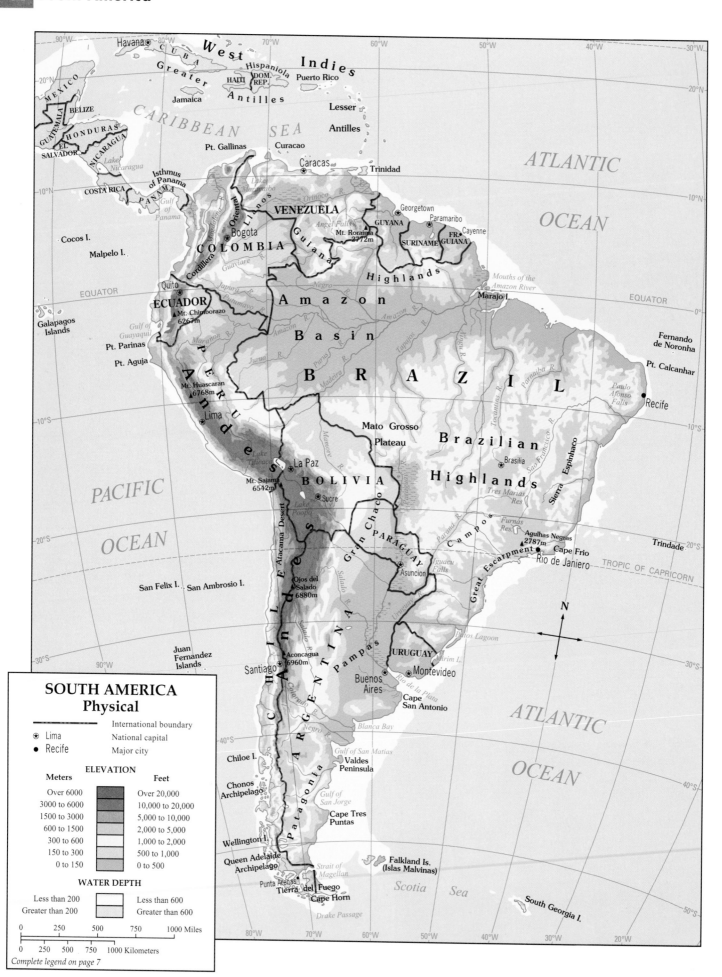

West Indies

Havana ⊛
CUBA
Greater
MEXICO
Hispaniola
HAITI DOM. REP.
BELIZE
Puerto Rico
GUATEMALA
HONDURAS
Jamaica
Lesser Antilles
EL SALVADOR
NICARAGUA
Lake Nicaragua
COSTA RICA
Isthmus of Panama
PANAMA
Gulf of Panama

CARIBBEAN SEA

Pt. Gallinas
Curacao
Caracas
Trinidad

ATLANTIC OCEAN

Cocos I.
Malpelo I.

VENEZUELA
Lake Maracaibo
Llanos
Orinoco R.
Angel Falls
Mt. Roraima 2772m
GUYANA
Georgetown
Paramaribo
Cayenne
SURINAME
FR. GUIANA

Bogota
COLOMBIA
Cordillera Oriental
Guiana
Highlands

Quito
ECUADOR
Mt. Chimborazo 6267m
Galapagos Islands
Gulf of Guayaquil
Pt. Parinas
Pt. Aguja

EQUATOR

Amazon Basin
Negro
Japura
Putumayo
Maranon
Amazon
Jurua
Purus
Madeira

Amazon R.
Tapajos R.
Xingu R.
Mouths of the Amazon River
Marajo I.

Fernando de Noronha

BRAZIL

Pt. Calcanhar

PERU
Mt. Huascaran 6768m
Lima ⊛

Paulo Afonso Falls
Recife ●

ANDES

Lake Titicaca
La Paz
Mt. Sajama 6542m
BOLIVIA
Sucre
Lake Poopo
Mamore R.

Mato Grosso Plateau

Brazilian Highlands

Brasilia ⊛
San Francisco R.
Sierra Espinhaco
Tres Marias Res

PACIFIC OCEAN

Atacama Desert
Gran Chaco
PARAGUAY
Asuncion
Iguacu Falls
Parana R.
Salado
Campos
Furnas Res
Agulhas Negras 2787m
Cape Frio
Rio de Janiero
Great Escarpment

Trindade

TROPIC OF CAPRICORN

San Felix I.
San Ambrosio I.

Ojos del Salado 6880m
Salado

ARGENTINA

Uruguay R.
Patos Lagoon
Mirim L.

N

Juan Fernandez Islands

Aconcagua 6960m
Santiago
Pampas
Buenos Aires
URUGUAY
Montevideo
Rio de la Plata
Cape San Antonio

ATLANTIC OCEAN

Colorado
Negro R.
Blanca Bay

Chiloe I.
Valdes Peninsula
Gulf of San Matias

CHILE
Patagonia
Chonos Archipelago
Gulf of San Jorge
Cape Tres Puntas

Wellington I.

Queen Adelaide Archipelago
Strait of Magellan
Punta Arenas
Tierra del Fuego
Cape Horn
Drake Passage

Falkland Is. (Islas Malvinas)
Scotia Sea
South Georgia I.

SOUTH AMERICA
Physical

—————— International boundary
⊛ Lima   National capital
● Recife   Major city

ELEVATION

Meters		Feet
Over 6000		Over 20,000
3000 to 6000		10,000 to 20,000
1500 to 3000		5,000 to 10,000
600 to 1500		2,000 to 5,000
300 to 600		1,000 to 2,000
150 to 300		500 to 1,000
0 to 150		0 to 500

WATER DEPTH

Less than 200		Less than 600
Greater than 200		Greater than 600

0   250   500   750   1000 Miles

0   250   500   750   1000 Kilometers

Complete legend on page 7

ATLANTIC OCEAN

PACIFIC OCEAN

CARIBBEAN SEA

CUBA
Havana ⊛
MEXICO
BELIZE
GUATEMALA
HONDURAS
EL SALVADOR
NICARAGUA
Lake Nicaragua
COSTA RICA
PANAMA
Gulf of Panama
Cocos I. (Costa Rica)
Malpelo I. (Colombia)

JAMAICA
HAITI
DOM. REP.
Puerto Rico (U.S.)
Anguilla (U.K.)
ST. KITTS AND NEVIS
ANTIGUA AND BARBUDA
Guadeloupe (Fr.)
DOMINICA
Martinique (Fr.)
ST. VINCENT AND THE GRENADINES
ST. LUCIA
BARBADOS
Curacao (Neth.)
GRENADA
TRINIDAD AND TOBAGO

Barranquilla
Maracaibo
Lake Maracaibo
Caracas
Barquisimeto
VENEZUELA
Bucaramanga
Medellín
Bogota ⊛
COLOMBIA
Cali
Orinoco R.
Angel Falls
Ciudad Bolivar
Georgetown
GUYANA
Paramaribo
SURINAME
FR. GUIANA (Fr.)
Cayenne
Guaviare R.
Boa Vista
Macapa
Mouths of the Amazon

EQUATOR

Quito ⊛
ECUADOR
Guayaquil
Gulf of Guayaquil
Galapagos Islands (Ecuador)
Iquitos
Piura
Chiclayo
Trujillo
PERU
Lima ⊛
Callao
Huancayo
Cuzco
Arequipa

Japura R.
Putumayo R.
Negro R.
Manaus
Amazon
Maranon R.
Jurua R.
Purus R.
Madeira R.
Rio Branco
Porto Velho
B R A Z I L
Santarem
Tapajos R.
Xingu R.
Belem
Sao Luis
Fortaleza
Teresina
Parnaiba R.
Natal
Joao Pessoa
Recife
Maceio
Paulo Afonso Falls
Aracaju
Feira de Santana
Salvador
Itabuna
Fernando de Noronha

Tocantins R.
Cuiaba
Brasilia ⊛
Goiania
Sao Francisco R.
Montes Claros
Belo Horizonte
Uberaba
Tres Marias Res.
Furnas Res.
Nova Iguacu
Vitoria
Campos
Trindade (Brazil)

La Paz ⊛
Mamore R.
Lake Titicaca
Arica
Iquique
B O L I V I A
Sucre ⊛
Santa Cruz
Potosi
Lake Poopo
Paraguay R.
Campo Grande
P A R A G U A Y
Asuncion ⊛
Iguacu Falls
Campinas
Parana R.
Sao Paulo
Santos
Curitiba
Rio de Janeiro

TROPIC OF CAPRICORN

Antofagasta
San Felix I. (Chile)
San Ambrosio I. (Chile)
Salta
Tucuman
Salado R.
Santiago del Estero
Resistencia
Uruguay R.
Santa Maria
Florianopolis
Porto Alegre
Patos Lagoon

La Serena
San Juan
Salado R.
Santa Fe
Salto
URUGUAY
Mirim L.
Vina del Mar
Valparaiso
Mendoza
Cordoba
Rosario
Montevideo
C H I L E
Santiago ⊛
San Luis
A R G E N T I N A
Buenos Aires ⊛
San Justo
La Plata
Rio de la Plata
Juan Fernandez Is. (Chile)

Talcahuano
Concepcion
Colorado R.
Mar del Plata
Temuco
Negro R.
Bahia Blanca
Blanca Bay
Viedma
Puerto Montt
Gulf of San Matias

Comodoro Rivadavia
Gulf of San Jorge

Rio Gallegos
Strait of Magellan
Punta Arenas
Falkland Is. (Islas Malvinas) (U.K.)
Scotia Sea
South Georgia (U.K.)
Drake Passage

N

SOUTH AMERICA
Political

BOUNDARIES

——————— International boundary

CITIES

● Sao Paulo
● Fortaleza
• Cuzco   A city's relative size is shown by the size of its symbol and lettering.
⊛ Lima   National capital

0   250   500   750   1000 Miles

0   250   500   750   1000 Kilometers

Complete legend on page 7

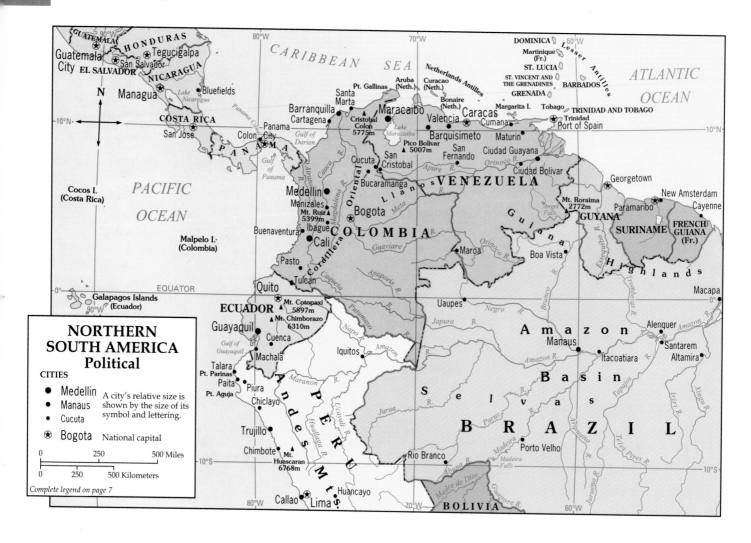

NORTHERN SOUTH AMERICA Political

CITIES

● **Medellin**   A city's relative size is shown by the size of its symbol and lettering.

■ **Manaus**

• Cucuta

✪ **Bogota**   National capital

```
0        250        500 Miles
0    250    500 Kilometers
```

Complete legend on page 7

Drug Trade

▨ Coca (cocaine) growing area

▢ Major drug-trafficking route

SOUTH AMERICA Area Comparison

The continent of South America is twice the size of the United States. Its largest country, Brazil, is larger than the contiguous United States.

South America	6,878,000 sq. mi. (17 818 700 sq. km)
Contiguous U.S.	3,021,295 sq. mi. (7 825 112 sq. km.)

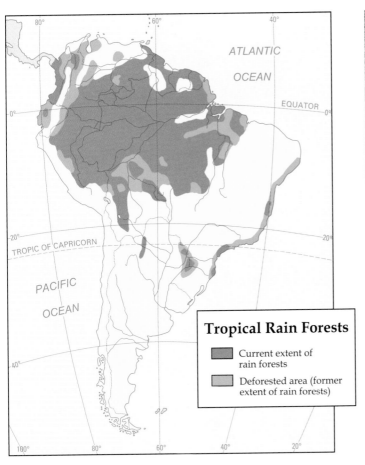

Tropical Rain Forests

Current extent of rain forests

Deforested area (former extent of rain forests)

Brazil's economic development often comes at the expense of the Amazon rain forest. Deforestation increases annually as trees are cut down to make way for farms and highways.

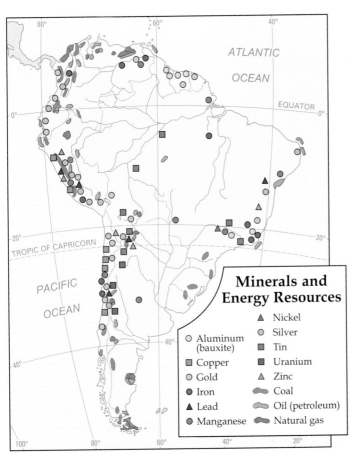

Minerals and Energy Resources

○ Aluminum (bauxite)
■ Copper
○ Gold
● Iron
▲ Lead
● Manganese
▲ Nickel
○ Silver
■ Tin
■ Uranium
▲ Zinc
Coal
Oil (petroleum)
Natural gas

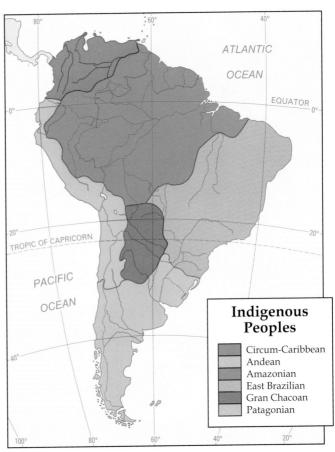

Indigenous Peoples

Circum-Caribbean
Andean
Amazonian
East Brazilian
Gran Chacoan
Patagonian

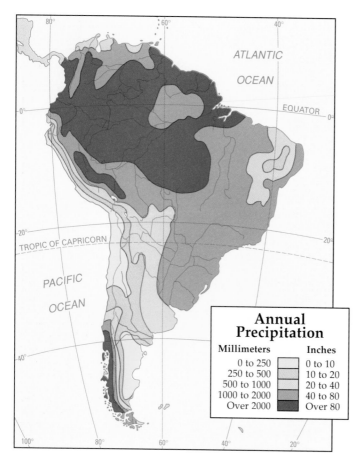

Annual Precipitation

Millimeters	Inches
0 to 250	0 to 10
250 to 500	10 to 20
500 to 1000	20 to 40
1000 to 2000	40 to 80
Over 2000	Over 80

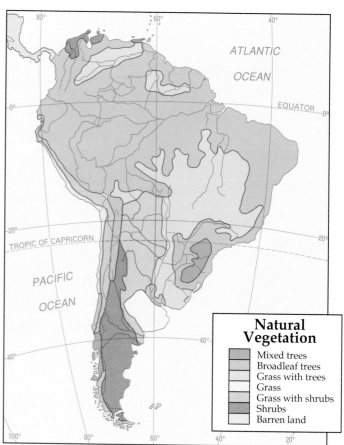

Natural Vegetation

Mixed trees
Broadleaf trees
Grass with trees
Grass
Grass with shrubs
Shrubs
Barren land

Brazil's urban population is a diverse mixture of European, African, and Indian ancestry.

VENEZUELA
Balance of Trade

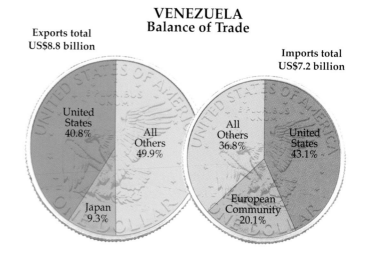

Exports total US$8.8 billion

United States 40.8%
All Others 49.9%
Japan 9.3%

Imports total US$7.2 billion

All Others 36.8%
United States 43.1%
European Community 20.1%

Cross Section of South America

ELEVATION

Meters		Feet
Over 6000		Over 20,000
3000 to 6000		10,000 to 20,000
1500 to 3000		5,000 to 10,000
600 to 1500		2,000 to 5,000
300 to 600		1,000 to 2,000
150 to 300		500 to 1,000
0 to 150		0 to 500
Below sea level		Below sea level

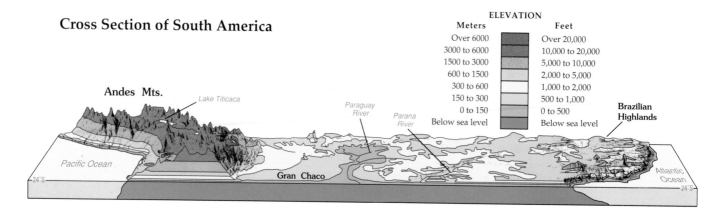

Andes Mts.
Lake Titicaca
Paraguay River
Parana River
Brazilian Highlands
Pacific Ocean
Gran Chaco
Atlantic Ocean
24°S
24°S

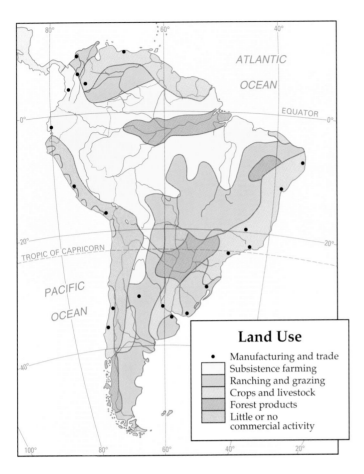

Land Use

- • Manufacturing and trade
- Subsistence farming
- Ranching and grazing
- Crops and livestock
- Forest products
- Little or no commercial activity

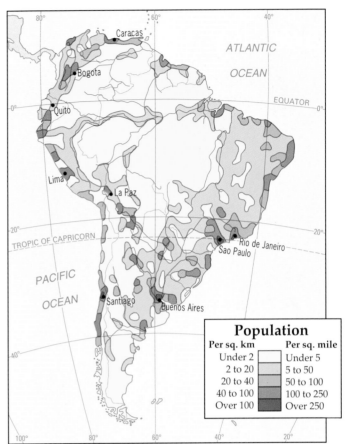

Population

Per sq. km	Per sq. mile
Under 2	Under 5
2 to 20	5 to 50
20 to 40	50 to 100
40 to 100	100 to 250
Over 100	Over 250

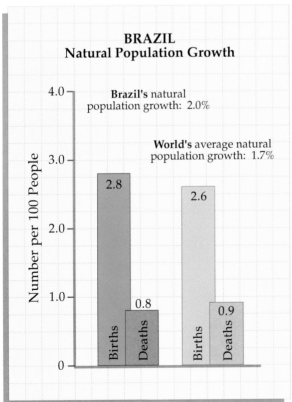

BRAZIL
Natural Population Growth

Brazil's natural population growth: 2.0%

World's average natural population growth: 1.7%

Number per 100 People

- 2.8 Births
- 0.8 Deaths
- 2.6 Births
- 0.9 Deaths

CHILE
Balance of Trade

Exports total US$6.9 billion

- European Community 29%
- All Others 51.2%
- United States 19.8%

Imports total US$5.3 billion

- United States 19.5%
- European Community 12.9%
- All Others 67.6%

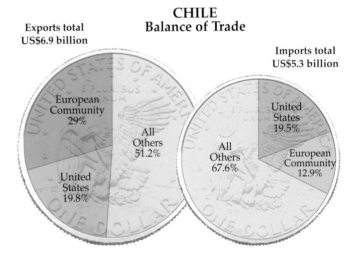

More Indians live in Peru than in any other South American country. Many still farm and bring goods to market in the highlands where their ancestors, the Incas, once reigned.

ARCTIC

Lofoten
Is.

NORWEGIAN
SEA

ARCTIC CIRCLE

PRIME MERIDIAN

Reykjavik

ICELAND

Surtsey I.   Hekla
             ▲1491m

N

NORWAY

Trondheims Fiord

Sogne Fiord

Hardanger Fiord

Faeroe
Islands

Bokna Fiord

SWEDEN

Rockall

Shetland
Islands

Oslo

L. Mälaren

NORTH
SEA

Gotaland   Gotlan

Hebrides

Orkney Is.

Grampian Mts.

Jutland   Skagerrak

Vänern
Vättern

Baltic

IRELAND   Great Britain   UNITED
                            KINGDOM

Irish Sea

DENMARK   Kattegat   Copenhagen

Bornholm   TO
              RUSS

British Isles

Cambrian Mts.

London

Thames R.

Frisian Is.

Netherlands

Elbe R.

Northern   POLA

Wars

Celtic
Sea

English Channel

Strait of Dover

NETHERLANDS

GERMANY

Channel Is.

Seine R.

BELGIUM

LUXEMBOURG

Rhine R.

Ore
Mts.

Elbe R.

Vist

CZECH REPUBLIC

Loire R.

Paris Basin ● Paris

FRANCE

Danube R.

Carpa
SLOVAK

Cape Finisterre

Bay of
Biscay

Munich ●

AUSTRIA

HUNGARY

Aquitaine Basin

Massif
Central

Mt. Blanc
4807m

SWITZERLAND LIECH.

A l p s

Great Hunga

Cantabrian Mts.

Pyrenees

Rhône R.

Geneva

SLOVENIA

CROATIA

Douro R.

ANDORRA

Po R.

BOSNIA

Duero R.

Ebro R.

MONACO

SAN
MARINO

Dinaric

PORTUGAL

SPAIN

Tagus R. ● Madrid

Gulf of
Lion

Ligurian
Sea

Apennines

YUGOSLAVI

Alp

Lisbon

Iberian

Guadiana R.

Corsica

VATICAN CITY ⊛ Rome

Adriatic
Sea

MACEDO

Cape St. Vincent

Peninsula

Balearic Sea

Tiber R.

ITALY

ALBANIA

Guadalquivir

Balearic Islands

Sardinia

Vesuvius
1277m

Gulf of
Taranto

Indus R

Strait of
Gibraltar

GIBRALTAR (U.K.)

Tyrrhenian
Sea

Ionian
Sea

G

MEDITERRANEAN

MOROCCO

A
F
R
I
C
A

Algiers

Sicily

Ionian Is.

Peloponnes

Tunis

ALGERIA

TUNISIA

MALTA
Maltese Islands

WESTERN
SAHARA

OCEAN

North Cape

Novaya Zemlya

Kolguyev I.

Barents Sea

Pechora Basin

Kanin Pen.

Kola Pen.

White Sea

Archangel

RUSSIA

Ural Mountains

FINLAND

L. Inari

Lapland

Kamskoye Res.

Kama Upland

L. Onega

Lake Ladoga

Lake Region

Gulf of Finland

St. Petersburg (Leningrad)

ESTONIA

L. Peipus

Rybinsk Res.

Gorki Res.

Kuybyshev Res.

Riga

LATVIA

Moscow

LITHUANIA

European

Central Russian Upland

Oka-Don Plain

Volga Upland

KAZAKHSTAN

Plain

BELARUS

Pripyat Marshes

Volgograd Res.

ASIA

Aral Sea

UZBEKISTAN

Syr Darya

Bug R.

UKRAINE

Lowland

Dnepr

Dnestr

Donets

Don R.

Ural R.

Caspian Depression

MOLDOVA

Prut R.

Black Sea Lowland

Volga R. Delta

Amu Darya

TURKMENISTAN

ROMANIA

Transylvanian Alps

Black

Odessa

Sea of Azov

Crimea Pen.

Caspian Sea

Bucharest

Danube

Caucasus Mountains

Mt. Elbrus 5642m

GEORGIA

Balkan Mts.

BULGARIA

Balkan Peninsula

Black Sea

ARMENIA

AZERBAIJAN

Baku

Bosporus

Istanbul

Sea of Marmara

TURKEY

Lake Van

Lake Urmia

Tehran

Olympus 17m

Dardanelles

Euboea

Aegean Sea

IRAN

Sporades

Cyclades

L. Tuz

SYRIA

IRAQ

Rhodes

Crete

SEA

CYPRUS

LEBANON

EUROPE
Physical

————————	International boundary
- - - - - - - -	Other boundary
⊗ Copenhagen	National capital
● Odessa	Major city

ELEVATION

Meters	Feet
Over 3000	Over 10,000
1,500 to 3000	5,000 to 10,000
600 to 1500	2,000 to 5,000
300 to 600	1,000 to 2,000
150 to 300	500 to 1,000
0 to 150	0 to 500
Below sea level	Below sea level

WATER DEPTH

Less than 200	Less than 600
Greater than 200	Greater than 600

0 100 200 300 400 500 Miles

0 100 200 300 400 500 Kilometers

Complete legend on page 7

ICELAND

Reykjavik

Surtsey I.
(Iceland)

N

ARCTIC CIRCLE

PRIME MERIDIAN

ARCTIC

NORWEGIAN SEA

Trondheims Fiord

Trondheim

Lofoten
Is.

Na

NORWAY

SWEDE

Faeroe Is.
(Den.)

Sogne Fiord

Bergen

Lillehammer

Hardanger Fiord

Bokna Fiord

Oslo

Stavanger

L. Vanern

L. Malaren

Stock

Rockall
(U.K.)

Shetland Is.
(U.K.)

Orkney Is.
(U.K.)

NORTH
SEA

Skagerrak

Goteborg

Norrkopmg

Kattegat

SCOTLAND

Glasgow

Edinburgh

Arhus

DENMARK

Copenhagen

Malmo

Bornholm
(Den.)

Balti

NORTHERN
IRELAND

Belfast

UNITED

KINGDOM

Gdansk

TO
RUSS

IRELAND

Dublin

Irish Sea

Leeds

Liverpool

ENGLAND

Cork

WALES

Birmingham

Amsterdam

The Hague

IJsselmeer

Hamburg

Elbe R.

Berlin

Poznan

POLA

Wars

Cardiff

Bristol

London

Thames

Rotterdam

NETHERLANDS

Essen

Cologne

GERMANY

Leipzig

Wroclaw

Krakow

Southampton

English Channel

Strait of Dover

Brussels

BELGIUM

Bonn

Frankfurt

Prague

CZECH REPUBLIC

Channel Is.
(U.K.)

Le Havre

Lille

LUXEMBOURG

Rhine R.

Luxembourg

Stuttgart

SLOVA

Nantes

Seine R.

Paris

Orleans

Munich

Vienna

Bratislava

Budat

FRANCE

Loire R.

Limoges

Bern

SWITZERLAND

LIECH.

Vaduz

AUSTRIA

Graz

HUNGARY

Bay of
Biscay

Danube R.

La Coruna

Bordeaux

Geneva

Lyon

L. Geneva

Szeged

Toulouse

Rhone R.

Milan

Turin

Venice

Ljubljana

SLOVENIA

Drava R.

Porto

Douro R.

Bilbao

Po R.

Genoa

CROATIA

Zagreb

Lisbon

PORTUGAL

Duero R.

Saragossa

Ebro R.

ANDORRA

Barcelona

Marseille

Gulf of
Lion

MONACO

Ligurian
Sea

SAN
MARINO

Florence

Adriatic

BOSNIA

Belgr

SPAIN

Madrid

Tagus R.

Guadiana

R.

Valencia

Bastia

Corsica
(Fr.)

VATICAN CITY

Tiber R.

Sarajevo

YUGOSLAV

Seville

Guadalquivir

R.

Balearic Sea

Palma

Rome

ITALY

Naples

Malaga

GIBRALTAR (U.K.)

Strait of
Gibraltar

Balearic Islands
(Spain)

Sardinia
(Italy)

Tyrrhenian
Sea

Bari

Tirane

MACED

Sk

ALBANIA

MEDITERRANEAN

Cagliari

Palermo

Messina

Sicily

Gulf of
Taranto

Ionian
Sea

Rabat

Algiers

Tunis

MOROCCO

AF

ALGERIA

TUNISIA

MALTA

Valletta

ATLANTIC
OCEAN

Celtic
Sea

WESTERN
SAHARA

EUROPE
Political

BOUNDARIES

International boundary

Internal boundary

Other boundary
(disputed or undefined)

CITIES

● Barcelona   A city's relative size is
● Liverpool   shown by the size of
• Constanta   its symbol and lettering.

⊛ Moscow   National capital

0   100   200   300   400   500 Miles
0 100 200 300 400 500 Kilometers

Complete legend on page 7

OCEAN

Barents Sea

Novaya Zemlya

Kolguyev I.

•merfest

• Vardo

• Murmansk

L. Inari

iruna

Oulu

FINLAND

L. Saimaa

Vaasa

Tampere

Turku

Helsinki

ESTONIA

Tallinn

L. Peipus

Riga

LATVIA

Pskov

LITHUANIA

Vilnius

Neman R.

Minsk

BELARUS

Pripyat Marshes

Pripyat R.

Bug R.

Chernobyl

L'vov

Kiev

UKRAINE

Dnepr R.

MOLDOVA

Chisinau

Dnestr R.

Prut R.

Cluj-Napoca

OMANIA

Bucharest

Danube

Sofia

BULGARIA

Plovdiv

Varna

Constanta

Dnepropetrovsk

Odessa

Sevastopol

E

alonika

Istanbul

Bosporus

Sea of Marmara

uboea

Athens

Dardanelle

Crete (Greece)

SEA

Aegean Sea

L. Tuz

Ankara

TURKEY

White Sea

Archangel

Onega R.

L. Onega

Northern Dvina R.

Sukhona R.

Pechora R.

Ob R.

RUSSIA

Syktyvkar

Kamskoye Res.

Perm

Kyatka R.

Kama R.

Ufa

St. Petersburg
(Leningrad)

Gulf of Finland

Lake Ladoga

Rybinsk Res.

Yaroslavl

Gorkiy Res.

Nizhniy Novgorod

Volga R.

Kazan

Kuybyshev Res.

Moscow

Oka R.

Samara

Orenburg

Tula

Ural R.

Bryansk

Orel

Uralsk

Voronezh

Saratov

KAZAKHSTAN

A S I A

Volgograd Res.

Kharkov

Donets R.

Volgograd

Ural R.

Donetsk

Don R.

Rostov-on-Don

Astrakhan

Aral Sea

Syr Darya

UZBEKISTAN

Sea of Azov

Kerch

Novorossiysk

Krasnodar

Groznyy

Volga R. Delta

Amu Darya

TURKMENISTAN

Black Sea

GEORGIA

Tbilisi

Baku

Caspian Sea

ARMENIA

Yerevan

AZERBAIJAN

Lake Van

Lake Urmia

Tehran

IRAN

Nicosia

CYPRUS

SYRIA

IRAQ

LEBANON

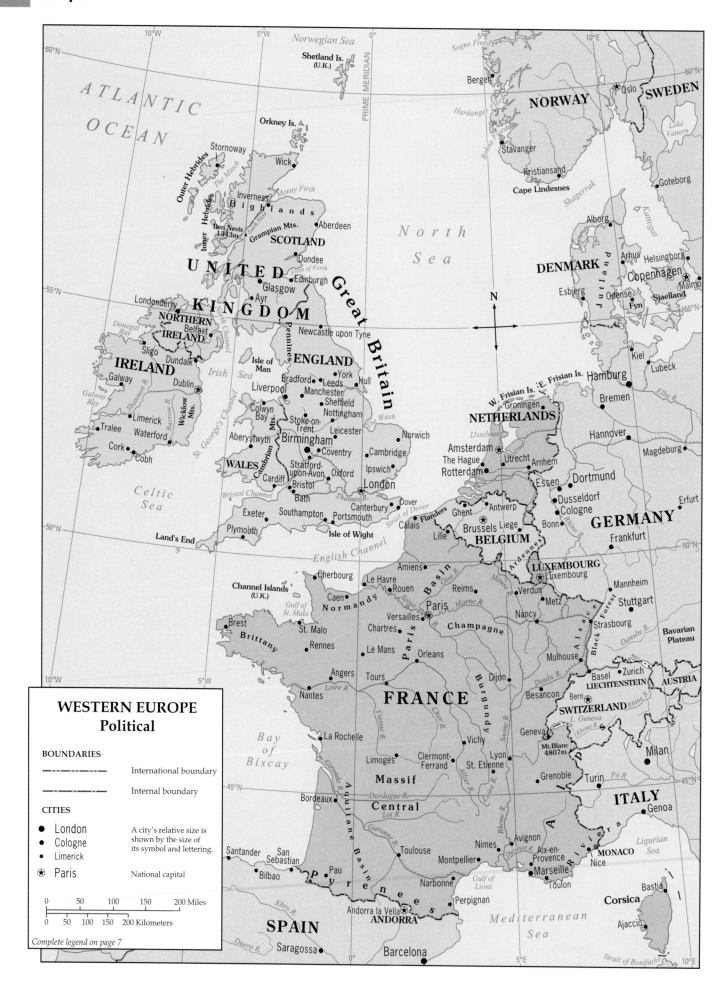

ATLANTIC
OCEAN

Norwegian Sea

Shetland Is.
(U.K.)

NORWAY   Oslo ✪   SWEDEN

Bergen

Sogne Fiord

Hardanger Fiord

Lake Vanern

Stavanger

Orkney Is.

Stornoway

Wick

Kristiansand

Cape Lindesnes

Skagerrak

Goteborg

Kattegat

Alborg

Inverness

Moray Firth

Highlands

Aberdeen

*North
Sea*

DENMARK

Arhus   Helsingborg

SCOTLAND

Ben Nevis
1343m

Grampian Mts.

Dundee

Esbjerg

Jutland

Odense   Copenhagen

Fyn   Sjaelland

Malmo

The Minch

Inner Hebrides

Outer Hebrides

Glasgow

Edinburgh

Firth of Forth

UNITED

Ayr

Kiel

Lubeck

Londonderry

NORTHERN
IRELAND

Belfast

*Donegal
Bay*

Sligo

Dundalk

IRELAND

Galway

*Galway
Bay*

Dublin ✪

Limerick

Tralee

Waterford

Cork

Cobh

KINGDOM

North Channel

*Irish
Sea*

Isle of
Man

Pennines

Newcastle upon Tyne

Great
Britain

ENGLAND

York   Hull

Bradford   Leeds

Liverpool   Manchester

Sheffield

Nottingham

Colwyn
Bay

Cambrian Mts.

Stoke-on-
Trent

Leicester

Birmingham

Coventry

Norwich

Cambridge

W. Frisian Is. E. Frisian Is.

Groningen

NETHERLANDS

IJsselmeer

Amsterdam ✪

The Hague   Utrecht

Rotterdam   Arnhem

Hamburg

Bremen

Hannover

Magdeburg

Erfurt

Essen   Dortmund

Dusseldorf

Cologne

GERMANY

Aberystwyth

WALES

Cardiff

Stratford-
upon-Avon

Bristol

Oxford

Ipswich

London ✪

Thames R.

Rhine R.

Bonn

Frankfurt

*Celtic
Sea*

St. George's Channel

Bristol Channel

Bath

Exeter

Southampton

Canterbury

Dover

Strait of Dover

Calais

Ghent

Flanders

Antwerp

Lille

Brussels Liege

BELGIUM

Ardennes

LUXEMBOURG

Luxembourg

Mannheim

Stuttgart

Plymouth

Portsmouth

Isle of Wight

Land's End

Amiens

Oise R.

Meuse R.

Verdun

Metz

Black Forest

Strasbourg

Danube R.

Bavarian
Plateau

English Channel

Cherbourg

Le Havre

Rouen

Reims

Nancy

Channel Islands
(U.K.)

Caen

Seine R.

Marne R.

Paris ✪

Versailles

Champagne

Alsace

Mulhouse

*Gulf of
St. Malo*

Normandy

Brest

St. Malo

Chartres

Paris Basin

Besancon

Doubs R.

Basel   Zurich

LIECHTENSTEIN   AUSTRIA

Brittany

Rennes

Le Mans

Orleans

Dijon

Burgundy

Saone R.

SWITZERLAND

Bern

Rhine R.

Angers

Tours

Cher R.

FRANCE

Loire R.

L. Geneva

Geneva

Rhone R.

Nantes

Loire R.

Vienne R.

Mt.Blanc
4807m

*Bay
of
Biscay*

La Rochelle

Vichy

Lyon

Grenoble

Milan

Limoges

Clermont-
Ferrand

St. Etienne

Allier R.

Turin

Po R.

Bordeaux

Massif

Central

Dordogne R.

Lot R.

Gironde R.

Garonne R.

Aquitaine Basin

Santander

San
Sebastian

Bilbao

Pau

Toulouse

Montpellier

Rhone R.

Nimes

Avignon

Durance R.

Aix-en-
Provence

Riviera

Marseille

Nice

MONACO

Alps

Genoa

ITALY

*Ligurian
Sea*

Narbonne

*Gulf of
Lions*

Toulon

Perpignan

Pyrenees

Andorra la Vella ✪

ANDORRA

SPAIN

Ebro R.

Saragossa

Barcelona

Duero R.

Corsica

Bastia

Ajaccio

*Mediterranean
Sea*

Strait of Bonifacio

N

PRIME MERIDIAN

WESTERN EUROPE
Political

BOUNDARIES

—·—·—·—   International boundary

————   Internal boundary

CITIES

● **London**

● Cologne

• Limerick

✪ **Paris**

A city's relative size is
shown by the size of
its symbol and lettering.

National capital

| 0 | 50 | 100 | 150 | 200 Miles |

| 0 | 50 | 100 | 150 | 200 Kilometers |

Complete legend on page 7

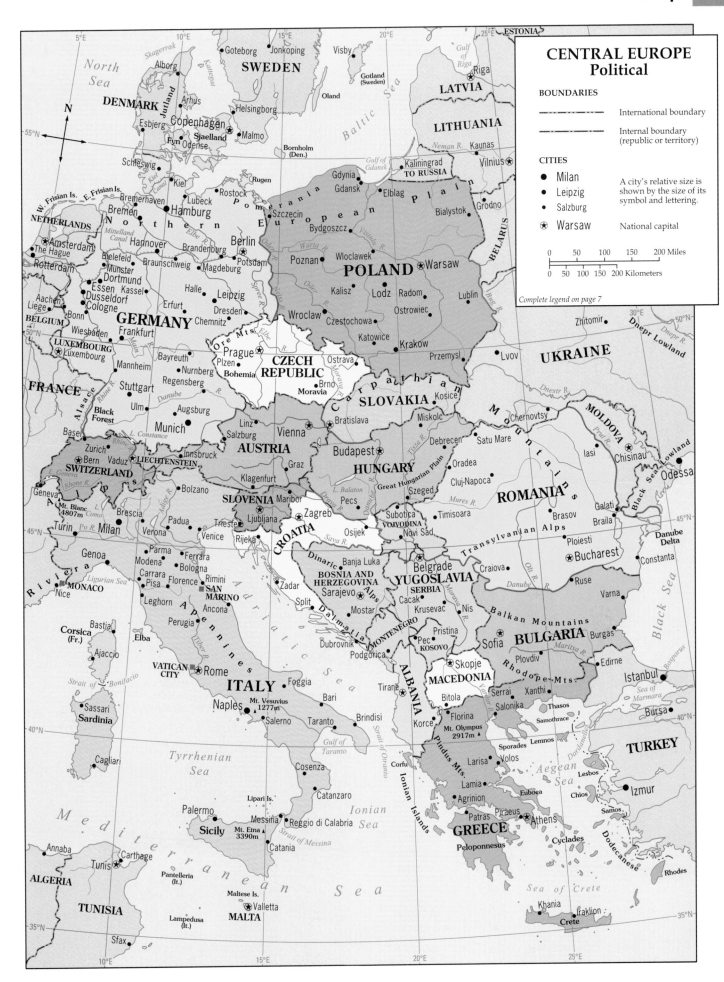

CENTRAL EUROPE
Political

BOUNDARIES

International boundary

Internal boundary
(republic or territory)

CITIES

● Milan

● Leipzig

• Salzburg

⊛ Warsaw

A city's relative size is
shown by the size of its
symbol and lettering.

National capital

| 0 | 50 | 100 | 150 | 200 Miles |

| 0 | 50 | 100 | 150 | 200 Kilometers |

Complete legend on page 7

North Sea

DENMARK

Skagerrak

Goteborg Jonkoping

SWEDEN

Visby

Gotland (Sweden)

Oland

Gulf of Riga

ESTONIA

Riga

LATVIA

LITHUANIA

Kattegat

Alborg

Arhus

Helsingborg

Malmo

Copenhagen

Esbjerg

Sjaelland

Fyn Odense

Schleswig

Jutland

Kiel Canal

Bornholm (Den.)

Kaunas

Neman R.

Vilnius

Baltic Sea

Kaliningrad TO RUSSIA

Gulf of Gdansk

Gdynia

Gdansk

Elblag

Grodno

BELARUS

NETHERLANDS

W. Frisian Is. E. Frisian Is.

Bremerhaven

Bremen

Hamburg

Lubeck

Rostock

Kiel

Rugen

Pomerania

Szczecin

European

Plain

Bialystok

Amsterdam

The Hague

Rotterdam

Bielefeld

Munster

Dortmund

Essen Kassel

Dusseldorf

Hannover

Brandenburg

Magdeburg

Berlin

Potsdam

Elbe R.

Oder R.

Warta R.

Bydgoszcz

Poznan

Wloclawek

Visula R.

POLAND

⊛ Warsaw

Aachen

Liege

Bonn

Cologne

Wiesbaden

Halle

Leipzig

Erfurt

Dresden

Spree R.

Kalisz

Lodz

Radom

Lublin

BELGIUM

GERMANY

Frankfurt

Chemnitz

Wroclaw

Czestochowa

Katowice

Krakow

Ostrowiec

Bug R.

LUXEMBOURG

Luxembourg

Bayreuth

Nurnberg

Ore Mts.

Prague

Plzen

CZECH REPUBLIC

Bohemia

Brno

Moravia

Ostrava

Morava R.

Przemysl

Lvov

UKRAINE

Zhitomir

Dnepr R.

Dnepr Lowland

FRANCE

Alsace

Rhine R.

Mannheim

Stuttgart

Regensberg

Main R.

Danube

Ulm

Augsburg

Munich

SLOVAKIA

Kosice

Miskolc

Carpathian

Mountains

Chernovtsy

Prut R.

Dnestr R.

MOLDOVA

Iasi

Chisinau

Black Forest

Basel

Zurich

Bern

Vaduz

LIECHTENSTEIN

Innsbruck

Linz

Salzburg

AUSTRIA

Vienna

Graz

Bratislava

Budapest

HUNGARY

Debrecen

Satu Mare

Oradea

Cluj-Napoca

Black Sea Lowland

Odessa

SWITZERLAND

L. Constance

Rhine R.

L. Geneva

Geneva

Rhone R.

Alps

Mt. Blanc 4807m

L. Como

Brescia

Turin

Po R.

Milan

Bolzano

Klagenfurt

SLOVENIA

Maribor

Ljubljana

Zagreb

Drava R.

Great Hungarian Plain

L. Balaton

Pecs

Szeged

Subotica

VOJVODINA

Novi Sad

Timisoara

Mures R.

ROMANIA

Tisza R.

Brasov

Galati

Braila

Black Sea

Danube Delta

Genoa

Parma

Modena

Bologna

Carrara

Florence

Pisa

Padua

Verona

Venice

Trieste

Rijeka

Adige R.

CROATIA

Osijek

Sava R.

Dinaric

Banja Luka

BOSNIA AND HERZEGOVINA

Sarajevo

Alps

Mostar

Belgrade

YUGOSLAVIA

SERBIA

Cacak

Krusevac

Nis

Morava R.

Danube

Craiova

Olt R.

Transylvanian Alps

Ploiesti

⊛ Bucharest

Constanta

Riviera

MONACO

Nice

Ligurian Sea

Leghorn

Apennines

Ancona

Perugia

Rimini

SAN MARINO

Zadar

Split

Dalmatia

Dubrovnik

MONTENEGRO

Podgorica

Pec

KOSOVO

Pristina

Sofia

Balkan Mountains

Ruse

Varna

Maritsa R.

BULGARIA

Burgas

Corsica (Fr.)

Bastia

Ajaccio

Elba

VATICAN CITY

Rome

Tiber R.

Foggia

ITALY

Bari

ALBANIA

Tirane

Korce

Skopje

MACEDONIA

Bitola

Florina

Vardar R.

Rhodope Mts.

Plovdiv

Serrai

Xanthi

Edirne

Istanbul

Sea of Marmara

Bursa

Sassari

Sardinia

Cagliari

Strait of Bonifacio

Naples

Mt. Vesuvius 1277m

Salerno

Taranto

Brindisi

Gulf of Taranto

Strait of Otranto

Corfu

Ionian Islands

Pindus Mts.

Mt. Olympus 2917m

Larisa

Volos

Sporades

Lemnos

Thasos

Samothrace

Salonika

TURKEY

Aegean Sea

Izmur

Lesbos

Chios

Tyrrhenian Sea

Palermo

Lipari Is.

Messina

Reggio di Calabria

Sicily

Mt. Etna 3390m

Catania

Strait of Messina

Cosenza

Catanzaro

Ionian Sea

Lamia

Agrinion

Euboea

Patras

Piraeus

Athens

GREECE

Peloponnesus

Cyclades

Samos

Dodecanese

Rhodes

Mediterranean Sea

Annaba

Tunis

Carthage

ALGERIA

TUNISIA

Pantelleria (It.)

Sfax

Lampedusa (It.)

Maltese Is.

MALTA

Valletta

Sea of Crete

Khania

Iraklion

Crete

ATLANTIC OCEAN

ARCTIC OCEAN

ARCTIC CIRCLE

U.K.
NETH.
GERMANY
Berlin
CZ. REP.
SL.
POLAND
Warsaw
Copenhagen
DENMARK
North Sea
NORWAY
Oslo
SWEDEN
Stockholm
Baltic Sea
LITHUANIA
Kaliningrad (To Russia)
Vilnius
TO RUSSIA
LATVIA
Riga
ESTONIA
Tallinn
Helsinki
St. Petersburg (Leningrad)
Pskov
FINLAND
Lake Ladoga
Lake Onega
Murmansk
Kola Peninsula
White Sea
Barents Sea
Svalbard (Nor.)
Franz Josel Land
Novaya Zemlya
Kara Sea
Severnaya Zemlya
N
New Siberian Is.
Chersk
Laptev Sea
Tiksi
Verkhoyansk
Verkhoyansk Range
East

BELARUS
Minsk
UKRAINE
Kiev
Chernobyl
Lvov
MOLDOVA
Chisinau
Odessa
Dnepropetrovsk
Donetsk
Crimea
Sevastopol
Yalta
Black Sea
Kharkov
Kursk
Voronezh
Rostov-on-Don
Krasnodar
Novorossiysk
Batumi
GEORGIA
Tbilisi
Grozny
CAUCASUS Mts.
ARMENIA
Yerevan
AZERBAIJAN
Baku
TURKEY
Smolensk
Tver
Yaroslavl
Moscow
Novgorod
Nizhny
Kirov
Great Russian Plains
Penza
Tula
Orel
Kazan
Izhevsk
Perm
Samara
Saratov
Ufa
Volgograd
Astrakhan
Uralsk
Orenburg
Atyrau
Caspian Sea
Dnieper R.
Dniester R.
Dvina R.
Don R.
Volga R.
Ural R.
Kama R.
Pechora R.
Ob R.
Ural Mountains
Vorkuta
Salekhard
Sergino
Tobolsk
Yekaterinburg
Kurgan
Chelyabinsk
Omsk
West Siberian Plain
Norilsk
Central Siberian Plateau
Lower Tunguska
Yenisey R.
Lena R.
Aldan R.
Irtysh R.
Taymyr Peninsula
RUSSIA
Siberia
Yakutsk
Stanovoy Mts.
Verkhoyansk Range
Tomsk
Novosibirsk
Novokuznetsk
Krasnoyarsk
Tayshet
Ust-Kut
Irkutsk
L. Baikal
Yablanovyy Mts.
Chita
Amur R.

Kirgiz Steppe
KAZAKHSTAN
Tselinograd
Karaganda
Semey
Balkhash
L. Balkhash
L. Zaysan
Altai Mts.
Sayan Mts.
Barnaul
Aralsk
Aral Sea
Kara Kum Desert
Kyzyl Kum Desert
UZBEKISTAN
Krasnovodsk
TURKMENISTAN
Ashgabat
Syr Darya
Amu Darya R.
Samarkand
Tashkent
Bishkek
KYRGYZSTAN
Almaty
Tien Shan
TAJIKISTAN
Dushanbe
AFGHANISTAN
Hindu Kush
PAKISTAN
INDIA
Himalayas
Zagros Mountains
IRAN
Tehran
CHINA
MONGOLIA
Ulan Bator
CHINA
Beijing

At the end of 1991, after 69 years of history, the Union of Soviet Socialist Republics dissolved. The former republics of the U.S.S.R. are separated here by color.

FORMER REPUBLICS OF THE SOVIET UNION
Political

BOUNDARIES

——— International boundary

CITIES

● Perm — A city's relative size is shown by the size of its symbol and lettering.
• Vladivostok
· Verkhoyansk

⊛ Moscow — National capital

0   250   500   750
0   250   500   750 Kilometers

Complete legend on page 7

In November 1989, Germans tore down the Berlin Wall. It was an event that symbolized the collapse of over 40 years of Communist rule in Eastern Europe.

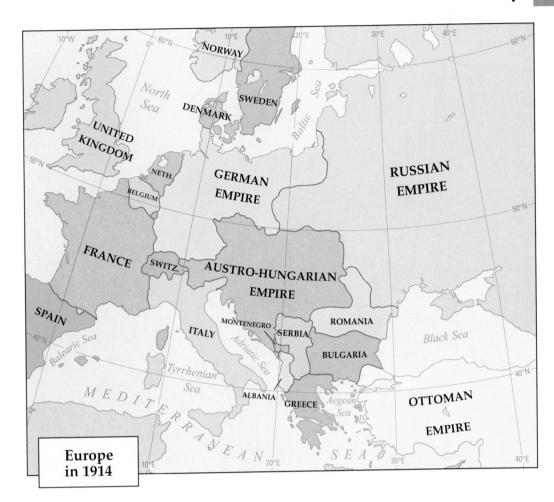

Europe in 1914

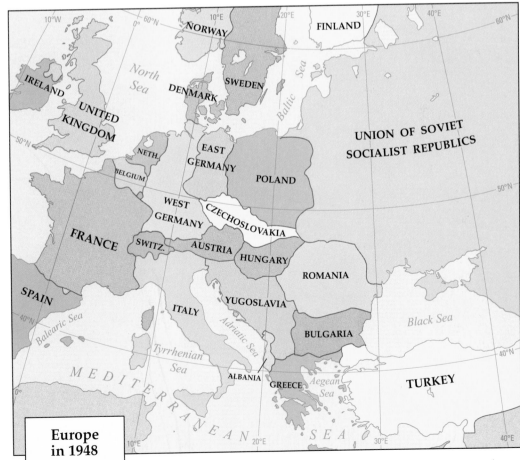

Twentieth-century Europe has seen radical changes in governments and boundaries. World War I brought the break-up of imperialistic monarchies and the formation of new, smaller states. Some of these, like Czechoslovakia, acquired democratic governments only to fall to Communism after World War II. Then, between 1989 and 1992, all the Communist governments of Europe were overthrown, and again new nations were formed.

Europe in 1948

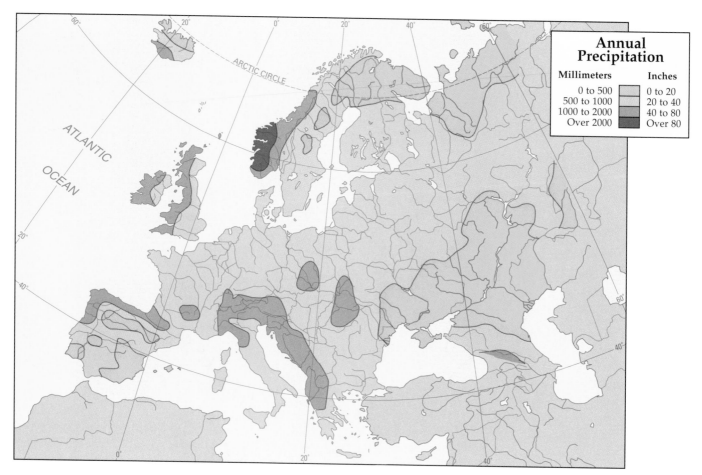

Annual Precipitation

Millimeters	Inches
0 to 500	0 to 20
500 to 1000	20 to 40
1000 to 2000	40 to 80
Over 2000	Over 80

ATLANTIC OCEAN

ARCTIC CIRCLE

Sources of Electrical Energy

Each country's position on the triangle shows its relative reliance on three sources of electrical energy. For example, Hungary gets about as much electricity from fossil fuel as from nuclear power and none from hydroelectricity.

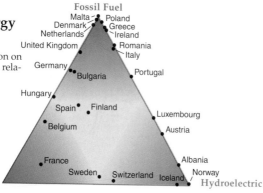

Fossil Fuel

Malta · Poland
Denmark · Greece
Netherlands · Ireland
United Kingdom · Romania
· Italy
Germany
· Bulgaria · Portugal
Hungary
· Spain · Finland
Belgium · Luxembourg
· Austria
· France · Albania
Sweden · Switzerland · Iceland · Norway

Nuclear   Hydroelectric

EUROPE Area Comparison

Although the entire continent of Europe is larger than the United States, the British Isles are smaller than America's Great Basin.

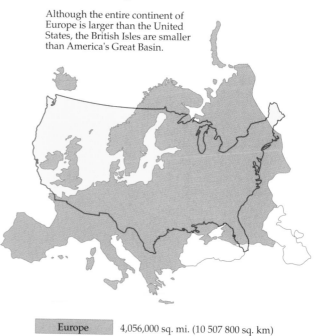

Europe	4,056,000 sq. mi. (10 507 800 sq. km)
Contiguous U.S.	3,021,295 sq. mi. (7 825 112 sq. km)

The Alps are an important region for farming and industry as well as a major tourist attraction. Railways crisscross the mountains that were a barrier to travel for centuries.

Vienna, Austria's capital, is the most prosperous city in Central Europe. Austria stands at the crossroads between former Communist states and democratically governed countries.

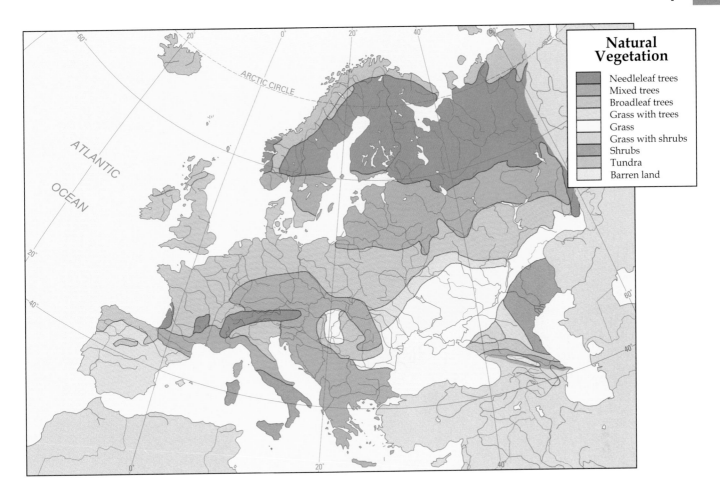

Natural Vegetation

- Needleleaf trees
- Mixed trees
- Broadleaf trees
- Grass with trees
- Grass
- Grass with shrubs
- Shrubs
- Tundra
- Barren land

ARCTIC CIRCLE

ATLANTIC OCEAN

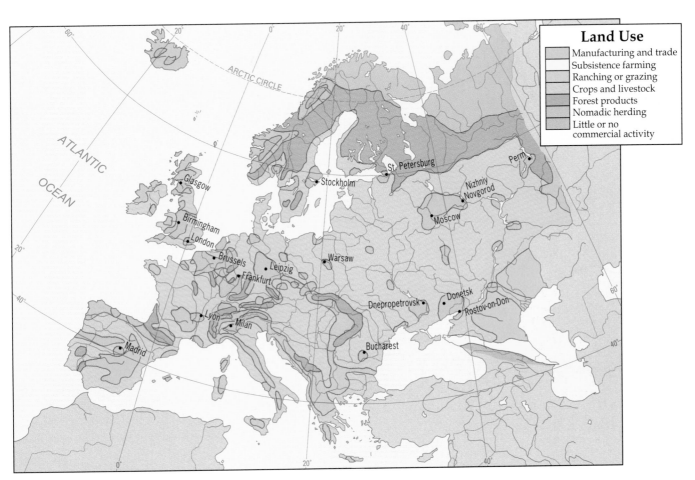

Land Use

- Manufacturing and trade
- Subsistence farming
- Ranching or grazing
- Crops and livestock
- Forest products
- Nomadic herding
- Little or no commercial activity

ARCTIC CIRCLE

ATLANTIC OCEAN

Glasgow
Birmingham
London
Brussels
Frankfurt
Leipzig
Lyon
Milan
Madrid
Stockholm
St. Petersburg
Perm
Nizhniy Novgorod
Moscow
Warsaw
Dnepropetrovsk
Donetsk
Rostov-on-Don
Bucharest

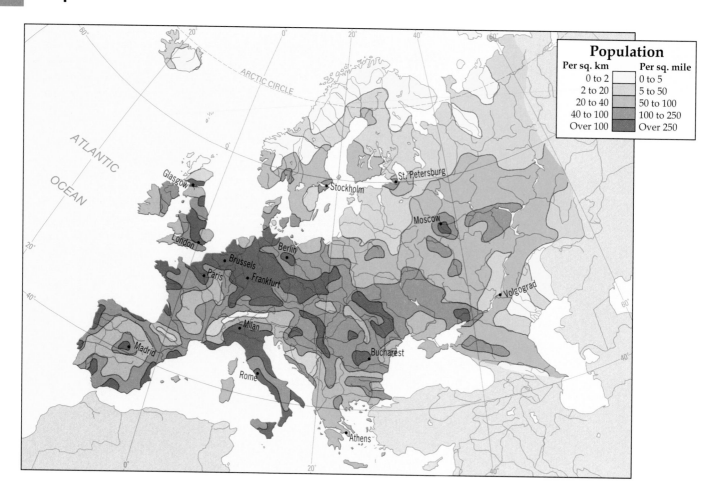

Population

Per sq. km	Per sq. mile
0 to 2	0 to 5
2 to 20	5 to 50
20 to 40	50 to 100
40 to 100	100 to 250
Over 100	Over 250

GREECE
Balance of Trade

Imports total
US$14.7 billion

Exports total
US$6 billion

All Others 44.7%

European Community 55.3%

All Others 43.3%

European Community 56.7%

POLAND
Balance of Trade

Imports total
US$7.7 billion

Exports total
US$5.7 billion

European Community 23.4%

Soviet Union 22.7%

All Others 53.9%

European Community 21.2%

All Others 58%

Soviet Union 20.8%

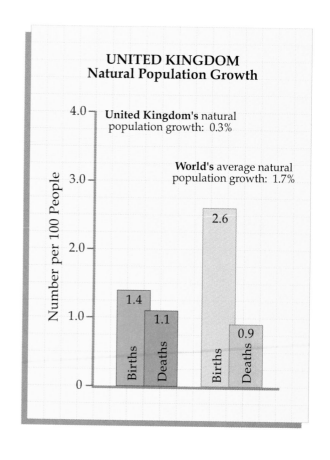

UNITED KINGDOM
Natural Population Growth

United Kingdom's natural population growth: 0.3%

World's average natural population growth: 1.7%

Number per 100 People

Births 1.4
Deaths 1.1
Births 2.6
Deaths 0.9

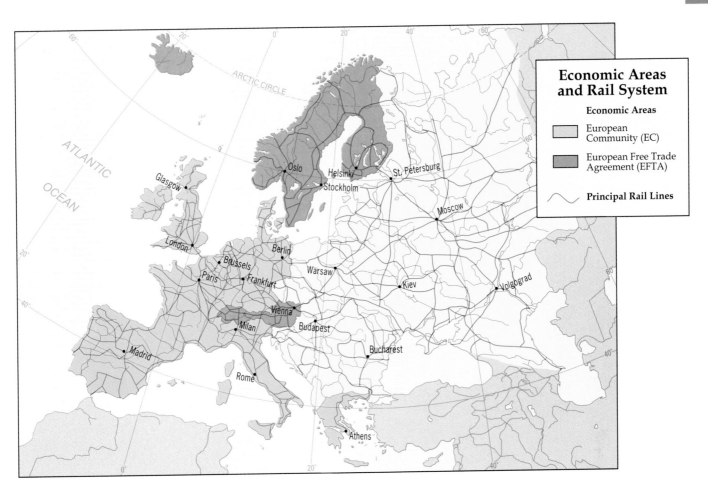

Economic Areas and Rail System

Economic Areas

European Community (EC)

European Free Trade Agreement (EFTA)

〜 Principal Rail Lines

Western European Imperialism

Colonizing countries of Western Europe

Past and present colonies and other territories of Western European countries

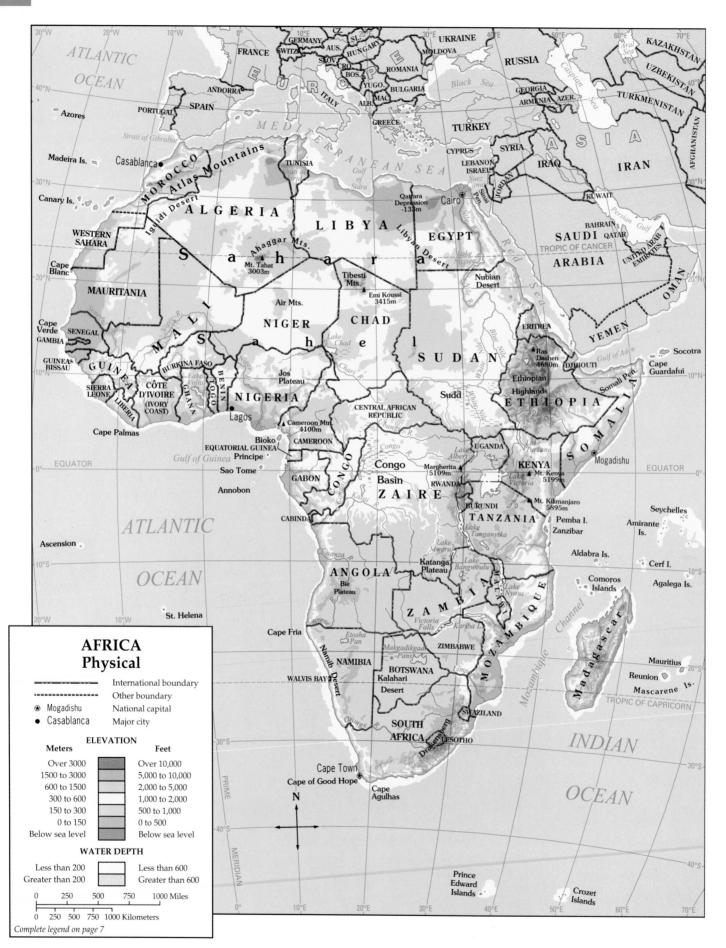

AFRICA
Physical

- - - - - International boundary
- - - - - Other boundary
⊛ Mogadishu — National capital
● Casablanca — Major city

ELEVATION

Meters	Feet
Over 3000	Over 10,000
1500 to 3000	5,000 to 10,000
600 to 1500	2,000 to 5,000
300 to 600	1,000 to 2,000
150 to 300	500 to 1,000
0 to 150	0 to 500
Below sea level	Below sea level

WATER DEPTH

Less than 200	Less than 600
Greater than 200	Greater than 600

0 250 500 750 1000 Miles

0 250 500 750 1000 Kilometers

Complete legend on page 7

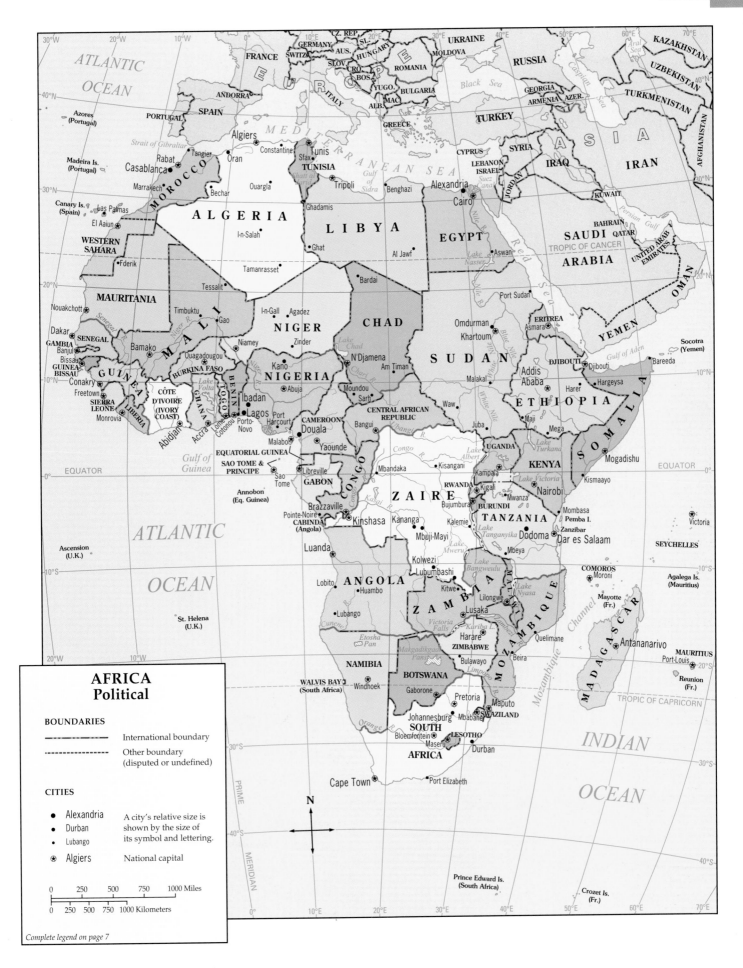

AFRICA
Political

BOUNDARIES

International boundary

Other boundary
(disputed or undefined)

CITIES

● Alexandria
● Durban
· Lubango

⊛ Algiers

A city's relative size is
shown by the size of
its symbol and lettering.

National capital

0   250   500   750   1000 Miles
0   250   500   750   1000 Kilometers

Complete legend on page 7

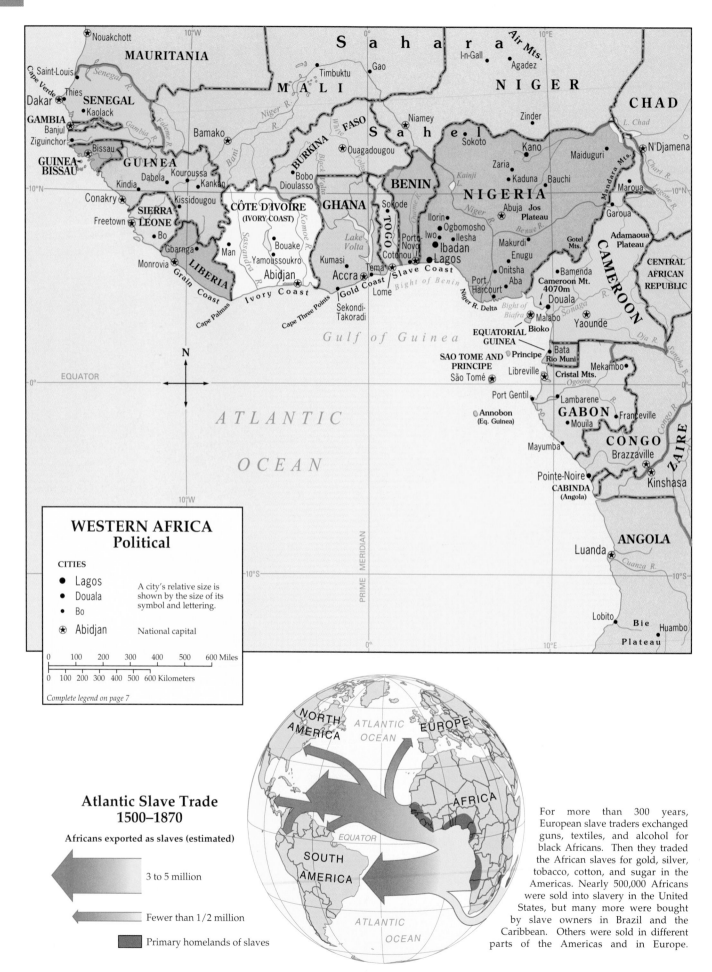

WESTERN AFRICA
Political

CITIES

● **Lagos**   A city's relative size is
                     shown by the size of its
● **Douala**   symbol and lettering.

• Bo

⊛ **Abidjan**   National capital

| 0 | 100 | 200 | 300 | 400 | 500 | 600 Miles |

| 0 | 100 | 200 | 300 | 400 | 500 | 600 Kilometers |

Complete legend on page 7

Atlantic Slave Trade
1500–1870

Africans exported as slaves (estimated)

➤ 3 to 5 million

➤ Fewer than 1/2 million

■ Primary homelands of slaves

For more than 300 years, European slave traders exchanged guns, textiles, and alcohol for black Africans. Then they traded the African slaves for gold, silver, tobacco, cotton, and sugar in the Americas. Nearly 500,000 Africans were sold into slavery in the United States, but many more were bought by slave owners in Brazil and the Caribbean. Others were sold in different parts of the Americas and in Europe.

SOUTH AFRICA
Political

CITIES

- Soweto — A city's relative size is shown by the size of its symbol and lettering.
- Bisho
- ✪ Pretoria — National capital

```
0      100      200      300 Miles
0   100   200   300 Kilometers
```

Complete legend on page 7

PWV: Pretoria/Witwatersrand/Vaal

SOUTH AFRICA
Balance of Trade

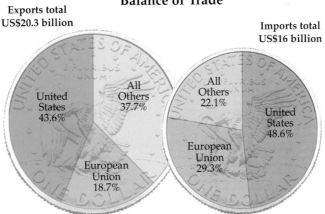

Exports total US$20.3 billion

- United States 43.6%
- All Others 37.7%
- European Union 18.7%

Imports total US$16 billion

- All Others 22.1%
- United States 48.6%
- European Union 29.3%

Ethnic Composition of South Africa

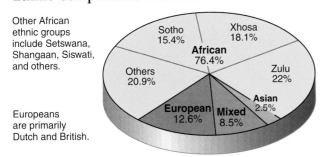

Other African ethnic groups include Setswana, Shangaan, Siswati, and others.

Europeans are primarily Dutch and British.

South Africa's total population: 39.1 million

- African 76.4%
  - Sotho 15.4%
  - Xhosa 18.1%
  - Zulu 22%
- Asian 2.5%
- Mixed 8.5%
- European 12.6%
- Others 20.9%

With the end of legal apartheid in 1994, a new future lies ahead for the children of South Africa.

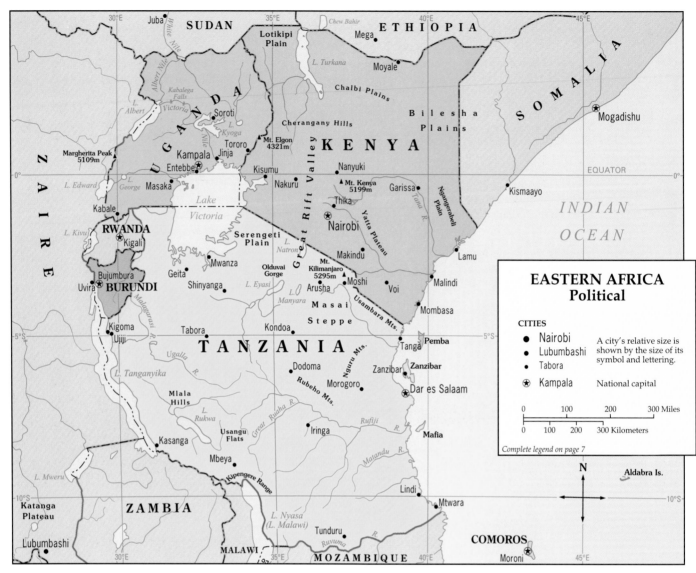

Eastern Africa
Political

CITIES

- Nairobi
- Lubumbashi
- Tabora
- ⊛ Kampala

A city's relative size is shown by the size of its symbol and lettering.

National capital

| 0 | 100 | 200 | 300 Miles |
| 0 | 100 | 200 | 300 Kilometers |

Complete legend on page 7

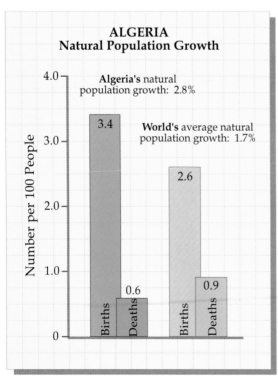

ALGERIA
Natural Population Growth

Algeria's natural population growth: 2.8%

World's average natural population growth: 1.7%

Number per 100 People

3.4 Births
0.6 Deaths
2.6 Births
0.9 Deaths

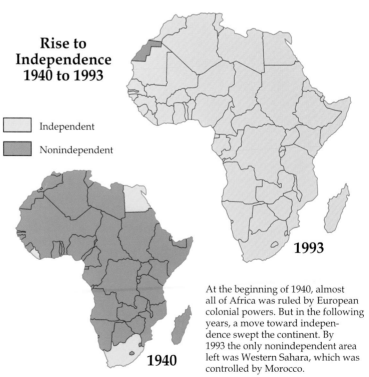

Rise to Independence
1940 to 1993

- Independent
- Nonindependent

1993

1940

At the beginning of 1940, almost all of Africa was ruled by European colonial powers. But in the following years, a move toward independence swept the continent. By 1993 the only nonindependent area left was Western Sahara, which was controlled by Morocco.

The cheetah, a hunter of incredible speed, is losing both its habitat and prey to human encroachment into its territory.

Endangered Species

Present range of species

- Cheetah
- Black Rhinoceros
- Mountain Gorilla
- North African Ostrich

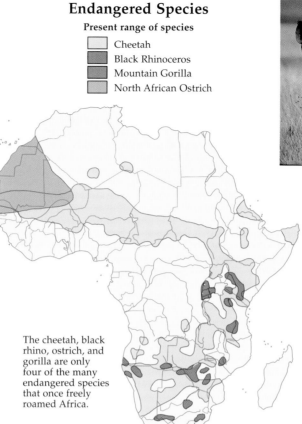

The cheetah, black rhino, ostrich, and gorilla are only four of the many endangered species that once freely roamed Africa.

The black rhinoceros lives on grassland and brush vegetation. Its distinctive horn makes it a target for poachers.

The flightless ostrich can roam the plains for long periods without water. Demand for its skin and plumes threaten its survival in the wild.

The mountain gorilla leads a quiet life, living off forest vegetation. It has no real enemies except human beings.

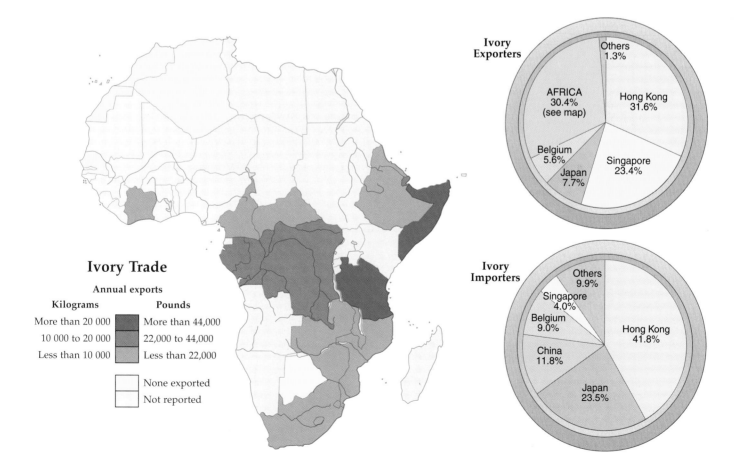

Ivory Trade

Annual exports

Kilograms	Pounds
More than 20 000	More than 44,000
10 000 to 20 000	22,000 to 44,000
Less than 10 000	Less than 22,000
None exported	
Not reported	

Ivory Exporters

- Others 1.3%
- Hong Kong 31.6%
- AFRICA 30.4% (see map)
- Singapore 23.4%
- Belgium 5.6%
- Japan 7.7%

Ivory Importers

- Others 9.9%
- Singapore 4.0%
- Belgium 9.0%
- China 11.8%
- Hong Kong 41.8%
- Japan 23.5%

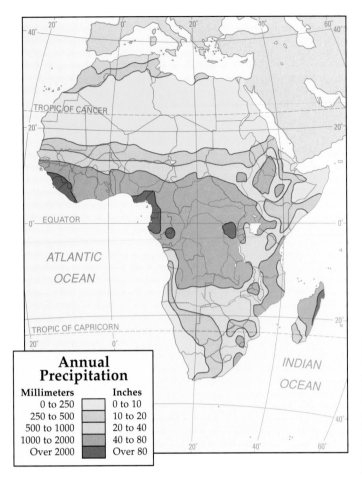

Annual Precipitation

Millimeters	Inches
0 to 250	0 to 10
250 to 500	10 to 20
500 to 1000	20 to 40
1000 to 2000	40 to 80
Over 2000	Over 80

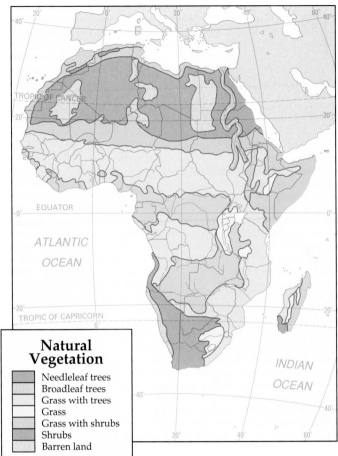

Natural Vegetation

- Needleleaf trees
- Broadleaf trees
- Grass with trees
- Grass
- Grass with shrubs
- Shrubs
- Barren land

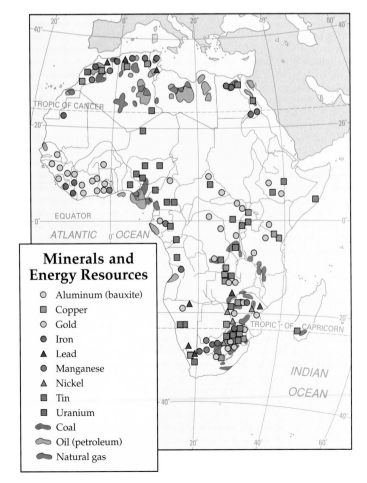

Minerals and Energy Resources

- ○ Aluminum (bauxite)
- ▢ Copper
- ○ Gold
- ● Iron
- ▲ Lead
- ● Manganese
- ▲ Nickel
- ▢ Tin
- ▢ Uranium
- ▬ Coal
- ▬ Oil (petroleum)
- ▬ Natural gas

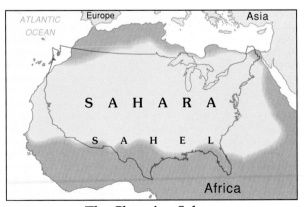

A Moroccan market displays locally grown produce and handwoven carpets. Many Moroccans and other North Africans dress in traditional Islamic style.

The Changing Sahara

The Sahara stretches across a greater area than the contiguous United States. During droughts it expands southward and in wet periods it shrinks back. Most recent years have been dry.

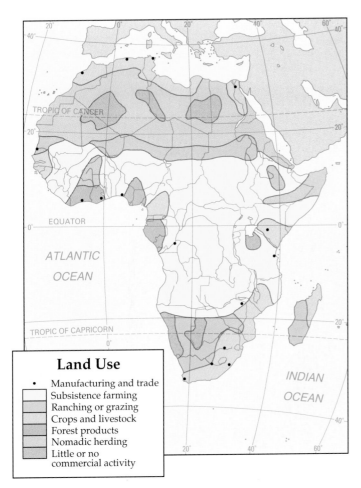

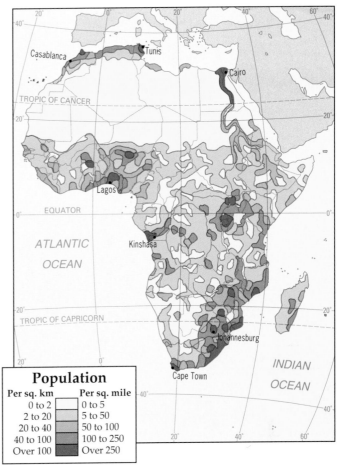

Land Use
- • Manufacturing and trade
- Subsistence farming
- Ranching or grazing
- Crops and livestock
- Forest products
- Nomadic herding
- Little or no commercial activity

Population

Per sq. km	Per sq. mile
0 to 2	0 to 5
2 to 20	5 to 50
20 to 40	50 to 100
40 to 100	100 to 250
Over 100	Over 250

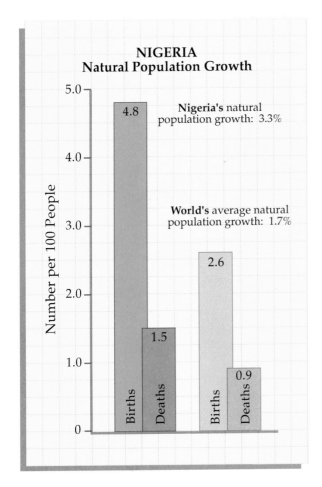

NIGERIA
Natural Population Growth

Nigeria's natural population growth: 3.3%

World's average natural population growth: 1.7%

Number per 100 People

Births 4.8 · Deaths 1.5 · Births 2.6 · Deaths 0.9

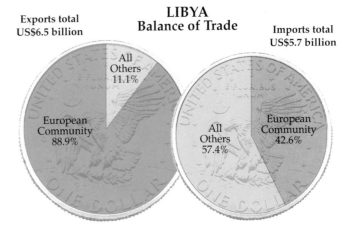

LIBYA
Balance of Trade

Exports total US$6.5 billion — All Others 11.1%, European Community 88.9%

Imports total US$5.7 billion — All Others 57.4%, European Community 42.6%

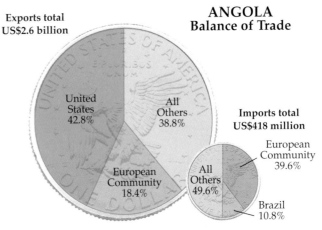

ANGOLA
Balance of Trade

Exports total US$2.6 billion — United States 42.8%, All Others 38.8%, European Community 18.4%

Imports total US$418 million — European Community 39.6%, All Others 49.6%, Brazil 10.8%

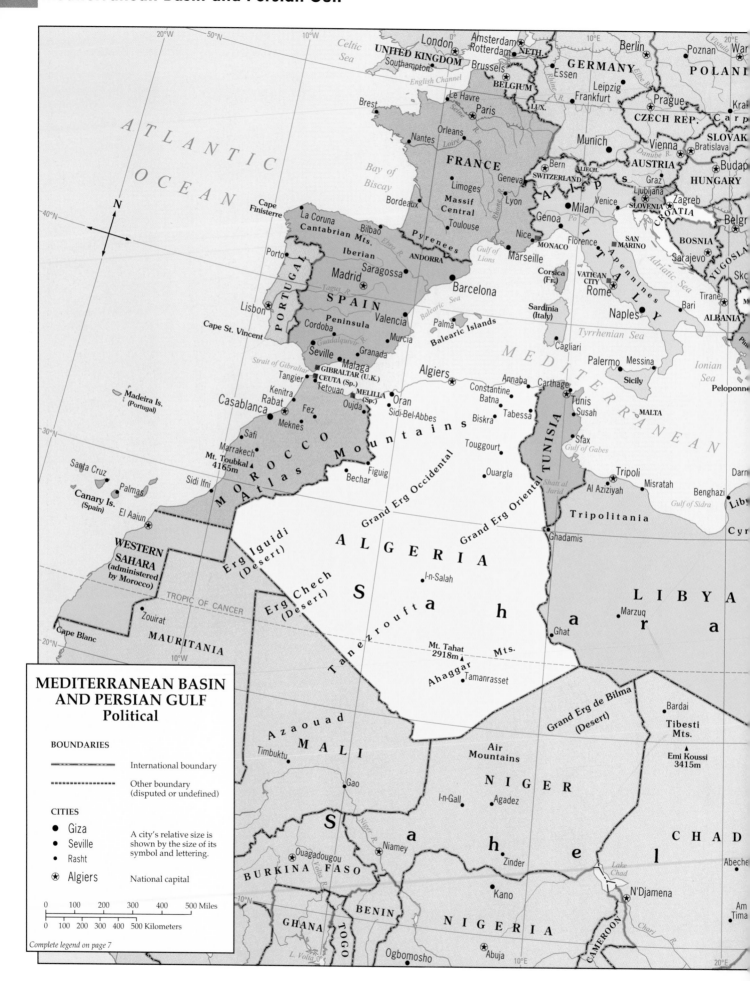

ATLANTIC OCEAN

Celtic Sea

UNITED KINGDOM
London
Southampton
English Channel
Amsterdam
Rotterdam
NETH.
Brussels
BELGIUM
Le Havre
Paris
LUX.
Berlin
GERMANY
Essen
Leipzig
Frankfurt
Munich
Poznan
POLAND
Prague
CZECH REP.
Kra...
Carp
SLOVAK...
Vienna
Bratislava
AUSTRIA
Graz
Budap...
HUNGARY
SWITZERLAND
Bern
Geneva
LIECH.
Ljubljana
SLOVENIA
Zagreb
CROATIA
Venice
Milan
Genoa
Nice
MONACO
Florence
SAN MARINO
BOSNIA
Sarajevo
YUGOSLA...
Belgr...

Brest
Bay of Biscay
Nantes
Orleans
Loire
Bordeaux
FRANCE
Limoges
Massif Central
Toulouse
Lyon
Rhône R.

Cape Finisterre
La Coruña
Bilbao
Cantabrian Mts.
Iberian
Porto
PORTUGAL
Madrid
Saragossa
Pyrenees
ANDORRA
SPAIN
Peninsula
Tagus R.
Lisbon
Cordoba
Valencia
Cape St. Vincent
Guadalquivir
Seville
Granada
Malaga
Murcia
Barcelona
Balearic Sea
Palma
Balearic Islands

Gulf of Lions
Marseille
Corsica (Fr.)
VATICAN CITY
Rome
ITALY
Apennines
Naples
Bari
ALBANIA
Tirane
Adriatic Sea
Sardinia (Italy)
Tyrrhenian Sea
Cagliari
Palermo
Messina
Sicily
MALTA
Ionian Sea
Peloponn...

MEDITERRANEAN

Madeira Is. (Portugal)

Strait of Gibraltar
GIBRALTAR (U.K.)
Tangier
CEUTA (Sp.)
Tetouan
MELILLA (Sp.)
Kenitra
Rabat
Casablanca
Fez
Oujda
Oran
Sidi-Bel-Abbes
Algiers
Annaba
Constantine
Carthage
Tunis
Batna
Tabessa
Susah
TUNISIA
Sfax
Gulf of Gabes
Tripoli
Misratah
Benghazi
Gulf of Sidra
Darn...
Liby...
Cyr...

Santa Cruz
Palmas
Canary Is. (Spain)
El Aaiun

Safi
Marrakech
Mt. Toubkal 4165m
MOROCCO
Atlas Mountains
Figuig
Bechar

Biskra
Touggourt
Ouargla
Grand Erg Occidental
Grand Erg Oriental
Al Aziziyah
Shatt al Jarid
Ghadames
Tripolitania

Sidi Ifni
Erg Iguidi (Desert)

WESTERN SAHARA (administered by Morocco)

TROPIC OF CANCER

Erg Chech (Desert)
ALGERIA
S
I-n-Salah
a
h
LIBYA
Marzuq
Ghat
a
r
a

Zouirat
Cape Blanc
MAURITANIA

Tanezrouft
Mt. Tahat 2918m
Ahaggar
Tamanrasset
Mts.

Grand Erg de Bilma (Desert)
Bardai
Tibesti Mts.
Emi Koussi 3415m

Azaouad
MALI
Timbuktu
Gao
S
Air Mountains
I-n-Gall
Agadez
NIGER
CHAD
Abeche

Niger R.
a
h
e
l
Niamey
Zinder
Lake Chad
N'Djamena
Am...
Tima...

BURKINA FASO
Ouagadougou
Volta R.
GHANA
TOGO
BENIN
Kano
NIGERIA
Abuja
Ogbomosho
L. Volta
Chari R.
CAMEROON

40°N
30°N
20°N

10°W 0° 10°E 20°E

MEDITERRANEAN BASIN AND PERSIAN GULF
Political

BOUNDARIES

—————— International boundary

- - - - - - - - Other boundary (disputed or undefined)

CITIES

● Giza

● Seville

• Rasht

⊛ Algiers

A city's relative size is shown by the size of its symbol and lettering.

National capital

0   100   200   300   400   500 Miles
0 100 200 300 400 500 Kilometers

Complete legend on page 7

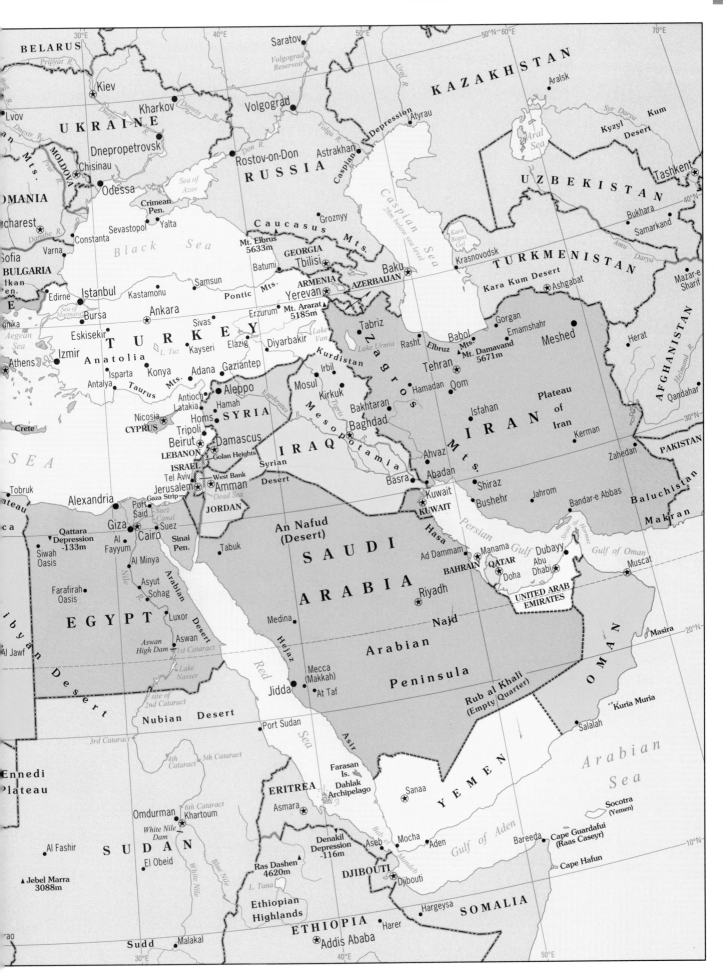

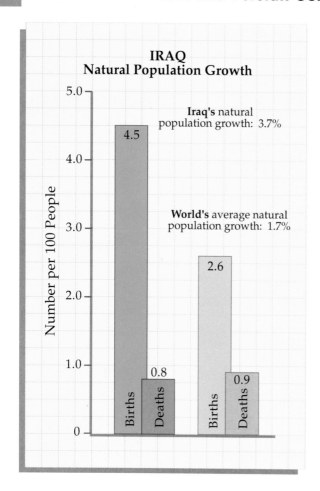

IRAQ
Natural Population Growth

Iraq's natural population growth: 3.7%

World's average natural population growth: 1.7%

(Number per 100 People)

- Births: 4.5
- Deaths: 0.8
- Births: 2.6
- Deaths: 0.9

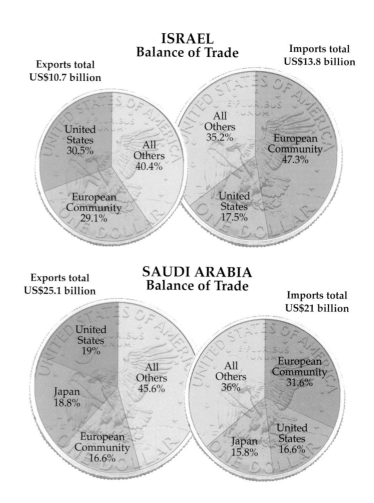

ISRAEL
Balance of Trade

Exports total US$10.7 billion
- United States 30.5%
- All Others 40.4%
- European Community 29.1%

Imports total US$13.8 billion
- All Others 35.2%
- European Community 47.3%
- United States 17.5%

SAUDI ARABIA
Balance of Trade

Exports total US$25.1 billion
- United States 19%
- All Others 45.6%
- Japan 18.8%
- European Community 16.6%

Imports total US$21 billion
- All Others 36%
- European Community 31.6%
- Japan 15.8%
- United States 16.6%

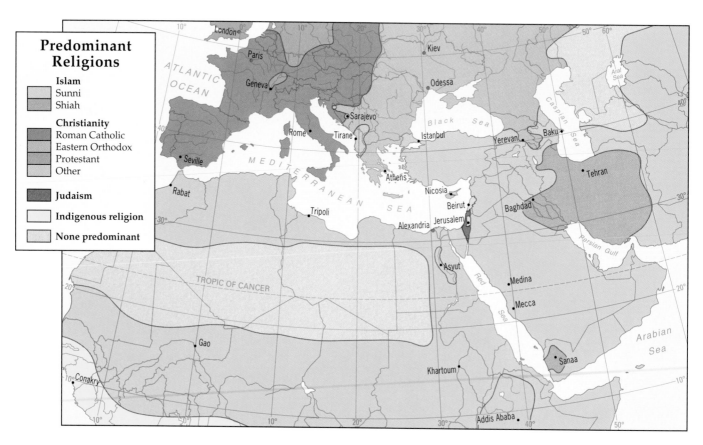

Predominant Religions

Islam
- Sunni
- Shiah

Christianity
- Roman Catholic
- Eastern Orthodox
- Protestant
- Other

Judaism

Indigenous religion

None predominant

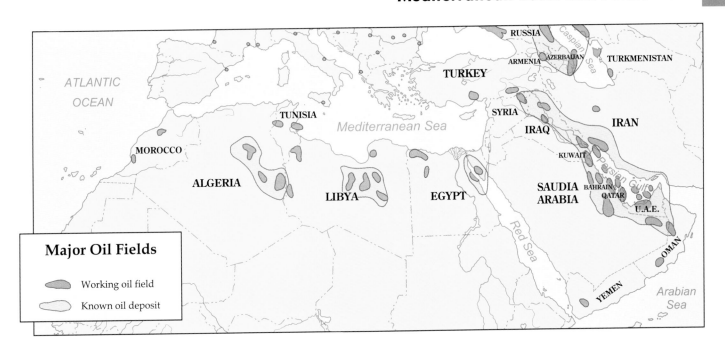

Major Oil Fields

Working oil field

Known oil deposit

Annual OPEC exports (number of barrels)		Percentage of total OPEC exports
2,640,200,000	All other countries	44.2%
256,400,000	Germany	4.3%
295,600,000	France	4.9%
407,900,000	Italy	6.8%
1,069,700,000	Japan	17.9%
1,306,000,000	United States	21.9%

Dependence on OPEC Oil

Japan and Italy import more than 80% of the oil they use from OPEC countries. The United States also relies on OPEC oil, but gets 73.5% of its oil from other sources.

OPEC: Organization of Petroleum Exporting Countries

Changing Boundaries

Israel occupied the area shown in dark orange until 1967. After the Six Day War of that year, it also controlled the parts of Egypt, Jordan, and Syria shown in light orange.

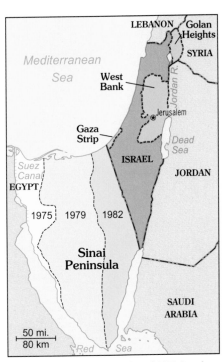

In stages during 1975, 1979, and 1982, Israel returned the Sinai Peninsula to Egypt. But Israel remained in control of the Gaza Strip, West Bank, and Golan Heights.

In 1993 Israeli and Palestinian leaders signed an agreement that would lead to self-rule for Palestinians living in Gaza and the city of Jericho.

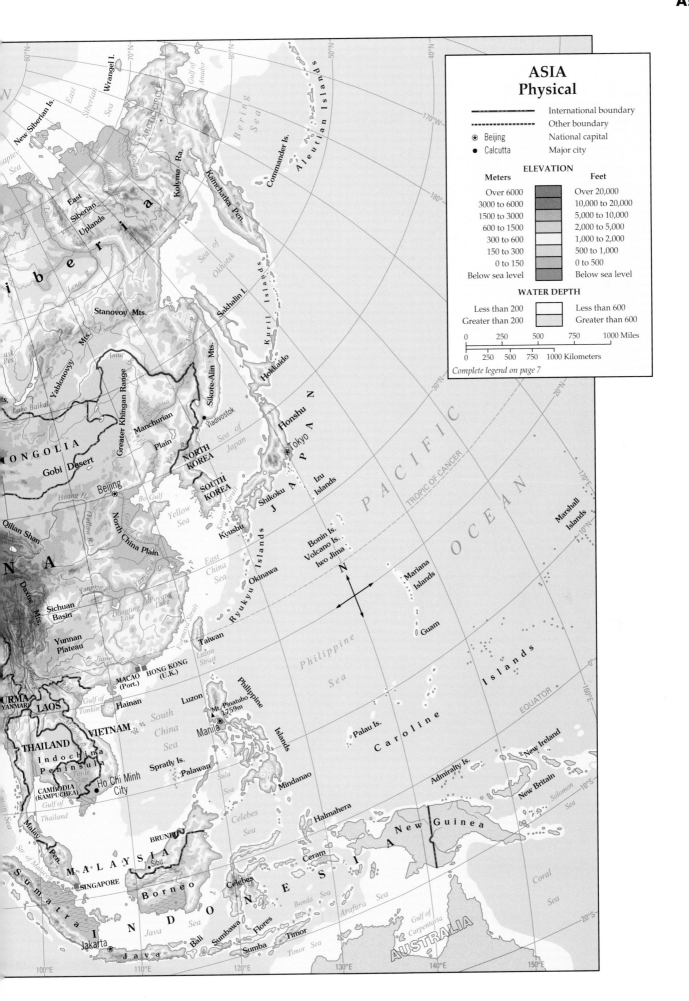

ASIA
Physical

——————— International boundary

- - - - - - - - - Other boundary

⊛ Beijing   National capital

● Calcutta   Major city

ELEVATION

Meters		Feet
Over 6000		Over 20,000
3000 to 6000		10,000 to 20,000
1500 to 3000		5,000 to 10,000
600 to 1500		2,000 to 5,000
300 to 600		1,000 to 2,000
150 to 300		500 to 1,000
0 to 150		0 to 500
Below sea level		Below sea level

WATER DEPTH

Less than 200		Less than 600
Greater than 200		Greater than 600

0   250   500   750   1000 Miles

0 250 500 750 1000 Kilometers

Complete legend on page 7

Wrangel I.

New Siberian Is.

East Siberian Sea

Laptev Sea

S i b e r i a

East Siberian Uplands

Kolyma Ra.

Kamchatka Pen.

Gulf of Anadyr

ARCTIC CIRCLE

Bering Sea

Commander Is.

Aleutian Islands

Stanovoy Mts.

Stanovoy Mts.

Sea of Okhotsk

Sakhalin I.

Kuril Islands

Amur

MONGOLIA

Yablonovyy Mts.

Greater Khingan Range

Manchurian Plain

Sikote-Alin Mts.

Hokkaido

Lake Baikal

Gobi Desert

Vladivostok

NORTH KOREA

SOUTH KOREA

Sea of Japan

Honshu

J A P A N

Tokyo

Qilian Shan

Huang He

Beijing

Bo Gulf

Yellow Sea

Korea Strait

Shikoku

Izu Islands

P A C I F I C

TROPIC OF CANCER

Marshall Islands

Grand Canal

North China Plain

Yellow R.

Kyushu

O C E A N

C H I N A

Daxue Mts.

Sichuan Basin

Yangtze R.

Dongting Lake

Poyang Lake

Taiwan

Ryukyu Islands

Okinawa

Bonin Is.

Volcano Is.

Iwo Jima

Mariana Islands

Yunnan Plateau

Min Jiang

East China Sea

Formosa Strait

Luzon Strait

N

Guam

MACAO (Port.)

HONG KONG (U.K.)

Philippine Sea

Islands

BURMA (MYANMAR)

LAOS

Gulf of Tonkin

Hainan

Luzon

Mt. Pinatubo 1759m

Manila

Palau Is.

Caroline

VIETNAM

South China Sea

New Ireland

THAILAND

Indochina Peninsula

Spratly Is.

Palawan

Islands

I s l a n d s

Admiralty Is.

New Britain

CAMBODIA (KAMPUCHEA)

Tonle Sap

Ho Chi Minh City

Sulu Sea

Mindanao

New Guinea

Solomon Sea

Gulf of Thailand

Halmahera

I N D O N E S I A

Coral Sea

Malay Pen.

BRUNEI

Celebes Sea

Ceram

Sibu

Celebes

Banda Sea

Str. of Malacca

Sumatra

MALAYSIA

SINGAPORE

B o r n e o

Java Sea

Flores

Sumbawa

Sumba

Timor

Arafura Sea

Gulf of Carpentaria

AUSTRALIA

Jakarta

J a v a

Bali

Timor Sea

EQUATOR

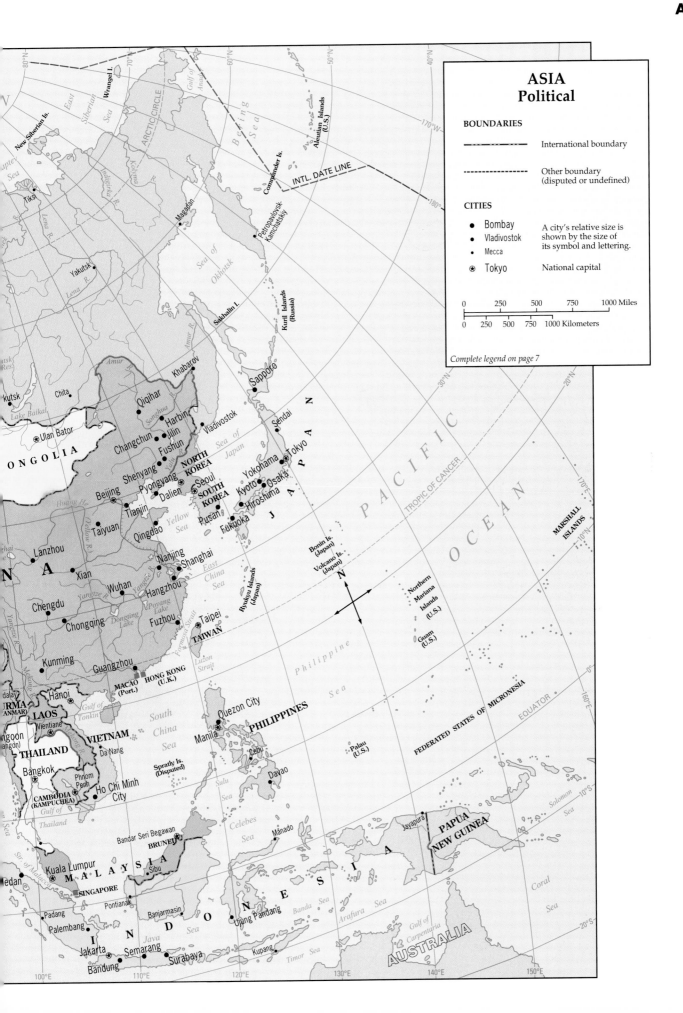

ASIA
Political

BOUNDARIES

—··—··—··— International boundary

------------ Other boundary
(disputed or undefined)

CITIES

● Bombay

• Vladivostok

· Mecca

⊛ Tokyo   National capital

A city's relative size is
shown by the size of
its symbol and lettering.

0   250   500   750   1000 Miles

0   250   500   750   1000 Kilometers

Complete legend on page 7

Map labels

INTL. DATE LINE

New Siberian Is.
Wrangel I.
ARCTIC CIRCLE
East Siberian Sea
Tiksi
Gulf of Anadyr
Bering Sea
Aleutian Islands (U.S.)
Commander Is.
Petropavlovsk-Kamchatskiy
Sea of Okhotsk
Magadan
Yakutsk
Kolyma R.
Indigirka R.
Lena R.
Lake Baikal
Chita
kutsk
Ulan Bator
MONGOLIA
Qiqihar
Songhua
Harbin
Changchun
Jilin
Fushun
Shenyang
NORTH KOREA
Pyongyang
Beijing
Dalian
Seoul
SOUTH KOREA
Tianjin
Taiyuan
Qingdao
Yellow Sea
Pusan
Fukuoka
Lanzhou
Huang He R.
Yangtze R.
Xian
Nanjing
Shanghai
Wuhan
Hangzhou
Poyang Lake
Chengdu
Chongqing
Dongting Lake
Fuzhou
Kunming
Guangzhou
MACAO (Port.)
HONG KONG (U.K.)
CHINA
dalay
Hanoi
BURMA (MYANMAR)
LAOS
Vientiane
VIETNAM
Da Nang
THAILAND
Bangkok
Phnom Penh
CAMBODIA (KAMPUCHEA)
Ho Chi Minh City
Gulf of Thailand
angon
ngoon
Gulf of Tonkin
Khabarov
Amur R.
Vladivostok
Sakhalin I.
Sea of Japan
Sapporo
Kuril Islands (Russia)
Sendai
Tokyo
Yokohama
Kyoto
Osaka
Hiroshima
JAPAN
Ryukyu Islands (Japan)
Taipei
TAIWAN
Formosa Strait
East China Sea
Luzon Strait
Bonin Is. (Japan)
Volcano Is. (Japan)
TROPIC OF CANCER
PACIFIC OCEAN
Northern Mariana Islands (U.S.)
Guam (U.S.)
MARSHALL ISLANDS
N
Philippine Sea
Quezon City
Manila
PHILIPPINES
Cebu
Davao
Palau (U.S.)
FEDERATED STATES OF MICRONESIA
EQUATOR
Spratly Is. (Disputed)
South China Sea
Sulu Sea
Celebes Sea
Manado
Bandar Seri Begawan
BRUNEI
Kuala Lumpur
MALAYSIA
Sibu
SINGAPORE
Pontianak
edan
Medan
Padang
Palembang
Banjarmasin
Ujung Pandang
Banda Sea
Arafura Sea
Jayapura
PAPUA NEW GUINEA
Solomon Sea
Coral Sea
INDONESIA
Java Sea
Jakarta
Semarang
Surabaya
Bandung
Kupang
Timor Sea
Gulf of Carpentaria
AUSTRALIA
Str. of Malacca

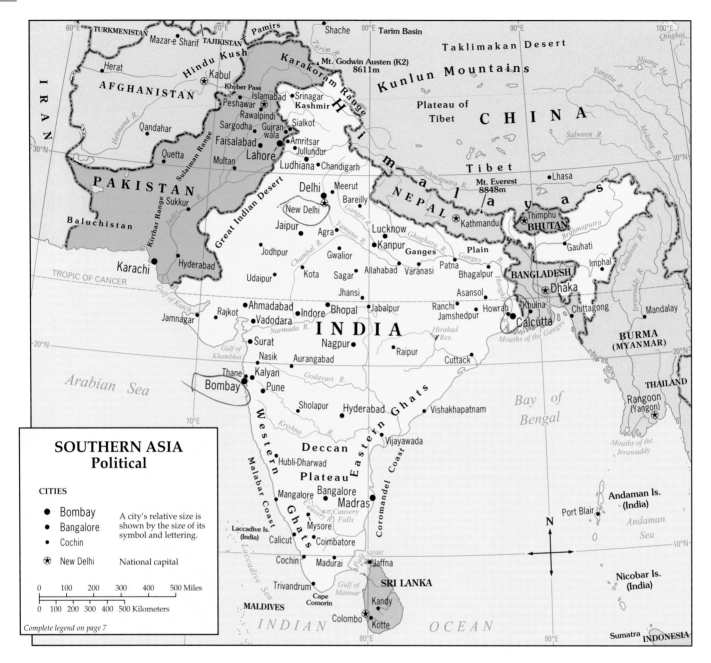

SOUTHERN ASIA
Political

CITIES

● Bombay

● Bangalore

· Cochin

⊛ New Delhi

A city's relative size is shown by the size of its symbol and lettering.

National capital

| 0 | 100 | 200 | 300 | 400 | 500 Miles |

| 0 | 100 | 200 | 300 | 400 | 500 Kilometers |

Complete legend on page 7

India's Ganges River is considered sacred by Hindus, who bathe in its waters to purify themselves.

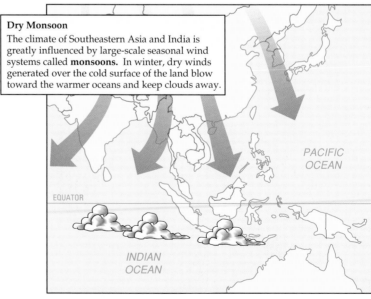

Dry Monsoon

The climate of Southeastern Asia and India is greatly influenced by large-scale seasonal wind systems called **monsoons.** In winter, dry winds generated over the cold surface of the land blow toward the warmer oceans and keep clouds away.

H i m a l a y a s
90°E
★Thimphu
BHUTAN
INDIA
BANGLADESH
Dhaka
Calcutta
Brahmaputra R.
Ganges
100°E
Myitkyina
Chindwin R.
Irrawaddy R.
Salween R.
Namtu
Mandalay
Yunnan Plateau
Kunming
Mekong R.
Chongqing
Zunyi
110°E
Changsha
CHINA
Yangtze R.
Wuzhou
Xi Jiang
Guangzhou
TROPIC OF CANCER
MACAO
(Port.)
**HONG
KONG**
(U.K.)
120°E
20°N
N
*Bay
of
Bengal*
**BURMA
(MYANMAR)**
Thayetmyo
Myanaung
Rangoon
(Yangon)
Pegu
Bassein
Moulmein
*Mouths of
the Irrawaddy*
Chiang Rai
Chiang Mai
Ping R.
Dien Bien Phu
Louangphrabang
LAOS
Vientiane
(Viangchan)
Mekong R.
Red R.
Black R.
Hanoi
★
Haiphong
Nam Dinh
Vinh
*Gulf of
Tonkin*
Haikou
Hainan
Paracel Is.
(disputed)
Luzon Strait
Luzon
THAILAND
Khon Kaen
Nakhon
Ratchasima
Chao Phraya R.
Mun R.
Chi R.
Savannakhet
Annamite Mts.
Hue
Da Nang
Plateau of
Kontum
VIETNAM
Qui Nhon
*South
China
Sea*
Mt. Pinatubo
1759m
Quezon
City
Manila
Mindoro
Andaman Is.
(India)
Port Blair
*Andaman
Sea*
Thon Buri
★
Bangkok
Mergui
Archipelago
*Gulf
of
Thailand*
Tonle
Sap
**CAMBODIA
(KAMPUCHEA)**
Khone
Falls
Kratie
Phnom Penh
Bien Hoa
Nha Trang
Ho Chi Minh City (Saigon)
Isthmus
of Kra
Surat Thani
Long
Xuyen
Can
Tho
*Mouths of
the Mekong*
Con Son Is.
Spratly Is.
(disputed)
Palawan
PHILIPPINES
*Sulu
Sea*
10°N
Nicobar Is.
(India)
*INDIAN
OCEAN*
Songkhla
Malay
Pinang
(George Town)
Ipoh
Medan
Pematangsiantar
Simeulue
Kelang
Nias
Peninsula
M A L A Y S I A
Natuna I.
(Indonesia)
Kuala Lumpur
★
Johor Baharu
SINGAPORE
★
Strait of Malacca
Sumatra
Serasun Strait
Pontianak
I N D O N E S I A
Kota Kinabalu
Bandar Seri Begawan
BRUNEI
★
Sabah
Balabac Strait
Tarakan
Sandakan
*Celebes
Sea*
Sibu
Sarawak
Kuching
Kapuas R.
Rajang R.
Kayan R.
B o r n e o
Mahakam R.
Celebes
Makassar Strait
120°E
EQUATOR
0°
90°E
100°E
110°E

SOUTHEASTERN ASIA
Political

CITIES
● Calcutta
● Medan
• Ipoh

A city's relative size is
shown by the size of its
symbol and lettering.

⊛ Bangkok   National capital

0   100   200   300   400 Miles
0   100 200 300   400 Kilometers

Complete legend on page 7

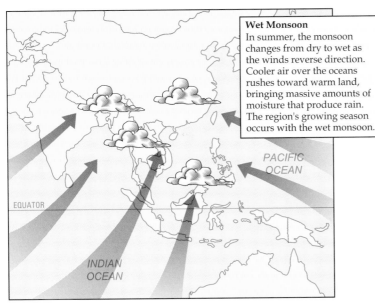

Wet Monsoon
In summer, the monsoon
changes from dry to wet as
the winds reverse direction.
Cooler air over the oceans
rushes toward warm land,
bringing massive amounts of
moisture that produce rain.
The region's growing season
occurs with the wet monsoon.

PACIFIC
OCEAN

EQUATOR

INDIAN
OCEAN

Terraces maximize the growing space for rice in hilly terrain.
Rice is the most important food crop in southeastern Asia.

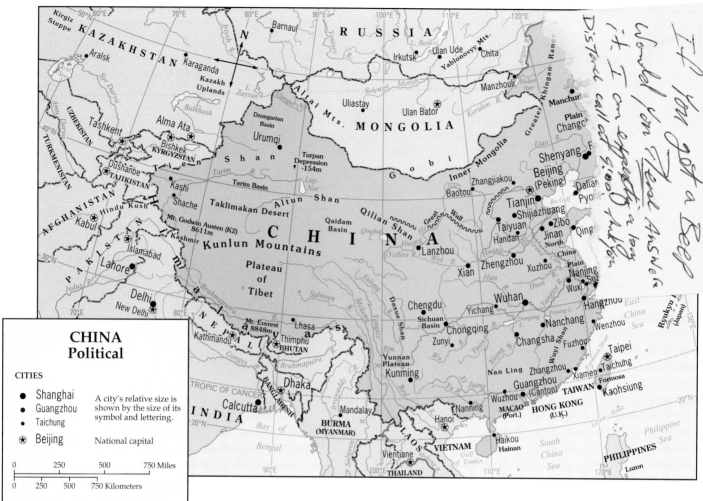

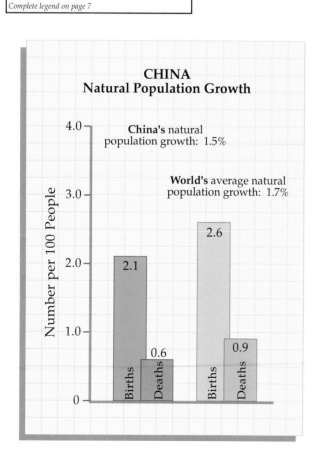

CHINA
Political

CITIES

A city's relative size is shown by the size of its symbol and lettering.

● Shanghai
● Guangzhou
▪ Taichung
✪ Beijing — National capital

| 0 | 250 | 500 | 750 Miles |

| 0 | 250 | 500 | 750 Kilometers |

Complete legend on page 7

CHINA
Natural Population Growth

China's natural population growth: 1.5%

World's average natural population growth: 1.7%

Number per 100 People

- Births 2.1
- Deaths 0.6
- Births 2.6
- Deaths 0.9

Bicycles in China

Number of bicycles in use: 369.2 million

Number of automobiles in use: 1.4 million

Nearly half of the people who work in urban China commute by bicycle.

CHINA
Area Comparison

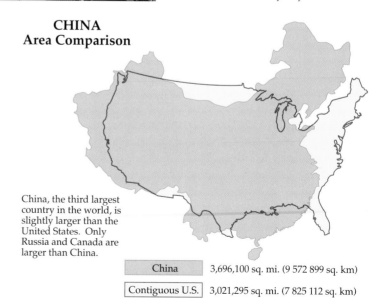

China, the third largest country in the world, is slightly larger than the United States. Only Russia and Canada are larger than China.

| China | 3,696,100 sq. mi. (9 572 899 sq. km) |
| Contiguous U.S. | 3,021,295 sq. mi. (7 825 112 sq. km) |

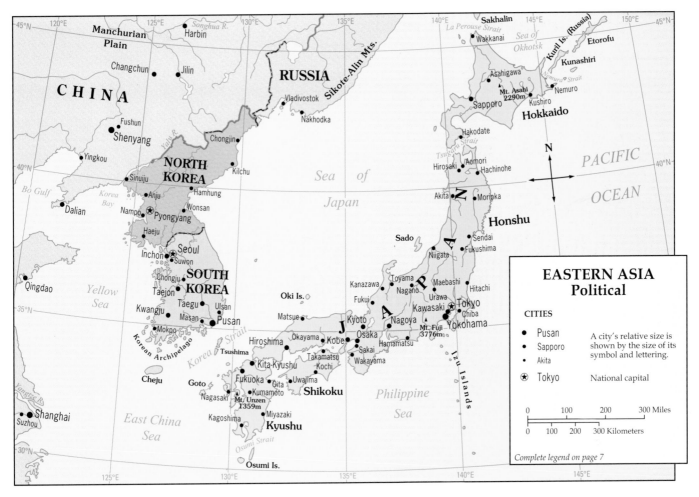

EASTERN ASIA
Political

CITIES

● Pusan

● Sapporo

● Akita

A city's relative size is shown by the size of its symbol and lettering.

✪ Tokyo — National capital

0   100   200   300 Miles

0   100   200   300 Kilometers

Complete legend on page 7

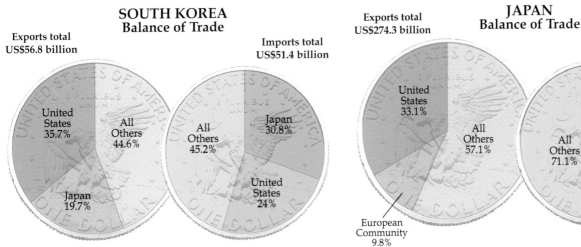

SOUTH KOREA
Balance of Trade

Exports total US$56.8 billion

United States 35.7%
All Others 44.6%
Japan 19.7%

Imports total US$51.4 billion

All Others 45.2%
Japan 30.8%
United States 24%

JAPAN
Balance of Trade

Exports total US$274.3 billion

United States 33.1%
All Others 57.1%
European Community 9.8%

Imports total US$210.4 billion

United States 22.5%
All Others 71.1%
European Community 6.4%

Leading Automobile Manufacturers

	Automobiles manufactured per year	Percentage of world production
Japan	9,584,000	27.2%
United States	6,113,000	17.4%
Germany	4,800,000	13.6%
France	3,297,000	9.4%
Italy	1,826,000	5.2%
Other countries	9,567,000	27.2%

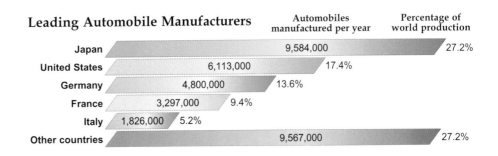

Japan's automakers have assembly plants in a number of locations in the United States.

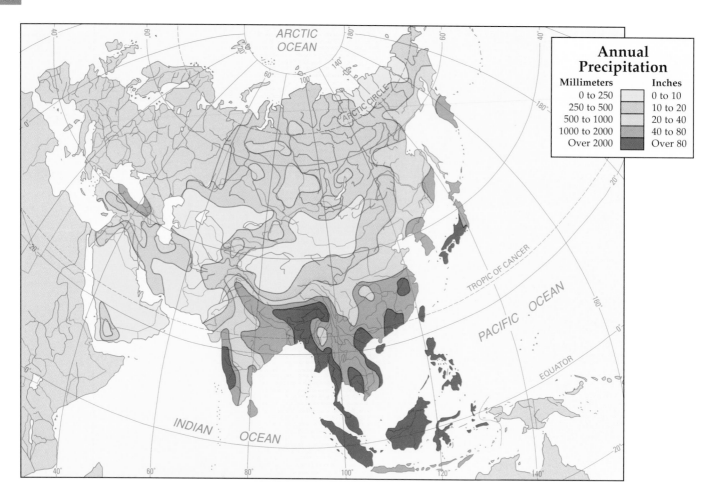

Annual Precipitation

Millimeters	Inches
0 to 250	0 to 10
250 to 500	10 to 20
500 to 1000	20 to 40
1000 to 2000	40 to 80
Over 2000	Over 80

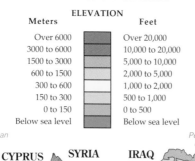

The Himalayas, located in southern Asia, are the world's highest mountain system.

INDONESIA
Area Comparison

The combined land area of Indonesia's 17,000 islands is about one-fourth the size of the contiguous United States. Three islands located partly or entirely in Indonesia—Sumatra, Borneo, and New Guinea—are each larger than all five Great Lakes combined.

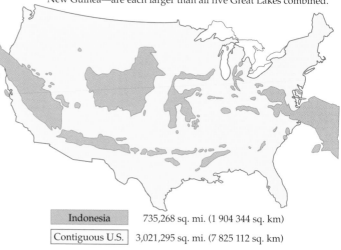

Indonesia	735,268 sq. mi. (1 904 344 sq. km)
Contiguous U.S.	3,021,295 sq. mi. (7 825 112 sq. km)

Cross Section of Asia

ELEVATION

Meters		Feet
Over 6000		Over 20,000
3000 to 6000		10,000 to 20,000
1500 to 3000		5,000 to 10,000
600 to 1500		2,000 to 5,000
300 to 600		1,000 to 2,000
150 to 300		500 to 1,000
0 to 150		0 to 500
Below sea level		Below sea level

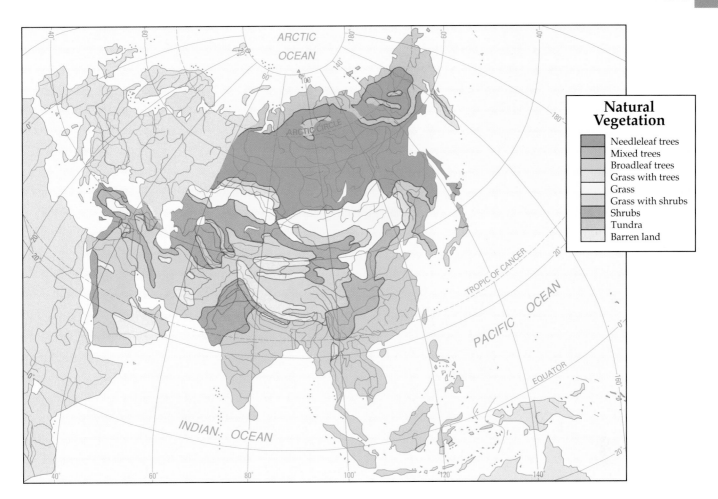

Natural Vegetation

- Needleleaf trees
- Mixed trees
- Broadleaf trees
- Grass with trees
- Grass
- Grass with shrubs
- Shrubs
- Tundra
- Barren land

INDIA
Balance of Trade

Exports total
US$8.7 billion

- United States 16.2%
- European Community 16%
- Soviet Union 15.9%
- All Others 51.9%

Imports total
US$12 billion

- European Community 23.1%
- United States 9.7%
- All Others 67.2%

CHINA
Balance of Trade

Exports total
US$46.5 billion

- Hong Kong 38.3%
- Japan 16.3%
- All Others 45.4%

Imports total
US$52.5 billion

- Hong Kong 20.6%
- Japan 20.4%
- All Others 59%

of   Tibet

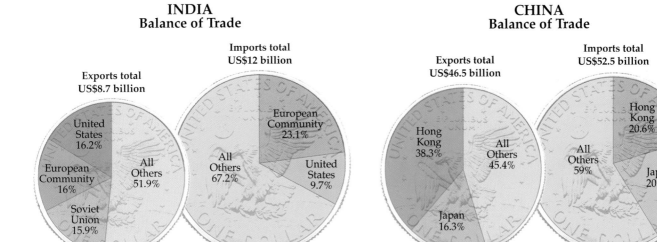

CHINA   KOREA   JAPAN

Yellow Sea   Pacific Ocean

28°N

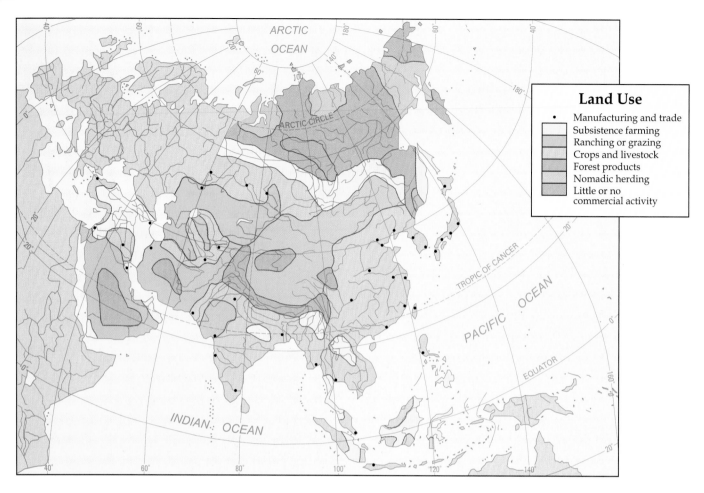

Land Use

- Manufacturing and trade
- Subsistence farming
- Ranching or grazing
- Crops and livestock
- Forest products
- Nomadic herding
- Little or no commercial activity

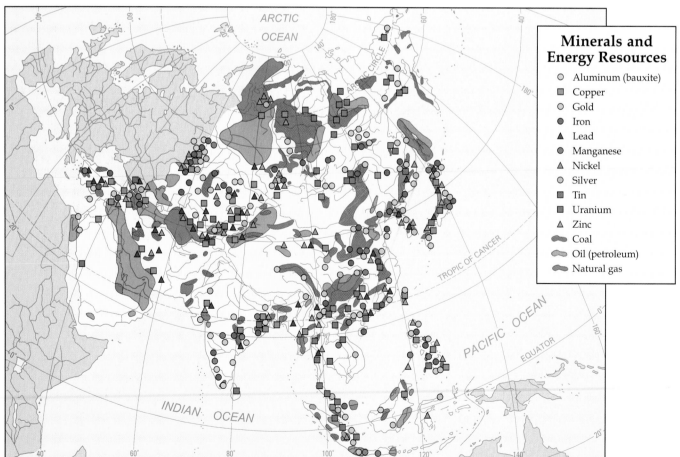

Minerals and Energy Resources

- Aluminum (bauxite)
- Copper
- Gold
- Iron
- Lead
- Manganese
- Nickel
- Silver
- Tin
- Uranium
- Zinc
- Coal
- Oil (petroleum)
- Natural gas

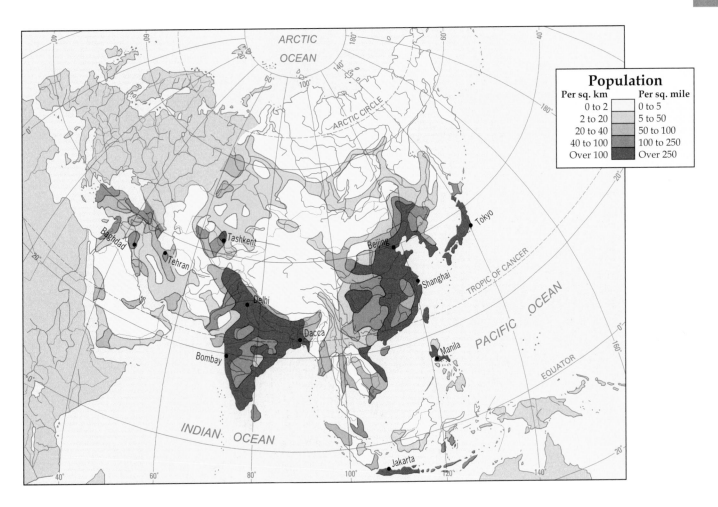

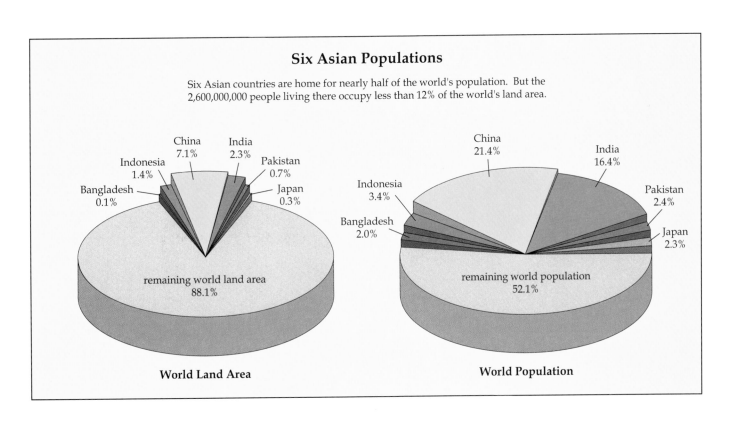

Six Asian Populations

Six Asian countries are home for nearly half of the world's population. But the 2,600,000,000 people living there occupy less than 12% of the world's land area.

World Land Area

Bangladesh 0.1%
Indonesia 1.4%
China 7.1%
India 2.3%
Pakistan 0.7%
Japan 0.3%
remaining world land area 88.1%

World Population

Indonesia 3.4%
Bangladesh 2.0%
China 21.4%
India 16.4%
Pakistan 2.4%
Japan 2.3%
remaining world population 52.1%

EQUATOR

PACIFIC

OCEAN

Espiritu Santo

Port-Vila Efate VANUATU

Loyalty Is.

New Caledonia

Norfolk I.

North Cape

Auckland North Island Wellington

Bay of Plenty

Cook Str.

Banks Pen.

NEW ZEALAND

Southern Alps

Mt. Cook 3764m

South Island

Foveaux Strait

Stewart I.

SOLOMON IS.

Honiara

Bougainville

Guadalcanal

Chesterfield Is.

Tasman Sea

New Ireland

New Britain

Bismarck Sea

Solomon Sea

Admiralty Is.

Port Moresby

Gulf of Papua

PAPUA NEW GUINEA

New Guinea

Maoke Mts.

Java Pk. 5030m

Coral Sea

Great Barrier Reef

Fraser I.

Brisbane

Great Dividing Range

Sydney

Lord Howe I.

Canberra

Mt. Kosciuszko 2228m

Australian Alps

Furneaux Group

TASMANIA

Mt. Ossa 1617m

King I.

Bass Strait

Great Dividing Range

Great Artesian Basin

Lowlands

Central

Townsville

Cape York

Cape York Pen.

Torres Strait

Biak

Dolak

Aru Is.

Tanimbar Is.

Arafura Sea

Wellesley Is.

Gulf of Carpentaria

Groote Eylandt

Cobourg Pen.

Arnhem Land

Barkly Tableland

Flinders

Melbourne

Adelaide

Kangaroo I.

Flinders Ranges

Spencer Gulf

Lake Eyre

Simpson Desert

Desert

MacDonnell Ranges

Musgrave Range

Alice Springs

Darling Range

Plain

Nullarbor

Great Australian Bight

INDIAN OCEAN

Gulf St. Vincent

Darwin

Melville I.

Joseph Bonaparte Gulf

Kimberley Plateau

Halmahera

Ceram Sea

Ceram

Buru

Wetar

Timor

Timor Sea

Flores

AUSTRALIA

Plateau

Western

Great Sandy Desert

Gibson Desert

Great Victoria Desert

Lake Disappointment

Lake Mackay

Hamersley Ranges

Eighty Mile Beach

Great Sandy Desert

Roebuck Bay

North West Cape

Shark Bay

Perth

Cape Leeuwin

INDONESIA

Celebes

Celebes Sea

Molucca Sea

Banda Sea

Sumbawa

Sumba

Bali

Java

Java Sea

Makassar Strait

Borneo

MALAYSIA

Kuala Lumpur

SINGAPORE

Sumatra

Bangka I.

Jakarta

Mentawai Is.

Nias

Strait of Malacca

Karimata Strait

Christmas I.

Mt. Tambora 2821m

Krakatoa 813m

Sunda Strait

Flores Sea

Savu Sea

Bali Sea

INDIAN OCEAN

TROPIC OF CAPRICORN

Christmas I.

Banks Pen.

N

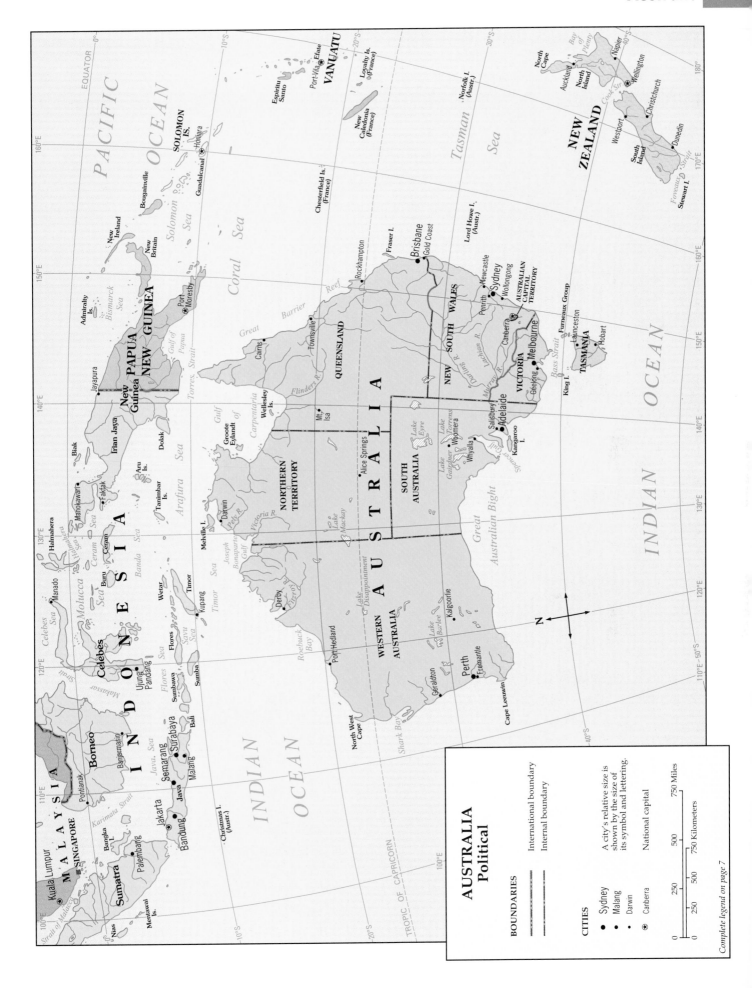

EQUATOR

PACIFIC OCEAN

Bougainville
New Ireland
New Britain
Admiralty Is.
Bismarck Sea
Solomon Sea

SOLOMON IS.
Guadalcanal Honiara

VANUATU
Espiritu Santo
Port-Vila Efate
New Caledonia (France)
Loyalty Is. (France)
Norfolk I. (Austr.)

Chesterfield Is. (France)

Coral Sea

NEW ZEALAND
North Cape
Auckland
North Island
Napier
Wellington
Christchurch
South Island
Westport
Dunedin
Foveaux Str. Stewart I.
Cook Str.
Bay of Plenty

Tasman Sea

INDONESIA
MALAYSIA
Kuala Lumpur
SINGAPORE
Sumatra
Bangka I.
Palembang
Mentawai Is.
Nias
Borneo
Pontianak
Banjarmasin
Java Sea
Jakarta
Bandung
Java
Semarang
Surabaya
Malang
Bali
Sumbawa
Sumba
Flores
Flores Sea
Savu Sea
Timor
Timor Sea
Kupang
Wetar
Celebes
Celebes Sea
Ujung Pandang
Manado
Molucca Sea
Halmahera
Buru
Ceram
Ceram Sea
Banda Sea
Buton
Aru Is.
Fakfak
Manokwari
Biak
Irian Jaya
New Guinea
Jayapura

Makassar Strait
Karimata Strait
Strait of Malacca

Christmas I. (Austr.)

PAPUA NEW GUINEA
Port Moresby
Gulf of Papua
Torres Strait
Arafura Sea
Tanimbar Is.
Dolak
Melville I.
Darwin

Gulf of Carpentaria
Groote Eylandt
Wellesley Is.

NORTHERN TERRITORY

Victoria R.
Joseph Bonaparte Gulf
Derby
Fitzroy R.
Roebuck Bay
Port Hedland
North West Cape
Shark Bay
Geraldton
Perth
Fremantle
Cape Leeuwin

WESTERN AUSTRALIA

Lake Disappointment
Lake Carnegie
Kalgoorlie
Lake Barlee

A U S T R A L I A

Alice Springs
Mt. Isa
Mackay
Lake Mackay

SOUTH AUSTRALIA
Lake Eyre
Lake Torrens
Lake Gairdner
Woomera
Whyalla
Salisbury
Adelaide
Kangaroo I.
Spencer Gulf

Great Australian Bight

QUEENSLAND
Cairns
Townsville
Flinders R.
Great Barrier Reef
Rockhampton
Fraser I.
Brisbane
Gold Coast

NEW SOUTH WALES
Darling R.
Lachlan R.
Murray R.
Newcastle
Sydney
Wollongong
Penrith
Canberra
AUSTRALIAN CAPITAL TERRITORY

VICTORIA
Melbourne
Geelong

Lord Howe I. (Austr.)

Bass Strait
King I.
Furneaux Group
Launceston
TASMANIA
Hobart

INDIAN OCEAN

N

AUSTRALIA Political

BOUNDARIES
International boundary
Internal boundary

CITIES
A city's relative size is shown by the size of its symbol and lettering.

- Sydney
- Malang
- Darwin
⊛ Canberra   National capital

0   250   500   750 Miles
0   250   500   750 Kilometers

TROPIC OF CAPRICORN

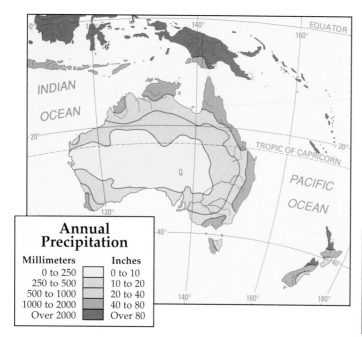

Annual Precipitation

Millimeters	Inches
0 to 250	0 to 10
250 to 500	10 to 20
500 to 1000	20 to 40
1000 to 2000	40 to 80
Over 2000	Over 80

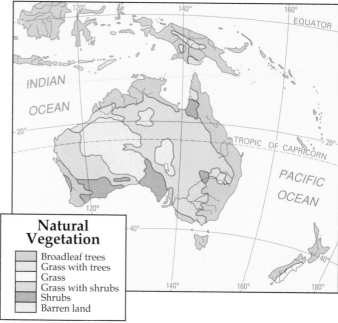

Natural Vegetation

- Broadleaf trees
- Grass with trees
- Grass
- Grass with shrubs
- Shrubs
- Barren land

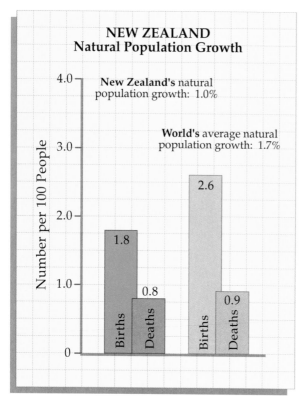

NEW ZEALAND
Natural Population Growth

New Zealand's natural population growth: 1.0%

World's average natural population growth: 1.7%

Number per 100 People

4.0

3.0

2.6

2.0

1.8

1.0

0.8

0.9

0

Births — Deaths — Births — Deaths

Sydney is Australia's largest city. Its Opera House and Harbour Bridge are internationally recognized landmarks.

Isolated Australia is home to many unique animals, including marsupials such as the kangaroo.

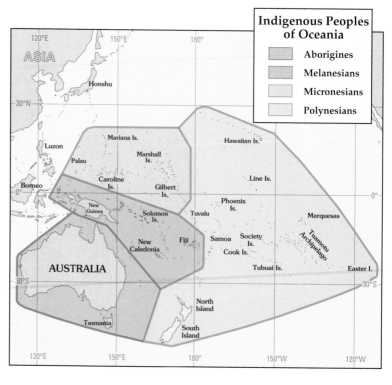

Indigenous Peoples of Oceania

- Aborigines
- Melanesians
- Micronesians
- Polynesians

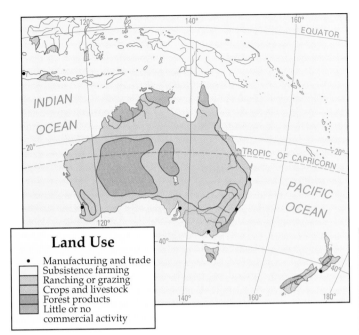

Land Use

- Manufacturing and trade
- Subsistence farming
- Ranching or grazing
- Crops and livestock
- Forest products
- Little or no commercial activity

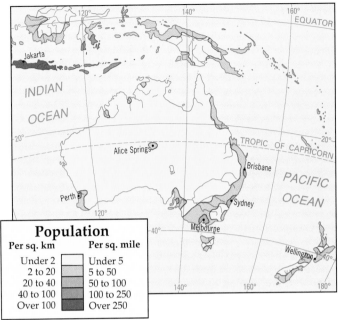

Population

Per sq. km	Per sq. mile
Under 2	Under 5
2 to 20	5 to 50
20 to 40	50 to 100
40 to 100	100 to 250
Over 100	Over 250

Australia's Isolation

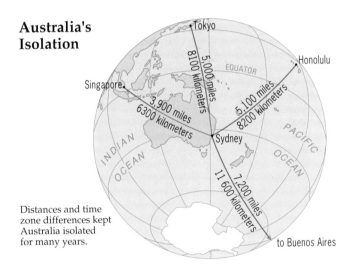

Tokyo
5,000 miles
8100 kilometers

Honolulu
5,100 miles
8200 kilometers

Singapore
3,900 miles
6300 kilometers

Sydney

7,200 miles
11 600 kilometers
to Buenos Aires

Distances and time zone differences kept Australia isolated for many years.

AUSTRALIA
Balance of Trade

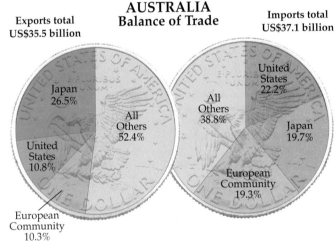

Exports total US$35.5 billion

Japan 26.5%
All Others 52.4%
United States 10.8%
European Community 10.3%

Imports total US$37.1 billion

United States 22.2%
All Others 38.8%
Japan 19.7%
European Community 19.3%

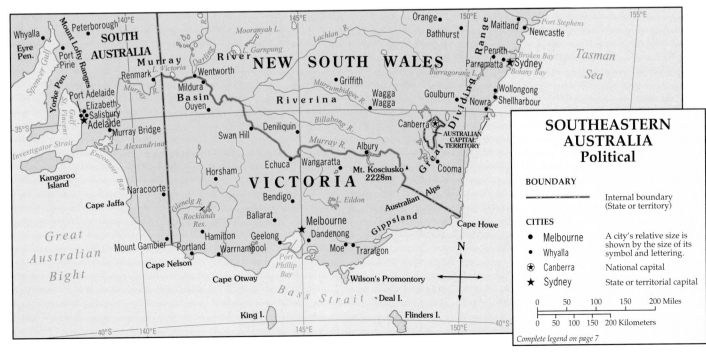

SOUTHEASTERN AUSTRALIA
Political

BOUNDARY

———— Internal boundary (State or territory)

CITIES

- ● Melbourne — A city's relative size is shown by the size of its symbol and lettering.
- • Whyalla
- ⊛ Canberra — National capital
- ★ Sydney — State or territorial capital

0   50   100   150   200 Miles

0   50 100 200 Kilometers

Complete legend on page 7

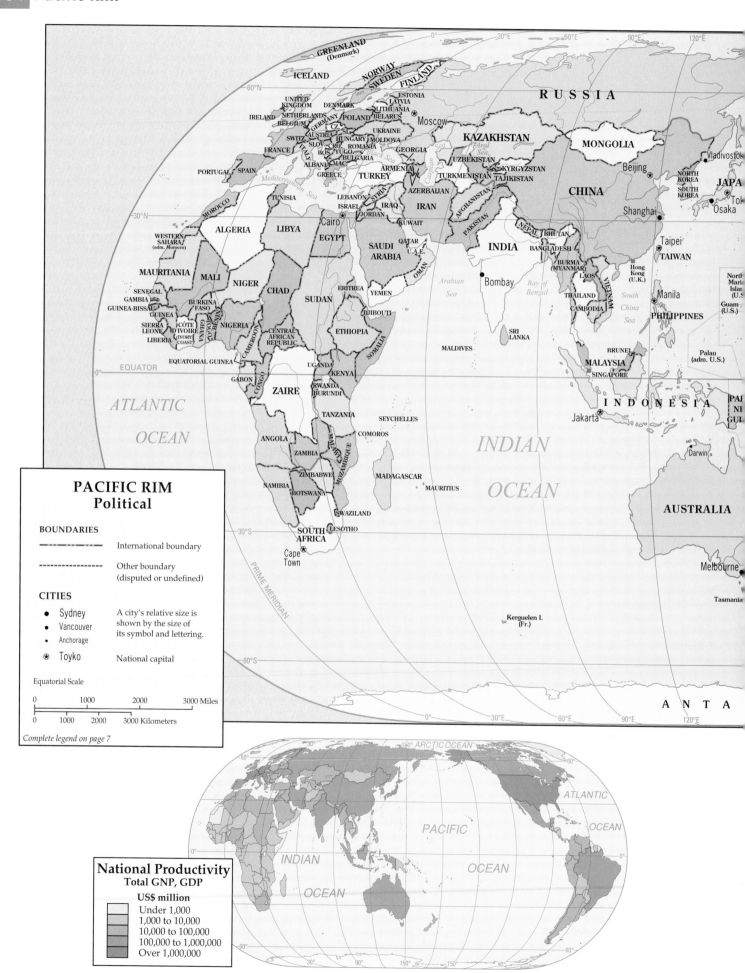

PACIFIC RIM
Political

BOUNDARIES

——————— International boundary

- - - - - - - - Other boundary
(disputed or undefined)

CITIES

● Sydney

● Vancouver

· Anchorage

⊛ Toyko   National capital

A city's relative size is
shown by the size of
its symbol and lettering.

Equatorial Scale

| 0 | 1000 | 2000 | 3000 Miles |

| 0 | 1000 | 2000 | 3000 Kilometers |

Complete legend on page 7

National Productivity
Total GNP, GDP

US$ million

Under 1,000
1,000 to 10,000
10,000 to 100,000
100,000 to 1,000,000
Over 1,000,000

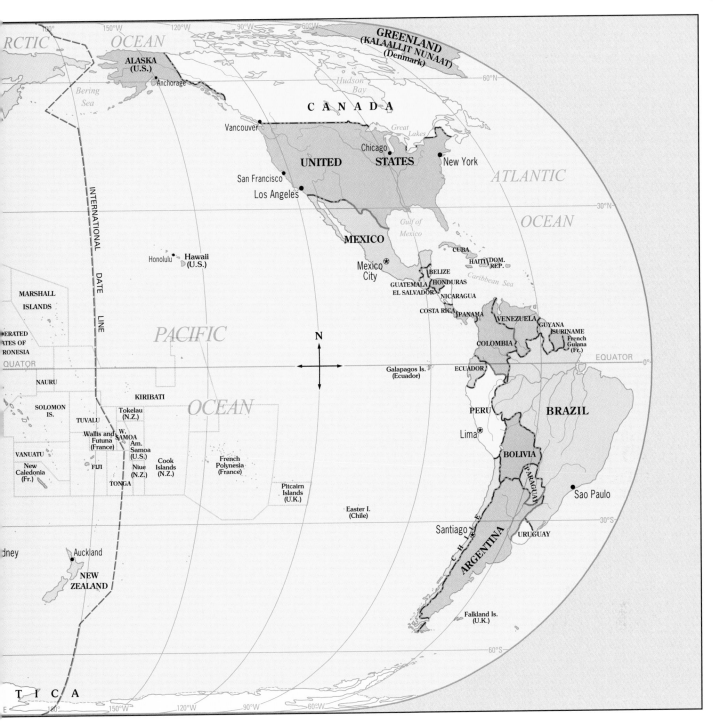

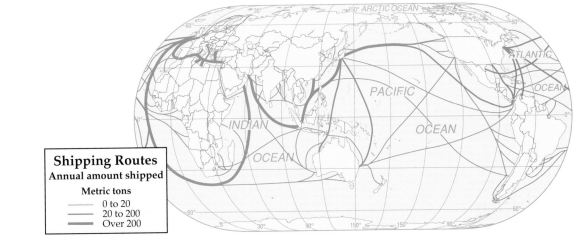

Shipping Routes
Annual amount shipped

Metric tons

—— 0 to 20
—— 20 to 200
—— Over 200

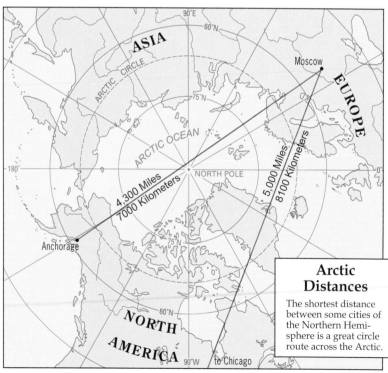

JAPAN
CHINA
120°E
90°E
60°E
KAZAKHSTAN
45°N
TURKEY

R U S S I A
60°N
Volga R.
Moscow ⊛
Black Sea
30°E

Sea of Okhotsk
Kuril Is.
Amur R.
Verkhoyansk Ra.
Lena R.
Ob R.
Ural Mountains
UKRAINE
ROMANIA
BELARUS

Magadan
ARCTIC CIRCLE
75°N
Kara Sea
Norilsk
Barents Sea
Novaya Zemlya
EST.
LAT. LITH.
POLAND
HUNGARY
AUSTRIA

Kamchatka Pen.
New Siberian Is.
Severnaya Zemlya
Murmansk
FINLAND
Helsinki ⊛
Baltic Sea
SWEDEN
GERMANY
CZECH REP.

Aleutian Islands
180°
A R C T I C   O C E A N
NORTH POLE
PRIME MERIDIAN
DENMARK
NORWAY
LUXEMBOURG
NETHERLANDS
BELGIUM
FRANCE

Bering Sea
Bering Strait
Chukchi Sea
Greenland Sea
Jan Mayen
ICELAND
North Sea
London
UNITED KINGDOM
0°

Brooks Range
ALASKA (U.S.)
Beaufort Sea
Queen Elizabeth Is.
Ellesmere I.
GREENLAND (KALAALLIT NUNAAT) (Denmark)
IRELAND

Alaska
Anchorage
Alaska Ra.
Yukon R.
Baffin Bay
30°W

PACIFIC OCEAN
150°W
Gulf of Alaska
Mackenzie R.
75°N
Baffin I.
Godthab (Nuuk)
Davis Strait

Rocky Mountains
C A N A D A
ARCTIC CIRCLE

Edmonton
60°N
Hudson Bay
120°W
90°W
60°W

THE ARCTIC
Physical

– – – – – – – International boundary

ELEVATION

Meters		Feet
Over 3000		Over 10,000
1500 to 3000		5,000 to 10,000
600 to 1500		2,000 to 5,000
300 to 600		1,000 to 2,000
150 to 300		500 to 1,000
0 to 150		0 to 500

WATER DEPTH

Less than 200		Less than 600
Greater than 200		Greater than 600

0   500   1000 Miles

0   500   1000 Kilometers

Complete legend on page 7

ASIA
60°N
90°E

ARCTIC CIRCLE
75°N
Moscow
EUROPE

ARCTIC OCEAN
180
4,300 Miles 7000 Kilometers
NORTH POLE
5,000 Miles 8100 Kilometers

75°N
Anchorage

NORTH AMERICA
60°N
90°W
to Chicago

Arctic Distances

The shortest distance between some cities of the Northern Hemisphere is a great circle route across the Arctic.

Polar bears roam the frozen wastes of the Arctic. These hunters can smell prey up to ten miles away.

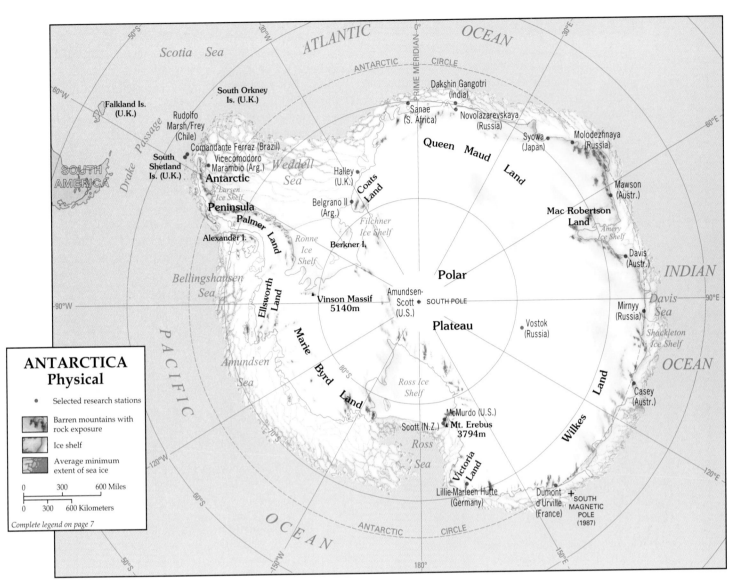

ANTARCTICA
Physical

- • Selected research stations
- Barren mountains with rock exposure
- Ice shelf
- Average minimum extent of sea ice

| 0 | 300 | 600 Miles |
| 0 | 300 | 600 Kilometers |

Complete legend on page 7

Map labels:

Scotia Sea
ATLANTIC OCEAN
PRIME MERIDIAN 0°
ANTARCTIC CIRCLE
Falkland Is. (U.K.)
South Orkney Is. (U.K.)
Dakshin Gangotri (India)
Sanae (S. Africa)
Novolazarevskaya (Russia)
Rudolfo Marsh/Frey (Chile)
Comandante Ferraz (Brazil)
Vicecomodoro Marambio (Arg.)
South Shetland Is. (U.K.)
SOUTH AMERICA
Drake Passage
Antarctic
Weddell Sea
Halley (U.K.)
Coats Land
Queen Maud Land
Syowa (Japan)
Molodezhnaya (Russia)
Mawson (Austr.)
Larsen Ice Shelf
Peninsula
Belgrano II (Arg.)
Mac Robertson Land
Palmer Land
Alexander I.
Ronne Ice Shelf
Filchner Ice Shelf
Berkner I.
Amery Ice Shelf
Davis (Austr.)
INDIAN
Bellingshausen Sea
Polar
Vinson Massif 5140m
Amundsen-Scott (U.S.)
SOUTH POLE
Vostok (Russia)
Mirnyy (Russia)
Davis Sea
90°E
PACIFIC
Ellsworth Land
Plateau
Shackleton Ice Shelf
OCEAN
Amundsen Sea
Marie Byrd Land
Ross Ice Shelf
Wilkes Land
Casey (Austr.)
McMurdo (U.S.)
Scott (N.Z.)
Mt. Erebus 3794m
Victoria Land
Lillie-Marleen Hutte (Germany)
Dumont d'Urville (France)
SOUTH MAGNETIC POLE (1987)
ANTARCTIC CIRCLE
180°
Ross Sea

Antarctica's Ice Cap

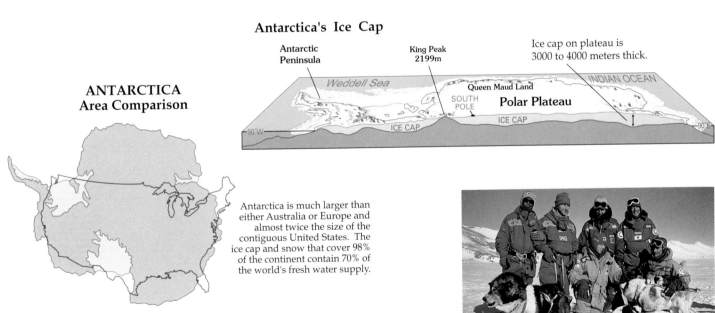

Antarctic Peninsula

King Peak 2199m

Ice cap on plateau is 3000 to 4000 meters thick.

Weddell Sea

Queen Maud Land

INDIAN OCEAN

SOUTH POLE

Polar Plateau

90° W

ICE CAP

ICE CAP

90° E

ANTARCTICA
Area Comparison

Antarctica is much larger than either Australia or Europe and almost twice the size of the contiguous United States. The ice cap and snow that cover 98% of the continent contain 70% of the world's fresh water supply.

| Antarctica | 5,500,000 sq. mi. (14 248 700 sq. km) |
| Contiguous U.S. | 3,021,295 sq. mi. (7 825 112 sq. km) |

Expeditions to the interior of Antarctica provide scientists with information about the earth's coldest region.

MAP PROJECTIONS

Map projections are the means by which the curved surface of a globe is transferred to the flat surface of a map. Because the earth is a sphere, a globe is its only perfect model. Even though there are an infinite number of map projections, none can be as accurate as a globe. A globe simultaneously shows accurate shapes, sizes, distances, and directions. No single world map can show all four of these properties accurately. Every world map distorts one or more of them. For example, a world map that shows correct shapes cannot show correct sizes, and vice versa.

The projections illustrated here can be classified according to their map properties. *Conformal* projections show true shapes, but distort sizes. (You can remember this term's meaning by associating *shape* with the word *form* in *conformal*.) *Equal-area* projections show all areas in their true relative sizes, but distort shapes. *Compromise* projections allow some size distortions in order to portray shapes more accurately. For all types of world map projections, distortion is generally least near the center of the map and greatest at its edges.

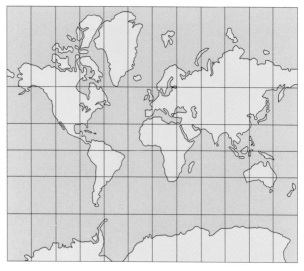

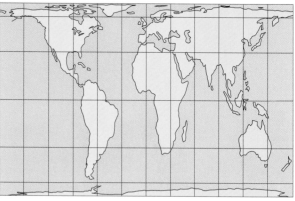

Gall-Peters: An equal-area projection first produced in the 1850s, the Gall-Peters greatly distorts shapes near the Equator as well as near the poles. Features near the Equator are stretched vertically, while features near the poles are flattened horizontally. The resulting shapes are quite different from those on the globe.

Mercator: First published in 1569, the Mercator is a conformal projection. North and South Poles are shown not as points, but as lines the same length as the Equator. The result is extreme size distortion in the higher latitudes. The Mercator map was designed for navigation, and the true compass direction between any two points can be determined by a straight line.

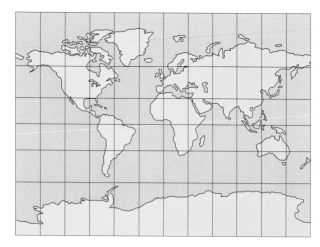

Armadillo: The Armadillo is a compromise projection that is intended to give young students the impression of a map being peeled from a globe. Because its unique appearance results in severe distortions, especially at the map's outer edges, it has seldom been used outside the classroom.

Miller Cylindrical: The Miller is a compromise projection based on the Mercator. Its shapes are not as accurate as those on the Mercator map, but it has much less size distortion in the higher latitiudes. The Miller cylindrical projection is frequently used when mapping world time zones.

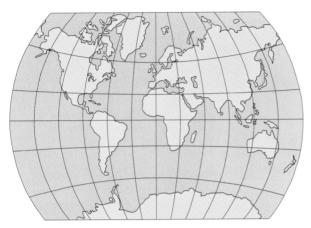

Van der Grinten: The Van der Grinten is a compromise between the Mercator and the Mollweide. The full projection is shaped like a circle, but the polar areas are normally not shown. Shapes, sizes, and directions are reasonably accurate between 60°N and 60°S, where most of the world's people live. The Van der Grinten has long been used for general reference maps.

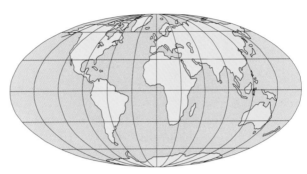

Mollweide: An equal-area projection, the Mollweide has an oval shape that reminds the viewer of a globe. The Mollweide projection is frequently used for world distribution maps. (A distribution map shows the relative location and extent of something—such as crops, livestock, or people—across the face of the earth.)

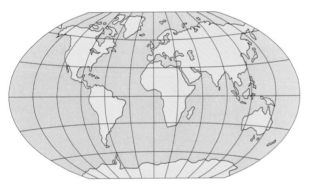

Winkel "Tripel": The Winkel "Tripel" is a compromise projection. Its oval shape and curving parallels result in a map with realistic shapes and minor size distortions at all latitudes. The Winkel has less size distortion than the Van der Grinten (above) and less shape distortion than the Robinson (below).

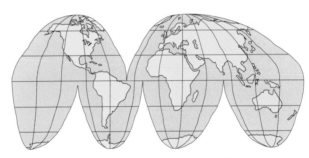

Goode's Homolosine: Goode's is an equal-area map that also shows shapes extremely well. Shapes can be shown more accurately than on most equal-area maps because the grid is *interrupted* or split in the ocean areas. The interruptions allow land areas to be shown with less stretch or distortion.

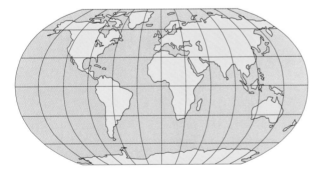

Robinson: First used in 1963, the Robinson is a compromise projection. Because it presents a reasonable overall picture of the world, it is often used for maps in educational materials. It looks similar to the Eckert IV (at right), but the Robinson is easily distinguished by its size distortion in the polar areas.

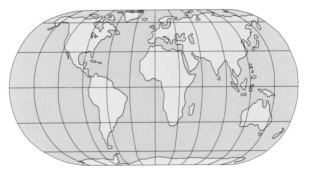

Eckert IV: An equal-area projection, the Eckert IV has relatively minor shape distortions near the Equator and the poles. The result is a map that is well-suited either for general reference or for showing world distributions. It has been used in several atlases to show world climates and other themes.

COUNTRY TABLES

COUNTRY	CAPITAL(S)	PRINCIPAL LANGUAGE(S)	POPULATION	AREA MI.² KM²	POP. DENSITY PER MI.² PER KM²	NATURAL POP. GROWTH PER 100 PEOPLE BIRTHS – DEATHS = % GAIN		
Africa								
ALGERIA	Algiers	Arabic, French, Berber	26,401,000	919,595 2 381 741	28.7 11.1	3.4	0.6	2.8
ANGOLA	Luanda	Ovimbundu, Portuguese, Mbundu, Kongo	10,609,000	481,354 1 246 700	22.0 8.5	4.7	2.0	2.7
BENIN	Porto-Novo, Cotonou	Fon, French, Yoruba, Adja	4,928,000	43,450 112 600	113.4 43.8	4.9	1.8	3.1
BOTSWANA	Gaborone	Tswana, English, Shona	1,359,000	224,607 581 730	6.1 2.3	4.6	1.1	3.5
BURKINA FASO	Ouagadougou	Voltaic, Mande, Fulani, French	9,515,000	105,946 274 400	89.8 34.7	4.7	1.8	2.9
BURUNDI	Bujumbura	Rundi, French	5,657,000	10,740 27 816	526.7 203.4	4.7	1.5	3.2
CAMEROON	Yaounde	Fang, Bamileke, French, Duala, Fulani, Tikar, English	12,622,000	179,714 465 458	70.5 27.2	4.5	1.5	3.0
CAPE VERDE	Praia	Crioulo, Portuguese	346,000	1,557 4 033	222.2 85.8	3.2	0.8	2.4
CENTRAL AFRICAN REPUBLIC	Bangui	Banda, Baya, Sango, French, Ngbandi, Mbaka	2,930,000	240,324 622 436	12.2 4.7	4.5	1.8	2.7
CHAD	N'Djamena	Sara, Bagirmi, Kraish, Arabic, French	5,961,000	495,755 1 284 000	12.0 4.6	4.4	1.9	2.5
COMOROS	Moroni	Comorian, French, Arabic	497,000	719 1 862	691.2 266.9	4.7	1.3	3.4
CONGO	Brazzaville	Monokutuba, Kongo, French, Teke	2,692,000	132,047 342 000	20.4 7.9	4.5	1.5	3.0
CÔTE D'IVOIRE (IVORY COAST)	Abidjan	Akan, French, Kru, Gur Hindi	12,951,000	123,847 320 763	104.6 40.4	4.7	1.3	3.4
DJIBOUTI	Djibouti	Somali, Afar, French, Arabic	557,000	8,950 23 200	62.2 24.0	4.6	1.7	2.9
EGYPT	Cairo	Arabic	55,979,000	385,229 997 739	145.3 56.1	3.9	0.9	3.0
EQUATORIAL GUINEA	Malabo	Fana, Bubi, Spanish	367,000	10,831 28 051	33.9 13.1	4.3	1.8	2.5
ERITREA	Asmara	Amharic, Tigrinya	3,332,000	17,413 45 100	91.4 35.3	4.7	2.1	2.6
ETHIOPIA	Addis Ababa	Amharic, Oromo, Tigrinya, Gurage	50,745,000	483,123 1 251 282	111.9 43.2	4.7	2.1	2.6
GABON	Libreville	Fang, French, Puna/Sira/Nzebi	1,253,000	103,347 267 667	12.1 4.7	4.0	1.6	2.4
GAMBIA	Banjul	Malinke, Fulani, English	921,000	4,127 10 689	223.2 86.2	4.6	2.1	2.5
GHANA	Accra	Hausa, Akan, Mole-Dagbani, English	15,237,000	92,098 238 533	165.4 63.9	4.4	1.3	3.1
GUINEA	Conakry	Fulani, Malinke, Susu, French	7,232,000	94,926 245 857	76.2 29.4	4.8	2.2	2.6
GUINEA-BISSAU	Bissau	Crioulo, Fulani, Balante, Portuguese	1,015,000	13,948 36 125	72.8 28.1	4.2	2.0	2.2
KENYA	Nairobi	Swahili, Kikuyu, Luhya, Luo, Kamba, Kalenjin	26,985,000	224,961 582 646	120.0 46.3	4.9	1.1	3.8
LESOTHO	Maseru	Sotho, Zulu, English	1,854,000	11,720 30 355	158.2 61.1	4.1	1.2	2.9
LIBERIA	Monrovia	Krio, English, Kepelle, Bassa, Grebo	2,780,000	38,250 99 067	72.7 28.1	4.6	1.4	3.2

Country: all independent countries, as well as selected dependencies. **Principal Language(s):** all official languages, as well as other primary languages spoken by a substantial proportion of the population. **Pop. Density:** population density, computed as population divided by area; given per square mile and per square kilometer.
Natural Pop. Growth: annual population increase per 100 people; does not include population change due to immigration or emigration.

COUNTRY	CAPITAL(S)	PRINCIPAL LANGUAGE(S)	POPULATION	AREA MI.² KM²	POP. DENSITY PER MI.² PER KM²	NATURAL POP. GROWTH PER 100 PEOPLE BIRTHS − DEATHS = % GAIN		
LIBYA	Tripoli	Arabic, Berber	4,447,000	678,400 1 757 000	6.6 2.5	4.5	0.8	3.7
MADAGASCAR	Antananarivo	Malagasy, French	12,803,000	226,658 587 041	56.5 21.8	4.6	1.4	3.2
MALAWI	Lilongwe, Zomba	Chewa, English, Lomwe, Yao, Ngoni	9,484,000	45,747 118 484	207.3 80.0	5.5	2.0	3.5
MALI	Bamako	Bambara, Fulani, Sehufo, Soninke, French	8,464,000	482,077 1 248 574	17.6 6.8	5.0	2.0	3.0
MAURITANIA	Nouakchott	Arabic, Wolof, French, Tukulor	2,108,000	398,000 1 030 700	5.3 2.0	4.7	1.9	2.8
MAURITIUS	Port-Louis	French Creole, Bhojpuri, Hindi, French, Tamil, Urdu, Telugu, English	1,081,000	788 2 040	1,371.8 529.9	2.0	0.6	1.4
MOROCCO	Rabat	Arabic, Berber	26,239,000	177,117 458 730	148.1 57.2	3.5	0.9	2.6
MOZAMBIQUE	Maputo	Makua, Tsonga, Senoc, Lomwe, Portuguese	14,842,000	313,661 812 379	47.3 18.3	4.5	1.8	2.7
NAMIBIA	Windhoek	Ovambo, Kavango, English	1,431,000	317,818 823 144	4.5 1.7	4.3	1.2	3.1
NIGER	Niamey	Hausa, Songhai/Zerma, French	8,281,000	458,075 1 186 408	18.1 7.0	5.1	2.0	3.1
NIGERIA	Abuja	English, Hausa, Yoruba, Igbo, Fulani	89,666,000	356,669 923 768	251.4 97.1	4.8	1.5	3.3
RWANDA	Kigali	Kwanda, French	7,347,000	10,169 26 338	722.5 279.0	5.1	1.7	3.4
SAO TOME AND PRINCIPE	Sao Tome	Crioulo, Portuguese	126,000	386 1 001	326.4 125.9	3.8	0.8	3.0
SENEGAL	Dakar	Wolof, Fulani, Serer Dyola, French, Malinke	7,691,000	75,951 196 712	101.3 39.1	4.5	1.8	2.7
SEYCHELLES	Victoria	Seselwa	71,000	175 453	405.7 156.7	2.4	0.8	1.6
SIERRA LEONE	Freetown	Mende, Temne, English, Krio	4,373,000	27,699 71 740	157.9 61.0	4.8	2.3	2.5
SOMALIA	Mogadishu	Somali, Arabic, English	7,872,000	246,000 637 000	32.0 12.4	4.9	1.9	3.0
SOUTH AFRICA	Cape Town, Pretoria, Bloemfontein	Zulu, Xhosa, Afrikaans, Sotho, English	39,085,000	473,290 1 225 815	82.1 31.7	3.3	0.9	2.4
SUDAN	Khartoum	Arabic, Dinka, Nubian, Beja, Nuer, Azande	29,971,000	966,757 2 503 890	31.0 12.0	4.5	1.5	3.0
SWAZILAND	Mbabane	Swazi, Zulu, English	826,000	6,704 17 364	123.2 47.6	4.7	1.2	3.5
TANZANIA	Dar es Salaam	Swahili, English, Nyamwezi	25,809,000	364,017 942 799	70.9 27.4	5.0	1.4	3.6
TOGO	Lome	Ewe-Adja, French, Tem-Kabre, Gurma	3,701,000	21,925 56 785	168.8 65.2	4.7	1.4	3.3
TUNISIA	Tunis	Arabic, French	8,413,000	59,664 154 530	141.0 54.4	2.6	0.5	2.1
UGANDA	Kampala	Swahili, Ganda, Teso, Soga, Nkole	17,194,000	93,070 241 040	184.7 71.3	5.1	1.5	3.6
WESTERN SAHARA (adm. Morocco)	El Aaiun	Arabic	209,000	97,344 252 120	2.1 0.8	4.8	2.3	2.5
ZAIRE	Kinshasa	Lingala, Swahili, Luba, Mongo, French	41,151,000	905,446 2 345 095	45.4 17.5	4.6	1.4	3.2
ZAMBIA	Lusaka	Bemba, Tonga, Lozi, English, Chewa, Nyamja	8,303,000	290,586 752 614	28.6 11.0	5.1	1.3	3.8
ZIMBABWE	Harare	Shona, Ndebele, Nyanja, English	9,871,000	150,873 390 759	65.4 25.3	4.0	1.0	3.0

Country: all independent countries, as well as selected dependencies. **Principal Language(s):** all official languages, as well as other primary languages spoken by a substantial proportion of the population. **Pop. Density:** population density, computed as population divided by area; given per square mile and per square kilometer. **Natural Pop. Growth:** annual population increase per 100 people; does not include population change due to immigration or emigration.

COUNTRY	CAPITAL(S)	PRINCIPAL LANGUAGE(S)	POPULATION	AREA MI.² KM²	POP. DENSITY PER MI.² PER KM²	NATURAL POP. GROWTH PER 100 PEOPLE BIRTHS – DEATHS = % GAIN		
Asia								
AFGHANISTAN	Kabul	Pashto, Dari, Uzbek, Turkmen	18,052,000	251,825 652 225	71.7 27.7	4.4	2.0	2.4
ARMENIA	Yerevan	Armenia	3,426,000	11,500 29 800	297.9 115.0	2.2	0.6	1.6
AZERBAIJAN	Baku	Azerbaijani, Russian, Armenian	7,237,000	33,400 86 600	216.7 83.6	2.6	0.6	2.0
BAHRAIN	Manama	Arabic	531,000	267 692	1,988.8 767.3	3.0	0.4	2.6
BANGLADESH	Dhaka	Bengali	110,602,000	55,598 143 998	1,989.3 768.1	3.6	1.2	2.4
BHUTAN	Thimphu, Paro	Dzongkha, Assamese	1,511,000	18,150 47 000	83.3 32.1	3.8	1.6	2.2
BRUNEI	Bandar Seri Begawan	Malay, Chinese, English	268,000	2,226 5 765	120.4 46.5	2.8	0.3	2.5
BURMA (MYANMAR)	Rangoon (Yangon)	Burmese, Shan, Karen	43,446,000	261,228 676 577	166.4 64.2	3.2	1.2	2.0
CAMBODIA (KAMPUCHEA)	Phnom Penh	Khmer	8,974,000	70,238 181 916	127.8 49.3	4.2	1.7	2.5
CHINA	Beijing	Han: Mandarin; Han: other; Zhuang	1,165,888,000	3,696,100 9 572 900	315.4 121.8	2.1	0.6	1.5
CYPRUS	Nicosia	Greek, Turkish	756,000	3,572 9 251	211.6 81.7	1.9	0.9	1.0
GEORGIA	Tbilisi	Georgian, Russian, Armenian, Azerbaijani	5,482,000	26,900 69 700	203.8 78.7	1.7	0.8	0.9
HONG KONG (U.K.)	Victoria	Cantonese, English, Mandarin	5,799,000	415 1 075	13,974.3 5 395.5	1.2	0.5	0.7
INDIA	New Delhi	Hindi, Telugu, Bengali, Maratha, Tamil	889,700,000	1,222,243 3 165 596	727.9 281.1	3.1	1.0	2.1
INDONESIA	Jakarta	Sundanese, Bahasa Indonesia	184,796,000	741,052 1 919 317	249.4 96.3	2.9	1.1	1.8
IRAN	Tehran	Farsi, Azerbaijani, Kurdish, Gilaki	59,570,000	632,457 1 638 057	94.2 36.4	4.4	1.0	3.4
IRAQ	Baghdad	Arabic, Kurdish	18,838,000	167,975 435 052	112.1 43.3	4.5	0.8	3.7
ISRAEL	Jerusalem	Hebrew, Arabic, Yiddish, Russian	5,237,000	7,992 20 700	655.5 253.1	2.2	0.6	1.6
JAPAN	Tokyo	Japanese	124,330,000	145,883 377 835	852.3 329.1	1.0	0.7	0.3
JORDAN	Amman	Arabic	3,636,000	34,342 88 946	105.9 40.9	3.9	0.6	3.3
KAZAKHSTAN	Almaty	Russian, Kazakh	17,008,000	1,049,200 2 717 300	16.2 6.3	2.2	0.8	1.4
KUWAIT	Kuwait	Arabic	1,190,000	6,880 17 818	173.0 66.8	2.7	0.2	2.5
KYRGYZSTAN	Bishkek	Kyrgyz, Russian, Uzbek	4,533,000	76,600 198 500	59.2 22.8	2.9	0.7	2.2
LAOS	Vientiane	Lao, Mon-Khmer, Miao and Munt	4,409,000	91,400 236 800	48.2 18.6	4.0	1.6	2.4
LEBANON	Beirut	Arabic, French, Armenian	2,803,000	3,950 10 230	709.6 274.0	2.9	0.7	2.2
MACAO (Port.)	Macao	Chinese, Portuguese	367,000	6.9 18.0	53,188.4 20 388.9	1.7	0.3	1.4
MALAYSIA	Kuala Lumpur	Malay, English, Chinese, Tamil	18,630,000	127,584 330 442	146.0 56.4	2.9	0.5	2.4
MALDIVES	Male	Divehi	230,000	115 298	2,000.0 771.8	4.2	0.9	3.3

Country: all independent countries, as well as selected dependencies. **Principal Language(s):** all official languages, as well as other primary languages spoken by a substantial proportion of the population. **Pop. Density:** population density, computed as population divided by area; given per square mile and per square kilometer. **Natural Pop. Growth:** annual population increase per 100 people; does not include population change due to immigration or emigration.

COUNTRY	CAPITAL(S)	PRINCIPAL LANGUAGE(S)	POPULATION	AREA MI.² KM²	POP. DENSITY PER MI.² PER KM²	NATURAL POP. GROWTH PER 100 PEOPLE BIRTHS – DEATHS = % GAIN		
MONGOLIA	Ulan Bator	Khalkar, Kazakh	2,182,000	604,800 1 566 500	3.6 1.4	3.7	0.9	2.8
NEPAL	Kathmandu	Nepali, Maithili, Bhojpuri	19,795,000	56,827 147 181	348.3 134.5	3.9	1.5	2.4
NORTH KOREA	Pyongyang	Korean	22,227,000	47,400 122 762	468.9 181.1	2.5	0.6	1.9
OMAN	Muscat	Arabic, Baluchi	1,640,000	118,150 306 000	13.9 5.4	4.4	0.9	3.5
PAKISTAN	Islamabad	Paunjabi, Pashto, Sindhi, Urdu	130,129,000	339,697 879 811	383.1 147.9	4.2	1.0	3.2
PHILIPPINES	Manila	Tagalog, English, Cebuanco	63,609,000	115,800 300 000	549.3 212.0	3.4	0.8	2.6
QATAR	Doha	Arabic	520,000	4,412 11 427	117.9 45.5	3.1	0.2	2.9
SAUDI ARABIA	Riyadh	Arabic	15,267,000	865,000 2 240 000	17.6 6.8	3.7	1.1	2.6
SINGAPORE	Singapore	Mandarin, English, Bahasa, Malaysian, Tamil	2,792,000	240 622	1,633.3 4 488.7	1.9	0.5	1.4
SOUTH KOREA	Seoul	Korean	43,663,000	38,326 99 263	1,139.3 439.9	1.7	0.6	1.1
SRI LANKA	Colombo, Kotte	Sinhalese, Tamil, English	17,464,000	25,332 65 610	689.4 266.2	2.2	0.6	1.6
SYRIA	Damascus	Arabic, Kurdish, Armenian	12,958,000	71,498 185 180	181.2 70.0	4.4	0.7	3.7
TAIWAN	Taipei	Min, Mandarin, Hakka	20,727,000	13,969 36 179	1,483.8 572.9	1.6	0.5	1.1
TAJIKISTAN	Dushanbe	Tajik, Uzbek, Russian	5,568,000	55,300 143 100	100.7 38.9	3.9	0.6	3.3
THAILAND	Bangkok	Thai, Lao, Chinese, Mon-Khmer	56,801,000	198,115 513 115	286.7 110.7	2.1	0.7	1.4
TURKEY	Ankara	Turkish, Kurdish, Arabic	58,584,000	300,948 779 452	194.7 75.2	2.8	0.7	2.1
TURKMENISTAN	Ashgabat	Turkmenian, Russian, Uzbek	3,859,000	188,500 488 100	20.5 7.9	3.4	0.7	2.7
UNITED ARAB EMIRATES	Abu Dhabi	Arabic	1,989,000	30,000 77 700	66.3 25.6	3.2	0.4	2.8
UZBEKISTAN	Tashkent	Uzbek, Russian, Tajik, Kazakh	21,363,000	172,700 447 400	123.7 47.7	3.4	0.6	2.8
VIETNAM	Hanoi	Vietnamese, Tay, Tai	69,052,000	127,246 329 566	542.7 209.5	3.1	0.9	2.2
YEMEN	Sanaa	Arabic	12,147,000	205,356 531 869	59.2 22.8	5.1	1.9	3.2

Australia and Oceania

COUNTRY	CAPITAL(S)	PRINCIPAL LANGUAGE(S)	POPULATION	AREA MI.² KM²	POP. DENSITY PER MI.² PER KM²	BIRTHS	DEATHS	% GAIN
AUSTRALIA	Canberra	English	17,562,000	2,966,200 7 682 300	5.9 2.3	1.5	0.7	0.8
FIJI	Suva	Fijian, Hindi, English	748,000	7,056 18 274	106.0 40.9	2.7	0.5	2.2
FRENCH POLYNESIA (Fr.)	Papeete	Polynesian, French, Chinese	206,000	1,544 4 000	133.4 51.5	2.7	0.5	2.2
KIRIBATI	Tarawa (Bairiki)	Kiribati, English	75,000	313 811	238.7 92.1	3.2	0.9	2.3
MARSHALL ISLANDS	Majuro	Marshallese, English	50,000	70 181	714.3 276.2	4.2	0.6	3.6
MICRONESIA	Palikir	Chuukese, Pohnpeian, English	114,000	271 701	420.7 162.6	3.4	0.5	2.9
NAURU	Yaren	Nauruan, Kiribati	10,000	8.2 21.2	1,170.7 452.8	2.1	0.5	1.6

Country: all independent countries, as well as selected dependencies. **Principal Language(s):** all official languages, as well as other primary languages spoken by a substantial proportion of the population. **Pop. Density:** population density, computed as population divided by area; given per square mile and per square kilometer. **Natural Pop. Growth:** annual population increase per 100 people; does not include population change due to immigration or emigration.

COUNTRY	CAPITAL(S)	PRINCIPAL LANGUAGE(S)	POPULATION	AREA MI.² KM²	POP. DENSITY PER MI.² PER KM²	NATURAL POP. GROWTH PER 100 PEOPLE BIRTHS – DEATHS = % GAIN		
NEW CALEDONIA (Fr.)	Noumea	English, Maori, Malanesian, Polynesian	174,000	7,172 18 576	24.3 9.4	1.8	0.8	1.8
NEW ZEALAND	Wellington	English, Maori	3,481,000	104,454 270 534	33.3 12.9	2.1	0.6	1.0
PALAU (adm. U.S.)	Koror	Palauan, English	16,000	188 488	83.5 32.2	2.5	0.6	1.9
PAPUA NEW GUINEA	Port Moresby	Papuan, English, Melanesian	3,834,000	178,704 462 840	21.5 8.3	3.5	1.2	2.3
SOLOMON ISLANDS	Honiara	Melanesian, Papuan, English	339,000	10,954 28 370	30.9 11.9	4.4	1.0	3.4
TONGA	Nukualofa	Tongan, English	97,000	301 780	323.3 124.7	3.0	0.7	2.3
TUVALU	Funafuti	Tuvaluan, English, Kiribati	10,000	9.3 24.0	1,021.5 395.8	2.9	1.0	1.9
VANUATU	Port-Vila	Melanesian, English	154,000	4,707 12 190	32.7 12.6	4.1	0.8	3.3
WESTERN SAMOA	Apia	Samoan, English	160,000	1,093 2 831	146.4 56.5	3.3	0.7	2.6

Europe

COUNTRY	CAPITAL(S)	PRINCIPAL LANGUAGE(S)	POPULATION	AREA MI.² KM²	POP. DENSITY PER MI.² PER KM²	BIRTHS	DEATHS	% GAIN
ALBANIA	Tirane	Albanian	3,357,000	11,100 28 748	302.4 116.8	2.5	0.5	2.0
ANDORRA	Andorra la Vella	Spanish, Catalan, French, Portuguese	57,000	181 468	315.5 122.0	1.4	0.4	1.0
AUSTRIA	Vienna	German, Serbo-Croatian	7,857,000	32,378 83 859	242.7 93.7	1.2	1.1	0.1
BELARUS	Minsk	Belorussian, Russian	10,321,000	80,200 207 600	128.7 49.7	1.4	1.1	0.3
BELGIUM	Brussels	Dutch, French	10,021,000	11,787 30 528	850.2 328.3	1.2	1.1	0.1
BOSNIA AND HERZEGOVINA	Sarajevo	Serbo-Croatian	4,397,000	19,741 51 129	222.7 86.0	1.4	0.6	0.8
BULGARIA	Sofia	Bulgarian, Turkish	8,985,000	42,855 110 994	209.7 81.0	1.2	1.2	0.0
CROATIA	Zagreb	Serbo-Croatian	4,808,000	21,829 56 538	220.3 85.0	1.2	1.1	0.1
CZECH REPUBLIC	Prague	Czech, Moravian, Slovak, Hungarian	10,323,000	30,450 78 864	339.0 130.9	1.4	1.2	0.2
DENMARK	Copenhagen	Danish	5,167,000	16,638 43 093	310.6 119.9	1.2	1.2	0.0
ESTONIA	Tallinn	Estonian, Russian	1,592,000	17,413 45 100	91.4 35.3	1.4	1.2	0.2
FINLAND	Helsinki	Finnish, Swedish	5,033,000	130,559 338 145	38.5 14.9	1.3	1.0	0.3
FRANCE	Paris	French, Arabic	57,289,000	210,026 543 965	272.8 105.3	1.4	0.9	0.5
GERMANY	Berlin	German, Turkish	79,122,000	137,822 356 957	574.1 221.7	1.1	1.1	0.0
GREECE	Athens	Greek	10,288,000	50,949 131 957	201.9 78.0	1.0	0.9	0.1
HUNGARY	Budapest	Hungarian, Romany	10,318,000	35,920 93 033	287.2 110.9	1.2	1.4	−0.2
ICELAND	Reykjavik	Icelandic	261,000	39,699 102 819	6.6 2.5	1.9	0.7	1.2
IRELAND	Dublin	English, Irish	3,519,000	27,137 70 285	129.7 50.1	1.5	0.9	0.6
ITALY	Rome	Italian, Sardinian	57,158,000	116,324 301 277	491.4 189.7	1.0	0.9	0.1

Country: all independent countries, as well as selected dependencies. **Principal Language(s):** all official languages, as well as other primary languages spoken by a substantial proportion of the population. **Pop. Density:** population density, computed as population divided by area; given per square mile and per square kilometer. **Natural Pop. Growth:** annual population increase per 100 people; does not include population change due to immigration or emigration.

COUNTRY	CAPITAL(S)	PRINCIPAL LANGUAGE(S)	POPULATION	AREA MI.² KM²	POP. DENSITY PER MI.² PER KM²	NATURAL POP. GROWTH PER 100 PEOPLE BIRTHS – DEATHS = % GAIN		
LATVIA	Riga	Latvian, Russian	2,685,000	24,900 64 500	107.8 41.6	1.4	1.3	0.1
LIECHTENSTEIN	Vaduz	German	30,000	62 160	477.4 185.0	1.3	0.6	0.7
LITHUANIA	Vilnius	Lithuanian, Russian, Polish	3,801,000	25,213 65 301	150.8 58.2	1.5	1.1	0.4
LUXEMBOURG	Luxembourg	Luxemburgian, French, Portuguese, Italian, French, German	387,000	999 2 586	387.4 149.7	1.2	1.0	0.2
MACEDONIA	Skopje	Macedonian, Albanian, Serbo-Croatian, Turkish	2,050,000	9,928 25 713	206.5 79.7	1.7	0.7	1.0
MALTA	Valletta	Maltese, English	360,000	122 316	2,950.8 1 139.2	1.5	0.8	0.7
MOLDOVA	Chisinau	Moldovan, Russian, Ukrainian, Gagauz	4,394,000	13,000 33 700	338.0 130.4	1.8	1.0	0.8
MONACO	Monaco	French, Italian, Monegasque, English	30,000	0.75 1.95	40,400.0 15 538.5	2.2	1.8	0.4
NETHERLANDS	Amsterdam, The Hague	Dutch, Frisian, Turkish, Arabic	15,163,000	16,163 41 863	938.1 362.2	1.3	0.9	0.4
NORWAY	Oslo	Norwegian	4,283,000	125,050 323 878	34.3 13.2	1.4	1.1	0.3
POLAND	Warsaw	Polish	38,429,000	120,727 312 683	318.3 122.9	1.5	1.0	0.5
PORTUGAL	Lisbon	Portuguese	10,429,000	35,672 92 389	292.4 112.9	1.2	0.9	0.3
ROMANIA	Bucharest	Romanian, Hungarian	23,332,000	91,699 237 500	254.4 98.2	1.5	1.1	0.4
RUSSIA	Moscow	Russian	149,469,000	6,592,800 17 075 400	22.7 8.8	1.3	1.1	0.2
SAN MARINO	San Marino	Italian	24,000	24 61	983.3 386.9	1.0	0.7	0.3
SLOVAKIA	Bratislava	Slovak, Hungarian, Czech	5,282,000	18,932 49 035	279.0 107.7	1.4	1.2	0.2
SLOVENIA	Ljubljana	Slovene, Serbo-Croatian	1,985,000	7,821 20 256	353.8 98.0	1.2	1.0	0.2
SPAIN	Madrid	Castilian Spanish, Catalan, Galician, Basque	39,085,000	194,898 504 783	200.5 77.4	1.1	0.8	0.3
SWEDEN	Stockholm	Swedish	8,673,000	173,732 449 964	49.9 19.3	1.4	1.1	0.3
SWITZERLAND	Bern	German, French, Italian, Romansch	6,911,000	15,943 41 293	433.5 167.4	1.2	0.9	0.3
UKRAINE	Kiev	Ukrainian, Russian	52,135,000	233,100 603 700	223.7 86.4	1.3	1.2	0.1
UNITED KINGDOM	London	English, Welsh, Scots-Gaelic	57,730,000	94,251 244 110	612.5 236.5	1.4	1.1	0.3
VATICAN CITY	Vatican City	Italian, Latin	1,000	0.17 0.44	4,576.5 1 768.2	0.0	0.0	0.0
YUGOSLAVIA	Belgrade	Serbo-Croatian, Albanian, Hungarian	10,394,000	39,449 102 173	263.5 101.7	1.5	0.9	0.6

North America

COUNTRY	CAPITAL(S)	PRINCIPAL LANGUAGE(S)	POPULATION	AREA MI.² KM²	POP. DENSITY PER MI.² PER KM²	BIRTHS	DEATHS	% GAIN
ANTIGUA AND BARBUDA	St. John's	English	64,000	171 442	374.3 144.8	1.4	0.5	0.9
ARUBA (Neth.)	Oranjestad	Dutch, Papiamento	69,000	75 193	921.3 358.0	1.8	0.6	1.1
BAHAMAS	Nassau	English, French	264,000	5,382 13 939	49.1 18.9	1.9	0.5	1.4

Country: all independent countries, as well as selected dependencies. **Principal Language(s):** all official languages, as well as other primary languages spoken by a substantial proportion of the population. **Pop. Density:** population density, computed as population divided by area; given per square mile and per square kilometer. **Natural Pop. Growth:** annual population increase per 100 people; does not include population change due to immigration or emigration.

COUNTRY	CAPITAL(S)	PRINCIPAL LANGUAGE(S)	POPULATION	AREA MI.² KM²	POP. DENSITY PER MI.² PER KM²	NATURAL POP. GROWTH PER 100 PEOPLE BIRTHS – DEATHS = % GAIN		
BARBADOS	Bridgetown	English	259,000	166 430	1,560.2 602.3	1.6	0.9	0.7
BELIZE	Belmopan	English, Spanish, Mayan, Garifuna	196,000	8,867 22 965	22.1 8.5	3.8	0.5	3.3
CANADA	Ottawa	English, French, Italian, German	27,737,000	3,849,674 9 970 610	7.2 2.8	1.4	0.7	0.7
COSTA RICA	San Jose	Spanish	3,161,000	19,730 51 100	160.2 61.9	2.8	0.4	2.4
CUBA	Havana	Spanish	10,848,000	42,804 110 861	253.4 97.9	1.8	0.6	1.2
DOMINICA	Roseau	English, French	72,000	18,704 48 443	399.4 154.2	3.0	0.7	2.3
DOMINICAN REPUBLIC	Santo Domingo	Spanish	7,471,000	18,704 48 443	399.4 154.2	3.0	0.7	2.3
EL SALVADOR	San Salvador	Spanish	5,460,000	8,124 21 041	672.1 259.5	3.4	0.8	2.6
GREENLAND (KALAALLIT NUNAAT) (Den.)	Godthab (Nuuk)	Greenlandic, Danish	57,000	840,000 2 175 600	0.1 0.0	2.2	0.8	1.4
GRENADA	St. George's	English	91,000	134 348	678.4 261.2	3.2	0.8	2.4
GUADELOUPE (Fr.)	Basse-Terre	French	400,000	687 1 780	582.2 224.7	2.0	0.6	1.4
GUATEMALA	Guatemala City	Spanish, Mayan, Black Carib	9,442,000	42,042 108 889	224.6 86.7	3.9	0.7	3.2
HAITI	Port-au-Prince	French	6,764,000	10,695 27 700	632.4 244.2	3.5	1.3	2.2
HONDURAS	Tegucigalpa	Spanish	4,996,000	43,277 112 088	115.4 44.6	3.8	0.7	3.1
JAMAICA	Kingston	English	2,445,000	4,244 10 991	576.1 222.5	2.5	0.6	1.9
MARTINIQUE (Fr.)	Fort-de-France	French	369,000	436 1 128	846.3 327.1	1.9	0.6	1.3
MEXICO	Mexico City	Spanish	84,439,000	756,066 1 958 201	111.7 43.1	3.3	0.5	2.8
NETHERLANDS ANTILLES (Neth.)	Willemstad	Dutch, Papiamento, English	191,000	308 800	620.1 238.8	2.4	0.6	1.5
NICARAGUA	Managua	Spanish, Miskito	4,131,000	50,464 130 700	81.9 31.6	3.9	0.7	3.2
PANAMA	Panama City	Spanish, English, Chibchan	2,515,000	29,157 75 517	86.3 33.3	2.5	0.5	2.0
PUERTO RICO (U.S.)	San Juan	Spanish, English	3,581,000	3,515 9 104	1,018.8 393.3	1.9	0.7	1.2
ST. KITTS AND NEVIS	Basseterre	English	43,000	104 269	414.4 160.2	2.2	1.1	1.1
ST. LUCIA	Castries	English, French	135,000	238 617	567.2 218.8	2.5	0.6	1.9
ST. VINCENT AND THE GRENADINES	Kingstown	English	109,000	150 389	726.7 280.2	2.6	0.6	2.0
TRINIDAD AND TOBAGO	Port-of-Spain	English	1,261,000	1,980 5 128	636.9 245.9	2.2	0.7	1.5
UNITED STATES OF AMERICA	Washington, D.C.	English, Spanish	255,414,000	3,679,192 9 529 063	69.4 26.8	1.6	0.9	0.7

Country: all independent countries, as well as selected dependencies. **Principal Language(s):** all official languages, as well as other primary languages spoken by a substantial proportion of the population. **Pop. Density:** population density, computed as population divided by area; given per square mile and per square kilometer. **Natural Pop. Growth:** annual population increase per 100 people; does not include population change due to immigration or emigration.

COUNTRY	CAPITAL(S)	PRINCIPAL LANGUAGE(S)	POPULATION	AREA MI.² KM²	POP. DENSITY PER MI.² PER KM²	NATURAL POP. GROWTH PER 100 PEOPLE BIRTHS – DEATHS = % GAIN		

South America

COUNTRY	CAPITAL(S)	PRINCIPAL LANGUAGE(S)	POPULATION	AREA MI.² / KM²	POP. DENSITY PER MI.² / PER KM²	BIRTHS	DEATHS	% GAIN
ARGENTINA	Buenos Aires	Spanish	33,070,000	1,073,518 / 2 780 400	30.8 / 11.9	2.0	0.9	1.1
BOLIVIA	La Paz, Sucre	Spanish, Quechua, Aymara	7,739,000	424,164 / 1 098 581	18.2 / 7.0	4.3	1.4	2.9
BRAZIL	Brasilia	Portuguese	151,381,000	3,286,500 / 8 511 996	46.1 / 17.8	2.8	0.8	2.0
CHILE	Santiago, Valparaiso	Spanish, Mapuche	13,599,000	292,135 / 756 626	46.6 / 18.0	2.3	0.6	1.7
COLOMBIA	Bogota	Spanish	34,252,000	440,831 / 1 141 748	77.7 / 30.0	2.7	0.7	2.0
ECUADOR	Quito	Spanish, Quechua	10,607,000	104,505 / 270 667	101.5 / 39.2	3.5	0.8	2.7
FRENCH GUIANA (Fr.)	Cayenne	French	123,000	33,399 / 86 504	3.7 / 1.4	3.0	0.5	2.5
GUYANA	Georgetown	English, Hindi	748,000	83,044 / 215 083	9.0 / 3.5	2.4	0.6	1.8
PARAGUAY	Asuncion	Guarani, Spanish, Portuguese	4,519,000	157,048 / 406 752	28.8 / 11.1	3.4	0.7	2.7
PERU	Lima	Spanish, Quechua, Aymara	22,454,000	496,225 / 1 285 216	45.2 / 17.5	3.3	0.8	2.5
SURINAME	Paramaribo	Sranantonga, Dutch	404,000	63,251 / 163 820	6.4 / 2.5	2.6	0.6	2.0
URUGUAY	Montevideo	Spanish	3,130,000	68,037 / 176 215	46.0 / 17.8	1.8	1.0	0.8
VENEZUELA	Caracas	Spanish	20,184,000	352,144 / 912 050	57.3 / 22.1	2.8	0.4	2.4

Country: all independent countries, as well as selected dependencies. **Principal Language(s):** all official languages, as well as other primary languages spoken by a substantial proportion of the population. **Pop. Density:** population density, computed as population divided by area; given per square mile and per square kilometer. **Natural Pop. Growth:** annual population increase per 100 people; does not include population change due to immigration or emigration.

acid rain Rain or snow that carries acids formed from chemical pollutants in the atmosphere.

Antarctic Circle An imaginary line of latitude located at 66½°S, approximately 1,630 miles (2620 kilometers) from the South Pole.

Arctic Circle An imaginary line of latitude located at 66½°N, approximately 1,630 miles (2620 kilometers) from the North Pole.

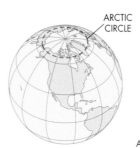 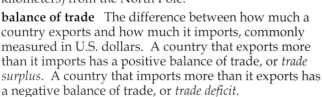 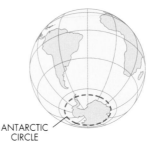

balance of trade The difference between how much a country exports and how much it imports, commonly measured in U.S. dollars. A country that exports more than it imports has a positive balance of trade, or *trade surplus*. A country that imports more than it exports has a negative balance of trade, or *trade deficit*.

center of population The location from which a country's population is equally distributed north, south, east, and west. The center of population changes as the population shifts from one region to another.

climate The usual weather conditions for a large area over a long period of time and through all seasons. Climate is affected by latitude, elevation, topography, ocean currents, and wind.

climograph Graph showing annual patterns of temperature and precipitation.

commodity One of the goods sold on the world market. Commodities may be agricultural products, manufactured items, or such natural resources as minerals.

deforestation Massive removal of trees from a forest.

elevation Height above sea level.

emigration Movement of people away from their native country or region to a new home elsewhere. The people moving away are called *emigrants*.

Equator An imaginary line that divides the earth into the Northern and Southern Hemispheres. All points along the Equator have a latitude of 0°.

European Community (EC) A group of 12 European nations whose main goal is to establish themselves for trading purposes as a single market. EC members are Belgium, Denmark, France, Germany, Greece, Ireland, Italy, Luxembourg, the Netherlands, Portugal, Spain, and the United Kingdom.

export The sale of goods to a foreign country.

fossil fuels Natural fuels that were formed from the remains of plants and animals over millions of years. Principal fossil fuels are petroleum, natural gas, and coal.

gross domestic product (GDP) Annual value of all goods and services produced within a country's borders. GDP includes production by foreign-owned facilities.

gross national product (GNP) Annual value of all goods and services produced by companies that are owned by a country's citizens. GNP includes production in facilities operated by the nation's citizens in other countries.

immigration Movement of people into a new country of residence. The people moving in are called *immigrants*.

imperialism Action taken by one country to control or influence another country or territory in order to gain economic or political advantage.

import The purchase of goods produced in a foreign country.

indigenous Native to a particular region. Indigenous peoples are related to the earliest inhabitants of a region.

land use How people use the earth's surface and natural resources for economic purposes. Regions are identified by the dominant form of economy, such as farming, herding, or manufacturing.

latitude Distance from the Equator measured in degrees. Lines of latitude, or *parallels*, are numbered north and south from the Equator and appear on maps as east-west lines.

life expectancy The average number of years that a group of people may expect to live based on the prevailing death rates for that population. Life expectancy reflects the group's general health and welfare.

literacy The ability to both read and write. The percentage of literate people is a good indicator of a country's educational level, although literacy standards vary by country.

longitude Distance from the Prime Meridian measured in degrees. Lines of longitude, or *meridians*, are numbered east and west from the Prime Meridian and appear on maps as north-south lines.

map projection Any system for drawing lines of latitude and longitude onto a map. Projections are never completely accurate, distorting either sizes or shapes of the earth's land and water features.

natural population growth Annual population increase for a region or country. It is the difference between the number of births and the number of deaths and does not include change due to population movement.

natural vegetation The type of vegetation that can grow in a specific region's climate and soil without benefit of human intervention or cultivation.

Oceania Collective name for islands of the central and southern Pacific Ocean, usually including New Zealand and sometimes also including Australia.

Organization of Petroleum Exporting Countries (OPEC) Association of 12 nations that control most of the world's known oil reserves. OPEC members are Algeria, Gabon, Indonesia, Iran, Iraq, Kuwait, Libya, Nigeria, Qatar, Saudi Arabia, United Arab Emirates, and Venezuela.

ozone A form of oxygen that occurs naturally in the atmosphere in small amounts. The layer of ozone in the upper atmosphere blocks most of the sun's harmful ultraviolet rays.

precipitation Water from the atmosphere that accumulates on the earth's surface as dew, rain, hail, sleet, or snow. For annual measures, ten inches of snow, sleet, or hail are counted as one inch of rain.

Prime Meridian The 0° meridian, which passes through Greenwich, England.

Sahel The drought-ridden area south of Africa's Sahara and extending east-west between Somalia and Senegal.

staple food A foodstuff that constitutes a major part of the diet for a region's population.

Tropic of Cancer An imaginary line of latitude located at 23½°N. It marks the northern boundary of the earth's tropical zone.

Tropic of Capricorn An imaginary line of latitude located at 23½°S. It marks the southern boundary of the earth's tropical zone.

wetlands A transition zone between land and water where the water level remains near or above the ground's surface for most of the year. Wetlands include swamps, marshes, and bogs.

Abbreviations

adm.	administered	km	kilometers	Oreg.	Oregon
Ala.	Alabama	Ky.	Kentucky	Pa.	Pennsylvania
Alb.	Albania	L., l.	Lake	Pen., pen.	Peninsula
Am. Samoa	American Samoa	La.	Louisiana	Pk., pk.	Peak
Ang.	Angola	Lat.	Latvia	Port.	Portugal
Arg.	Argentina	lat.	latitude	poss.	possession
Ariz.	Arizona	Liech.	Liechtenstein	Prov., prov.	Province
Ark.	Arkansas	Lith.	Lithuania	Pt.	Point
Aus.	Austria	long.	longitude	R., r.	River
Austr.	Australia	Lux.	Luxembourg	R.I.	Rhode Island
Azer.	Azerbaijan	m	meters	Ra.	Range
Bos.	Bosnia and Herzegovina	Mac.	Macedonia	Res., res.	Reservoir
		Mass.	Massachusetts	S. Afr.	South Africa
C.	Cape	Md.	Maryland	S. Dak.	South Dakota
C. Afr. Rep.	Central African Republic	Mex.	Mexico	S.C.	South Carolina
		mi.	miles	Sl., Slovak.	Slovakia
Calif.	California	Mich.	Michigan	Slov.	Slovenia
Colo.	Colorado	Minn.	Minnesota	Sp.	Spain
Conn.	Connecticut	Miss.	Mississippi	sq.	square
Cro.	Croatia	Mo.	Missouri	St., Ste.	Saint, Sainte
Cz., Cz. Rep.	Czech Republic	Mont.	Montana	Str.	Strait
D.C.	District of Columbia	Mt., Mts.	Mount, Mont, Mountain, Mountains	Switz.	Switzerland
Del.	Delaware			Tenn.	Tennessee
Den.	Denmark	N.C.	North Carolina	Terr., terr.	Territory
Dom. Rep.	Dominican Republic	N. Dak.	North Dakota	Tex.	Texas
Eq. Guinea	Equatorial Guinea	N.H.	New Hampshire	U.A.E.	United Arab Emirates
Est.	Estonia	N.J.	New Jersey	U.K.	United Kingdom
Fk.	Fork	N.M.	New Mexico	U.S.	United States
Fla.	Florida	N.P.	National Park	US$	United States dollars
Fr.	France, French	N.W.T.	Northwest Territories	U.S.S.R.	Union of Soviet Socialist Republics
ft.	feet	N.Y.	New York		
Ga.	Georgia	N.Z.	New Zealand	Va.	Virginia
I., Is.	Island, Islands	Nebr.	Nebraska	Vt.	Vermont
Ill.	Illinois	Neth.	Netherlands	W. Va.	West Virginia
Ind.	Indiana	Nev	Nevada	Wash.	Washington
Intl.	International	Nor.	Norway	Wis.	Wisconsin
It.	Italy	O.	Ocean	Wyo.	Wyoming
Kans.	Kansas	Okla.	Oklahoma	Yugo.	Yugoslavia

INDEX

The index lists all the place names that appear in the book. Each entry includes a brief description of what or where it is, its latitude and longitude, and its main page reference. Many of the entries also include phonetic pronunciations. The key to the system of phonetic respelling is given on the inside back cover, so it can be turned to easily.

The entry for a physical feature is alphabetized by the proper part of its name, not by the descriptive part. For example, Lake Superior is listed as *Superior, L.,* and Mount Etna is listed as *Etna, Mt.* The entry for a city, however, is alphabetized by the first word in its name, no matter what it is, so that the city of Lake Charles, Louisiana, is listed as *Lake Charles.* Similarly, foreign names such as Rio Grande are alphabetized by the first word in the name.

Names beginning with *St.* are spelled *Saint* in the index. Abbreviations that are used in the index and in other parts of the book are listed on page 149.

Name (Pronunciation), *Description* (Lat., Long.) — Page

A

Aachen (AH kuhn), *Germany* (51°N, 6°E) 99
Aba (ah BAH), *Nigeria* (5°N, 7°E) 108
Abadan, *Iran* (30°N, 49°E) 115
Abeche, *Chad* (14°N, 21°E) 114
Abeokuta (AB ee OH kuht uh), *Nigeria* (7°N, 3°E) 108
Aberdeen, *Scotland* (57°N, 2°W) 98
Aberdeen, *S. Dak.* (46°N, 99°W) 62
Aberdeen, *Wash.* (47°N, 124°W) 60
Aberystwyth (AB uh RIS TWITH), *Wales* (52°N, 4°W) 98
Abidjan (AB ih JAHN), *Côte d'Ivoire* (5°N, 4°W) 108
Abilene (AB uh LEEN), *Kans.* (39°N, 97°W) 64
Abilene, *Tex.* (32°N, 100°W) 66
Abitibi, L. (AB uh TIHB ee), *Ontario* (49°N, 80°W) 46
Abitibi R. , *Ontario* (51°N, 81°W) 46
Absaroka Range (ab SAHR uh kuh), *Wyo.* (44°N, 110°W) 61
Abu Dhabi (AHB oo DAHB ee), *United Arab Emirates* (24°N, 55°E) 115
Abuja (ah BOO juh), *Nigeria* (9°N, 8°E) 108
Abuna R. (ah boo NAH), *South America* (10°S, 67°W) 90
Acadia N.P. (uh KAY dee uh), *Maine* (44°N, 68°W) 73
Acapulco (AH kah POOL koh), *Mexico* (17°N, 100°W) 84
Accra, *Ghana* (6°N, 0°) 108
Aconcagua (AH kawng KAH gwah), *mt. in South America* (33°S, 70°W) 88
Ad Dammam, *Saudi Arabia* (27°N, 50°E) 115
Adamaoua Plateau (AH duh MAH wuh), *Africa* (8°N, 15°E) 108
Adams, Mt., *Wash.* (46°N, 121°W) 60
Adana, *Turkey* (37°N, 35°E) 115
Addis Ababa (AD ihs AB uh buh), *Ethiopia* (9°N, 39°E) 107
Adelaide (AD uh LAYD), *Australia* (35°S, 138°E) 133
Aden (AHD uhn), *Yemen* (13°N, 45°E) 115
Aden, Gulf of, *Arabian Sea* (13°N, 48°E) 115
Adige R. (AHD jay), *Italy* (46°N, 11°E) 99
Adirondack Mts., *N.Y.* (44°N, 74°W) 72
Admiralty I., *Papua New Guinea* (2°S, 147°E) 130
Adriatic Sea, *Europe* (44°N, 13°E) 99
Aegean Sea, *Mediterranean Sea* (38°N, 25°E) 99
Afghanistan, *country in Asia* (34°N, 65°E) 120
Africa, *continent* 7
Agadez, *Niger* (17°N, 8°E) 107
Agalega Is., *Indian Ocean* (10°S, 57°E) 106
Agra, *India* (27°N, 78°E) 122
Agrinion (ah GREEN yawn), *Greece* (39°N, 21°E) 99
Aguanus R. (ah GWAHN uhs), *Quebec* (50°N, 62°W) 47
Aguasabon R., *Ontario* (49°N, 87°W) 46
Aguascalientes (AH wuh SKAHL YEN tuhs), *Mexico* (22°N, 102°W) 84
Aguja, Point (ah GOO hah), *Peru* (6°S, 81°W) 90
Agulhas, Cape (uh GUHL uhs), *South Africa* (35°S, 20°E) 109
Agulhas Negras, *mt. in Brazil* (22°S, 46°W) 88

Ahaggar Mts., *Africa* (24°N, 6°E) 114
Ahmadabad, *India* (23°N, 73°E) 122
Ahvaz, *Iran* (31°N, 49°E) 115
Air Mts., *Niger* (18°N, 8°E) 106
Aix-en-Provence (AYK SAHN pruh VAHNS), *France* (44°N, 5°E) 98
Ajaccio (ah YAHCH OH), *Corsica* (42°N, 9°E) 98
Akimiski I., *James Bay* (53°N, 80°W) 46
Akita (ah KEET uh), *Japan* (40°N, 140°E) 125
Akron, *Ohio* (41°N, 81°W) 71
Al Aziziyah (al AZ ee ZEE yuh), *Libya* (33°N, 13°E) 114
Al Fashir (AL FAH shuhr), *Sudan* (14°N, 25°E) 115
Al Fayyum (AL fay YOOM), *Egypt* (29°N, 31°E) 115
Al Jawf, *Libya* (24°N, 23°E) 115
Al Minya, *Egypt* (28°N, 31°E) 115
Alabama, *state in U.S.* (33°N, 87°W) 10
Alabama R., *Ala.* (32°N, 88°W) 68
Alamogordo (AL uh muh GAWRD oh), *N. Mex.* (33°N, 106°W) 59
Aland Is., *Finland* (60°N, 21°E) 95
Alaska, *state in U.S.* (65°N, 155°W) 57
Alaska, Gulf of, *Pacific O.* (59°N, 145°W) 57
Alaska Pen., *Alaska* (55°N, 164°W) 57
Alaska Range, *Alaska* (63°N, 150°W) 57
Albania, *Europe* (41°N 20°E) 99
Albany, *Ga.* (32°N, 84°W) 11
Albany, *N.Y.* (43°N, 74°W) 72
Albany, *Oreg.* (45°N, 123°W) 60
Albany R., *Ontario* (51°N, 82°W) 46
Albemarle Sound, *N.C.* (36°N, 76°W) 71
Albert, L., *Africa* (2°N, 31°E) 110
Albert Nile, *r. in Uganda* (3°N, 31°E) 110
Alberta, *prov. in Canada* (57°N, 115°W) 44-45
Alborg (AWL BAWRG), *Denmark* (57°N, 10°E) 98
Albuquerque (AL buh kur kee), *N. Mex.* (35°N, 107°W) 59
Albury, *Australia* (36°S, 147°E) 133
Aldabra Is., *Indian O.* (9°S, 46°E) 106
Aldan R., *Russia* (63°N, 133°E) 101
Alenquer (ah leng KEHR), *Brazil* (2°S, 55°W) 90
Alenuihaha Channel (AHL uh NOO ee HAH HAH), *Hawaii* (20°N, 156°W) 57
Aleppo, *Syria* (36°N, 37°E) 115
Aleutian Is., (uh LOO shuhn), *Alaska* (52°N, 180°) 57
Alexander Archipelago, *Alaska* (57°N, 135°W) 57
Alexander I., *Antarctica* (70°S, 70°W) 137
Alexandria, *Egypt* (31°N, 30°E) 115
Alexandria, *La.* (32°N, 93°W) 67
Alexandria, *Minn.* (46°N, 95°W) 62
Alexandria, *Va.* (39°N, 77°W) 71
Alexandrina, L., *Australia* (36°S, 139°E) 133
Algeria, *country in Africa* (28°N, 3°E) 114
Algiers (al JEERS), *Algeria* (37°N, 3°E) 114
Alice Springs, *Australia* (24°S, 134°E) 131
Allahabad (AL uh huh BAD), *India* (26°N, 82°E) 122
Allatoona L., *Ga.* (34°N, 85°W) 68
Allegheny Mts. (AL uh GAY nee), *U.S.* (38°N, 80°W) 71

Allegheny Plateau, *U.S.* (39°N, 80°W) 71
Allegheny Res., *U.S.* (42°N, 79°W) 72
Allegheny R., *Pa.* (41°N, 80°W) 72
Allentown, *Pa.* (41°N, 75°W) 72
Alliance, *Nebr.* (42°N, 103°W) 64
Alliance, *Ohio* (41°N, 81°W) 71
Allier R. (al YAY), *France* (46°N, 3°E) 98
Alma, *Quebec* (48°N, 72°W) 47
Almaty, *Kazakhstan* (43°N, 77°E) 100
Alpena, *Mich.* (45°N, 83°W) 63
Alpine, *Tex.* (30°N, 104°W) 66
Alps, *mt. range in Europe* (46°N, 10°E) 99
Alsace (al SAS), *region of France* (48°N, 8°E) 98
Altai Mts. (AL ty), *Asia* (49°N, 90°E) 118
Altamaha R., *Ga.* (32°N, 82°W) 69
Altamira, *Brazil* (3°S, 52°W) 90
Altamonte Springs (AL tuh MAHNT), *Fla.* (29°N, 81°W) 69
Alton, *Ill.* (39°N, 90°W) 65
Altona, *Manitoba* (49°N, 98°W) 45
Altoona, *Pa.* (40°N, 78°W) 72
Altun Shan (ahl toon shahn), *mts. in China* (40°N, 90°E) 124
Alvaro Abregon Res., *Mexico* (28°N, 110°W) 82
Am Timan, *Chad* (11°N, 20°E) 107
Amarillo, *Tex.* (35°N, 102°W) 66
Amazon Basin, *South America* (4°S, 65°W) 58
Amazon, Mouths of the, *Brazil* (0°, 50°W) 88
Amazon R., *South America* (3°S, 59°W) 90
American Falls Res., *Idaho* (43°N, 113°W) 61
American Samoa, *poss. of U.S.* (14°S, 170°W) 135
Americus, *Ga.* (32° 84°W) 69
Amery Ice Shelf, *Antarctica* (70°S, 70°E) 137
Ames, *Iowa* (42°N, 94°W) 65
Amherst, *Nova Scotia* (46°N, 64°W) 47
Amiens (AM ee uhnz), *France* (50°N, 2°E) 98
Amirante Is. (AM uh RANT), *Indian O.* (5°S, 53°E) 106
Amisk L., *Saskatchewan* (55°N, 102°W) 45
Amistad Res., *Mexico and U.S.* (30°N, 101°W) 66
Amman, *Jordan* (32°N, 36°E) 115
Amritsar (uhm RIHT suhr), *India* (32°N, 75°E) 122
Amsterdam, *Netherlands* (53°N, 5°E) 98
Amsterdam I., *Indian O.* (38°S, 78°E) 11
Amu Darya (AHM oo DAHR yuh), *r. in Asia* (40°N, 63°E) 100
Amundsen Gulf, *Beaufort Sea* (71°N, 125°W) 40
Amundsen Sea, *Antarctica* (70°S, 110°W) 137
Amur R. (ah MOOR), *Asia* (53°N, 123°E) 119
An Nafud (AN nuh FOOD), *desert in Saudi Arabia* (28°N, 40°E) 115
Anadyr (an uh DIR), *Russia* (65°N, 178°E) 101
Anadyr, Gulf of, *Bering Sea* (65°N, 178°W) 101
Anaheim (AN uh HYM), *Calif.* (34°N, 118°W) 58
Anatolia (AN uh TOH lee uh), *region of Turkey* (38°N, 30°E) 115
Anchorage, *Alaska* (61°N, 150°W) 57
Ancona (ang KOH nuh), *Italy* (44°N, 14°E) 99
Andaman Is., *Bay of Bengal* (12°N, 93°E) 122
Andaman Sea, *Indian O.* (12°N, 96°E) 122
Anderson, *Ind.* (40°N, 86°W) 70
Anderson, *S.C.* (35°N, 83°W) 69

Name (Pronunciation), Description (Lat, Long)	Page

Andes, *mt. range in South America* (10°S, 77°W) — 88
Andorra, *country in Europe* (43°N, 2°E) — 98
Andorra la Vella (an DAWR uh lah VEL ah), *Andorra* (43°N, 2°E) — 98
Andros I., *Atlantic O.* (24°N, 78°W) — 83
Androscoggin R., *Maine* (44°N, 71°W) — 73
Anegada Passage, *Caribbean Sea* (18°N, 64°W) — 83
Angel de la Guarda I., *Mexico* (29°N, 113°W) — 82
Angel Falls, *waterfall in Venezuela* (6°N, 63°W) — 90
Angelina, *Tex.* (30°N, 94°W) — 67
Angers (ahn ZHAY), *France* (47°N, 1°W) — 98
Angola, *country in Africa* (12°S, 17°E) — 107
Angostura Res., *Mexico* (16°N, 92°W) — 82
Anguilla (ang GWIL uh), *island in Caribbean Sea* (18°N, 63°W) — 83
Anju (AHN joo), *N. Korea* (40°N, 126°E) — 125
Ankara, *Turkey* (40°N, 33°E) — 115
Ann, Cape, *Mass.* (43°N, 71°W) — 73
Ann Arbor, *Mich.* (42°N, 84°W) — 63
Annaba (an NAHB uh), *Algeria* (37°N, 8°E) — 114
Annamite Mts., *Asia* (17°N, 106°E) — 123
Annapolis, *Md.* (39°N, 76°W) — 71
Anniston, *Ala.* (34°N, 86°W) — 68
Annobon, *island in Atlantic O.* (2°S, 6°E) — 108
Antalya (ANT uhl YAH), *Turkey* (37°N, 31°E) — 115
Antananarivo (AHN tuh NAH nuh REE voh), *Madagascar* (19°S, 47°E) — 107
Antarctic Pen., *Antarctica* (66°S, 60°W) — 137
Antarctica, *continent* — 7
Anticosti I., *Quebec* (49°N, 62°W) — 47
Antigua and Barbuda, *country in Caribbean Sea* (18°N, 62°W) — 85
Antioch, *Turkey* (36°N, 36°E) — 115
Antofagasta, *Chile* (24°S, 70°W) — 89
Antwerp, *Belgium* (51°N, 4°E) — 98
Aomori (OW muh ree), *Japan* (41°N, 141°E) — 125
Apalachee Bay, *Fla.* (30°N, 85°W) — 69
Apalachicola (AP uh LACH uh KOHL uh), *Fla.* (30°N, 85°W) — 68
Apalachicola R., *Fla.* (30°N, 85°W) — 68
Apaporis R. (AHP uh POHR ees), *Colombia* (1°S, 70°W) — 90
Apennines, *mt. range in Italy* (43°N, 13°E) — 99
Apostle Is. (uh PAHS uhl), *L. Superior* (47°N, 91°W) — 63
Appalachian Mts., *U.S.* (37°N, 82°W) — 53
Appleton, *Wis.* (44°N, 88°W) — 63
Apure R. (uh POOR uh), *Venezuela* (8°N, 68°W) — 90
Aquitaine Basin, *France* (44°N, 1°W) — 98
Arabian Desert, *Egypt* (26°N, 34°E) — 115
Arabian Pen., *Asia* (20°N, 45°E) — 115
Arabian Sea, *Indian O.* (15°N, 65°E) — 118
Aracaju (AR uh kuh ZHOO), *Brazil* (11°S, 37°W) — 89
Arafura Sea (ar uh FOOR uh), *Indian O.* (9°S, 135°E) — 130
Aral Sea (AR uhl), *Asia* (45°N, 60°E) — 118
Aralsk, *Kazakhstan* (47°N, 62°E) — 100
Ararat, Mt., *Turkey* (40°N, 44°E) — 115
Arbuckle Mts., *Okla.* (34°N, 97°W) — 67
Arcadia, *Fla.* (27°N, 84°W) — 69
Archangel (AHRK AYN juhl), *Russia* (65°N, 41°E) — 100
Arches N. P., *Utah* (39°N, 110°W) — 59
Arctic Ocean — 7
Ardennes (ahr DEN), *mts. in Belgium* (50°N, 5°E) — 98
Ardmore, *Okla.* (34°N, 97°W) — 67
Arequipa (AR uh KEE pah), *Peru* (16°S, 72°W) — 89
Argentina, *country in South America* (35°S, 65°W) — 89
Arhus (AWR hoos), *Denmark* (56°N, 10°E) — 96
Arica (uh REE kuh), *Chile* (19°S, 70°W) — 89
Aripuana R. (AR uhp wuh NA), *Brazil* (5°S, 60°W) — 90
Arizona, *state in U.S.* (34°N, 114°W) — 58-59

Arkabutla L. (ahr kuh BUHT lay), *Miss.* (35°N, 90°W) — 68
Arkansas, *state in U.S.* (35°N, 94°W) — 67
Arkansas R., *U.S.* (37°N, 93°W) — 52-53
Arlington, *Tex.* (33°N, 97°W) — 67
Arlington, *Va.* (39°N, 77°W) — 71
Arlington Heights, *Ill.* (42°N, 88°W) — 65
Armenia, *country in Asia* (40°N, 45°E) — 100
Armstrong, *Ontario* (50°N, 89°W) — 46
Arnhem (AHRN hem), *Netherlands* (52°N, 6°E) — 98
Arnhem Land, *Australia* (13°S, 134°E) — 130
Aroostook R. (uh ROOS tuhk), *Maine* (47°N, 68°W) — 73
Aru Is., *Arafura Sea* (6°S, 134°E) — 130
Aruba, *overseas part of Neth.* (12°N, 70°W) — 83
Arusha (uh ROOSH uh), *Tanzania* (3°S, 37°E) — 110
Arvada, *Colo.* (40°N, 105°W) — 59
Arviat, *Northwest Terr.* (62°N, 94°W) — 45
Asahi, Mt. (ah SAH hee) *Japan* (44°N, 143°E) — 125
Asahikawa (ah SAH hee KAY wuh), *Japan* (44°N, 142°E) — 125
Asansol (AHS uhn SOHL), *India* (24°N, 87°E) — 122
Asbury Park, *N.J.* (40°N, 74°W) — 72
Ascension (uh SEHN shuhn), *island in Atlantic O.* (8°S, 14°W) — 106
Aseb, *Eritrea* (13°N, 44°E) — 115
Asheboro, *N.C.* (36°N, 80°W) — 71
Asheville, *N.C.* (36°N, 83°W) — 70-71
Asheweig R., *Ontario* (59°N, 87°W) — 46
Ashgabat, *Turkmenistan* (38°N, 58°E) — 100
Ashland, *Ky.* (38°N, 83°W) — 70
Ashland, *Wis.* (47°N, 91°W) — 63
Ashtabula (ASH tuh BYOO luh), *Ohio* (42°N, 81°W) — 71
Ashuanipi, L. (ASH wuh NIHP ee), *Newfoundland* (52°N, 67°W) — 47
Ashuapmushuan R. (uh SHAH muhsh WAHN), *Quebec* (49°N, 73°W) — 47
Asia, *continent* — 7
Asir, *region of Saudi Arabia* (18°N, 42°E) — 115
Asmara, *Ethiopia* (15°N, 39°E) — 107
Aspen, *Colo.* (39°N, 107°W) — 59
Assateague I. (AS uh TEEG), *Atlantic O.* (38°N, 75°W) — 71
Assiniboine, Mt. (uh SIHN uh BOYN), *British Columbia* (51°N, 116°W) — 44
Assiniboine R., *Canada* (52°N, 102°W) — 45
Astoria, *Oreg.* (46°N, 124°W) — 40
Astrakhan, *Russia* (46°N, 48°E) — 100
Asuncion (AH SOON see awn), *Paraguay* (25°S, 57°W) — 89
Aswan, *Egypt* (24°N, 33°E) — 115
Aswan High Dam, *Egypt* (24°N, 33°E) — 115
Asyut (AS ee YOOT) *Egypt* (27°N, 31°E) — 115
At Taif (at TAY if), *Saudi Arabia* (21°N, 41°E) — 115
Atacama Desert, *South America* (23°S, 69°W) — 88
Atbara R., *Africa* (17°N, 35°E) — 106
Atchafalaya Bay (uh CHAF uh LY uh), *La.* (30°N, 92°W) — 67
Atchafalaya R., *La.* (31°N, 92°W) — 67
Atchison, *Kans.* (40°N, 95°W) — 65
Athabasca, L., *Canada* (60°N, 109°W) — 45
Athabasca R., *Canada* (58°N, 111°W) — 45
Athens, *Ga.* (34°N, 83°W) — 69
Athens, *Greece* (38°N, 24°E) — 99
Athens, *Ohio* (39°N, 82°W) — 71
Atikokan, *Ontario* (49°N, 92°W) — 46
Atikonak, L., *Newfoundland* (52°N, 64°W) — 47
Atlanta, *Ga.* (34°N, 84°W) — 68-69
Atlantic City, *N.J.* (39°N, 75°W) — 72
Atlantic Coastal Plain, *U.S.* (32°N, 81°W) — 53
Atlantic Ocean — 7
Atlas Mts., *Africa* (32°N, 6°W) — 114
Attawapiskat (AT uh wuh PIHS kuht), *Ontario* (53°N, 82°W) — 46
Attawapiskat R., *Ontario* (53°N, 86°W) — 46

Attikamagen L., *Newfoundland* (55°N, 67°W) — 47
Attleboro, *Mass.* (42°N, 71°W) — 73
Atyrau, *Kazakhstan* (47°N, 52°E) — 100
Au Sable R. (oh SAY buhl), *Mich.* (45°N, 84°W) — 63
Au Sable R. , *N.Y.* (44°N, 74°W) — 72
Auburn (AW buhrn), *Ala.* (33°N, 85°W) — 68
Auburn, *Maine* (44°N, 70°W) — 73
Auburn, *Nebr.* (40°N, 96°W) — 65
Auburn, *N.Y.* (43°N, 77°W) — 72
Auburn, *Wash.* (47°N, 122°W) — 60
Auckland (AWK luhnd), *New Zealand* (37°S, 175°E) — 131
Auglaize R. (oh GLAYZ), *Ohio* (41°N, 84°W) — 70
Augsburg (AWGZ buhrg), *Germany* (48°N, 11°E) — 99
Augusta, *Ga.* (33°N, 82°W) — 69
Augusta, *Maine* (44°N, 70°W) — 73
Aurangabad (ow RUNG uh BAHD), *India* (20°N, 76°E) — 122
Aurora, *Colo.* (40°N, 105°W) — 59
Aurora, *Ill.* (42°N, 88°W) — 65
Austin, *Minn.* (44°N, 93°W) — 63
Austin, *Tex.* (30°N, 98°W) — 67
Australia, *country and continent* — 7
Australian Alps, *Australia* (37°S, 148°E) — 133
Australian Capital Terr., *Australia* (36°S, 149°E) — 133
Austria, *country in Europe* (47°N, 14°E) — 99
Avignon (ah vee NYAWN), *France* (44°N, 5°E) — 98
Axel Heiberg I., *Arctic O.* (80°N, 92°W) — 43
Ayr, *Scotland* (55°N, 5°W) — 98
Azerbaijan, *country in Europe and Asia* (41°N, 48°E) — 100
Azores, *islands in Atlantic O.* (38°N, 25°W) — 106
Azov, Sea of, *Europe* (46°N, 37°E) — 95

B

B. Everett Jordan L., *N.C.* (36°N, 79°W) — 71
Babine L. (BAH been), *British Columbia* (55°N, 126°W) — 44
Babol (bah BOHL), *Iran* (37°N, 53°E) — 115
Bad R., *S. Dak.* (44°N, 101°W) — 62
Badlands, *S. Dak.* (44°N, 103°W) — 62
Badlands N.P., *S. Dak.* (44°N, 102°W) — 62
Baffin Bay, *Arctic O.* (74°N, 65°W) — 41
Baffin I., *Baffin Bay* (70°N, 72°W) — 41
Baghdad, *Iraq* (33°N, 44°E) — 115
Bahama Is., *Atlantic O.* (24°N, 76°W) — 83
Bahamas, *country in Atlantic O.* (24°N, 76°W) — 85
Bahia Blanca (bu HEE uh BLANG kuh), *Argentina* (39°S, 62°W) — 89
Bahrain, *country in Asia* (27°N, 51°E) — 115
Baie-Comeau (bay KOH moh), *Quebec* (49°N, 68°W) — 47
Baikal, L., *Russia* (52°N, 105°E) — 100
Baja California (BAH hah), *region of Mexico* (30°N, 115°W) — 82
Baker, *Ore.* (45°N, 118°W) — 60
Baker Lake, *Northwest Terr.* (65°N, 96°W) — 42
Bakersfield, *Calif.* (35°N, 119°W) — 58
Bakhtaran, *Iran* (34°N, 47°E) — 115
Baku, *Azerbaijan* (40°N, 50°E) — 100
Balabac Strait (buh LAHB AHK), *Borneo and Palawan* (8°N, 117°E) — 123
Balaton (BAL uh TAHN), *lake in Hungary* (47°N, 18°E) — 99
Baldy Peak, *Ariz.* (34°N, 110°W) — 59
Balearic Is., *Mediterranean Sea* (39°N, 3°E) — 114
Balearic Sea, *Europe* (40°N, 2°E) — 114
Baleine, River de la, *Quebec* (55°N, 77°W) — 46-47
Bali, *island in Flores Sea* (8°S, 105°E) — 130
Balkan Mts., *Europe* (43°N, 24°E) — 99
Balkan Pen., *Europe* (42°N, 25°E) — 95
Balkhash, *Kazakhstan* (47°N, 75°E) — 100
Balkhash, L., *Kazakhstan* (47°N, 75°E) — 100

Name (Pronunciation), *Description* (Lat., Long.)	Page
Ballarat, *Australia* (38°S, 144°E)	133
Balmertown, *Ontario* (51°N, 94°W)	46
Balsas R., *Mexico* (18°N, 100°W)	82
Baltic Sea, *Europe* (55°N, 18°E)	94-95
Baltimore, *Md.* (39°N, 77°W)	71
Baluchistan (buh LOO chih STAN), *region of Pakistan* (27°N, 66°E)	122
Bamako, *Mali* (13°N, 8°W)	107
Bamenda, *Cameroon* (6°N, 10°E)	108
Bancroft, *Ontario* (45°N, 78°W)	46
Banda Sea, *Indian O.* (5°S, 128°E)	130
Bandar Seri Begawan, *Brunei* (5°N, 115°E)	123
Bandar-e Abbas, *Iran* (27°N, 56°E)	115
Bandung, *Indonesia* (7°S, 108°E)	31
Banff, *Alberta* (51°N, 115°W)	44
Banff N. P. (BAMF), *Alberta* (51°N, 116°W)	44
Bangalore, *India* (13°N, 78°E)	122
Bangka, *island in Karimata Strait* (2°S, 106°E)	130
Bangkok, *Thailand* (14°N, 100°E)	123
Bangladesh, *country in Asia* (24°N, 90°E)	122
Bangor, *Maine* (45°N, 69°W)	73
Bangui (bahng GEE), *Central African Republic* (4°N, 19°E)	107
Bangweulu, L. (BANG wee OO loo), *Zambia* (11°S, 30°E)	106
Banja Luka (BAHN yuh LOO kuh), *Bosnia and Herzegovina* (45°N, 17°E)	99
Banjarmasin (bahn jur MAH sihn), *Indonesia* (3°S, 114°E)	131
Banjul (BAHN jool), *Gambia* (13°N, 17°W)	108
Banks I., *Arctic O.* (73°N, 120°W)	42
Banks I., *Hecate Strait* (53°N, 130°W)	44
Banks Pen., *New Zealand* (44°S, 173°E)	130
Baotou (bow toh), *China* (40°N, 110°E)	124
Bar Harbor, *Maine* (44°N, 68°W)	73
Baranof I., *Gulf of Alaska* (57°N, 135°W)	57
Barbados (bahr BAY dohz), *country in Caribbean Sea* (14°N, 59°W)	85
Barberton, *Ohio* (41°N, 82°W)	71
Barcelona (bahr suh LOH nuh), *Spain* (41°N, 2°E)	114
Bardai (bahr DY), *Chad* (22°N, 17°E)	107
Bareeda, *Somalia* (12°N, 51°E)	107
Bareilly (buh RAY lee), *India* (28°N, 79°E)	122
Barents Sea (BAR uhnts), *Arctic O.* (69°N, 40°E)	95
Bari, *Italy* (41°N, 17°E)	99
Barkley, L., *U.S.* (37°N, 88°W)	71
Barkly Tableland, *plateau in Australia* (16°S, 134°E)	130
Barlee, L., *Australia* (31°S, 121°E)	130
Barnaul (bahr nuh OOL), *Russia* (53°N, 83°E)	100
Barnstable, *Mass.* (42°N, 70°W)	73
Barquisimeto (BAHR kee see MAY toh), *Venezuela* (10°N, 69°W)	90
Barranquilla (BAHR uhn KEE uh), *Colombia* (11°N, 75°W)	90
Barrie, *Ontario* (44°N, 80°W)	46
Barrow, Point, *Alaska* (71°N, 156°W)	57
Barrow R., *Ireland* (52°N, 7°W)	98
Barstow (BAHR stoh), *Calif.* (35°N, 117°W)	58
Bartholomew Bayou, *r. in U.S.* (33°N, 92°W)	67
Bartlesville, *Okla.* (37°N, 96°W)	67
Bartlett, *Tenn.* (37°N, 90°W)	70
Basel (BAHZ uhl), *Switzerland* (48°N, 8°E)	99
Baskatong Res., *Quebec* (47°N, 76°W)	47
Basra, *Iraq* (31°N, 48°E)	115
Bass Strait, *Australia and Tasmania* (40°S, 145°E)	133
Bassein (buh SAYN), *Burma* (17°N, 95°E)	123
Bastia, *Corsica* (43°N, 9°E)	98
Bastrop, *La.* (33°N, 92°W)	67
Bata, *Equatorial Guinea* (2°N, 10°E)	108
Batabano Gulf (baht uh buh NOH), *Caribbean Sea* (22°N, 83°W)	83
Bath, *England* (51°N, 2°W)	98
Bathurst (BATH urst), *Australia* (34°S, 150°E)	133
Bathurst, *New Brunswick* (48°N, 66°W)	47
Bathurst I., *Arctic O.* (76°N, 100°W)	40
Batna, *Algeria* (36°N, 6°E)	114
Baton Rouge (BAT uhn ROOZH), *La.* (31°N, 91°W)	67
Battle Creek, *Mich.* (42°N, 85°W)	63
Battle R., *Alberta* (52°N, 112°W)	44-45
Batumi, *Georgia* (41°N, 42°E)	100
Bauchi (BOW chee), *Nigeria* (10°N, 10°E)	108
Bay City, *Mich.* (44°N, 84°W)	63
Bayou d'Arbonne L. (BY yoo DAHR BON), *La.* (33°N, 92°W)	67
Bayreuth (by ROYT), *Germany* (50°N, 12°E)	99
Baytown, *Tex.* (30°N, 95°W)	67
Beals Creek, *r. in Tex.* (32°N, 103°W)	66
Bear I., *James Bay.* (54°N, 81°W)	46
Bear L., *U.S.* (42°N, 111°W)	59
Bear Lodge Mts., *Wyo.* (45°N, 104°W)	61
Bear R., *Idaho* (43°N, 112°W)	61
Beatrice (bee AH trus), *Nebr.* (40°N, 97°W)	64
Beaufort Sea, *Arctic O.* (72°N, 135°W)	57
Beaumont (BOH mont), *Tex.* (30°N, 94°W)	67
Beauport (bo PAWR), *Quebec* (47°N, 71°W)	47
Beaver I., *L. Michigan* (46°N, 86°W)	63
Beaver L., *Ark.* (36°N, 94°W)	67
Beaver R., *Canada* (54°N, 111°W)	45
Beaverhead Mts., *Idaho* (44°N, 113°W)	61
Beaverton, *Oreg.* (45°N, 123°W)	60
Bechar (bay SHAHR), *Algeria* (32°N, 2°W)	114
Beckley, *W. Va.* (38°N, 81°W)	71
Bedford, *Ind.* (39°N, 87°W)	70
Beijing (bay JIHNG), *China* (40°N, 116°E)	124
Beira (BAY ruh), *Mozambique* (20°S, 35°E)	107
Beirut (bay ROOT), *Lebanon* (33°N, 36°E)	115
Belarus (BEHL ah ruhs), *country in Europe* (52°N, 27°E)	97
Belcher Is., *Hudson Bay* (56°N, 79°W)	97
Belem (buh LEM), *Brazil* (1°S, 48°W)	89
Belfast, *Northern Ireland* (55°N, 6°W)	98
Belgium (BEL jum), *country in Europe* (51°N, 5°E)	98
Belgrade, *Yugoslavia* (45°N, 21°E)	99
Belize (buh LEEZ), *country in Central America* (17°N, 89°W)	84
Bell R., *Quebec* (50°N, 78°W)	47
Bella Coola, *British Columbia* (52°N, 127°W)	44
Belle Glade, *Fla.* (27°N, 81°W)	69
Belle Isle, Strait of, *Canada* (52°N, 57°W)	41
Bellefontaine (behl FOWNT uhn), *Ohio* (40°N, 84°W)	70
Belleville, *Ill.* (39°N, 90°W)	65
Belleville, *Ontario* (44°N, 77°W)	46
Bellevue (BEHL vyoo), *Nebr.* (41°N, 96°W)	64
Bellevue, *Wash.* (48°N, 122°W)	60
Bellingham, *Wash.* (49°N, 123°W)	60
Bellingshausen Sea (BEH lingz HOWZ ehn), *Antarctica* (68°S, 85°W)	137
Belmopan (BEL moh PAN), *Belize* (17°N, 89°W)	84
Belo Horizonte (BAY loh HAWR uh ZAHN tee), *Brazil* (20°S, 44°W)	89
Beloit (buh LOYT), *Wis.* (43°N, 89°W)	63
Bemidji (buh MIJ ee), *Minn.* (47°N, 95°W)	62
Ben Nevis, *mt. in Scotland* (57°N, 5°W)	98
Bend, *Oreg.* (44°N, 121°W)	60
Bendigo, *Australia* (37°S, 146°E)	133
Bengal, Bay of (ben GAWL), *Indian O.* (17°N, 90°E)	122
Benghazi (ben GAH zee), *Libya* (32°N, 20°E)	114
Benin, *country in Africa* (8°N, 2°E)	108
Benin, Bight of, *gulf in Africa* (6°N, 3°E)	108
Bennington, *Vt.* (43°N, 73°W)	73
Benton Harbor, *Mich.* (42°N, 87°W)	63
Benue R. (BAYN way), *Africa* (8°N, 9°E)	108
Berea (buh REE uh), *Ky.* (38°N, 84°W)	70
Berens R., *Canada* (52°N, 97°W)	45
Bergen, *Norway* (60°N, 5°E)	96
Bering Sea (BAYR ing), *Pacific O.* (57°N, 175°W)	136
Bering Strait, *U.S. and Russia* (65°N, 168°W)	57
Berkeley, *Calif.* (38°N, 122°W)	58
Berkner I., *Antarctica* (80°S, 45°W)	137
Berkshire Hills, *Mass.* (42°N, 73°W)	73
Berlin, *Germany* (52°N, 13°E)	99
Berlin, *N.H.* (44°N, 71°W)	73
Bermuda Is. (buhr MYOO duh), *Atlantic O.* (32°N, 65°W)	36
Bern, *Switzerland* (47°N, 7°E)	99
Besancon (buh ZAN suhn), *France* (47°N, 6°E)	98
Bessemer, *Ala.* (33°N, 87°W)	68
Bethany, *Mo.* (40°N, 94°W)	65
Bethel, *Alaska* (61°N, 162°W)	57
Bethel Park, *Pa.* (40°N, 80°W)	72
Bethesda (buh THES duh), *Md.* (39°N, 77°W)	71
Bethlehem, *Pa.* (41°N, 75°W)	72
Bettendorf, *Iowa* (42°N, 91°W)	65
Bhagalpur (BAHG uhl POOR), *India* (25°N, 87°E)	122
Bhopal (boh PAHL), *India* (23°N, 77°E)	122
Bhutan (boo TAHN), *country in Asia* (28°N, 91°E)	122
Biafra, Bight of (bee AHF ruh), *gulf in Africa* (4°N, 8°E)	108
Biak (bee YAK), *island in Pacific O.* (1°S, 136°E)	130
Bialystok (bee AHL uh STAWK), *Poland* (53°N, 23°E)	99
Biddeford, *Maine* (43°N, 69°W)	73
Bie Plateau, *Angola* (13°S, 17°E)	106
Bielefeld (BEE luh FELT), *Germany* (52°N, 9°E)	99
Bien Hoa (bee EHN WAH), *Vietnam* (11°N, 107°E)	123
Bienville, L. (bee EHN VIHL), *Quebec* (55°N, 73°W)	47
Big Belt Mts., *Mont.* (46°N, 111°W)	61
Big Bend Dam, *S. Dak.* (44°N, 100°W)	62
Big Bend N. P., *Tex.* (29°N, 103°W)	66
Big Black R., *Miss.* (33°N, 90°W)	68
Big Blue R., *U.S.* (41°N, 97°W)	64
Big Cypress Swamp, *Fla.* (26°N, 81°W)	69
Big L., *Maine* (45°N, 68°W)	73
Big Lost R., *Idaho* (44°N, 114°W)	61
Big Muddy R., *Ill.* (38°N, 89°W)	65
Big Sandy R., *U.S.* (38°N, 83°W)	70
Big Sioux R. (SOO), *S. Dak.* (44°N, 97°W)	62
Big Spring, *Tex.* (32°N, 102°W)	66
Big Stone L., *Minn.* (45°N, 97°W)	62
Big Trout L., *Ontario* (59°N, 90°W)	46
Bighorn L., *U.S.* (45°N, 108°W)	61
Bighorn Mts., *U.S.* (45°N, 108°W)	61
Bighorn R., *U.S.* (44°N, 108°W)	61
Bilbao (bil BAH oh), *Spain* (43°N, 3°W)	114
Billabong R., *Australia* (35°S, 145°E)	133
Billings, *Mont.* (46°N, 109°W)	61
Biloxi, *Miss.* (30°N, 89°W)	68
Bimini Is. (BIHM uh nee), *Straits of Florida,* (26°N, 79°W)	69
Binghamton, *N.Y.* (42°N, 76°W)	72
Bioko (bee OH koh), *island in Gulf of Guinea* (4°N, 9°E)	108
Birau, *Central African Rep.* (10°N, 23°E)	115
Birch Mts., *Alberta* (58°N, 113°W)	44
Birmingham, *Ala.* (34°N, 87°W)	68
Birmingham, *England* (53°N, 2°W)	98
Biscay, Bay of (BIS kay), *Europe* (45°N, 5°W)	98
Biscayne N.P. (bis KAYN), *Fla.* (25°N, 80°W)	69
Biscotasi L., *Ontario* (47°N, 82°W)	46
Bishkek, *Kyrgyzstan* (43°N, 75°E)	100
Bisho (BEE shoh), *South Africa* (33°S, 27°E)	109
Bishop, *Calif.* (37°N, 118°W)	58
Biskra, *Algeria* (35°N, 6°E)	114
Bismarck, *N. Dak.* (47°N, 101°W)	62
Bismarck Sea, *Pacific O.* (4°S, 147°E)	130
Bissau (bih SAW), *Guinea-Bissau* (12°N, 16°W)	108
Bitola (BEET uhl YAH), *Macedonia* (41°N, 21°E)	99
Bitterroot Range, *U.S.* (47°N, 115°W)	60-61
Bitterroot R., *Mont.* (46°N, 114°W)	61
Black Forest, *region of Germany* (48°N, 8°E)	99
Black Hills, *S. Dak.* (44°N, 104°W)	62
Black L., *Saskatchewan* (59°N, 105°W)	45
Black Mesa (MAY suh), *Ariz.* (37°N, 110°W)	59
Black R., *Ark.* (36°N, 91°W)	67
Black R., *N.Y.* (44°N, 77°W)	72
Black R., *Vietnam* (22°N, 104°E)	123
Black Sea, *Europe and Asia* (43°N, 35°E)	95
Black Sea Lowland, *Ukraine* (46°N, 30°E)	95
Black Volta R., *Africa* (12°N, 3°W)	108
Black Warrior R., *Ala.* (34°N, 87°W)	68
Blackfoot R., *Mont.* (47°N, 113°W)	61

Name (Pronunciation), *Description* (Lat., Long.) **Page**

Blacksburg, *Va.* (37°N, 81°W) 71
Blair, *Nebr.* (42°N, 96°W) 64
Blanc, Cape (blangk), *Africa* (21°N, 18°W) 106
Blanc, Mont (blahn, mawn), *France and Italy* (45°N, 7°E) 98
Blanca Bay (BLAHNG kuh), *Argentina* (39°S, 62°W) 88
Blanchard R., *Ohio* (41°N, 84°W) 70
Blanco, Cape (BLANG koh), *Oreg.* (43°N, 125°W) 60
Blind River, *Ontario* (46°N, 83°W) 46
Bloemfontein (BLOOM fahn tayn), *South Africa* (29°S, 26°E) 66
Bloodvein R., *Canada* (52°N, 96°W) 45
Bloomington, *Ill.* (41°N, 89°W) 65
Bloomington, *Ind.* (39°N, 87°W) 70
Bloomington, *Minn.* (44°N, 96°W) 62-63
Blue Mt., *Pa.* (41°N, 76°W) 72
Blue Mts., *U.S.* (45°N, 119°W) 60
Blue Nile, *r. in Africa* (14°N, 34°E) 106
Blue Ridge Mts., *U.S.* (36°N, 82°W) 71
Bluefield, *W. Va.* (37°N, 81°W) 71
Bluefields, *Nicaragua* (12°N, 84°W) 85
Blytheville, *Ark.* (36°N, 90°W) 67
Bo, *Sierra Leone* (8°N, 11°W) 108
Bo Gulf, *Yellow Sea* (38°N, 120°E) 124
Boa Vista (boh uh VEESH tuh), *Brazil* (3°N, 61°W) 90
Bobo Dioulasso (BOH BOH doo LAS oh), *Burkina Faso* (11°N, 4°W) 108
Boca Raton (BOH kuh ruh TOHN), *Fla.* (26°N, 80°W) 69
Bogalusa (BOH guh LOO suh), *La.* (31°N, 90°W) 67
Bogota (boh guh TAH), *Colombia* (4°N, 74°W) 90
Bohemia (boh HEE mee uh), *region of Czech Rep.* (50°N, 14°E) 99
Boise (BOY zee), *Idaho* (44°N, 116°W) 60
Boise R., *Idaho* (44°N, 116°W) 60
Bokna Fiord, *Norway* (59°N, 6°E) 94
Bolivia (boh LIHV ee uh), *country in South America* (17°S, 65°W) 89
Bologna (buh LOHN yuh), *Italy* (44°N, 11°E) 99
Bolzano (bohlt SAHN oh), *Italy* (47°N, 11°E) 99
Bombay, *India* (19°N, 73°E) 122
Bonifacio, Strait of (BAHN uh FAHCH oh), *Mediterranean Sea* (41°N, 9°E) 99
Bonin Is., *Philippine Sea* (27°N, 141°E) 119
Bonn, *Germany* (51°N, 7°E) 99
Bonneville Dam, *Wash.* (46°N, 122°W) 60
Boothia, Gulf of (BOO thee uh), *Northwest Terr.* (72°N, 91°W) 41
Boothia Pen., *Northwest Terr.* (71°N, 94°W) 41
Borah Pk., *Idaho* (44°N, 114°W) 61
Bordeaux (bawr DOH), *France* (45°N, 1°W) 98
Borgne L. (BAWRN), *La.* (30°N, 90°W) 67
Borneo, *island in South China Sea* (0°, 113°E) 119
Bornholm, *island in Baltic Sea* (55°N, 15°E) 96
Bosnia and Herzegovina (HERT suh goh VEE nuh), *country in Europe* (44°N, 18°E) 99
Bosporus (BAHS puhr uhs), *strait in Turkey* (41°N, 29°E) 95
Bossier City (BOH zhur), *La.* (33°, 94°W) 67
Boston, *Mass.* (42°N, 71°W) 73
Boston Mts., *Ark.* (36°N, 93°W) 67
Botany Bay, *Australia* (34°S, 151°E) 133
Bothnia, Gulf of, *Baltic Sea* (62°N, 20°E) 94-95
Botswana, *country in Africa* (22°S, 24°E) 107
Bouake (BWAH KAY), *Côte d'Ivoire* (7°N, 5°W) 108
Bougainville (BOO guhn VIHL), *island in Solomon Sea* (6°S, 155°E) 130
Boulder (BOHL duhr), *Colo.* (40°N, 105°W) 59
Boulder City, *Nev.* (36°N, 115°W) 58
Bountiful, *Utah* (41°N, 112°W) 59
Bow R. (BOH), *Alberta* (51°N, 113°W) 44-45
Bowling Green, *Ky.* (37°N, 86°W) 70
Bowling Green, *Ohio* (41°N, 84°W) 70
Boysen Res., *Wyo.* (43°N, 108°W) 61
Bozeman (BOHZ muhn), *Mont.* (46°N, 110°W) 61
Bradenton, *Fla.* (27°N, 83°W) 69
Bradford, *England* (54°N, 2°W) 98
Brahmaputra R., (brah muh POO truh), *Asia* (27°N, 92°E) 122

Braila (bruh EE luh), *Romania* (45°N, 28°E) 99
Brainerd, *Minn.* (46°N, 94°W) 62
Brampton, *Ontario* (44°N, 80°W) 46
Branco R. (brang koh), *South America* (0°N, 62°W) 90
Brandenburg, *Germany* (52°N, 13°E) 99
Brandon, *Manitoba* (50°N, 100°W) 45
Branford, *Fla.* (30°N, 83°W) 69
Branson, *Mo.* (37°N, 93°W) 65
Brantford, *Ontario* (43°N, 80°W) 46
Bras d'Or L. (brad AWR), *Nova Scotia* (46°N, 61°W) 47
Brasilia (brah SEEL yuh), *Brazil* (16°S, 48°W) 89
Brasov (brah SHAWV), *Romania* (46°N, 26°E) 99
Bratislava (BRAH tuh SLAH vuh), *Slovakia* (48°N, 17°E) 99
Bratsk Res., *Russia* (55°N, 102°E) 119
Brattleboro, *Vt.* (43°N, 73°W) 73
Braunschweig (BROWN shvyg), *Germany* (52°N, 10°E) 99
Brawley, *Calif.* (33°N, 115°W) 58
Brazil, *country in South America* (10°S, 55°W) 89
Brazilian Highlands, *Brazil* (17°S, 48°W) 88
Brazos R. (BRAZ uhs), *Tex.* (32°N, 97°W) 66-67
Brazzaville, *Congo* (4°S, 15°E) 107
Bremen (BREHM uhn), *Germany* (53°N, 9°E) 99
Bremerhaven (brem uhr HAHV uhn), *Germany* (54°N, 9°E) 99
Bremerton, *Wash.* (48°N, 123°W) 60
Brescia (BRESH uh), *Italy* (46°N, 10°E) 99
Brest, *France* (48°N, 5°W) 98
Breton Sound (BREHT uhn), *Gulf of Mexico* (29°N, 89°W) 67
Brewton, *Ala.* (31°N, 87°W) 68
Bridgeport, *Conn.* (41°N, 73°W) 73
Brindisi (BRIN duh zee), *Italy* (41°N, 18°E) 99
Brisbane (BRIHS bayn), *Australia* (27°S, 153°E) 131
Bristol, *England* (51°N, 3°W) 60
Bristol, *Va. and N.C.* (37°N, 80°W) 71
Bristol Bay, *Alaska* (58°N, 159°W) 57
Bristol Channel, *United Kingdom* (51°N, 3°W) 98
British Columbia, *prov. in Canada* (55°N, 125°W) 44
British Isles, *Europe* (52°N, 7°W) 94
Brittany, *region of France* (48°N, 4°W) 98
Brno (BUHR noh), *Czech Republic* (49°N, 17°E) 99
Broadback R., *Quebec* (51°N, 79°W) 46
Brockton, *Mass.* (42°N, 71°W) 73
Brockville, *Ontario* (45°N, 76°W) 47
Broken Arrow, *Okla.* (36°N, 96°W) 67
Broken Bay, *Australia* (34°S, 151°E) 133
Broken Bow L., *Okla.* (34°N, 95°W) 67
Broken Bow Res., *Okla.* (34°N, 95°W) 67
Brookings, *S. Dak.* (44°N, 97°W) 62
Brooks Range, *Alaska* (67°N, 155°W) 57
Brownsville, *Tex.* (26°N, 97°W) 67
Brownwood, *Tex.* (32°N, 99°W) 66
Bruce Peninsula N. P., *Ontario* (45°N, 81°W) 46
Brunei (broon EYE), *country in Asia* (4°N, 114°E) 123
Brunswick, *Ga.* (31°N, 81°W) 69
Brunswick, *Maine* (44°N, 70°W) 73
Brussels, *capital of Belgium* (51°N, 4°E) 98
Bryan, *Tex.* (31°N, 96°W) 67
Bryansk (bree ANSK), *Russia* (53°N, 34°E) 97
Bryce Canyon N. P. (BRYS), *Utah* (38°N, 112°W) 59
Bucaramanga (boo kuh ruh MAHNG guh), *Colombia* (7°N, 73°W) 90
Buchanan, L., *Tex.* (31°N, 98°W) 66
Bucharest (BYOO kuh REST), *Romania* (44°N, 26°E) 99
Budapest (BOO duh PEST), *Hungary* (47°N, 19°E) 99
Buenaventura (BWAY nuh vehn TOOR uh), *Colombia* (4°N, 77°W) 90
Buenos Aires (BWAY nohs EYE rays), *Argentina* (35°S, 58°W) 89
Buffalo, *N.Y.* (43°N, 79°W) 72
Buffalo, *S. Dak.* (46°N, 104°W) 62
Buffalo, *Wyo.* (44°N, 107°W) 61
Buffalo Narrows, *Saskatchewan* (57°N, 109°W) 45
Bug River (boog), *Europe* (53°N, 22°E) 99
Bujumbura (boo juhm BOOR uh), *Burundi* (3°S, 29°E) 110

Bukhara (boo KAHR uh), *Uzbekistan* (40°N, 64°E) 115
Bulawayo (boo luh WAH yo), *Zimbabwe* (20°S, 29°E) 107
Bulgaria, *country in Europe* (43°N, 25°E) 99
Bull Shoals L., *U.S.* (36°N, 93°W) 67
Bun Plains, *Kenya* (1°N, 41°E) 110
Bureinskiy Mts., *Russia* (50°N, 135°E) 101
Burgas (boor GAHS), *Bulgaria* (42°N, 27°E) 99
Burgundy, *region of France* (47°N, 4°E) 98
Burkina Faso (bur KEE nuh FAH soh), *country in Africa* (12°N, 4°W) 108
Burlington, *Iowa* (41°N, 91°W) 65
Burlington, *N.C.* (36°N, 80°W) 71
Burlington, *Vt.* (45°N, 73°W) 73
Burma, *country in Asia* (22°N, 95°E) 123
Burnaby, *British Columbia* (49°N, 123°W) 44
Burntwood R., *Manitoba* (56°N, 98°W) 45
Burragorang L., *Australia* (36°S, 150°E) 133
Bursa, *Turkey* (40°N, 29°E) 115
Buru (BOO roo), *island in Molucca Sea* (3°S, 127°E) 130
Burundi (buh RUHN dee), *country in Africa* (3°S, 30°E) 110
Bushehr (boo SHEHR), *Iran* (29°N, 51°E) 115
Butte (BYOOT), *Montana* (46°N, 113°W) 61
Bydgoszcz (BID GAWSH), *Poland* (53°N, 18°E) 99

C

Caballo Res. (kuh BAH yoh), *N. Mex.* (33°N, 107°W) 59
Cabinda (kuh BEEN duh), *terr. of Angola* (5°S, 12°E) 107
Cabonga Res., *Quebec* (47°N, 77°W) 47
Cacak (CHAH chawk), *Yugoslavia* (44°N, 20°E) 99
Caddo L. (KAD oh), *U.S.* (33°N, 94°W) 67
Cadillac, *Mich.* (44°N, 85°W) 63
Caen (kahn), *France* (49°N, 0°) 98
Cagliari (KAHL yuh ree), *Sardinia* (39°N, 9°E) 99
Cairns (kayrns), *Australia* (17°S, 146°E) 131
Cairo (KY roh), *Egypt* (30°N, 31°E) 115
Cairo (KAY roh), *Ill.* (37°N, 89°W) 65
Calais (KAL ay), *France* (51°N, 2°E) 98
Calcanhar, Point, *Brazil* (5°S, 35°W) 88
Calcasieu L. (KAL kuh SHOO), *La.* (30°N, 94°W) 67
Calcasieu R., *La.* (31°N, 93°W) 67
Calcutta (kal KUT uh), *India* (23°N, 88°E) 122
Caldwell, *Idaho* (44°N, 117°W) 60
Calexico, *Calif.* (33°N, 116°W) 58
Calgary (KAL guh ree), *Alberta* (51°N, 114°W) 44
Cali (KAH lee), *Colombia* (3°N, 77°W) 90
Calicut, *India* (11°N, 76°E) 122
California, *state in U.S.* (38°N, 121°W) 58
California, Gulf of, *Pacific O.* (30°N, 114°W) 82
California Aqueduct, *Calif.* (36°N, 120°W) 58
Callao (kah YAH oh), *Peru* (12°S, 77°W) 90
Caloosahatchee R. (kuh LOO suh HACH ee), *Fla.* (27°N, 82°W) 69
Calumet City (KAL yuh MEHT), *Ill.* (42°N, 88°W) 65
Calvinia (kal VIHN ee uh), *South Africa* (31°S, 20°E) 109
Cambodia, *country in Asia,* (13°N, 105°E) 123
Cambrian Mts. (KAM bree uhn), *Wales* (52°N, 4°E) 98
Cambridge (KAYM brihj), *England* (52°N, 0°) 98
Cambridge, *Mass.* (42°N, 71°W) 73
Cambridge, *Ohio* (40°N, 82°W) 71
Cambridge Bay, *Northwest Terr.* (69°N, 105°W) 42
Camden, *N.J.* (40°N, 75°W) 72
Cameroon (kam uh ROON), *country in Africa* (6°N, 12°E) 108
Cameroon Mt., *Cameroon* (5°N, 9°E) 108
Campbell River, *British Columbia* (50°N, 125°W) 44
Campbellton, *New Brunswick* (48°N, 67°W) 47
Campeche (kam PAY chay), *Mexico* (20°N, 91°W) 84
Campeche, Bay of, *Gulf of Mexico* (18°N, 94°W) 84
Campinas (kam PEE nuhs), *Brazil* (23°S, 47°W) 89
Campo Grande (KAHM poo GRAN dee), *Brazil* (20°S, 55°W) 89
Campos (KAM puhs), *Brazil* (22°S, 41°W) 89

Name (Pronunciation), *Description* (Lat., Long.)	Page

Campos, *plain in South America* (22°S, 50°W) — 88
Can Tho (kuhn TOH), *Vietnam* (10°N, 105°E) — 123
Canada, *country in North America* (60°N, 100°W) — 42-43
Canadian R., *U.S.* (36°N, 102°W) — 52-53
Canadian Shield, *region of Canada* (60°N, 101°W) — 40-41
Canandaigua L. (KAN uhn DAY gwuh), *N.Y.* (43°N, 77°W) — 72
Canary Is., *Atlantic O.* (28°N, 16°W) — 114
Canaveral, Cape, *Fla.* (29°N, 80°W) — 69
Canberra (KAN behr uh), *Australia* (35°S, 149°E) — 131
Candlewood, L., *Conn.* (41°N, 74°W) — 72-73
Caniapiscau Res. (KAN ee uh PIHS koh), *Quebec* (54°N, 70°W) — 47
Caniapiscau R., *Quebec* (55°N, 70°W) — 47
Cannonball R., *N. Dak.* (46°N, 102°W) — 62
Canso, *Nova Scotia* (45°N, 61°W) — 47
Cantabrian Mts. (kan TAH bree uhn), *Spain* (43°N, 6°W) — 114
Canterbury, *England* (51°N, 1°E) — 98
Canton (KAN tuhn), *Ohio* (41°N, 81°W) — 71
Canyon Ferry L., *Mont.* (46°N, 112°W) — 61
Canyonlands N. P., *Utah* (38°N, 110°W) — 59
Cape Breton Highlands N.P., *Nova Scotia* (47°N, 63°W) — 47
Cape Breton I., *Nova Scotia* (47°N, 61°W) — 47
Cape Coral, *city in Fla.* (27°N, 82°W) — 69
Cape Fear R., *N.C.* (35°N, 79°W) — 71
Cape Girardeau (juh RAHR doh), *Mo.* (37°N, 90°W) — 65
Cape Province, *South Africa* (31°S, 21°E) — 109
Cape Town, *South Africa* (34°S, 18°E) — 109
Cape Verde, *country in Atlantic O.* (16°N, 25°W) — 10
Cape York Pen., *Australia* (13°S, 143°E) — 130
Capitol Reef N. P., *Utah* (38°N, 111°W) — 59
Caqueta R. (KAH kuh TAH), *Colombia* (0°, 73°W) — 90
Caracas (kuh RAH kuhs), *Venezuela* (11°N, 67°W) — 90
Caratasca Lagoon (KAHR uh TAHS kuh), *Honduras* (15°N, 83°W) — 83
Carbondale, *Ill.* (38°N, 89°W) — 65
Cardiff (KAHR dif), *Wales* (52°N, 3°W) — 98
Cardston, *Alberta* (49°N, 113°W) — 44
Caribbean Sea (KAR uh BEE uhn), *Atlantic O.* (16°N, 80°W) — 83
Caribou (KAR uh BOO), *Maine* (47°N, 68°W) — 73
Caribou Mts., *Alberta* (59°N, 115°W) — 44
Carlsbad, *N. Mex.* (32°N, 104°W) — 59
Carlsbad Caverns N. P., *N. Mex.* (32°N, 105°W) — 59
Carlyle L. (kahr LYL), *Ill.* (39°N, 89°W) — 65
Carnarvon (kahr NAHR vuhn), *South Africa* (31°S, 22°E) — 109
Carpathian Mts. (kahr PAY thee un), *Europe* (49°N, 19°E) — 99
Carpentaria, Gulf of, *Australia* (14°S, 140°E) — 130
Carrara, *Italy* (44°N, 10°E) — 99
Carson City, *Nev.* (39°N, 120°W) — 58
Carson R., *U.S.* (39°N, 120°W) — 58
Carson Sink, *seasonal lake of Nev.* (40°N, 118°W) — 58
Cartagena, *Colombia* (10°N, 75°W) — 90
Carthage, *Tunisia* (37°N, 10°E) — 114
Cary, *N.C.* (36°N, 79°W) — 71
Casa Grande (KAS uh GRAN dee), *Ariz.* (33°N, 112°W) — 59
Casablanca (KAS uh BLANG kuh), *Morocco* (34°N, 8°W) — 114
Cascade Range (kas KAYD), *U.S.* (42°N, 122°W) — 60
Cascade Res., *Idaho* (45°N, 116°W) — 60
Casco Bay (KAS koh), *Maine* (44°N, 70°W) — 73
Casper, *Wyo.* (43°N, 106°W) — 61
Caspian Depression, *Russia* (47°N, 47°E) — 95
Caspian Sea, *Europe and Asia* (42°N, 50°E) — 95
Cassiar Mts., *Canada* (59°N, 130°W) — 44
Cat I., *Bahamas* (24°N, 75°W) — 69
Catania, *Sicily* (38°N, 15°E) — 99
Catanzaro, *Italy* (39°N, 17°E) — 99
Catoche, Cape (kuh TOH chee), *Mexico* (22°N, 87°W) — 82
Catskill Mts., *N.Y.* (42°N, 75°W) — 72
Cauca R., *Colombia* (7°N, 76°W) — 90

Caucasus Mts. (KAW kuh suhs), *Europe and Asia* (44°N, 41°E) — 95
Cauvery Falls (KOH vuh ree), *India* (12°N, 77°E) — 122
Cauvery R., *India* (11°N, 79°E) — 122
Cayenne (ky EHN), *Fr. Guiana* (5°N, 52°W) — 90
Cayman Is. (KAY muhn), *Caribbean Sea* (19°N, 81°W) — 83
Cayos Miskitos, *islands in Caribbean Sea* (15°N, 83°W) — 83
Cayuga L. (kuh OO guh), *N.Y.* (42°N, 77°W) — 72
Cebu (seh BOO), *Philippines* (10°N, 124°E) — 121
Cedar City (SEED uhr), *Utah* (38°N, 113°W) — 58
Cedar Creek L., *Tex.* (32°N, 96°W) — 67
Cedar Falls, *Iowa* (42°N, 92°W) — 65
Cedar L., *Manitoba* (53°N, 100°W) — 45
Cedar Rapids, *Iowa* (42°N, 92°W) — 65
Cedar R., *Iowa* (42°N, 92°W) — 65
Cedros I. (SAY druhs), *Mexico* (28°N, 115°W) — 82
Celebes (SEL uh BEEZ), *island in Molucca Sea* (2°S, 120°E) — 84
Celebes Sea, *Asia* (3°N, 122°E) — 119
Celtic Sea (KEL tik), *Europe* (50°N, 8°W) — 98
Center Hill L., *Tenn.* (36°N, 86°W) — 70
Central African Republic, *country in Africa* (7°N, 20°E) — 107
Central Lowland, *U.S.* (41°N, 90°W) — 53
Central Lowlands, *Australia* (22°S, 142°E) — 130
Central Patricia, *Ontario* (51°N, 90°W) — 46
Central Russian Upland, *Russia* (55°N, 34°E) — 95
Central Siberian Plateau, *Russia* (68°N, 98°E) — 100
Ceram (SAY rahm), *island in Banda Sea* (3°S, 129°E) — 84
Ceram Sea, *Indian O.* (2°S, 130°E) — 130
Cerf I., *Indian O.* (9°S, 51°E) — 106
Ceuta (SAY OO tuh), *terr. of Spain* (36°N, 5°W) — 114
Chaco Canyon (CHAHK oh), *N. Mex.* (36°N, 108°W) — 59
Chad, *country in Africa* (15°N, 18°E) — 107
Chad, L., *Africa* (13°N, 14°E) — 108
Chadron (SHAD ruhn), *Nebr.* (43°N, 103°W) — 64
Chagos Archipelago, *island group in Indian O.* (6°S, 73°E) — 120
Chalbi Plains, *Kenya* (3°N, 37°E) — 110
Chaleur Bay (shuh LOOR), *Canada* (48°N, 65°W) — 47
Chambal R., *India* (25°N, 76°E) — 122
Chamberlain L., *Maine* (46°N, 71°W) — 73
Champagne (sham PAYN), *region of France* (49°N, 4°E) — 98
Champaign (sham PAYN), *Ill.* (40°N, 88°W) — 65
Champlain, L. (sham PLAYN), *North America* (45°N, 73°W) — 73
Chandeleur Is. (SHAN duh LOOR), *Gulf of Mexico* (30°N, 89°W) — 67
Chandeleur Sound, *Gulf of Mexico* (30°N, 89°W) — 67
Chandigarh, *India* (31°N, 77°E) — 122
Chandler, *Ariz.* (33°N, 112°W) — 59
Chandler, *Quebec* (48°N, 65°W) — 47
Changchun, *China* (44°N, 125°E) — 124
Changsha (chahng shah), *China* (28°N, 113°E) — 124
Channel Is., *English Channel* (49°N, 3°W) — 98
Channel Is., *Pacific O.* (34°N, 120°W) — 58
Channel Is. N.P., *Calif.* (34°N, 120°W) — 58
Chao Phraya (chow PRY uh), *r. in Thailand* (15°N, 100°E) — 123
Chapala, L., *Mexico* (20°N, 103°W) — 82
Chapel Hill, *N.C.* (36°N, 79°W) — 71
Chapleau (chap LOH), *Ontario* (48°N, 83°W) — 46
Chari River (SHAHR ee), *Africa* (11°N, 16°E) — 106
Chariton R. (SHAR uht uhn), *U.S.* (40°N, 93°W) — 65
Charles, Cape, *Va.* (37°N, 76°W) — 71
Charlesbourg (sharl BOOR), *Quebec* (47°N, 71°W) — 47
Charleston, *Ill.* (40°N, 88°W) — 65
Charleston, *S.C.* (33°N, 80°W) — 69
Charleston, *W. Va.* (38°N, 82°W) — 71
Charlestown, *Ind.* (38°N, 86°W) — 70
Charlevoix (SHAHR luh voy), *Mich.* (45°N, 85°W) — 63
Charlotte, *N.C.* (35°N, 81°W) — 71
Charlottesville, *Va.* (38°N, 78°W) — 71

Charlottetown, *Prince Edward I.* (47°N, 62°W) — 47
Charlton I., *James Bay* (52°N, 79°W) — 46
Chartres (SHAHR truh), *France* (48°N, 2°E) — 98
Chatham (CHAT uhm), *Ontario* (42°N, 82°W) — 46
Chattahoochee R., *U.S.* (32°N, 85°W) — 68-69
Chattanooga, *Tenn.* (35°N, 85°W) — 70
Chaudiere R. (shoh DYER), *Quebec* (46°N, 71°W) — 47
Chautauqua L. (shuh TAW kwuh), *N.Y.* (42°N, 79°W) — 72
Cheat R., *W. Va.* (40°N, 80°W) — 71
Chehalis R. (chih HAY luhs), *Wash.* (47°N, 123°W) — 60
Cheju (CHAY JOO), *island in East China Sea* (34°N, 126°E) — 125
Chelan, L., *Wash.* (48°N, 120°W) — 60
Chelyabinsk, *Russia* (55°N, 61°E) — 100
Chemnitz, *Germany* (51°N, 13°E) — 99
Chemung R. (shi MUHNG), *N.Y.* (42°N, 77°W) — 72
Cheney Res. (CHEE nee), *Kans.* (38°N, 98°W) — 64
Chengdu, *China* (31°N, 104°E) — 124
Cher R. (SHEHR), *France* (47°N, 2°E) — 98
Cherangany Hills, *Kenya* (2°N, 37°E) — 110
Cherbourg (SHEHR boorg), *France* (50°N, 2°W) — 98
Chernovtsky, *Ukraine* (48°N, 26°E) — 99
Chernobyl (chuhr NOH buhl), *Ukraine* (51°N, 30°E) — 100
Cherokee L., *Tenn.* (36°N, 84°W) — 70
Cherokees, Lake O' the, *Okla.* (37°N, 95°W) — 67
Cherskiy Range, *Russia* (70°N, 145°E) — 101
Chesapeake (CHES uh peek), *Va.* (37°N, 76°W) — 71
Chesapeake Bay, *U.S.* (37°N, 76°W) — 71
Chester, *Pa.* (40°N, 75°W) — 72
Chesterfield Inlet, *Hudson Bay* (63°N, 91°W) — 41
Chesterfield I., *Pacific O.* (19°S, 160°E) — 131
Chesuncook L. (chuh SUHN KOOK), *Maine* (46°N, 71°W) — 73
Chetumal Bay (CHAY tyoo MAHL), *Caribbean Sea* (18°N, 88°W) — 82-83
Chew Bakir, *l. in Africa* (5°N, 38°E) — 110
Cheyenne (shy AN), *Wyo.* (41°N, 105°W) — 61
Chi R. (CHEE), *Thailand* (16°N, 104°E) — 123
Chiang Mai (chee AHNG MY), *Thailand* (19°N, 99°E) — 123
Chiang Rai (chee AHNG RY), *Thailand* (20°N, 100°E) — 123
Chiba (CHEE buh), *Japan* (36°N, 140°E) — 125
Chibougamau (shuh BOO guh moh), *Quebec* (50°N, 74°W) — 47
Chic-Choc Mts., *Quebec* (49°N, 67°W) — 47
Chicago, *Ill.* (42°N, 88°W) — 65
Chickamauga L. (CHIK uh MAW guh), *Tenn.* (35°N, 85°W) — 70
Chickasawhay R. (CHIK uh SAW way), *Miss.* (31°N, 89°W) — 68
Chiclayo (chuh KLY OH), *Peru* (7°S, 80°W) — 90
Chico (CHEE koh), *Calif.* (40°N, 122°W) — 58
Chicoutimi (shuh KOOT uh mee), *Quebec* (48°N, 71°W) — 47
Chidley, Cape (CHID lee), *Canada* (61°N, 64°W) — 41
Chihuahua (chih WAH wah), *Mexico* (29°N, 106°W) — 84
Chile, *country in South America* (35°S, 71°W) — 89
Chillicothe (CHIHL uh KAHTH ee), *Mo.* (40°N, 94°W) — 65
Chillicothe , *Ohio* (39°N, 83°W) — 70
Chilliwack (CHIL uh WAK), *British Columbia* (49°N, 122°W) — 44
Chiloe I. (CHEE luh WAY), *Chile* (43°S, 74°W) — 88
Chimborazo, Mt., *Ecuador* (2°S, 79°W) — 90
Chimbote (chim BOH tee), *Peru* (9°S, 79°W) — 90
China, *country in Asia* (35°N, 105°E) — 124
Chinchaga R., *Canada* (58°N, 119°W) — 44
Chincoteague Bay (SHING kuh TEEG), *Atlantic O.* (38°N, 75°W) — 71
Chindwin R., *Burma* (24°N, 95°E) — 123
Chinle Wash, *U.S.* (37°N, 110°W) — 59
Chios (KEE aws), *island in Aegean Sea* (38°N, 26°E) — 99
Chippewa R., *Minn.* (45°N, 96°W) — 62
Chippewa R., *Wis.* (45°N, 91°W) — 63
Chiputneticook Lakes (SHIP uht NET ih KOOK), *North America* (46°N, 68°W) — 73

Name (Pronunciation), *Description* (Lat., Long.)	Page
Chisasibi, *Quebec*, (54°N, 79°W)	47
Chisinau, *Moldova* (47°N, 29°E)	100
Chita, *Russia* (52°N, 114°E)	100
Chittagong, *Bangladesh* (22°N, 91°E)	122
Choctawhatchee R. (CHAHK tuh HACH ee), *U.S.* (31°N, 86°W)	68
Chongjin (CHUNG JEEN), *North Korea* (42°N, 130°E)	125
Chongju, *South Korea* (37°N, 127°E)	125
Chongqing (chuhng chihng), *China* (29°N, 106°E)	124
Chonos Archipelago, *island group in Chile* (45°S, 74°W)	88
Chowan R. (chuh WAHN), *U.S.* (36°N, 77°W)	71
Christchurch, *New Zealand* (43°S, 173°E)	131
Christmas I., *Indian O.* (11°S, 106°E)	130
Chukchi Peninsula (CHUHK chee), *Russia* (66°N, 175°E)	101
Chukchi Sea, *Arctic O.* (70°N, 170°W)	57
Chula Vista (CHOO luh VIS tuh), *Calif.* (33°N, 117°W)	58
Churchill, *Manitoba* (59°N, 93°W)	45
Churchill Falls, *city in Newfoundland* (53°N, 64°W)	47
Churchill Falls, *waterfall in Newfoundland* (54°N, 64°W)	47
Churchill L., *Saskatchewan* (56°N, 108°W)	45
Churchill R., *Manitoba* (59°N, 94°W)	45
Churchill R., *Newfoundland* (53°N, 63°W)	47
Cimarron R. (SIM uh ROHN), *U.S.* (37°N, 99°W)	66-67
Cincinnati, *Ohio* (39°N, 85°W)	70
Ciudad Bolivar (syoo DAHD boh LEE vahr), *Venezuela* (8°N, 64°W)	90
Ciudad Guayana, *Venezuela* (9°N, 63°W)	90
Claire, L., *Alberta* (59°N, 112°W)	45
Clarion, *Pa.* (41°N, 79°W)	72
Clark Fork, *r. in U.S.* (48°N, 116°W)	60-61
Clark Hill L., *U.S.* (34°N, 82°W)	69
Clarke City, *Quebec* (50°N, 67°W)	47
Clarks Fork, *r. in U.S.* (45°N, 109°W)	61
Clarksburg, *W. Va.* (39°N, 80°W)	71
Clarksdale, *Miss.* (34°N, 91°W)	68
Clarksville, *Tenn.* (37°N, 87°W)	70
Clarksville, *Va.* (37°N, 79°W)	71
Clear L., *Calif.* (39°N, 123°W)	58
Clearwater, *Fla.* (28°N, 83°W)	69
Clearwater Mts., *Idaho* (46°N, 116°W)	60
Clearwater R., *Canada* (57°N, 111°W)	45
Clearwater R., *Idaho* (46°N, 116°W)	60
Clermont-Ferrand (klehr MOHN fuh RAN), *France* (46°N, 3°E)	98
Cleveland, *Ohio* (42°N, 82°W)	71
Cleveland, *Tenn.* (35°N, 85°W)	70
Cleveland Heights, *Ohio* (41°N, 82°W)	71
Clinch R., *U.S.* (37°N, 83°W)	70-71
Clinton, *Iowa* (42°N, 90°W)	65
Clovis, *N. Mex.* (34°N, 105°W)	59
Cluj-Napoca, *Romania* (47°N, 24°E)	99
Clyde, *Northwest Terr.* (71°N, 69°W)	43
Coachella Canal (KOH CHEHL uh), *Calif.* (33°N, 115°W)	58
Coast Mts., *British Columbia* (53°N, 127°W)	44
Coast Ranges, *U.S.* (37°N, 122°W)	52
Coats I., *Hudson Bay* (62°N, 82°W)	35
Coats Land, *region of Antarctica* (78°S, 25°W)	137
Cobalt, *Ontario* (47°N, 80°W)	46
Cobh (KOHV), *Ireland* (52°N, 8°W)	98
Cobourg Pen., *Australia* (12°S, 135°E)	130
Cochin (koh CHIHN), *India* (10°N, 76°E)	122
Cochrane (KAWK ruhn), *Ontario* (49°N, 81°W)	46
Cockburn I. (KOH buhrn), *L. Huron* (46°N, 83°W)	46
Coco R., *North America* (14°N, 84°W)	83
Cocos I., *Pacific O.* (5°N, 87°W)	90
Cod, Cape, *Mass.* (42°N, 70°W)	73
Cody, *Wyo.* (44°N, 109°W)	61
Coeur d'Alene (KAWR duh LAYN), *Idaho* (48°N, 117°W)	60
Coeur d'Alene L., *Idaho* (47°N, 117°W)	60
Coffeyville, *Kans.* (37°N, 96°W)	65
Coiba I., *Panama* (7°N, 82°W)	83
Coimbatore (KOYM buh TOHR), *India* (11°N, 77°E)	122
Cold L., *Canada* (55°N, 110°W)	45
College, *Alaska* (65°N, 148°W)	57
College Station, *Tex.* (31°N, 96°W)	67
Cologne (koh LOHN), *Germany* (51°N, 7°E)	99
Colombia, *country in South America* (3°N, 73°W)	90
Colombo, *Sri Lanka* (7°N, 80°E)	122
Colon (koh LOHN), *Panama* (9°N, 80°W)	85
Colorado, *state in U.S.* (39°N, 107°W)	59
Colorado Plateau, *U.S.* (37°N, 112°W)	59
Colorado R., *Argentina* (38°S, 68°W)	88
Colorado R., *Tex.* (30°N, 97°W)	66-67
Colorado R., *U.S.* (34°N, 114°W)	52
Colorado River Aqueduct, *Calif.* (34°N, 115°W)	58
Colorado Springs, *Col.* (39°N, 105°W)	59
Columbia, *Md.* (39°N, 77°W)	71
Columbia, *Mo.* (39°N, 92°W)	65
Columbia, *S.C.* (34°N, 81°W)	69
Columbia, *Tenn.* (36°N, 87°W)	70
Columbia Mts., *British Columbia* (52°N, 119°W)	44
Columbia Plateau, *U.S.* (44°N, 118°W)	60
Columbia R., *North America* (47°N, 120°W)	60
Columbus, *Ga.* (32°N, 85°W)	68
Columbus, *Ind.* (39°N, 86°W)	70
Columbus, *Miss.* (33°N, 88°W)	68
Columbus, *Nebr.* (41°N, 97°W)	64
Columbus, *Ohio* (40°N, 83°W)	70
Colville R., *Alaska* (69°N, 156°W)	57
Colwyn Bay (KAWL wuhn), *Wales* (53°N, 4°W)	98
Commander Is., *Bering Sea* (55°N, 167°E)	121
Como, L. (KOH moh), *Italy* (46°N, 9°E)	99
Comodoro Rivadavia, *Arg.* (46°S, 68°W)	89
Comorin, Cape, *India* (8°N, 78°E)	122
Comoros, *country in Indian O.* (13°S, 43°E)	107
Con Son Is. (KOHN SOHN), *South China Sea* (9°N, 106°E)	123
Conakry, *Guinea* (10°N, 14°W)	108
Concepcion (kuhn SEP see OHN), *Chile* (37°S, 73°W)	89
Conception, Point, *Calif.* (35°N, 121°W)	58
Conchas Res. (KAHN chus), *N. Mex.* (35°N, 104°W)	59
Conchita Res. (KAHN CHEE tuh), *N. Mex.* (36°N, 106°W)	59
Conchos R., *Mexico* (29°N, 105°W)	82
Concord, *N.H.* (43°N, 71°W)	73
Concord, *N.C.* (35°N, 81°W)	71
Concordia (kuhn KAWRD ee uh), *Kans.* (40°N, 98°W)	64
Conecuh R. (kuh NAY kuh), *Ala.* (31°N, 87°W)	68
Conemaugh R. (KAHN uh MOH), *Pa.* (41°N, 79°W)	72
Congo, *country in Africa* (3°S, 15°E)	106
Congo Basin, *Africa* (0°, 20°E)	107
Congo R., *Africa* (2°N, 20°E)	106
Connecticut, *state in U.S.* (42°N, 73°W)	72-73
Connecticut R., *U.S.* (43°N, 73°W)	73
Conroe (KAHN ROH), *Tex.* (30°N, 95°W)	67
Constance L. (KAHN stuhns), *Europe* (48°N, 9°E)	99
Constanta, *Romania* (44°N, 29°E)	99
Constantine, *Algeria* (36°N, 7°E)	114
Conway, *Ark.* (35°N, 92°W)	67
Cook Inlet, *Alaska* (60°N, 153°W)	57
Cook Is., *poss. of N.Z.* (20°S, 158°W)	135
Cook, Mt., *New Zealand* (44°S, 170°E)	130
Cook Strait, *New Zealand* (40°S, 173°E)	130
Cooma, *Australia* (36°S, 149°E)	133
Cooper R., *S.C.* (33°N, 80°W)	69
Cooperstown, *N.Y.* (43°N, 75°W)	72
Coos Bay, *Oreg.* (43°N, 124°W)	60
Coosa R. (KOO suh), *Ala.* (34°N, 86°W)	68
Copenhagen, *Denmark* (56°N, 13°E)	96
Coral Gables, *Fla.* (26°N, 80°W)	69
Coral Sea, *Pacific O.* (13°S, 150°E)	130
Coral Springs, *Fla.* (26°N, 80°W)	69
Coralville Res., *Iowa* (42°N, 92°W)	65
Cordillera Oriental, *range of Andes* (3°N, 77°W)	90
Cordoba (KAWRD uh buh), *Argentina* (31°S, 64°W)	89
Cordoba, *Spain* (38°N, 5°W)	114
Cordova (kawr DOH vuh), *Alaska* (61°N, 146°W)	57
Corfu (kawr FOO), *island in Ionian Sea* (40°N, 20°E)	99
Corinth, *Miss.* (35°N, 88°W)	68
Cork, *Ireland* (52°N, 9°W)	98
Corner Brook, *Newfoundland* (49°N, 48°W)	43
Cornwall, *Ontario* (45°N, 75°W)	47
Coromandel Coast, *India* (15°N, 81°E)	122
Coronada Bay, *Costa Rica* (9°N, 85°W)	83
Coronation Gulf, *Northwest Terr.* (68°N, 112°W)	40
Corowa, *Australia* (36°S, 146°E)	133
Corpus Christi (KAWR puhs KRIHS tee), *Tex.* (28°N, 97°W)	67
Corpus Christi Bay, *Gulf of Mexico* (28°N, 97°W)	67
Corpus Christi, L., *Tex.* (28°N, 98°W)	67
Corrientes, Cape, *Mexico* (20°N, 105°W)	82
Corsica, *island in Mediterranean Sea* (42°N, 9°E)	98
Corsicana (KAWR sih KAHN uh), *Tex.* (32°N, 96°W)	67
Cortland, *N.Y.* (43°N, 76°W)	72
Corvallis, *Oreg.* (45°N, 123°W)	60
Cosenza (koh ZEN suh), *Italy* (39°N, 16°E)	99
Costa Rica, *country in Central America* (10°N, 84°W)	85
Côte d'Ivoire (koht deev WAHR), *country in Africa* (8°N, 5°W)	108
Cotonou (KOHT uh NOO), *Benin* (6°N, 2°E)	108
Cotopaxi, Mt., *Ecuador* (1°S, 78°W)	90
Cottonwood R., *Kans.* (38°N, 97°W)	64
Council Bluffs, *Iowa* (41°N, 96°W)	64-65
Coventry, *England* (52°N, 1°W)	98
Cowlitz R., *Wash.* (46°N, 123°W)	60
Cozumel I., *Mexico* (20°N, 87°W)	83
Craiova (kruh YOH vuh), *Romania* (44°N, 24°E)	99
Cranbrook, *British Columbia* (50°N, 116°W)	44
Crater Lake N.P., *Oreg.* (43°N, 122°W)	60
Crawford, *Nebr.* (43°N, 103°W)	64
Crawfordsville, *Ind.* (40°N, 87°W)	70
Cree L., *Saskatchewan* (57°N, 106°W)	45
Crete (kreet), *island in Mediterranean Sea* (34°N, 25°E)	99
Crete, Sea of, *Europe and Asia* (36°N, 25°E)	99
Crimean Pen. (kry MEE uhn), *Ukraine* (45°N, 34°E)	95
Cristobal Colon, Mt., *Colombia* (11°N, 74°W)	90
Croatia (kro AY shuh), *country in Europe* (46°N, 16°E)	99
Crooked R., *British Columbia* (55°N, 123°W)	44
Cross City, *Fla.* (30°N, 83°W)	69
Cross L., *Manitoba* (55°N, 97°W)	45
Crossville, *Tenn.* (36°N, 85°W)	70
Crow Agency, *Mont.* (46°N, 107°W)	61
Crozet Is. (kro ZAY), *Indian O.* (46°S, 50°E)	107
Crystal Mts., *Gabon* (1°N, 11°E)	108
Cuanza R. (KWAN zuh), *Angola* (9°S, 13°E)	106
Cuba (KYOO buh), *country in Caribbean Sea* (23°N, 80°W)	85
Cucuta (KOO kuht uh), *Colombia* (8°N, 73°W)	90
Cuenca (KWENG kuh), *Ecuador* (3°S, 79°W)	90
Cuiaba (KYOO yuh BAH), *Brazil* (16°S, 56°W)	89
Cumana, *Venezuela* (10°N, 64°W)	90
Cumberland, *Md.* (40°N, 79°W)	71
Cumberland Gap, *mt. pass in Ky. and Va.* (37°N, 84°W)	70
Cumberland, L., *Ky.* (37°N, 85°W)	70
Cumberland Plateau, *U.S.* (36°N, 84°W)	70-71
Cumberland R., *U.S.* (36°N, 84°W)	70
Cumberland Sound, *Labrador Sea* (66°N, 67°W)	41
Cunene R. (kyoo NAY nuh), *Angola* (17°S, 14°E)	106
Curitiba (KOOR ih TEE buh), *Brazil* (25°S, 49°W)	89
Current R., *U.S.* (37°N, 91°W)	65
Cuzco (KOOS koh), *Peru* (14°S, 72°W)	89
Cut Bank Creek, *Mont.* (49°N, 113°W)	61
Cuttack (KUHT uhk), *India* (21°N, 86°E)	122
Cyclades (SIK luh DEEZ), *islands in Aegean Sea* (37°N, 24°E)	99

Name (Pronunciation), *Description* (Lat., Long.)	**Page**
Cyprus (SY pruhs), *country in Mediterranean* Sea (35°N, 33°E)	115
Cyrenaica (SIH ruh NAY ih cuh), *region of Libya* (32°N, 22°E)	114
Czech Republic, *country in Europe* (49°N, 15°E)	99
Czestochowa (CHEN stuh KOH vuh), *Poland* (51°N, 19°E)	99

D

Da Nang, *Vietnam* (16°N, 108°E)	123
Dabola, *Guinea* (11°N, 11°W)	108
Dahlak Archipelago, *island group in Red Sea* (16°N, 90°E)	115
Dakar, *Senegal* (15°N, 17°W)	108
Dakhilah Oasis (DAHK luh), *Egypt* (25°N, 29°E)	115
Dale Hollow L., *Tenn.* (37°N, 85°W)	70
Dalhart, *Tex.* (36°N, 102°W)	66
Dalian (dah lehn), *China* (39°N, 122°E)	124
Dallas, *Tex.* (33°N, 97°W)	67
Dalles, The (DALZ), *Oreg.* (46°N, 121°W)	60
Dalmatia, *region of Europe* (43°N, 17°E)	99
Dalton, *Ga.* (35°N, 85°W)	68
Daly City, *Calif.* (38°N, 122°W)	58
Damascus, *Syria* (34°N, 36°E)	115
Damavand, Mt., *Iran* (36°N, 52°E)	115
Dan R., *U.S.* (37°N, 79°W)	71
Danbury, *Conn.* (41°N, 73°W)	73
Dandenong, *Australia* (38°S, 145°E)	133
Dansville, *N.Y.* (43°N, 78°W)	72
Danube R., *Europe* (44°N, 27°E)	99
Danville, *Ill.* (40°N, 88°W)	65
Danville, *Va.* (37°N, 79°W)	71
Dar es Salaam, *Tanzania* (7°S, 39°E)	110
Dardanelle L., *Ark.* (35°N, 93°W)	67
Dardanelles, *strait of Europe and Asia* (40°N, 25°E)	99
Darien, Gulf of, *Caribbean Sea* (9°N, 77°W)	83
Darling Range, *Australia* (33°S, 117°E)	130
Darling R., *Australia* (32°S, 143°E)	133
Darnah, *Libya* (33°N, 23°E)	114
Darwin, *Australia* (12°S, 131°E)	131
Dauphin (DAW fuhn), *Manitoba* (51°N, 100°W)	45
Davao, *Philippines* (7°N, 126°E)	121
Davenport, *Iowa* (42°N, 91°W)	65
Davie, *Fla.* (26°N, 80°W)	69
Davis, *Calif.* (39°N, 122°W)	58
Davis Mts., *Tex.* (31°N, 104°W)	66
Davis Sea, *Antarctica* (65°S, 90°E)	137
Davis Strait, *Canada and Greenland* (67°N, 59°W)	41
Dawson, *Yukon Terr.* (64°N, 140°W)	42
Dawson Creek, *British Columbia* (56°N, 120°W)	44
Daxue Shan (dah shyoo shahn), *mts. in China* (30°N, 102°E)	124
Dayton, *Ohio* (40°N, 84°W)	70
Daytona Beach, *Fla.* (29°N, 81°W)	69
De Aar (dee AHR), *South Africa* (31°S, 24°E)	109
Dead Sea, *Asia* (31°N, 35°E)	115
Deal I., *Bass Strait* (39°S, 148°E)	133
Dearborn, *Mich.* (42°N, 83°W)	63
Dease Lake (DEES), *British Columbia* (58°N, 130°W)	44
Death Valley, *Calif.* (36°N, 117°W)	58
Debrecen (DEB ruht SEHN), *Hungary* (47°N, 22°E)	99
Decatur (deh KAY tuhr), *Ala.* (35°N, 87°W)	68
Decatur, *Ga.* (34°N, 84°W)	69
Decatur, *Ill.* (40°N, 89°W)	65
Deccan Plateau, *India* (18°N, 77°E)	122
Decelles, Res., *Quebec* (48°N, 78°W)	46
Decorah (deh KOHR uh), *Iowa* (43°N, 92°W)	65
Defiance, *Ohio* (41°N, 84°W)	70
DeKalb, *Ill.* (42°N, 89°W)	65
Del Norte (del NOHRT), *Colo.* (38°N, 106°W)	59
Del Rio, *Tex.* (29°N, 101°W)	66
Delaware, *state in U.S.* (39°N, 76°W)	71
Delaware Bay, *U.S.* (39°N, 75°W)	71
Delaware R., *U.S.* (40°N, 75°W)	72
Delhi (DEL ee), *India* (29°N, 77°E)	122
Delmarva Pen., *U.S.* (38°N, 76°W)	71

Denakil Depression, *lowland in Ethiopia* (14°N, 40°E)	115
Denali N. P., *Alaska* (63°N, 150°W)	57
Deniliquin (duh NIHL uh kwihn), *Australia* (36°S, 145°E)	133
Denison, *Iowa* (42°N, 95°W)	65
Denmark, *country in Europe* (56°N, 9°E)	96
Denmark Strait, *Greenland and Iceland* (67°N, 27°W)	41
Dennison, *Ohio* (40°N, 81°W)	71
Denton, *Tex.* (33°N, 97°W)	67
Denver, *Colo.* (40°N, 105°W)	59
Derby, *Australia* (17°S, 124°E)	131
Derry, *N.H.* (43°N, 71°W)	73
Des Moines (di MOYN), *Iowa* (42°N, 94°W)	65
Des Moines R., *Iowa* (43°N, 94°W)	65
Deschutes R. (dih SHOOTS), *Oreg.* (45°N, 121°W)	60
Detroit, *Mich.* (42°N, 83°W)	63
Devils Tower, *mt. in Wyo.* (45°N, 105°W)	61
Devils L., *N. Dak.* (48°N, 99°W)	62
Devils R., *Tex.* (30°N, 101°W)	66
Devon I., *Baffin Bay* (75°N, 85°W)	41
Dhaka, *Bangladesh* (24°N, 90°E)	122
Dickinson, *N. Dak.* (47°N, 103°W)	62
Diefenbaker (DEE fuhn BAY kuhr), L., *Saskatchewan* (51°N, 107°W)	45
Dien Bien Phu (DYEN byen FOO), *Vietnam* (21°N, 103°E)	123
Digby, *Nova Scotia* (45°N, 66°W)	47
Dijon (dee ZHOHN), *France* (47°N, 5°E)	98
Dillingham, *Alaska* (59°N, 159°W)	57
Dillon Res., *Ohio* (40°N, 82°W)	71
Dinaric Alps, *mt. range in Europe* (44°N, 17°E)	99
Disappointment, L., *Australia* (24°S, 123°E)	130
District of Columbia, *U.S.* (39°N, 77°W)	71
Dixon Entrance, *strait between Alaska and British Columbia* (54°N, 133°W)	57
Diyarbakir, *Turkey* (38°N, 40°E)	115
Dja R. (JAH), *Africa* (3°N, 13°E)	108
Djibouti (jih BOO tee), *country in Africa* (12°N, 43°E)	107
Djibouti, *Djibouti* (12°N, 43°E)	107
Dnepr Lowland (NEE puhr), *Ukraine* (53°N, 29°E)	95
Dnepr R., *Ukraine* (49°N, 34°E)	95
Dnepropetrovsk (NEHP roh pih TRAWFSK), *Ukraine* (48°N, 35°E)	97
Dnestr R., (NEE stuhr), *Ukraine* (48°N, 28°E)	95
Dodecanese (doh DEK uh NEEZ), *islands in Aegean Sea* (37°N, 26°E)	99
Dodge City, *Kans.* (38°N, 100°W)	64
Dodoma, *Tanzania* (6°S, 36°E)	110
Doha, *Qatar* (25°N, 52°E)	115
Dolak, *island in Arafura Sea* (8°S, 139°E)	130
Dolores R. (duh LOHR uhs), *Colo.* (39°N, 109°W)	59
Dominica, *country in Caribbean Sea* (16°N, 61°W)	85
Dominican Republic, *country in Caribbean Sea* (19°N, 71°W)	85
Don R., *Russia* (47°N, 40°E)	95
Donegal Bay (DAHN ih GAWL), *Ireland* (55°N, 8°W)	98
Donets R., *Ukraine* (49°N, 38°E)	95
Donetsk, *Ukraine* (48°N, 38°E)	97
Dongting L., *China* (29°N, 112°E)	124
Door Pen., *Wis.* (45°N, 87°W)	63
Dordogne R. (dawr DOHN), *France* (45°N, 1°E)	98
Dortmund (DAWRT moont), *Germany* (52°N, 7°E)	99
Dothan, *Ala.* (31°N, 85°W)	68
Douala, *Cameroon* (4°N, 10°E)	108
Double Mountain Fork, *r. in Tex.* (34°N, 102°W)	66
Doubs R. (DOO), *France* (47°N, 5°E)	98
Douglas, *Ariz.* (31°N, 110°W)	59
Douglas, *Wyo.* (43°N, 105°W)	61
Douro R., *Portugal* (41°N, 8°W)	94
Dover (DOH vuhr), *Del.* (39°N, 75°W)	71
Dover, *England* (51°N, 1°E)	98
Dover, *N.H.* (43°N, 71°W)	73
Dover, Strait of, *England and France* (51°N, 1°E)	98
Drake Passage, *South America* (57°S, 65°W)	88

Drakensberg, *mt. range in South Africa* (31°S, 27°E)	109
Drava R., *Europe* (46°N, 17°E)	99
Dresden (DREZ dehn), *Germany* (51°N, 14°E)	99
Driftless Area, *U.S.* (43°N, 91°W)	63
Drumheller, *Alberta* (51°N, 113°W)	44-45
Drummond I., *L. Huron* (48°N, 84°W)	63
Drummondsville, *Quebec* (46°N, 73°W)	47
Dry Tortugas, *islands in Gulf of Mexico* (25°N, 83°W)	69
Dryden, *Ontario* (50°N, 93°W)	46
Dubawnt L., *Northwest Terr.* (63°N, 101°W)	45
Dubayy, *United Arab Emirates* (25°N, 55°E)	115
Dublin, *Ga.* (33°N, 83°W)	69
Dublin, *Ireland* (53°N, 6°W)	98
Dubrovnik (DOO BRAWV nik), *Croatia* (43°N, 18°E)	99
Dubuque (duh BYOOK), *Iowa* (43°N, 91°W)	65
Duck Mt. N. P., *Manitoba* (52°N, 101°W)	45
Duero R. (DWER oh), *Europe* (42°N, 3°W)	98
Duluth (duh LOOTH), *Minn.* (47°N, 92°W)	63
Dundalk (DUHN dawk), *Ireland* (54°N, 6°W)	98
Dundee (duhn DEE), *Scotland* (56°N, 3°W)	98
Dunedin, *New Zealand* (46°S, 171°E)	131
Durance R. (doo RAHNS), *France* (44°N, 5°E)	98
Durango, *Colo.* (37°N, 108°W)	59
Durant (doo RANT), *Okla.* (34°N, 96°W)	67
Durban, *South Africa* (30°S, 31°E)	109
Durham, *N.C.* (36°N, 79°W)	71
Dushanbe (du SHAM buh), *Tajikistan* (38°N, 69°E)	100
Dusseldorf (DOO suhl DAWRF), *Germany* (51°N, 7°E)	99
Dutch Harbor, *Alaska* (54°N, 167°W)	57
Dyersburg, *Tenn.* (36°N, 89°W)	70
Dzhugdzhur Range, *Russia* (58°N, 140°E)	101
Dzungarian Basin (ZUNG GAR ee uhn), *Asia* (45°N, 86°E)	124

E

Eagle L., *Maine* (46°N, 71°W)	73
Eagle Mountain L., *Tex.* (33°N, 98°W)	67
Eagle Pass, *Tex.* (29°N, 100°W)	66
Eagle R., *Newfoundland* (54°N, 57°W)	47
East Chicago, *Ind.* (42°N, 87°W)	70
East China Sea, *Asia* (30°N, 125°E)	125
East Fork White R., *Ind.* (39°N, 86°W)	70
East Frisian Is. (FRIZH uhn), *North Sea* (54°N, 7°E)	99
East Lansing, *Mich.* (43°N, 84°W)	63
East Liverpool, *Ohio* (41°N, 81°W)	71
East London, *South Africa* (33°S, 27°E)	109
East Nishnabotna R. (NISH nuh BAHT nuh), *Iowa* (41°N, 96°W)	64-65
East Point, *Ga.* (34°N, 84°W)	69
East Saint Louis, *Ill.* (39°N, 90°W)	65
East Siberian Sea, *Arctic O.* (73°N, 165°E)	119
East Siberian Uplands, *Siberia* (66°N, 135°E)	119
Easter I., *poss. of Chile* (27°S, 110°W)	135
Eastern Ghats, *mt. range in India* (13°N, 78°E)	122
Eastmain, *Quebec* (52°N, 79°W)	46
Eastmain R., *Quebec* (52°N, 76°W)	46-47
Easton, *Pa.* (41°N, 75°W)	72
Eastport, *Maine* (45°N, 69°W)	73
Eau Claire (oh KLAYR), *Wis.* (45°N, 92°W)	63
Ebro R., *Spain* (42°N, 2°W)	114
Echuca (ee CHOO kah), *Australia* (36°S, 145°E)	133
Ecuador (EHK wuh dohr), *country in South America* (1°S, 78°W)	90
Edinburg, *Tex.* (26°N, 98°W)	66
Edinburgh (ED ihn BUH ruh), *Scotland* (56°N, 3°W)	98
Edirne (ay DIHR nuh), *Turkey* (42°N, 27°E)	115
Edmond, *Okla.* (36°N, 97°W)	67
Edmonds, *Wash.* (48°N, 122°W)	60
Edmonton, *Alberta* (54°N, 113°W)	44
Edmundston, *New Brunswick* (47°N, 68°W)	47
Edward, L., *Africa* (0°, 30°E)	110
Edwards Plateau, *Tex.* (31°N, 101°W)	66
Eel R., *Calif.* (41°N, 124°W)	58

Name (Pronunciation), *Description* (Lat., Long.)	Page
Efate (ay FAHT ee), *island in Pacific O.* (18°S, 169°E)	130
Effingham, *Ill.* (39°N, 88°W)	65
Egypt, *country in Africa* (25°N, 30°E)	114
Eighty Mile Beach, *Australia* (21°S, 119°E)	130
Eildon, L. (EEL duhn), *Australia* (37°S, 146°E)	133
Ekwan R., *Ontario* (53°N, 82°W)	46
El Aaiun (EHL ah YOON), *Western Sahara* (27°N, 13°W)	112
El Chicon (chee KOHN), *mt. in Mexico* (17°N, 93°W)	82
El Dorado (EHL duh RAH doh), *Ark.* (33°N, 93°W)	67
El Obeid, *Sudan* (13°N, 30°E)	115
El Paso, *Tex.* (32°N, 106°W)	66
El Salvador, *country in Central America* (13°N, 89°W)	84
Elazig (EHL uh ZUH), *Turkey* (39°N, 39°E)	115
Elba, *island in Tyrrhenian Sea* (43°N, 10°E)	99
Elbe R., *Europe* (54°N, 10°E)	99
Elbert, Mt., *Colo.* (39°N, 106°W)	59
Elblag (EL BLAWNG), *Poland* (54°N, 19°E)	99
Elbrus, Mt., *Russia* (43°N, 42°E)	95
Elburz Mts., *Iran* (36°N, 52°E)	114
Elephant Butte Res., *N. Mex.* (33°N, 107°W)	59
Eleuthera I., *Bahamas* (25°N, 76°W)	69
Elgin (EL jihn), *Ill.* (42°N, 88°W)	65
Elgon, Mt., *Africa* (1°N, 34°E)	110
Elizabeth, *Australia* (35°S, 138°E)	133
Elizabeth, *N.J.* (41°N, 74°W)	72
Elizabeth City, *N.C.* (36°N, 76°W)	71
Elizabethton, *Tenn.* (36°N, 82°E)	71
Elizabethtown, *N.C.* (35°N, 79°W)	71
Elk City, *Okla.* (35°N, 99°W)	66
Elk City Res., *Kans.* (37°N, 96°W)	64
Elk Is. N. P., *Alberta* (54°N, 113°W)	44-45
Elkhart, *Ind.* (42°N, 86°W)	70
Elkhorn R., *Nebr.* (42°N, 98°W)	64
Elkins, *W. Va.* (39°N, 80°W)	71
Elko, *Nev.* (41°N, 116°W)	62
Elwell, L., *Mont.* (48°N, 111°W)	61
Ellef Ringnes I. (EL uhf RING nays), *Arctic O.* (79°N, 102°W)	40
Ellensburg, *Wash.* (47°N, 121°W)	60
Ellesmere I., *Arctic O.* (80°N, 77°W)	41
Ellsworth, *Maine* (45°N, 68°W)	73
Ellsworth Land, *region of Antarctica* (85°S, 90°W)	137
Elmhurst, *Ill.* (42°N, 88°W)	65
Elmira (el MY ruh), *N.Y.* (42°N, 77°W)	72
Elwell, L., *Mont.* (48°N, 111°W)	61
Ely (EE lee), *Minn.* (48°N, 92°W)	63
Ely, *Nev.* (39°N, 115°W)	58
Elyria (ih LIHR ee uh), *Ohio* (41°N, 82°W)	71
Emamshahr (eh MAHM SHAHR), *Iran* (36°N, 55°E)	115
Embarrass R. (AHM braw), *Ill.* (39°N, 88°W)	65
Emi Koussi (AY mee KYOO suh), *mt. in Chad* (20°N, 19°E)	106
Emporia (em POHR ee uh), *Kans.* (38°N, 96°W)	64
Encounter Bay, *Australia* (36°S, 138°E)	133
Enfield, *Conn.* (42°N, 73°W)	73
England, *part of United Kingdom* (53°N, 1°W)	98
English Channel, *England and France* (50°N, 2°W)	98
Enid (EE nid), *Okla.* (36°N, 98°W)	67
Ennadaj L., *Northwest Terr.* (61°N, 101°W)	45
Ennedi Plateau (EN uh DEE), *Africa* (18°N, 23°E)	115
Ensenada (EN suh NAHD uh), *Mexico* (32°N, 117°W)	58
Entebbe (ehn TEHB ih), *Uganda* (0°, 32°E)	110
Enugu (ah NOO goo), *Nigeria* (6°N, 7°E)	108
Equatorial Guinea, *country in Africa* (2°N, 9°E)	108
Erebus, Mt. (EHR uh buhs), *Antarctica* (78°S, 167°E)	137
Erfurt, *Germany* (51°N, 11°E)	99
Erg Chech, *desert in Africa* (25°N, 2°W)	114
Erg Iguidi, *desert in Africa* (26°N, 7°W)	114
Erie, *Pa.* (42°N, 80°W)	72
Erie, L., *North America* (42°N, 82°W)	46
Erie Canal (EER ee), *N.Y.* (43°N, 77°W)	72
Eritrea (EH rih TREE yuh), *country in Africa* (15°N, 39°E)	107
Esbjerg (EHS byerhg), *Denmark* (55°N, 30°E)	99
Erzurum (ERZ ROOM), *Turkey* (40°N, 41°E)	115
Escambia R., *Fla.* (31°N, 87°W)	68
Escanaba (ES kuh NAHB uh), *Mich.* (46°N, 87°W)	63
Escondido (EHS kun DEED oh), *Calif.* (33°N, 117°W)	58
Eskisehir (EHS kih shuh HIHR), *Turkey* (40°N, 30°E)	115
Espiritu Santo, *island in Pacific O.* (15°S, 167°E)	130
Essen, *Germany* (51°N, 7°E)	99
Essequibo R. (ES uh KWEE boh), *Guyana* (4°N, 58°W)	90
Essex, Mt., *Vt.* (45°N, 73°W)	73
Estevan (EHS tuh VAN), *Saskatchewan* (49°N, 103°W)	45
Estonia, *country in Europe* (59°N, 26°E)	97
Ethiopia, *country in Africa* (10°N, 40°E)	107
Ethiopian Highlands, *Africa* (10°N, 37°E)	106
Etna, Mt., *Sicily* (38°N, 15°E)	99
Etobicoke, *Ontario* (44°N, 80°W)	46
Etorofu (EHT uh ROH foo), *island in Sea of Okhotsk* (45°N, 147°E)	125
Etosha Pan, *dry lake in Namibia* (19°S, 16°E)	106
Euboea (EV yuh), *island in the Aegean Sea* (39°N, 24°E)	99
Euclid (YOO klid), *Ohio* (41°N, 82°W)	71
Eufaula L. (yoo FAW luh), *Okla.* (35°N, 96°W)	67
Eugene, *Oreg.* (44°N, 123°W)	60
Eugenia, Cape, *Mexico* (28°N, 115°W)	82
Euphrates R., *Asia* (35°N, 41°E)	115
Eureka, *Calif.* (41°N, 124°W)	62
Europe, *continent*	7
Eutsuk L. (OOT suhk), *British Columbia* (53°N, 126°W)	44
Evans Res., *Quebec* (51°N, 77°W)	46-47
Evanston, *Ill.* (42°N, 88°W)	65
Evanston, *Wyo.* (41°N, 111°W)	61
Evansville, *Ind.* (38°N, 88°W)	70
Everest, Mt., *China and Nepal* (28°N, 87°E)	122
Everett, *Wash.* (48°N, 122°W)	60
Everglades, The, *swamp in Fla.* (26°N, 81°W)	69
Everglades N.P., *Fla.* (25°N, 81°W)	69
Exeter (EHK suht uhr), *England* (51°N, 4°W)	98
Eyasi, L. (ay YAH say), *Tanzania* (3°S, 35°E)	110
Eyre, L. (AYR), *Australia* (29°S, 138°E)	130
Eyre Pen., *Australia* (33°S, 136°E)	133

F

Faeroe Is. (FAYR oh), *overseas part of Denmark* (62°N, 7°W)	94
Faffak, *Indonesia* (3°S, 132°E)	131
Fairbanks, *Alaska* (65°N, 148°W)	57
Fairmont, *Minn.* (44°N, 94°W)	62
Fairmont, *W. Va.* (39°N, 80°W)	71
Fairweather, Mt., *Yukon* (59°N, 138°W)	40
Faisalabad (FY SAHL uh BAHD), *Pakistan* (31°N, 73°E)	122
Falcon Res., *Tex.* (27°N, 99°W)	66
Faleme R. (fal uh MAY), *Africa* (13°N, 11°W)	108
Falfurrias (fal FYOOR ee uhs), *Tex.* (27°N, 98°W)	66
Falkland Is., *Atlantic O.* (52°S, 60°W)	89
Fall River, *Mass.* (42°N, 71°W)	73
Farafirah Oasis (fuh RAHF uh ruh), *Egypt* (27°N, 28°E)	115
Farasan Is., *Red Sea* (17°N, 42°E)	115
Farewell, Cape, *Greenland* (59°N, 43°W)	41
Fargo, *N. Dak.* (47°N, 97°W)	62
Farmington, *Maine* (45°N, 70°W)	73
Farmington, *N. Mex.* (37°N, 108°W)	59
Fawn R., *Ontario* (60°N, 88°W)	46
Fayette (fay EHT), *Iowa* (43°N, 92°W)	65
Fayetteville, *Ark.* (36°N, 94°W)	67
Fayetteville, *N.C.* (35°N, 79°W)	71
Fderik, *Mauritania* (23°N, 13°W)	107
Fear, Cape, *N.C.* (34°N, 78°W)	71
Federated States of Micronesia, *country in Pacific O.* (10°N, 150°E)	135
Feira de Santana (FAY uhr uh duh san TAN uh), *Brazil* (12°S, 39°W)	89
Fergus Falls, *Minn.* (46°N, 96°W)	62
Fernando de Noronha, *island in Atlantic O.* (4°S, 32°W)	89
Fernie, *British Columbia* (50°N, 115°W)	44
Ferrara, *Italy* (45°N, 12°E)	99
Feuilles R. (FOO yuh), *Quebec* (59°N, 71°W)	41
Fez, *Morocco* (34°N, 5°W)	114
Fifth Cataract, *waterfall in Sudan* (18°N, 34°E)	115
Figuig (fih GIHG), *Morocco* (32°N, 2°W)	114
Fiji, *country in Pacific O.* (20°S, 178°W)	135
Filchner Ice Shelf, *Antarctica* (82°S, 30°W)	137
Findlay, *Ohio* (41°N, 84°W)	70
Finisterre, Cape (FIN uh STEHR), *Spain* (43°N, 9°W)	114
Finland, *country in Europe* (62°N, 24°E)	97
Finland, Gulf of, *Baltic Sea* (60°N, 25°E)	95
Finlay R., *British Columbia* (58°N, 126°W)	44
Firebag Hills, *Canada* (57°N, 110°W)	45
First Cataract, *waterfall in Egypt* (24°N, 33°E)	115
Firth of Forth, *bay in Scotland* (56°N, 3°W)	108
Fitchburg, *Mass.* (43°N, 72°W)	73
Flagstaff, *Ariz.* (35°N, 112°W)	59
Flagstaff L., *Maine* (45°N, 70°W)	73
Flambeau R. (FLAM boh), *Wis.* (45°N, 91°W)	63
Flaming Gorge Res., *Wyo.* (41°N, 110°W)	61
Flanders, *region of Europe* (51°N, 2°E)	98
Flathead L., *Mont.* (48°N, 114°W)	61
Flathead R., *Mont.* (49°N, 114°W)	61
Flattery, Cape, *U.S.* (48°N, 125°W)	60
Flin Flon, *Manitoba* (55°N, 102°W)	45
Flinders I., *Bass Strait* (40°S, 148°E)	133
Flinders Ranges, *Australia* (33°S, 138°E)	130
Flinders R., *Australia* (18°S, 141°E)	130
Flint, *Mich.* (43°N, 84°W)	63
Flint Hills, *Kans.* (38°N, 97°W)	64
Flint R., *Ga.* (32°N, 84°W)	69
Florence, *Ala.* (35°N, 88°W)	68
Florence, *Italy* (44°N, 11°E)	99
Florence, *S.C.* (34°N, 80°W)	69
Flores, *island in Sava Sea* (9°S, 121°E)	130
Flores Sea, *Indian O.* (7°S, 120°E)	130
Florianopolis, *Brazil* (28°S, 49°W)	89
Florida, *state in U.S.* (30°N, 83°W)	68-69
Florida, Straits of, *U.S. and Cuba* (24°N, 81°W)	69
Florida Bay, *Fla.* (25°N, 81°W)	69
Florida Keys, *islands in Caribbean Sea* (25°N, 81°W)	69
Florina (FLAWR uh nuh), *Greece* (41°N, 21°E)	99
Florissant, *Mo.* (39°N, 90°W)	65
Floyd R., *Iowa* (43°N, 96°W)	64
Foggia (FAW juh), *Italy* (42°N, 16°E)	99
Folsom L., *Calif.* (39°N, 121°W)	58
Fond-du-Lac (FAHN duh LAK), *Saskatchewan* (59°N, 107°W)	45
Fond du Lac, *Wis.* (44°N, 89°W)	63
Fond-du-Lac R., *Saskatchewan* (59°N, 104°W)	45
Fonseca, Gulf of, *Pacific O.* (13°N, 88°W)	82-83
Forest City, *Iowa* (43°N, 94°W)	65
Forestville, *Quebec* (49°N, 69°W)	47
Forillon N. P. (FOH ree YOHN), *Quebec* (49°N, 64°W)	47
Formosa Strait, *Taiwan and China* (24°N, 120°E)	124
Fort Albany, *Ontario* (52°N, 82°W)	46
Fort Chipewyan, *Alberta* (59°N, 111°W)	45
Fort Collins, *Colo.* (41°N, 105°W)	59
Fort Dodge, *Iowa* (43°N, 94°W)	65
Fort Frances, *Ontario* (49°N, 93°W)	46
Fort Knox, *Ky.* (38°N, 86°W)	70
Fort Lauderdale, *Fla.* (26°N, 80°W)	69
Fort Liard (LEE AHRD), *Northwest Terr.* (60°N, 123°W)	44
Fort Loudoun L. (LOWD uhn), *Tenn.* (36°N, 84°W)	70
Fort McMurray, *Alberta* (57°N, 111°W)	45
Fort Myers, *Fla.* (27°N, 82°W)	69
Fort Nelson, *British Columbia* (59°N, 123°W)	44
Fort Nelson R., *British Columbia* (59°N, 123°W)	44
Fort Peck Dam, *Mont.* (48°N, 106°W)	61
Fort Peck L., *Mont.* (48°N, 107°W)	61
Fort Pierce, *Fla.* (27°N, 80°W)	69
Fort Randall Dam, *S. Dak.* (43°N, 99°W)	62
Fort Resolution, *Northwest Terr.* (61°N, 114°W)	44

Name (Pronunciation), *Description* (Lat., Long.)	Page
Fort Saint John, *British Columbia* (56°N, 121°W)	44
Fort Scott, *Kans.* (38°N, 95°W)	65
Fort Severn, *Ontario* (57°N, 88°W)	43
Fort Simpson, *Northwest Terr.* (62°N, 121°W)	44
Fort Smith, *Ark.* (35°N, 94°W)	67
Fort Smith, *Northwest Terr.* (60°N, 112°W)	45
Fort Stockton, *Tex.* (31°N, 103°W)	66
Fort Vermillion, *Alberta* (58°N, 116°W)	44
Fort Walton Beach, *Fla.* (30°N, 87°W)	68
Fort Wayne, *Ind.* (41°N, 85°W)	70
Fort Worth, *Tex.* (33°N, 97°W)	67
Fort Yukon (YOO KAHN), *Alaska* (67°N, 145°W)	57
Fortaleza, *Brazil* (4°S, 39°W)	89
Fourth Cataract, *waterfall in Sudan* (19°N, 32°E)	115
Foveaux Strait (FOH VOH), *New Zealand* (47°S, 168°E)	130
Fox R., *U.S.* (42°N, 88°W)	65
Fox R., *Wis.* (44°N, 89°W)	63
Foxe Basin, *Northwest Terr.* (67°N, 80°W)	41
Foxe Channel, *Northwest Terr.* (65°N, 80°W)	41
Foxe Pen., *Baffin I.* (65°N, 76°W)	41
Framingham (FRAY ming HAM), *Mass.* (42°N, 72°W)	73
France, *country in Europe* (47°N, 0°)	98
Franceville (frahns VEEL), *Gabon* (2°S, 14°E)	108
Francis Case, L., *S. Dak.* (43°N, 99°W)	62
Francois L. (FRANG SWUH), *British Columbia* (54°N, 126°W)	44
Frankfort, *Ky.* (38°N, 85°W)	70
Frankfurt, *Germany* (50°N, 9°E)	99
Franklin, *N.C.* (35°N, 83°W)	70
Franklin D. Roosevelt L., *Wash.* (48°N, 118°W)	60
Franz Josef Land, *island group in Arctic O.* (82°N, 55°E)	100
Fraser I., *Australia* (25°S, 153°E)	130
Fraser Plateau, *British Columbia* (53°N, 125°W)	44
Fraser R., *Canada* (51°N, 122°W)	44
Frederick, *Md.* (39°N, 77°W)	71
Fredericksburg, *Va.* (38°N, 77°W)	71
Fredericton, *New Brunswick* (46°N, 67°W)	47
Fredonia, *N.Y.* (42°N, 79°W)	72
Freemantle, *Australia* (32°S, 116°E)	131
Freeport, *Ill.* (42°N, 90°W)	65
Freetown, *Sierra Leone* (8°N, 13°W)	108
Fremont (FREE MAHNT), *Calif.* (38°N, 122°W)	58
Fremont, *Nebr.* (41°N, 96°W)	64
Fremont, *Ohio* (41°N, 83°W)	70
French Guiana (gee AH nuh), *overseas state of France* (4°N, 53°W)	90
French Lick, *Ind.* (39°N, 87°W)	70
French Polynesia, *poss. of France* (150°S, 140°W)	135
Frenchman R., *North America* (49°N, 108°W)	45
Fresno, *Calif.* (37°N, 120°W)	58
Fria, Cape, *Africa* (18°S, 12°E)	106
Frio, Cape, *Brazil* (23°S, 42°W)	88
Frisian Is., *Europe* (53°N, 5°E)	94
Frobisher Bay, *Canada* (63°N, 67°W)	41
Frobisher L., *Saskatchewan* (56°N, 108°W)	45
Front Range, *Colo.* (40°N, 106°W)	59
Fuerte R., *Mexico* (27°N, 109°W)	82
Fuji, Mt. (FOO jee), *Japan* (35°N, 139°E)	125
Fukui (foo KOO ee), *Japan* (36°N, 136°E)	125
Fukuoka, *Japan* (34°N, 130°E)	125
Fukushima (FOO kuh SHEE muh), *Japan* (37°N, 140°E)	125
Fulton, *Ky.* (37°N, 89°W)	70
Fundy, Bay of, *North America* (45°N, 65°W)	47
Fundy N.P., *New Brunswick* (46°N, 65°W)	47
Furnas Res., *Brazil* (21°S, 46°W)	88
Furneaux Group (FUHR noh), *islands in Bass Strait* (40°S, 148°E)	130
Fushun (fyu shoon), *China* (42°N, 124°E)	124
Fuzhou (FYU zhoo), *China* (26°N, 119°E)	124
Fyn (FIN), *island in Katlegat* (55°N, 10°E)	99

G

Gabes, Gulf of (GAHB uhs), *Tunisia* (34°N, 10°E)	114
Gabon, *country in Africa* (1°S, 12°E)	108
Gaborone (GAHB uh ROHN ee), *Botswana* (24°S, 26°E)	107
Gadsden, *Ala.* (34°N, 86°W)	68
Gagnon (gah NYON), *Quebec* (52°N, 68°W)	47
Gainesville, *Fla.* (30°N, 82°W)	69
Gairdner, L., *Australia* (32°S, 136°E)	130
Galapagos Is. (guh LAH puh GOHS), *Pacific O.* (0°, 91°W)	90
Galati (guh LATS ee), *Romania* (45°N, 28°E)	99
Galena (guh LEEN uh), *Ill.* (42°N, 90°W)	65
Galesburg (GAYLZ buhrg), *Ill.* (41°N, 90°W)	65
Gallatin R., *Mont.* (45°N, 111°W)	61
Gallinas, Point, *Colombia* (12°N, 72°W)	90
Gallup, *N. Mex.* (36°N, 109°W)	59
Galveston, *Tex.* (29°N, 95°W)	67
Galveston Bay, *Tex.* (30°N, 94°W)	67
Galway, *Ireland* (53°N, 9°W)	98
Galway Bay, *Ireland* (53°N, 9°W)	98
Gambia (GAM bee uh), *country in Africa* (13°N, 15°W)	108
Gambia R., *Africa* (13°N, 14°W)	108
Gamtoos R., *South Africa* (34°S, 25°E)	109
Ganges, Mouths of the (GAN jeez), *delta in Asia* (22°N, 89°E)	122
Ganges Plain, *India* (26°N, 84°E)	122
Ganges R., *India* (25°N, 86°E)	122
Gao, *Mali* (17°N, 0°)	107
Garden City, *Kans.* (38°N, 101°W)	64
Garibaldi, Mt. (GAR uh BAWL dee), *British Columbia* (50°N, 123°W)	44
Garissa, *Kenya* (1°S, 40°E)	110
Garland, *Tex.* (33°N, 97°W)	67
Garnpung, L., *Australia* (34°S, 143°E)	133
Garonne R. (guh RAHN), *France* (44°N, 1°E)	98
Garoua (guh ROO uh), *Cameroon* (9°N, 13°E)	108
Garrison Dam, *N. Dak.* (48°N, 101°W)	62
Gary, *Ind.* (42°N, 87°W)	70
Gasconade R. (GAS kuh NAYD), *Mo.* (38°N, 92°W)	65
Gaspe (gah SPAY), *Quebec* (49°N, 65°W)	47
Gaspe Pen., *Quebec* (48°N, 67°W)	47
Gastonia, *N.C.* (35°N, 81°W)	71
Gates of the Arctic N. P., *Alaska* (68°N, 154°W)	57
Gatineau R. (GAT uhn OH), *Quebec* (45°N, 76°W)	47
Gauhati, *India* (26°N, 92°E)	122
Gavin's Point Dam, *S. Dak.* (43°N, 97°W)	62
Gaza Strip, *terr. in Asia* (32°N, 34°E)	115
Gaziantep, *Turkey* (37°N, 37°E)	115
Gbarnga, *Liberia* (7°N, 9°W)	108
Gdansk (guh DAHNSK), *Poland* (54°N, 19°E)	99
Gdansk, Gulf of, *Poland* (55°N, 19°E)	99
Gdynia (guh DIN ee uh), *Poland* (54°N, 18°E)	99
Geelong (juh LAWNG), *Australia* (38°S, 144°E)	133
Geita, *Tanzania* (3°S, 32°E)	110
Genesee R. (JEN uh SEE), *N.Y.* (42°N, 78°W)	72
Geneseo (JEN uh SEE oh), *N.Y.* (43°N, 78°W)	72
Geneva, *Switzerland* (46°N, 6°E)	99
Geneva, L., *Switzerland* (46°N, 7°E)	99
Genoa (JEHN oh uh), *Italy* (44°N, 9°E)	99
George, L., *Fla.* (29°N, 82°W)	69
George, L., *N.Y.* (44°N, 73°W)	72
George, L., *Uganda* (0°, 30°E)	110
George Res., *U.S.* (32°N, 85°W)	68
George R., *Quebec* (58°N, 66°W)	41
George West, *Tex.* (28°N, 98°W)	66
Georgetown, *Guyana* (7°N, 58°W)	90
Georgetown, *Ky.* (38°N, 85°W)	70
Georgetown, *Md.* (39°N, 76°W)	71
Georgia, *country in Asia* (42°N, 43°E)	100
Georgia, *state in U.S.* (33°N, 83°W)	68-69
Georgia, Strait of, *British Columbia* (49°N, 125°W)	44
Georgian Bay, *Canada* (45°N, 81°W)	46
Georgian Bay Is. N.P., *L. Huron* (45°N, 80°W)	46
Geraldton, *Australia* (29°S, 115°E)	131
Germantown, *Tenn.* (37°N, 90°W)	70
Germany, *country in Europe* (52°N, 12°E)	99
Germiston (JEHR muh stuhn), *South Africa* (26°S, 28°E)	109
Gettysburg, *Pa.* (40°N, 77°W)	72
Ghadamis, *Libya* (30°N, 10°E)	114
Ghaghara R. (GAHG uh ruh), *Asia* (27°N, 83°E)	122
Ghana, *Africa* (8°N, 2°W)	108
Ghat, *Libya* (25°N, 10°E)	114
Ghent (gehnt), *Belgium* (51°N, 4°E)	98
Gibraltar (jih BRAWL tuhr), *terr. of United Kingdom* (36°N, 5°W)	114
Gibraltar, Strait of, *Europe and Africa* (36°N, 6°W)	114
Gibson Desert, *Australia* (24°S, 120°E)	130
Gila R. (HEE luh), *Ariz.* (33°N, 114°W)	58-59
Gillam, *Manitoba* (56°N, 95°W)	45
Gillette (juh LEHT), *Wyo.* (44°N, 106°W)	61
Gimli, *Manitoba* (51°N, 97°W)	45
Gippsland, *Australia* (37°S, 148°E)	133
Gironde R. (juh RAHND), *France* (45°N, 1°W)	98
Giza (GEE zuh), *Egypt* (30°N, 31°E)	115
Glacier Bay N.P. (GLAY shuhr), *Alaska* (59°N, 137°W)	57
Glacier N.P., *British Columbia* (51°N, 118°W)	44
Glacier N.P., *Mont.* (49°N, 114°W)	61
Glasgow (GLAS GOH), *Ky.* (37°N, 86°W)	70
Glasgow (GLAHZ goh), *Scotland* (56°N, 4°W)	98
Glen Canyon Dam, *Ariz.* (37°N, 111°W)	59
Glendale, *Ariz.* (34°N, 112°W)	59
Glendale, *Calif.* (34°N, 118°W)	58
Glendive (GLEHN DYV), *Mont.* (47°N, 105°W)	61
Glenelg R., *Australia* (37°S, 143°E)	133
Gobi Desert (GOH bee), *Asia* (44°N, 109°E)	119
Godavari R. (guh DAHV uh ree), *India* (19°N, 77°E)	122
Goderich (GAHD RICH), *Ontario* (44°N, 82°W)	46
Gods L., *Manitoba* (55°N, 94°W)	45
Gods R., *Manitoba* (55°N, 93°W)	45
Godthab (GAWT hob), *Greenland* (64°N, 51°W)	35
Godwin Austen, Mt., *China and Pakistan* (36°N, 77°E)	122
Gogebic Range (goh GEE bik), *Mich.* (47°N, 90°W)	63
Goiania (goy AN ee uh), *Brazil* (17°S, 49°W)	89
Golan Heights, *terr. in Asia* (33°N, 36°E)	115
Gold Coast, *Australia* (28°S, 153°E)	131
Gold Coast, *region in Africa* (5°N, 0°)	108
Goldsboro, *N.C.* (35°N, 78°W)	71
Good Hope, Cape of, *South Africa* (34°S, 18°E)	109
Goodland, *Kans.* (39°N, 102°W)	64
Goose L., *U.S.* (42°N, 121°W)	58
Gorgan (gohr GAHN), *Iran* (37°N, 54°E)	115
Gorki Res., *Russia* (57°N, 43°E)	95
Gotaland, *region of Sweden* (57°N, 13°E)	94
Goteborg (YUH tuh BAWR yuh), *Sweden* (58°N, 12°E)	99
Gotel Mts., *Africa* (7°N, 11°E)	108
Gotland, *island in Baltic Sea* (57°N, 19°E)	94
Goto I. (GOHT oh), *island in East China Sea* (33°N, 129°E)	125
Gott Peak, *British Columbia* (50°N, 122°W)	44
Gouin, Res. (GWAN), *Quebec* (48°N, 74°W)	47
Goulburn (GOHL buhrn), *Australia* (35°S, 150°E)	133
Graaff Reinet (GRAHF RY nut), *South Africa* (32°S, 25°E)	109
Grafton, *N. Dak.* (48°N, 97°W)	62
Graham, *Tex.* (33°N, 99°W)	66
Grahamstown, *South Africa* (33°S, 27°E)	109
Grain Coast, *region of Africa* (5°N, 10°W)	108
Grampian Mts., *Scotland* (57°N, 4°W)	98
Gran Chaco, *plains in central South America* (24°S, 63°W)	88
Granada, *Spain* (37°N, 4°W)	114
Granby, *Quebec* (45°N, 73°W)	47
Grand Bahama I., *Atlantic O.* (27°N, 78°W)	83
Grand Canal, *China* (36°N, 116°E)	124
Grand Canyon, *Ariz.* (36°N, 113°W)	58-59
Grand Canyon N.P., *Ariz.* (36°N, 112°W)	59
Grand Coulee Dam, *Wash.* (48°N, 119°W)	60
Grand Erg de Bilma, *desert in Africa* (19°N, 14°E)	114
Grand Erg Occidental, *desert in Algeria* (30°N, 1°E)	114
Grand Erg Oriental, *desert in Algeria* (31°N, 7°E)	114

Name (Pronunciation), *Description* (Lat., Long.)	**Page**
Grand Falls, *New Brunswick* (47°N, 68°W)	47
Grand Forks, *N. Dak.* (48°N, 97°W)	62
Grand Haven, *Mich.* (43°N, 86°W)	63
Grand I., *L. Superior* (47°N, 87°W)	63
Grand Island, *Nebr.* (41°N, 98°W)	64
Grand Junction, *Colo.* (39°N, 108°W)	59
Grand L., *La.* (30°N, 93°W)	67
Grand L., *New Brunswick* (46°N, 67°W)	47
Grand L., *Ohio* (41°N, 84°W)	70
Grand Manan I., *Bay of Fundy* (45°N, 67°W)	47
Grand Rapids, *Manitoba* (53°N, 99°W)	45
Grand Rapids, *Mich.* (43°N, 86°W)	63
Grand R., *Mich.* (43°N, 86°W)	63
Grand R., *S. Dak.* (46°N, 102°W)	62
Grand R., *U.S.* (40°N, 94°W)	65
Grand Teton N.P., *Wyo.* (44°N, 110°W)	61
Grand Traverse Bay, *Mich.* (45°N, 86°W)	63
Grande 4, Res. de la, *Quebec* (54°N, 73°W)	47
Grande Prairie, *Alberta* (55°N, 119°W)	44
Grande R., *Nicaragua* (14°N, 84°W)	83
Grande 3, Res. de la, *Quebec* (54°N, 75°W)	47
Grande 2, Res. de la, *Quebec* (54°N, 77°W)	46-47
Granville L., *Manitoba* (56°N, 100°W)	45
Grays Harbor, *Wash.* (47°N, 124°W)	60
Graz, *Austria* (47°N, 15°E)	99
Great Abaco I., *Atlantic O.* (27°N, 77°W)	83
Great Artesian Basin, *Australia* (24°S, 145°E)	130
Great Australian Bight, *gulf in Indian O.* (34°S, 130°E)	130
Great Barrier Reef, *Australia* (15°S, 146°E)	130
Great Basin, *U.S.* (39°N, 117°W)	58
Great Basin N.P., *Nev.* (39°N, 114°W)	58
Great Bear L., *Northwest Terr.* (66°N, 121°W)	40
Great Bend, *Kans.* (38°N, 99°W)	64
Great Britain, *island in North Sea* (52°N, 2°W)	98
Great Dismal Swamp, *U.S.* (37°N, 76°W)	71
Great Divide Basin, *Wyo.* (42°N, 108°W)	61
Great Dividing Range, *Australia* (34°S, 149°E)	133
Great Escarpment, *natural feature of Brazil* (27°S, 49°W)	88
Great Falls, *Mont.* (47°N, 111°W)	61
Great Fish R., *South Africa* (33°S, 27°E)	109
Great Hungarian Plain, *Europe* (46°N, 18°E)	99
Great Inagua I., *Atlantic O.* (21°N, 74°W)	83
Great Indian Desert, *India* (25°N, 71°E)	122
Great Karroo, *plateau in South Africa* (33°S, 23°E)	109
Great Lakes, *North America* (49°N, 86°W)	46-47
Great Plains, *North America* (50°N, 108°W)	36
Great Rift Valley, *Africa* (2°S, 35°E)	110
Great Ruaha R. (roo AH hah), *Tanzania* (8°S, 35°E)	110
Great Russian Plains, *Russia* (55°N, 45°E)	100
Great Salt L., *Utah* (41°N, 112°W)	59
Great Salt L. Desert, *U.S.* (41°N, 113°W)	58
Great Sandy Desert, *Australia* (19°S, 124°E)	130
Great Sandy Desert, *Oreg.* (44°N, 121°W)	60
Great Slave L., *Northwest Terr.* (62°N, 114°W)	44-45
Great Smoky Mts., *U.S.* (36°N, 85°W)	70-71
Great Smoky Mts. N.P., *U.S.* (36°N, 84°W)	70
Great Valley, *Appalachian Mts.* (38°N, 79°W)	70-71
Great Victoria Desert, *Australia* (28°S, 126°E)	130
Great Wall, *China* (38°N, 105°E)	124
Greater Antilles, *island group in Caribbean Sea* (20°N, 77°W)	83
Greater Khingan Range, *China* (44°N, 119°E)	124
Greece, *country in Europe* (38°N, 22°E)	99
Greeley, *Colo.* (40°N, 105°W)	59
Green Bay, *L. Michigan* (45°N, 88°W)	63
Green Bay, *city in Wis.* (44°N, 88°W)	63
Green Mts., *Vt.* (44°N, 73°W)	73
Green R., *Ky.* (37°N, 87°W)	70
Green R., *Wyo.* (42°N, 110°W)	61
Greenland, *overseas part of Denmark* (75°N, 40°W)	37
Greensboro, *N.C.* (36°N, 80°W)	71
Greensburg, *Ind.* (39°N, 86°W)	70
Greenville, *Miss.* (33°N, 91°W)	69
Greenville, *N.C.* (36°N, 77°W)	71
Greenville, *S.C.* (35°N, 82°W)	69
Greenwood, *Miss.* (33°N, 90°W)	68
Greenwood, *S.C.* (32°N, 84°W)	69

Name (Pronunciation), *Description* (Lat., Long.)	**Page**
Grenada, *country in Caribbean Sea* (12°N, 62°W)	85
Grenoble (gruh NOH buhl), *France* (45°N, 6°E)	98
Gresham, *Oreg.* (45°N, 122°W)	60
Griffith, *Australia* (34°S, 146°E)	133
Grodno, *Ukraine,* (54°N, 24°W)	99
Grinnell (gruh NEHL), *Iowa* (42°N, 93°W)	65
Groningen (GROH ning guhn), *Netherlands* (53°N, 7°E)	98
Groot Vloer (GROHT VLAWR), *l. in South Africa* (30°S, 21°E)	109
Groote Eylandt (gryoot EYE lund), *island in Gulf of Carpentaria* (14°S, 137°E)	130
Groton (GRAHT uhn), *Conn.* (41°N, 72°W)	73
Groundhog R., *Ontario* (48°N, 82°W)	46
Groznyy (GRAWZ nee), *Russia* (43°N, 46°E)	97
Guadalajara (GWAH duh luh HAHR uh), *Mexico* (21°N, 103°W)	84
Guadalcanal, *island in Solomon Sea* (9°S, 160°E)	130
Guadalquivir R., *Europe* (38°N, 6°W)	114
Guadalupe I. (GWAH duh LOOP), *Mexico* (29°N, 118°W)	82
Guadalupe Mts., *U.S.* (32°N, 105°W)	66
Guadalupe Mts. N.P., *U.S.* (32°N, 105°W)	66
Guadalupe Pk., *Tex.* (32°N, 105°W)	66
Guadalupe R. , *Tex.* (29°N, 97°W)	67
Guadeloupe (GWAH duh LOOP), *overseas state of France* (17°N, 62°W)	85
Guadiana R., *Spain* (39°N, 7°W)	114
Guam, *poss. of U.S.* (14°N, 143°E)	134
Guangzhou (gwahng joh), *China* (23°N, 113°E)	124
Guantanamo (gwahn TAH nuh MOH), *Cuba* (20°N, 75°W)	85
Guapore R. (GWAHP uh RAY), *South America* (12°S, 65°W)	90
Guardafui, Cape (GAHRD uf WEE), *Somalia* (12°N, 51°E)	106
Guatemala, *country in Central America* (15°N, 90°W)	84
Guatemala City, *Guatemala* (15°N, 91°W)	84
Guaviare R. (gwav YAHR ee), *South America* (3°N, 73°W)	90
Guayaquil (GWAH yah KEEL), *Ecuador* (2°S, 80°W)	90
Guayaquil, Gulf of, *Pacific O.* (3°S, 80°W)	90
Guiana Highlands (gee AH nuh), *South America* (4°N, 65°W)	90
Guinea (GIHN ee), *country in Africa* (10°N, 10°W)	108
Guinea-Bissau (GIHN ee bih SOW), *country in Africa* (12°N, 15°W)	108
Guinea, Gulf of, *Atlantic O.* (0°, 0°)	108
Gujranwala (GOOJ ruhn WAHL uh), *Pakistan* (32°N, 74°E)	122
Gulf Coastal Plain, *U.S.* (31°N, 94°W)	53
Gulf St. Vincent, *Australia* (35°S, 138°E)	133
Gulfport, *Miss.* (30°N, 89°W)	68
Gunisao R. (guhn ih SAY oh), *Manitoba* (54°N, 97°W)	45
Gunnison R., *Colo.* (39°N, 108°W)	59
Guntersville L., *Ala.* (34°N, 86°W)	68
Guyana, *country in South America* (5°N, 59°W)	90
Guymon (GY muhn), *Okla.* (37°N, 101°W)	66
Gwalior, *India* (26°N, 78°E)	122
Gydan Pen., *Russia* (70°N, 80°E)	118

H

Name (Pronunciation), *Description* (Lat., Long.)	**Page**
Habuna, *Brazil* (15°S, 39°W)	89
Hachinohe (HAHCH ih noh hay), *Japan* (40°N, 142°E)	125
Haeju (HY JOO), *North Korea* (38°N, 126°E)	125
Hafun, Cape (ha FOON), *Somalia* (10°N, 51°E)	115
Hagerstown, *Md.* (40°N, 78°W)	71
Hague, The, *Netherlands* (52°N, 4°E)	98
Hai Phong (HY FONG), *Vietnam* (21°N, 107°E)	123
Haikou (hy koh), *China* (20°N, 110°E)	124
Hainan, *island in South China Sea* (20°N, 110°E)	124
Haiti (HAY tee), *country in Caribbean Sea* (19°N, 72°W)	85
Hakodate (HAHK uh DAHT ee), *Japan* (42°N, 141°E)	125
Haleakala N. P. (HAHL ee AHK uh LAH), *Hawaii* (21°N, 156°W)	57

Name (Pronunciation), *Description* (Lat., Long.)	**Page**
Halifax, *Nova Scotia* (44°N, 63°W)	47
Halle (HAHL uh), *Germany* (52°N, 12°E)	99
Halmahera, *island in Philippine Sea* (1°N, 128°E)	130
Halmahera Sea, *Indian O.* (0°, 129°E)	130
Hamadan, *Iran* (35°N, 48°E)	115
Hamah, *Syria* (35°N, 37°E)	115
Hamamatsu (HAHM uh MAHT soo), *Japan* (35°N, 138°E)	125
Hamburg, *Germany* (54°N, 10°E)	99
Hamden, *Conn.* (41°N, 73°W)	73
Hamhung (HAHM HOONG), *North Korea* (40°N, 128°E)	125
Hamilton, *Ala.* (34°N, 88°W)	68
Hamilton, *Australia* (38°S, 142°E)	133
Hamilton, *Ohio* (39°N, 85°W)	70
Hamilton, *Ontario* (43°N, 80°W)	46
Hammerfest, *Norway* (71°N, 24°E)	97
Hammersley Ranges, *Australia* (22°S, 118°E)	130
Hammond, *Ind.* (42°N, 87°W)	70
Hampton, *Va.* (37°N, 76°W)	71
Han R. (hahn), *China* (33°N, 111°E)	124
Handan, *China* (37°N, 114°E)	124
Hangzhou, *China* (31°N, 120°E)	124
Hannibal, *Mo.* (40°N, 91°W)	65
Hannover, *Germany* (52°N, 10°E)	99
Hanoi, *Vietnam* (21°N, 106°E)	123
Happy Valley–Goose Bay, *Newfoundland* (53°N, 60°W)	47
Harare, *Zimbabwe* (18°S, 31°E)	107
Harbin, *China* (46°N, 127°E)	124
Hardanger Fiord (hahr DANG guhr), *Norway* (60°N, 6°E)	94
Harer, *Ethiopia* (9°N, 42°E)	107
Hargeysa, *Somalia* (9°N, 44°E)	107
Harlan, *Ky.* (37°N, 83°W)	70
Harlingen (HAHR ling uhn), *Tex.* (26°N, 98°W)	67
Harney Basin, *Oreg.* (43°N, 120°W)	60
Harney Pk., *S. Dak.* (44°N, 104°W)	62
Harper, *Liberia* (4°N, 8°W)	107
Harpers Ferry, *W. Va.* (39°N, 78°W)	71
Harricana R. (HAR ih KAN aw), *Quebec* (51°N, 79°W)	46
Harrisburg, *Pa.* (40°N, 77°W)	72
Harrisonburg, *Va.* (39°N, 79°W)	71
Hartford, *Conn.* (42°N, 73°W)	73
Hartwell L., *U.S.* (34°N, 83°W)	69
Hasa, *region of Saudi Arabia* (27°N, 48°E)	115
Hastings, *Nebr.* (41°N, 98°W)	64
Hatchie R., *U.S.* (36°N, 90°W)	70
Hatteras, Cape, *N.C.* (35°N, 76°W)	71
Hatteras I., *Pamlico Sound* (36°N, 76°W)	71
Hattiesburg, *Miss.* (31°N, 89°W)	68
Havana, *Cuba* (23°N, 82°W)	85
Havasu, L. (HAV uh SOO), *Ariz.* (34°N, 114°W)	58
Haverhill, *Mass.* (43°N, 71°W)	73
Havre (HAV uhr), *Mont.* (48°N, 110°W)	61
Havre-Saint-Pierre (HAV ruh SAN PYAIR), *Quebec* (50°N, 64°W)	47
Hawaii (huh WY ee), *island in Pacific O.* (20°N, 156°W)	57
Hawaii, *state in U.S.* (21°N, 157°W)	57
Hawaii Volcanoes N.P., *Hawaii* (20°N, 156°W)	57
Hay R., *Canada* (59°N, 119°W)	44
Hay River, *city in Northwest Terr.* (61°N, 116°W)	44
Hayes R., *Manitoba* (56°N, 93°W)	45
Hays, *Kans.* (39°N, 99°W)	64
Hayward, *Wis.* (46°N, 92°W)	63
Hazelton, *British Columbia* (55°N, 128°W)	44
Hearst, *Ontario* (50°N, 84°W)	46
Heart R., *N. Dak.* (47°N, 102°W)	62
Hebgen L., *Mont.* (45°N, 111°W)	61
Hebrides (HEHB rih DEEZ), *island group in Atlantic O.* (57°N, 7°W)	94
Hecate Strait (HEK uht), *British Columbia* (53°N, 131°W)	44
Hejaz, *region of Saudi Arabia* (24°N, 38°E)	115
Hekla, *mt. in Iceland* (64°N, 20°W)	94
Helena, *Mont.* (47°N, 112°W)	61
Hell's Canyon, *Snake R.* (45°N, 117°W)	60

Name (Pronunciation), *Description* (Lat., Long.)	Page
Helsingborg (HEHL sing BAWR), *Sweden* (56°N, 13°E)	99
Helsinki, *Finland* (60°N, 25°E)	97
Hempstead, *N.Y.* (41°N, 74°W)	72-73
Henderson, *Ky.* (38°N, 88°W)	70
Henderson, *Nev.* (36°N, 115°W)	58
Henderson, *N.C.* (36°N, 78°W)	71
Hendersonville, *Tenn.* (36°N, 87°W)	70
Henrietta Maria, Cape, *Ontario* (55°N, 82°W)	46
Henry Mts., *Utah* (38°N, 111°W)	59
Herat (heh RAHT), *Afghanistan* (34°N, 62°E)	120
Hereford (HUHR furd), *Tex.* (35°N, 102°W)	66
Hermosillo (EHR muh SEE yoh), *Mexico* (29°N, 111°W)	84
Hetch Hetchy Aqueduct, *Calif.* (38°N, 121°W)	58
Hialeah (HY uh LEE uh), *Fla.* (26°N, 80°W)	69
Hibbing, *Minn.* (47°N, 93°W)	63
Hickory, *N.C.* (36°N, 81°W)	71
Hickory, L., *N.C.* (36°N, 81°W)	71
High Point, *N.C.* (36°N, 80°W)	71
High Rock L., *N.C.* (36°N, 80°W)	71
Highlands, *region of Scotland* (57°N, 4°W)	98
Hillsboro, *Ohio* (39°N, 84°W)	70
Hilo, *Hawaii* (20°N, 155°W)	57
Himalayas, *mt. range in Asia* (28°N, 85°E)	122
Hindu Kush, *mt. range in Asia* (37°N, 72°E)	122
Hinton, *Alberta* (53°N, 118°W)	44
Hirakud Res., *India* (22°N, 84°E)	122
Hirosaki, *Japan* (41°N, 140°E)	125
Hiroshima (HEER oh SHEE muh), *Japan* (34°N, 132°E)	125
Hispaniola, *island in Caribbean Sea* (19°N, 72°W)	83
Hitachi, *Japan* (37°N, 141°E)	125
Hjalmar L. (YEHL muhr), *Northwest Terr.* (62°N, 115°W)	45
Ho Chi Minh City (ho chee mihn), *Vietnam* (11°N, 107°E)	123
Hobart, *Australia* (43°S, 147°E)	131
Hobbs, *N. Mex.* (33°N, 103°W)	59
Hoh R., *Wash.* (48°N, 124°W)	60
Hokkaido, *island in Sea of Japan* (43°N, 143°E)	125
Holguin (awl GEEN), *Cuba* (21°N, 76°W)	85
Holland, *Mich.* (43°N, 86°W)	63
Hollywood, *Fla.* (26°N, 80°W)	69
Holt, *Mo.* (39°N, 94°W)	65
Holyoke (HOHL YOHK), *Mass.* (42°N, 73°W)	73
Homestead, *Fla.* (25°N, 80°W)	69
Homs, *Syria* (35°N, 37°E)	115
Hondo R., *North America* (18°N, 89°W)	82
Honduras, *country in Central America* (15°N, 87°W)	84
Honduras, Gulf of, *Caribbean Sea* (16°N, 88°W)	82
Hong Kong, *poss. of United Kingdom* (22°N, 114°E)	124
Honiara (HOHN ee AHR ah), *Solomon Islands* (9°S, 160°E)	131
Honolulu, *Hawaii* (21°N, 158°W)	57
Honshu, *island in Sea of Japan* (38°N, 140°E)	125
Hood, Mt., *Oreg.* (45°N, 122°W)	60
Hooghly R. (HOO glee), *India* (23°N, 88°E)	122
Hoover, *Ala.* (33°N, 87°W)	68
Hoover Dam, *U.S.* (36°N, 115°W)	58
Hope, *Ark.* (34°N, 94°W)	67
Hopkinsville, *Ky.* (37°N, 87°W)	70
Hormuz, Strait of, *Persian Gulf and Gulf of Oman* (27°N, 57°E)	115
Horn, Cape, *South America* (56°S, 68°W)	88
Horn Mts., *Northwest Terr.* (62°N, 120°W)	44
Horsham, *Australia* (37°S, 143°E)	133
Hot Springs, *Ark.* (34°N, 93°W)	67
Hot Springs, *S. Dak.* (43°N, 103°W)	62
Hot Springs N.P., *Ark.* (34°N, 93°W)	67
Houghton (HOH tuhn), *Mich.* (47°N, 89°W)	63
Houma (HOH muh), *La.* (30°N, 91°W)	67
Houston, *Miss.* (34°N, 89°W)	68
Houston, *Tex.* (30°N, 95°W)	67
Howe, Cape, *Australia* (37°S, 150°E)	133
Howrah, *India* (23°N, 88°E)	122
Huai R. (hwy), *China* (33°N, 115°E)	124
Huallaga R. (wa YAG uh), *Peru* (8°S, 76°W)	90
Huambo, *Angola* (13°S, 16°E)	107
Huancayo, *Peru* (12°S, 75°W)	90
Huang He (WANG hee), *r. in China* (41°N, 110°E)	124
Huascaran, Mt. (WAHS kuh RAHN), *Peru* (9°S, 78°W)	90
Huber Heights, *Ohio* (40°N, 84°W)	70
Hubli-Dharward (HOOB lee dahr WAHRD), *India* (15°N, 75°E)	122
Hudson Bay, *Canada* (60°N, 85°W)	41
Hudson R., *N.Y.* (42°N, 74°W)	72
Hudson Strait, *Hudson Bay and Labrador Sea* (62°N, 70°W)	40
Hue (hoo AY), *Vietnam* (16°N, 107°E)	123
Hull, *England* (54°N, 0°)	98
Hull, *Quebec* (46°N, 76°W)	47
Humboldt R., *Nev.* (41°N, 117°W)	58
Humphreys Peak (HUHM freez), *Ariz.* (35°N, 112°W)	59
Hungary, *country in Europe* (47°N, 18°E)	99
Huntington, *W. Va.* (38°N, 82°W)	71
Huntington Beach, *Calif.* (34°N, 118°W)	58
Huntsville, *Ala.* (35°N, 87°W)	68
Huntsville, *Ontario* (45°N, 79°W)	46
Huntsville, *Tex.* (31°N, 96°W)	67
Huron (HYOO ruhn), *S. Dak.* (44°N, 98°W)	62
Huron, L., *North America* (45°N, 82°W)	46
Hutchinson, *Kans.* (38°N, 98°W)	64
Huttonsville, *W. Va.* (39°N, 80°W)	71
Hyco L., *N.C.* (36°N, 79°W)	71
Hyderabad, *India* (17°N, 78°E)	122
Hyderabad, *Pakistan* (25°N, 68°E)	122

I

Name (Pronunciation), *Description* (Lat., Long.)	Page
I-n-Gall, *Niger* (17°N, 6°E)	107
I-n-Salah, *Algeria* (28°N, 4°E)	107
Iasi (YASH ee), *Romania* (47°N, 28°E)	99
Ibadan, *Nigeria* (8°N, 4°E)	108
Ibague (EE buh GAY), *Colombia* (4°N, 75°W)	90
Iberian Pen., *Europe* (39°N, 5°W)	114
Iceland, *country in Atlantic O.* (65°N, 20°W)	96
Idaho, *state in U.S.* (44°N, 115°W)	60-61
Idaho Falls, *Idaho* (44°N, 112°W)	61
Iguacu Falls (ih GWAH syu), *waterfall in South America* (26°S, 54°W)	88
Iguidi Desert, *Africa* (28°N, 7°W)	106
IJsselmeer (EYE suhl MER), *l. in Netherlands* (53°N, 5°E)	98
Ilesha, *Nigeria* (8°N, 5°E)	108
Iliamna L. (IHL ee AM nuh), *Alaska* (59°N, 155°W)	57
Illinois, *state in U.S.* (40°N, 90°W)	65
Illinois R., *Ill.* (39°N, 91°W)	65
Ilorin (EE luh REEN), *Nigeria* (9°N, 5°E)	108
Imperial, *Nebr.* (41°N, 102°W)	64
Imperial Valley, *Calif.* (33°N, 116°W)	58
Imphal (IMP huhl), *India* (25°N, 94°E)	122
Inari, L., *Finland* (69°N, 28°W)	95
Inchon (IHN CHAHN), *South Korea* (37°N, 127°E)	125
Independence, *Mo.* (39°N, 94°W)	65
India, *country in Asia* (25°N, 80°E)	122
Indian L., *Ontario* (47°N, 82°W)	46
Indian Ocean	7
Indiana, *Pa.* (41°N, 79°W)	72
Indiana, *state in U.S.* (40°N, 86°W)	70
Indianapolis, *Ind.* (40°N, 86°W)	70
Indigirka R., *Russia* (68°N, 148°E)	119
Indio (IN dee OH), *Calif.* (34°N, 116°W)	58
Indochina Pen., *Asia* (15°N, 105°E)	119
Indonesia, *country in Asia* (3°S, 115°E)	121
Indore (ihn DOHR), *India* (23°N, 76°E)	122
Indus R., *Asia* (25°N, 68°E)	122
Infiernillo Res., *Mexico* (19°N, 102°W)	82
Inner Hebrides, *island group in Atlantic O.* (57°N, 6°W)	98
Inner Mongolia, *region of China* (42°N, 110°E)	124
Innsbruck (IHNZ bruk), *Austria* (47°N, 11°E)	99
International Falls, *Minn.* (49°N, 93°W)	62-63
Intracoastal Waterway, *canal in La.* (30°N, 93°W)	67
Inuvik (ih NOO vihk), *Northwest Terr.* (68°N, 134°W)	42
Inverness (IHN vuhr NEHS), *Scotland* (57°N, 4°W)	98
Investigator Strait, *Australia* (36°S, 137°E)	133
Ionian Is., *Greece* (38°N, 20°E)	99
Ionian Sea, *Europe* (38°N, 18°E)	99
Iowa, *state in U.S.* (42°N, 94°W)	64-65
Iowa City, *Iowa* (42°N, 92°W)	65
Iowa R., *Iowa* (42°N, 92°W)	65
Ipoh (EE poh), *Malaysia* (5°N, 101°E)	123
Ipswich, *England* (52°N, 1°E)	98
Iqaluit, *Northwest Terr.* (64°N, 68°W)	43
Iquique (ih KEE keh), *Chile* (20°S, 70°W)	89
Iquitos (ih KEET ohs), *Peru* (4°S, 73°W)	90
Iraklion, *Crete* (35°N, 25°E)	99
Iran, *country in Asia* (31°N, 54°E)	115
Iran, Plateau of, *Iran* (33°N, 59°E)	115
Iraq, *country in Asia* (32°N, 44°E)	115
Irazu, *mt. in Costa Rica* (10°N, 84°W)	83
Irbil, *Iraq* (36°N, 44°E)	115
Ireland, *country in Europe* (54°N, 8°W)	37
Irian Jaya, *region of Indonesia* (4°S, 138°E)	131
Iringa (ih RING guh), *Tanzania* (8°S, 36°E)	110
Iriri R. (IHR uh REE), *Brazil* (4°S, 53°W)	90
Irish Sea, *Europe* (54°N, 5°W)	98
Irkutsk, *Russia* (52°N, 104°E)	100
Iron River, *Mich.* (46°N, 89°W)	63
Ironton, *Ohio* (39°N, 83°W)	70
Ironwood, *Mich.* (46°N, 90°W)	62
Irrawaddy, Mouths of the, *delta in Burma* (16°N, 95°E)	123
Irrawaddy R., *Asia* (20°N, 94°E)	123
Irtysh R. (ir TISH), *Russia* (58°N, 70°E)	100
Irving, *Tex.* (33°N, 97°W)	67
Isfahan, *Iran* (33°N, 52°E)	115
Iskut R., *North America* (57°N, 132°W)	44
Isla de Providencia, *island in Caribbean Sea* (14°N, 82°W)	83
Islamabad, *Pakistan* (34°N, 73°E)	122
Island L., *Manitoba* (54°N, 94°W)	45
Isle of Youth, *Cuba* (22°N, 83°W)	83
Isle Royale, *Mich.* (48°N, 89°W)	63
Isle Royale N.P., *Mich.* (48°N, 89°W)	63
Isles de la Bahia (EEZ LAHS DAY lah buh HEE uh), *Honduras* (16°N, 87°W)	83
Isparta (is pahr TAH), *Turkey* (38°N, 31°E)	115
Israel, *country in Asia* (31°N, 35°E)	115
Istanbul, *Turkey* (41°N, 29°E)	115
Istokpoga, L. (IHS tahk POH guh), *Fla.* (27°N, 81°W)	69
Itacoatiara (ee ta kwa TYAH ra), *Brazil* (3°S, 58°W)	90
Italy, *country in Europe* (42°N, 13°E)	99
Itasca, L. (eye TAS kuh), *Minn.* (47°N, 95°W)	62
Ithaca, *N.Y.* (42°N, 76°W)	72
Ivory Coast, *region of Africa* (5°N, 5°W)	108
Iwo (EE WOH), *Nigeria* (8°N, 4°E)	108
Iwo Jima, *Pacific O.* (25°N, 142°E)	119
Izabal, L., *Guatemala* (15°N, 89°W)	82
Izhevsk, *Russia* (57°N, 53°E)	100
Izmir, *Turkey* (38°N, 27°E)	115
Izu Is. (EE zoo), *Philippine Sea* (34°N, 140°E)	125

J

Name (Pronunciation), *Description* (Lat., Long.)	Page
J. Percy Priest L., *Tenn.* (36°N, 87°W)	70
Jabalpur (JUHB uhl POOR), *India* (23°N, 80°E)	122
Jackson, *Ala.* (32°N, 88°W)	68
Jackson, *Mich.* (42°N, 84°W)	63
Jackson, *Miss.* (32°N, 90°W)	68
Jackson, *Ohio* (39°N, 83°W)	70
Jackson, *Tenn.* (36°N, 89°W)	70
Jackson, *Wyo.* (44°N, 110°W)	61
Jacksonville, *Fla.* (30°N, 82°W)	69
Jacksonville, *Ill.* (40°N, 90°W)	65
Jacksonville, *N.C.* (35°N, 77°W)	71

Name (Pronunciation), *Description* (Lat., Long.)	Page
Jaffa, Cape, *Australia* (37°S, 140°E)	133
Jaffna, *Sri Lanka* (10°N, 80°E)	122
Jahrom (yah ROHM), *Iran* (28°N, 54°E)	115
Jaipur (JY POOR), *India* (27°N, 76°E)	122
Jakarta, *Indonesia* (6°S, 107°E)	131
Jamaica, *country in Caribbean Sea* (18°N, 78°W)	85
Jamaica Channel, *Caribbean Sea* (19°N, 76°W)	83
James Bay, *Canada* (54°N, 81°W)	46
James R., *Mo.* (37°N, 93°W)	65
James R., *U.S.* (46°N, 98°W)	62
James R., *Va.* (38°N, 78°W)	71
Jamestown, *N.Y.* (42°N, 79°W)	72
Jamestown, *N. Dak.* (47°N, 99°W)	62
Jamestown, *Va.* (37°N, 75°W)	71
Jamnagar, *India* (22°N, 70°E)	122
Jamshedpur (JAHM shed POOR), *India* (23°N, 86°E)	122
Jan Mayen (yahn MY uhn), *island in Greenland Sea* (71°N, 8°W)	136
Janesville, *Wis.* (43°N, 89°W)	63
Japan, *country in Asia* (36°N, 138°E)	125
Japan, Sea of, *Asia* (40°N, 135°E)	125
Japura R., *South America* (0° 74°W)	90
Jasper, *Alberta* (53°N, 118°W)	44
Jasper N.P., *Alberta* (52°N, 117°W)	44
Java, *island in Java Sea* (8°S, 110°E)	130
Java Sea, *Indian O.* (6°S, 113°E)	130
Jaya Peak, *Indonesia* (4°S, 137°E)	130
Jayapura, *Indonesia* (2°S, 141°E)	131
Jefferson City, *Mo.* (39°N, 92°W)	65
Jefferson, Mt., *Oreg.* (45°N, 122°W)	60
Jefferson R., *Mont.* (46°N, 112°W)	61
Jeffersonville, *Ind.* (38°N, 86°W)	70
Jericho (JEHR uh koh), *West Bank* (32°N, 35°E)	117
Jerusalem, *Israel* (32°N, 35°E)	115
Jhansi, *India* (25°N, 79°E)	122
Jidda, *Saudi Arabia* (21°N, 39°E)	115
Jilin, *China* (44°N, 127°E)	124
Jinan (jyee nahn), *China* (37°N, 117°E)	124
Jinja, *Uganda* (0°, 33°E)	110
Joao Pessoa (ZHWOW puh SOH uh), *Brazil* (7°S, 35°W)	89
Jodhpur (JAHD puhr), *India* (26°N, 73°E)	122
Johannesburg, *South Africa* (26°S, 28°E)	109
John Day, *Oreg.* (44°N, 119°W)	60
John Day Dam, *Columbia R.* (46°N, 121°W)	60
John Day R., *Oreg.* (45°N, 120°W)	60
John H. Kerr Res., *U.S.* (37°N, 78°W)	71
John Redmond Res., *Kans.* (38°N, 96°W)	64
Johnson City, *Tenn.* (36°N, 82°W)	71
Johnstown, *Pa.* (40°N, 79°W)	72
Johor Baharu (juh HOHR BAHR oo), *Malaysia* (2°N, 104°E)	123
Joliet, *Ill.* (42°N, 88°W)	65
Joliette, *Quebec* (46°N, 73°W)	47
Jonesboro, *Ark.* (36°N, 91°W)	67
Jonkoping (YUHN chuh pihng), *Sweden* (58°N, 14°E)	99
Jonquiere (ZHOHN kee EHR), *Quebec* (48°N, 71°W)	47
Joplin, *Mo.* (37°N, 95°W)	65
Jordan, *country in Asia* (31°N, 37°E)	115
Jordan R., *Asia*	117
Jos Plateau, *Nigeria* (10°N, 9°E)	108
Joseph Bonaparte Gulf, *Indian O.* (14°S, 128°E)	130
Juan de Fuca, Strait of (hwahn duh FYOO kuh), *U.S. and Canada* (48°N, 125°W)	44
Juan Fernandez Is., *Pacific O.* (33°S, 80°W)	88
Juarez (HWAHR ehz), *Mexico* (32°N, 106°W)	84
Juazeiro (zhwu ZEE roo), *Brazil* (9°S, 41°W)	89
Juba, *Sudan* (5°N, 31°E)	107
Judith R., *Mont.* (48°N, 110°W)	61
Jullundur, *India* (31°N, 76°E)	122
Juneau (JOO noh), *Alaska* (58°N, 134°W)	57
Juniata R., *Pa.* (40°N, 78°W)	72
Jurua R. (zhoor WAH), *Brazil* (7°S, 70°W)	90
Juruena R. (ZHOOR WAY nuh), *Brazil* (7°S, 58°W)	90
Jutland, *pen. of Denmark* (56°N, 9°E)	99

K
Name (Pronunciation), *Description* (Lat., Long.)	Page
Kabale, *Uganda* (1°S, 30°E)	110
Kabalega Falls (kuh BAHL ih guh), *Uganda* (2°S, 32°E)	110
Kabinakagami R., *Ontario* (49°N, 84°W)	46
Kabul (KAH bool), *Afghanistan* (34°N, 69°E)	120
Kaduna (kuh DOO nuh), *Nigeria* (11°N, 7°E)	108
Kagoshima, *Japan* (32°N, 131°E)	125
Kahoolawe (kah HOH uh LAH wee), *island in Pacific O.* (21°N, 157°W)	57
Kailua (ky LOO uh), *Hawaii* (21°N, 158°W)	57
Kailua Kona (ky LOO uh KOH nuh), *Hawaii* (20°N, 156°W)	57
Kainji L., *Nigeria* (10°N, 5°E)	108
Kaiwi Channel (KY wee), *Hawaii* (21°N, 158°W)	57
Kalahari Desert, *Africa* (23°S, 22°E)	106
Kalamazoo, *Mich.* (42°N, 86°W)	63
Kalemie, *Zaire* (6°S, 29°E)	107
Kalgoorlie, *Australia* (31°S, 121°E)	131
Kaliningrad (kuh LEE nihn GRAD), *Russia* (55°N, 21°E)	100
Kalispell, *Mont.* (48°N, 114°W)	61
Kalisz (KAHL eesh), *Poland* (52°N, 18°E)	99
Kalyan (kuhl YAHN), *India* (19°N, 73°E)	122
Kama R., *Russia* (56°N, 53°E)	95
Kama Upland, *Russia* (58°N, 53°E)	95
Kamchatka Pen., *Russia* (55°N, 160°E)	119
Kamilukuak L., *Northwest Terr.* (62°N, 100°W)	45
Kamloops, *British Columbia* (51°N, 120°W)	57
Kampala, *Uganda* (0°, 33°E)	110
Kamskoye Res., *Russia* (59°N, 57°E)	95
Kamuela, *Hawaii* (20°N, 156°W)	57
Kanaaupscow R., *Quebec* (59°N, 73°W)	47
Kananga, *Zaire* (6°S, 22°E)	107
Kanazawa (kuh NAHZ uh wuh), *Japan* (37°N, 137°E)	125
Kandy, *Sri Lanka* (7°N, 81°E)	122
Kane Basin, *North America* (79°N, 70°W)	41
Kaneohe (KAHN ee OH ee), *Hawaii* (21°N, 158°W)	57
Kangaroo I., *Bass Strait* (36°S, 137°E)	133
Kanin Pen., *Russia* (68°N, 45°E)	95
Kankakee (KANG kuh KEE), *Ill.* (41°N, 88°W)	65
Kankakee R., *U.S.* (41°N, 88°W)	65
Kankan, *Guinea* (10°N, 9°W)	108
Kannapolis, *N.C.* (35°N, 81°W)	71
Kano, *Nigeria* (12°N, 8°E)	108
Kanpur, *India* (26°N, 80°E)	122
Kansas, *state in U.S.* (38°N, 100°W)	64-65
Kansas City, *Kans.* (39°N, 95°W)	65
Kansas City, *Mo.* (39°N, 95°W)	65
Kansas R., *U.S.* (39°N, 97°W)	64-65
Kaohsiung (kah oh SYOONG), *Taiwan* (23°N, 120°E)	124
Kaolack (KOW LAK), *Senegal* (14°N, 16°W)	108
Kapiskau R., *Ontario* (53°N, 82°W)	46
Kapuas R. (KAHP uh WAHS), *Indonesia* (1°N, 112°E)	123
Kapuskasing (KAP uh SKAY sing), *Ontario* (49°N, 82°W)	46
Kara Bogaz Gol, *gulf in Caspian Sea* (41°N, 53°E)	115
Kara Kum Desert, *Turkmenistan* (40°N, 57°E)	100
Kara Sea, *Arctic O.* (72°N, 62°E)	100
Karachi, *Pakistan* (25°N, 67°E)	122
Karakoram Range (KAR uh KOHR uhm), *Asia* (36°N, 76°E)	122
Kariba L., *Africa* (17°S, 28°E)	106
Karimata Strait, *Sumatra and Borneo* (1°S, 108°E)	130
Kasai R. (kuh SY), *Africa* (3°S, 17°E)	106
Kasanga (kuh SAHNG guh), *Tanzania* (8°S, 31°E)	110
Kasba L., *Northwest Terr.* (60°N, 102°W)	45
Kashechewan, *Ontario* (52°N, 82°W)	46
Kashi (kah shee), *China* (40°N, 76°E)	124
Kashmir, *region of Asia* (34°N, 75°E)	122
Kaskaskia R. (kas KAS kee uh), *Ill.* (39°N, 89°W)	65
Kassel, *Germany* (51°N, 9°E)	99
Kastamonu (KAHS tuh moh NOO), *Turkey* (41°N, 34°E)	115
Katahdin, Mt. (kuh TAHD uhn), *Maine* (46°N, 71°W)	73

Name (Pronunciation), *Description* (Lat., Long.)	Page
Katanga Plateau, *Zaire* (10°S, 26°E)	106
Kathmandu (kaht mahn DOO), *Nepal* (28°N, 85°E)	122
Katmai N. P. (KAT MY), *Alaska* (59°N, 155°W)	57
Katowice (KAHT uh VEET suh), *Poland* (50°N, 19°E)	99
Kattegat, *strait between Sweden and Denmark* (57°N, 11°E)	94
Kauai (KOW eye), *island in Pacific O.* (22°N, 159°W)	57
Kauai Channel, *Hawaii* (22°N, 159°W)	57
Kaulakahai Channel (KOW luh KAH HEE), *Hawaii* (22°N, 160°W)	57
Kaunakakai (KOW nuh KAH KEE), *Hawaii* (21°N, 157°W)	57
Kaunas, *Lithuania* (55°N, 24°E)	99
Kawartha Lakes (kuh WAWR thuh), *Ontario* (45°N, 78°W)	46
Kawasaki, *Japan* (36°N, 140°E)	125
Kayseri (KY zuh REE), *Turkey* (39°N, 35°E)	115
Kazakh Uplands, *Kazakhstan* (48°N, 75°E)	118
Kazakhstan, *country in Asia and Europe* (48°N, 65°E)	100
Kazan, *Russia* (56°N, 49°E)	97
Kearney (KAHR nee), *Nebr.* (41°N, 99°W)	64
Kechika R., *British Columbia* (59°N, 127°W)	44
Keene (KEEN), *N.H.* (43°N, 72°W)	73
Kejimkujik N. P. (KEHJ uh muh KOO jee), *Nova Scotia* (44°N, 65°W)	47
Kekaha (kay KAH HAH), *Hawaii* (22°N, 160°W)	57
Kelang, *Malaysia* (3°N, 102°E)	123
Kelowna (kih LOHN uh), *British Columbia* (50°N, 120°W)	44
Kemp, L., *Tex.* (34°N, 99°W)	66
Kempt, L., *Quebec* (52°N, 74°W)	47
Kenai Fjords N. P. (KEE NY), *Alaska* (60°N, 150°W)	57
Kenai Pen., *Alaska* (60°N, 150°W)	57
Kenitra (kuh NEE truh), *Morocco* (34°N, 7°W)	114
Kennebec R., *Maine* (45°N, 70°W)	73
Kenner, *La.* (30°N, 90°W)	67
Kennewick, *Wash.* (46°N, 119°W)	60
Kenogami R. (kuh NAHG uh mee), *Ontario* (50°N, 85°W)	46
Kenora, *Ontario* (50°N, 94°W)	46
Kenosha (kuh NOH shuh), *Wis.* (43°N, 88°W)	63
Kent, *Ohio* (41°N, 81°W)	71
Kent, *Wash.* (47°N, 122°W)	60
Kentucky, *state in U.S.* (37°N, 87°W)	70-71
Kentucky L., *U.S.* (37°N, 88°W)	71
Kentucky R., *Ky.* (38°N, 85°W)	70
Kenya, *country in Africa* (1°N, 37°E)	110
Kenya, Mt., *Kenya* (0°, 37°E)	110
Keokuk (KEE uh KUHK), *Iowa* (40°N, 91°W)	65
Kerch, *Ukraine* (45°N, 36°E)	97
Kerguelin I., *Indian O.* (56°S, 69°E)	9
Kerman, *Iran* (30°N, 57°E)	115
Kern R., *Calif.* (35°N, 119°W)	58
Kerulen R. (KEHR uh LEHN), *Asia* (48°N, 114°E)	124
Kesagami L. (kuh SAHG uh mee), *Ontario* (50°N, 80°W)	46
Ketchikan, *Alaska* (55°N, 132°W)	57
Kettering, *Ohio* (40°N, 84°W)	70
Keuka L. (KYOO kuh), *N.Y.* (42°N, 77°W)	72
Keweenaw Bay (KEE wih NAW), *L. Superior* (47°N, 88°W)	63
Keweenaw Pen., *Mich.* (47°N, 88°W)	63
Key West, *Fla.* (25°N, 82°W)	69
Khabarovsk, *Russia* (49°N, 135°E)	101
Khambai, Gulf of, *Arabian Sea* (21°N, 72°E)	122
Khania, *Crete* (35°N, 24°E)	99
Kharkov, *Ukraine* (50°N, 36°E)	97
Khartoum (kahr TOOM), *Sudan* (16°N, 33°E)	107
Khon Kaen (KAWN KAN), *Thailand* (17°N, 103°E)	123
Khone Falls, *Mekong R.* (14°N, 106°E)	123
Khulna (KOOL nuh), *Bangladesh* (23°N, 90°E)	122
Khyber Pass (KY buhr), *Asia* (34°N, 71°E)	122
Kiel (KEEL), *Germany* (54°N, 10°E)	99
Kiel Canal, *Germany* (54°N, 9°E)	99
Kiev, *Ukraine* (50°N, 31°E)	100
Kigali, *Rwanda* (2°S, 30°E)	110

Name (Pronunciation), *Description* (Lat., Long.)	Page
Kigoma (kih GOH muh), *Tanzania* (5°S, 30°E)	110
Kilauea (KEE low AY ah), *volcano in Hawaii* (19°N, 155°W)	57
Kilbuck Mts., *Alaska* (60°N, 160°W)	57
Kilchu (KIL choh), *N. Korea* (41°N, 129°E)	125
Kilimanjaro, Mt., *Africa* (3°S, 37°E)	110
Killeen (kil LEEN), *Tex.* (31°N, 98°W)	67
Kim R., *Cameroon* (7°N, 11°E)	108
Kimberley, *British Columbia* (50°N, 116°W)	44
Kimberley, *South Africa* (28°S, 25°E)	109
Kimberly Plateau, *Australia* (16°S, 127°E)	130
Kinabasket, L., *British Columbia* (52°N, 118°W)	44
Kindersley, *Saskatchewan* (51°N, 109°W)	45
Kindia (KIHN dee uh), *Guinea* (10°N, 13°W)	108
King I., *Bass Strait* (40°S, 144°E)	133
King William I., *Arctic O.* (69°N, 98°W)	42
Kingman, *Ariz.* (35°N, 114°W)	58
Kings Canyon N.P., *Calif.* (37°N, 119°W)	58
Kingsport, *Tenn.* (37°N, 83°W)	71
Kingston, *Jamaica* (18°N, 77°W)	85
Kingston, *Ontario* (44°N, 76°W)	47
Kinshasa, *Zaire* (4°S, 15°E)	107
Kinston, *N.C.* (35°N, 78°W)	71
Kipawa, L., *Quebec* (47°N, 79°W)	46
Kipengere Range (kip uhn GAY ruh), *Tanzania* (10°S, 35°E)	110
Kirgiz Steppe, *Kazakhstan* (48°N, 60°E)	100
Kiribati, *country in Pacific O.* (1°S, 173°W)	135
Kirkland Lake, *Ontario* (48°N, 80°W)	46
Kirksville, *Mo.* (40°N, 93°W)	65
Kirkuk (kihr KOOK), *Iraq* (35°N, 45°E)	113
Kirkwood, *Mo.* (39°N, 90°W)	65
Kirov, *Russia* (59°N, 50°E)	100
Kirthar Range (kir TAHR), *Pakistan* (27°N, 67°E)	122
Kiruna, *Sweden* (68°N, 20°E)	97
Kirwin Res., *Kans.* (40°N, 99°W)	64
Kisangani (KEE suhn GAYN ee), *Zaire* (1°N, 25°E)	107
Kismaayo (kis MY yoo), *Somalia* (0°, 42°E)	107
Kissidougou (KEE see DOO goo), *Guinea* (9°N, 10°W)	108
Kissimmee (kihs IHM ee), *Fla.* (28°N, 82°W)	69
Kissimmee, L., *Fla.* (28°N, 81°W)	69
Kissimmee R., *Fla.* (27°N, 81°W)	69
Kisumu (kih SOO moo), *Kenya* (0°, 35°E)	110
Kita-Kyushu (kee TAH KYOO shu), *Japan* (34°N, 131°E)	125
Kitchener, *Ontario* (43°N, 81°W)	46
Kitimat, *British Columbia* (54°N, 129°W)	44
Kittatinny Mts., *N.J.* (41°N, 75°W)	72
Kitty Hawk, *N.C.* (36°N, 76°W)	71
Kitwe (KEE tway), *Zambia* (13°S, 28°E)	107
Kivu, L. (KEE voo), *Africa* (2°S, 29°E)	110
Klagenfurt (KLAHG uhn FOORT), *Austria* (47°N, 14°E)	99
Klamath Falls (KLAM uth), *Ore.* (42°N, 122°W)	60
Klamath Mts., *U.S.* (42°N, 123°W)	58
Kluane N.P. (kloo AWN ee), *Yukon Terr.* (60°N, 138°W)	44
Knife R., *N. Dak.* (47°N, 102°W)	62
Knoxville, *Tenn.* (36°N, 84°W)	70
Kobe (KOH bee), *Japan* (35°N, 135°E)	125
Kobuk Valley N.P. (koh BOOK), *Alaska* (67°N, 160°W)	57
Kochi (KOH chee), *Japan* (34°N, 134°E)	125
Kodiak, *Alaska* (58°N, 153°W)	57
Kodiak I., *Alaska* (57°N, 154°W)	57
Kokomo (KOH kuh MOH), *Ind.* (41°N, 86°W)	70
Kola Pen., *Russia* (67°N, 38°E)	95
Kolguyev I., *Russia* (69°N, 49°E)	95
Kolwezi (kohl WAY zee), *Zaire* (11°S, 25°E)	106
Kolyma Mts. (kuh LEE muh), *Russia* (63°N, 160°E)	101
Kolyma R., *Russia* (67°N, 155°E)	101
Komoe R., *Africa* (10°N, 4°W)	108
Kondoa (kahn DOH uh), *Tanzania* (5°S, 36°E)	110
Kontum, Plateau of, *Vietnam* (13°N, 108°E)	123
Konya, *Turkey* (38°N, 33°E)	115
Kootenay N.P. (KOOT uh nay), *British Columbia* (51°N, 116°W)	44
Kootenay R., *North America* (50°N, 115°W)	44

Name (Pronunciation), *Description* (Lat., Long.)	Page
Korce (KAWR chuh), *Albania* (41°N, 21°E)	99
Korea Bay, *Asia* (39°N, 124°E)	125
Korea Strait, *South Korea and Japan* (34°N, 128°E)	125
Korean Archipelago, *is. in Korea Strait* (34°N, 127°E)	125
Koryak Mts., *Russia* (62°N, 170°E)	101
Kosciusko, Mt. (KAHZ ee UHS koh), *Australia* (37°S, 148°E)	133
Kosice (KAW shuht SAY), *Slovakia* (49°N, 21°E)	99
Kosovo, *prov. of Serbia* (43°N, 21°E)	99
Kota, *India* (25°N, 76°E)	122
Kota Kinabalu (KOHT uh KIHN uh buh LOO), *Malaysia* (6°N, 116°E)	123
Kotte (KOH tay), *Sri Lanka* (7°N, 80°E)	122
Kotzebue (KAHT suh BYOO), *Alaska* (67°N, 163°W)	57
Kotzebue Sound, *Alaska* (67°N, 164°W)	57
Kouchibouguac N.P. (koo SHEE boo GWAK), *New Brunswick* (47°N, 65°W)	47
Kouroussa (koo ROO suh), *Guinea* (11°N, 10°W)	108
Kra, Isthmus of, *Asia* (10°N, 99°E)	123
Krakatoa, *mt. in Indonesia* (6°S, 1°E)	130
Krakow (KRAK ow), *Poland* (50°N, 20°E)	99
Krasnodar, *Russia* (45°N, 39°E)	95
Krasnovodsk, *Turkmenistan* (40°N, 53°E)	100
Krasnoyarsk, *Russia* (56°N, 93°E)	100
Kratie (krah TYAH), *Cambodia* (12°N, 106°E)	123
Krishna R., *India* (16°N, 75°E)	122
Kristiansand, *Norway* (58°N, 8°E)	98
Kroonstad (KROHN STAT), *South Africa* (28°S, 27°E)	109
Krugersdorp, *South Africa* (26°S, 28°E)	109
Krusevac (KROO shuh VAHTS), *Yugoslavia* (44°N, 21°E)	99
Kuala Lumpur, *Malaysia* (3°N, 102°E)	123
Kuching, *Malaysia* (2°N, 110°E)	123
Kumamoto (KOOM uh MOH toh), *Japan* (33°N, 131°E)	125
Kumasi (koo MAHS ee), *Ghana* (7°N, 2°W)	108
Kunashiri, *island in Sea of Okhotsk* (45°N, 146°E)	125
Kunlun Mts., *China* (37°N, 80°E)	124
Kunming, *China* (25°N, 103°E)	124
Kupang (KOO PANG), *Indonesia* (10°S, 124°E)	131
Kurdistan (KOORD uh STAN), *region of Asia* (37°N, 44°E)	115
Kurgan, *Russia* (55°N, 65°E)	100
Kuria Muria I. (KOOR ee uh MOOR ee uh), *island in Arabian Sea* (17°N, 56°E)	115
Kuril Is. (KOO rihl), *Sea of Japan* (46°N, 152°E)	119
Kursk (KOORSK), *Russia* (52°N, 36°E)	100
Kuruman (KOOR uh MAHN), *South Africa* (27°S, 23°E)	109
Kushiro (KOOSH ee ROH), *Japan* (43°N, 144°E)	125
Kuskokwim Mts., *Alaska* (63°N, 156°W)	57
Kuskokwim R., *Alaska* (63°N, 155°W)	57
Kutch, Gulf of (KUCH), *India* (23°N, 70°E)	122
Kuujjuaq, *Quebec* (58°N, 69°W)	43
Kuujjuarapik, *Quebec* (56°N, 78°W)	46
Kuwait (koo WAYT), *country in Asia* (29°N, 48°E)	115
Kuwait, *Kuwait* (30°N, 48°E)	115
Kuybyshev Res. (KWEE buh shehf), *Russia* (55°N, 50°W)	93
Kwangju (GWAWNG JOO), *South Korea* (35°N, 126°E)	125
Kyoga, L. (kee OH guh), *Uganda* (2°N, 33°E)	110
Kyoto, *Japan* (35°N, 136°E)	125
Kyrgyzstan, *country in Asia* (42°N, 75°E)	100
Kyushu (kee YOO shoo), *island in East China Sea* (33°N, 131°E)	125
Kyzyl Kum Desert (kuh ZIHL KOOM), *Kazakhstan* (47°N, 62°E)	100

L

Name (Pronunciation), *Description* (Lat., Long.)	Page
La Coruna (LAHK uh ROON yuh), *Spain* (43°N, 8°W)	114
La Crosse, *Wis.* (44°N, 91°W)	63
La Grande R., *Quebec* (54°N, 78°W)	46
La Grange, *Ga.* (33°N, 85°W)	68
La Malbaie (lah mal BAY), *Quebec* (48°N, 70°W)	47
La Mauricie N. P. (luh MAWR ee SEE), *Quebec* (47°N, 73°W)	47
La Paz, *Bolivia* (16°S, 68°W)	89
La Paz, *Mexico* (24°N, 110°W)	84
La Perouse Strait (LAHP uh ROOZ), *Asia* (46°N, 142°E)	125
La Plata, *Argentina* (35°S, 58°W)	89
La Rochelle (lah roh SHEHL), *France* (46°N, 1°W)	98
La Ronge (luh ROHNZH), *Saskatchewan* (55°N, 105°W)	45
La Sarre, *Quebec* (49°N, 79°W)	46
La Serena, *Chile* (30°S, 71°W)	89
La Tuque (luh TYOOK), *Quebec* (47°N, 73°W)	47
Labrador, *region of North America* (54°N, 60°W)	47
Labrador City, *Newfoundland* (53°N, 67°W)	47
Labrador Sea, *Atlantic O.* (57°N, 50°W)	41
Lac La Ronge (LAK la RONZH), *Saskatchewan* (55°N, 105°W)	45
Lac Seul (lak SOHL), *Ontario* (50°N, 93°W)	45
Laccadive Is., *Laccadive Sea* (11°N, 73°E)	122
Laccadive Sea, *Indian O.* (10°N, 75°E)	122
Lachlan R. (LAHK luhn), *Australia* (33°S, 146°E)	133
Laconia (luh KOH nee uh), *N.H.* (43°N, 72°W)	73
Ladoga, L., *Russia* (61°N, 31°E)	95
Lafayette (LAHF ee ET), *Ind.* (40°N, 87°W)	70
Lafayette, *La.* (30°N, 92°W)	67
Lafourche Bayou (luh FOOSH), *r. in La.* (30°N, 91°W)	67
Lagos (LAH gohs), *Nigeria* (6°N, 3°E)	108
Lahore, *Pakistan* (32°N, 74°E)	122
Lake Charles, *Louisiana* (30°N, 93°W)	67
Lake City, *Minn.* (42°N, 92°W)	63
Lake Clark N.P., *Alaska* (61°N, 153°W)	57
Lake Havasu City (HAV uh SOO), *Ariz.* (34°N, 114°W)	58
Lake Region, *Finland* (63°N, 27°E)	95
Lakeland, *Fla.* (28°N, 82°W)	69
Lakewood, *Colo.* (40°N, 105°W)	59
Lakewood, *Ohio* (41°N, 82°W)	71
Lamar, *Colo.* (38°N, 103°W)	59
Lambarene (LAHM buh RAY nee), *Gabon* (1°S, 10°E)	108
Lamia (luh MEE uh), *Greece* (39°N, 22°E)	99
Lampedusa (LAM puh DOO suh), *island in Mediterranean Sea*, (36°N, 13°E)	99
Lampedusa, *Italy* (36°N, 13°E)	99
Lamu (LAHM oo), *Kenya* (2°S, 41°E)	110
Lanai, *island in Pacific O.* (21°N, 157°W)	57
Lanai City (luh NY), *Hawaii* (21°N, 157°W)	57
Lancaster, *Calif.* (35°N, 118°W)	58
Lancaster, *Ohio* (40°N, 83°W)	70
Lancaster, *Pa.* (40°N, 76°W)	72
Lancaster Sound, *Baffin Bay* (74°N, 85°W)	41
Lander, *Wyo.* (43°N, 109°W)	61
Land's End, *cape in England* (50°N, 6°W)	98
Lanier, L. (luh NIHR), *Ga.* (34°N, 84°W)	69
Lansing, *Mich.* (43°N, 85°W)	63
Lanzhou (lahn joh), *China* (36°N, 103°E)	124
Laos (LAH ohs), *country in Asia* (20°N, 102°E)	123
Lapland, *region of Europe* (68°N, 20°E)	94-95
Laptev Sea, *Arctic O.* (75°N, 125°E)	119
Laramie, *Wyo.* (41°N, 105°W)	61
Laramie Mts., *Wyo.* (42°N, 105°W)	61
Laredo, *Tex.* (28°N, 99°W)	66
Larisa, *Greece* (40°N, 22°E)	99
Larsen Ice Shelf, *Antarctica* (68°S, 60°W)	137
Las Cruces (lahs KROO sihs), *N. Mex.* (32°N, 107°W)	59
Las Palmas, *Canary Islands* (28°N, 15°W)	114
Las Vegas, *Nev.* (36°N, 115°W)	58
Lassen Volcanic N. P., *Calif.* (41°N, 121°W)	58
Latakia (LAT uh KEE uh), *Syria* (36°N, 36°E)	115
Latvia, *country in Europe* (57°N, 23°E)	97
Launceston, *Australia* (41°S, 147°E)	131
Laurel, *Miss.* (32°N, 89°W)	68
Laurentian Highlands (law REHN shuhn), *Quebec* (47°N, 74°W)	47
Laval (luh VAL), *Quebec* (46°N, 74°W)	47

Name (Pronunciation), *Description* (Lat., Long.)	Page
Lawrence, *Kans.* (39°N, 95°W)	65
Lawrence, *Mass.* (43°N, 71°W)	73
Lawrenceburg, *Tenn.* (35°N, 87°W)	70
Lawton, *Okla.* (35°N, 98°W)	66
Layton, *Utah* (41°N, 112°W)	59
Le Havre (luh HAHV ruh), *France* (49°N, 0°)	98
Le Mans (luh MAHN), *France* (48°N, 0°)	98
Leaf R., *Miss.* (31°N, 89°W)	68
Leavenworth (LEHV uh WUHRTH), *Kans.* (39°N, 95°W)	65
Lebanon, *country in Asia* (34°N, 37°E)	115
Lebanon, *N.H.* (44°N, 72°W)	73
Lee's Summit, *Mo.* (39°N, 94°W)	65
Leech L., *Minn.* (47°N, 94°W)	62
Leeds, *England* (54°N, 2°W)	98
Leeuwin, Cape (LYOO ihn), *Australia* (33°S, 115°E)	130
Leeward Is., *Caribbean Sea* (17°N, 62°W)	83
Leghorn, *Italy* (44°N, 10°E)	99
Leicester (LEHS tuhr), *England* (53°N, 1°W)	98
Leipzig, *Germany* (51°N, 12°E)	99
Lemhi Range (LEHM hy), *Idaho* (45°N, 114°W)	61
Lena R., *Russia* (69°N, 124°E)	119
Leon, *Mexico* (21°N, 102°W)	84
Lerma R., *Mexico* (20°N, 100°W)	82
Lesbos, *island in Aegean Sea* (39°N, 26°E)	99
Lesotho, *country in Africa* (30°S, 28°E)	107
Lesser Antilles, *island group in Caribbean Sea* (15°N, 62°W)	83
Lesser Slave L., *Alberta* (55°N, 115°W)	44
Lethbridge, *Alberta* (50°N, 112°W)	45
Levisa Fork (luh VY suh), *r. in Ky.* (38°N, 83°W)	70
Lewis and Clark L., *U.S.* (43°N, 98°W)	62
Lewis Range, *Mont.* (48°N, 113°W)	61
Lewis Smith L., *Ala.* (34°N, 87°W)	68
Lewiston, *Idaho* (46°N, 117°W)	60
Lewiston, *Maine* (44°N, 70°W)	73
Lewistown, *Mont.* (47°N, 109°W)	61
Lewisville, *Tex.* (33°N, 97°W)	67
Lewisville, L., *Tex.* (33°N, 97°W)	67
Lexington, *Ky.* (38°N, 85°W)	70
Lexington, *Va.* (38°N, 79°W)	71
Lhasa (LAH suh), *China* (30°N, 91°E)	124
Liao R. (lee OW), *China* (44°N, 120°E)	124
Liard R., *Canada* (59°N, 126°W)	44
Liberal, *Kans.* (37°N, 101°W)	64
Liberia, *country in Africa* (7°N, 10°W)	108
Libreville, *Gabon* (0°, 9°E)	108
Libya, *country in Africa* (26°N, 16°E)	114-115
Libyan Desert, *Africa* (25°N, 26°E)	115
Licking R., *Ky.* (39°N, 84°W)	70
Liechtenstein (LIHK tuhn STYN), *country in Europe* (47°N, 10°E)	99
Liege (lee AYZH), *Belgium* (51°N, 6°E)	98
Ligurian Sea (lih GYOO rih uhn), *Europe* (44°N, 9°E)	99
Lihue (lih HYOO ee), *Hawaii* (22°N, 159°W)	57
Lille (leel), *France* (51°N, 3°E)	98
Lillehammer (LIHL uh HAHM uhr), *Norway* (61°N, 10°E)	96
Lilongwe (lih LAWNG way), *Malawi* (14°S, 34°E)	107
Lima (LEE muh), *Peru* (12°S, 77°W)	90
Lima (LY muh), *Ohio* (41°N, 84°W)	70
Limerick, *Ireland* (53°N, 9°W)	98
Limnos, *island in Aegean Sea* (40°N, 25°E)	99
Limoges (lee MOHZH), *France* (46°N, 1°E)	98
Limon (LY muhn), *Colo.* (40°N, 105°W)	59
Limon (lih MAWN), *Costa Rica* (10°N, 83°W)	85
Limpopo R. (lihm POH poh), *Africa* (23°S, 32°E)	109
Lincoln, *Maine* (45°N, 68°W)	73
Lincoln, *Nebr.* (41°N, 97°W)	64
Lindenhurst, *N.Y.* (41°N, 73°W)	73
Lindesnes, Cape, *Norway* (58°N, 7°E)	98
Lindi (LIHN dee), *Tanzania* (10°S, 40°E)	110
Linz, *Austria* (48°N, 14°E)	99
Lions, Gulf of, *Mediterranean Sea* (43°N, 4°E)	98
Lipari Is., *Tyrrhenian Sea* (39°N, 15°E)	99
Lisbon, *Portugal* (39°N, 9°W)	114
Lithuania, *country in Europe* (55°N, 23°E)	97
Little Bighorn R., *Mont.* (45°N, 108°W)	61
Little Colorado R., *U.S.* (36°N, 111°W)	59
Little Current R., *Ontario* (51°N, 85°W)	46
Little Kanawha R. (kuh NAW wuh), *W. Va.* (39°N, 81°W)	71
Little Karroo, *plateau in South Africa* (34°S, 22°E)	109
Little Mecatina R., *Canada* (52°N, 61°W)	47
Little Missouri R., *N. Dak.* (47°N, 103°W)	62
Little Rock, *Ark.* (35°N, 92°W)	67
Little Sioux R. (SOO), *Iowa* (43°N, 95°W)	64-65
Little Tennessee R., *U.S.* (36°N, 84°W)	70
Little Wabash R., *Ill.* (38°N, 88°W)	65
Liverpool, *England* (53°N, 3°W)	98
Livingston, L., *Tex.* (31°N, 95°W)	67
Ljiji, *Tanzania* (5°S, 30°E)	110
Ljubljana (LYOO BLYAH nah), *Slovenia* (46°N, 14°E)	99
Llano Estacado (LAHN oh es tuh KAHD oh), *plain in U.S.* (33°N, 103°W)	89
Llano R., *Tex.* (30°N, 99°W)	66
Llanos (LAH nohz), *plain in South America* (7°N, 71°W)	90
Lloyd George, Mt., *British Columbia* (58°N, 125°W)	44
Lloydminster, *Alberta* (53°N, 110°W)	45
Lobito, *Angola* (12°S, 14°E)	107
Loch Ness (lawk nehs), *lake in Scotland* (57°N, 4°W)	98
Lodi (LAWD ee), *Calif.* (38°N, 121°W)	58
Lodz (LOOJ), *Poland* (52°N, 19°E)	99
Lofoten Is., *Norway* (69°N, 15°E)	96
Logan, *Utah* (42°N, 112°W)	59
Logan, *W. Va.* (38°N, 82°W)	71
Logan, Mt., *Yukon Terr.* (61°N, 140°W)	44
Logan Mts., *Yukon Terr.* (62°N, 128°W)	44
Logansport, *Ind.* (41°N, 86°W)	70
Loire R. (lwahr), *France* (48°N, 1°W)	98
Lome (loh MAY), *Togo* (6°N, 1°E)	108
Lompoc (LAHM pahk), *Calif.* (35°N, 120°W)	58
London, *England* (52°N, 0°)	98
London, *Ontario* (43°N, 81°W)	46
Londonderry, *Northern Ireland* (55°N, 7°W)	98
Long Bay, *S.C.* (34°N, 79°W)	69
Long Beach, *Calif.* (34°N, 118°W)	58
Long Branch, *N.J.* (40°N, 74°W)	72
Long I., *Hudson Bay* (55°N, 80°W)	46
Long I., *N.Y.* (41°N, 73°W)	72-73
Long I. Sound, *U.S.* (41°N, 73°W)	73
Long Xuyen (lowng SWEE uhn), *Vietnam* (10°N, 105°E)	123
Longfellow Mts., *Maine* (45°N, 70°W)	73
Longlac, *Ontario* (50°N, 87°W)	46
Longmont, *Colo.* (40°N, 105°W)	59
Longs Pk., *Colo.* (40°N, 106°W)	59
Longueuil (lawng GAYL), *Quebec* (46°N, 74°W)	47
Longview, *Tex.* (32°N, 95°W)	67
Longview, *Wash.* (46°N, 123°W)	60
Lookout, Cape, *N.C.* (35°N, 76°W)	71
Lop Nor (lawp nawr), *l. in China* (40°N, 90°E)	124
Lorain, *Ohio* (41°N, 82°W)	71
Lord Howe I., *Tasman Sea* (31°S, 159°E)	130
Los Alamos (law SAL uh MOHS), *N. Mex.* (36°N, 106°W)	59
Los Angeles, *Calif.* (34°N, 118°W)	58
Los Angeles Aqueduct, *Calif.* (35°N, 118°W)	58
Lot R. (LAHT), *France* (44°N, 1°E)	98
Lotikipi Plains, *Africa* (4°N, 35°E)	110
Louangphrabang (LWAHNG prah BAHNG), *Laos* (20°N, 102°E)	123
Louisiana, *state in U.S.* (32°N, 93°W)	67
Louisville, *Ky.* (38°N, 86°W)	70
Lowell (LOH uhl), *Mass.* (43°N, 71°W)	73
Lower Arrow L., *British Columbia* (50°N, 118°W)	44
Lower Pen., *Mich.* (44°N, 85°W)	63
Lower Red Lake, *Minn.* (48°N, 95°W)	62
Lower Tunguska R., *Russia* (65°N, 92°E)	118-119
Loyalty Is., *Pacific O.* (21°S, 168°E)	130
Luanda, *Angola* (9°S, 13°E)	107
Lubango, *Angola* (15°S, 13°E)	107
Lubbock, *Texas* (34°N, 102°W)	66
Lubeck, *Germany* (54°N, 11°E)	99
Lublin, *Poland* (51°N, 23°E)	99
Lubumbashi, *Zaire* (12°S, 27°E)	107
Lucknow (LUHK NOW), *India* (27°N, 81°E)	122
Ludhiana (LOOD ee AHN ah), *India* (31°N, 76°E)	122
Ludington, *Mich.* (44°N, 86°W)	63
Lufkin, *Tex.* (31°N, 95°W)	67
Lule R. (LOO luh), *Sweden* (66°N, 21°E)	95
Lunenburg (LOO nuhn BURG), *Nova Scotia* (44°N, 64°W)	47
Lusaka, *Zambia* (15°S, 28°E)	107
Luxembourg (LUHK sum BURG), *country in Europe* (50°N, 6°E)	98
Luxembourg, *Luxembourg* (49°N, 6°E)	98
Luxor, *Egypt* (26°N, 33°E)	115
Luzon, *island in Philippine Sea* (17°N, 121°E)	119
Luzon Strait, *Philippines and Taiwan* (21°N, 121°E)	119
Lvov (luh VAWF), *Ukraine* (50°N, 24°E)	97
Lyall, Mt., *Canada* (50°N, 115°W)	44
Lynchburg, *Va.* (37°N, 79°W)	71
Lyndon B. Johnson, L., *Tex.* (31°N, 98°W)	66
Lynn (LIN), *Mass.* (42°N, 71°W)	73
Lynn Lake, *Manitoba* (57°N, 101°W)	45
Lyon (lyawn), *France* (46°N, 5°E)	98

M

Name (Pronunciation), *Description* (Lat., Long.)	Page
Macao, (muh KOW), *poss. of Portugal* (22°N, 113°E)	124
Macapa (MAHK uh PAH), *Brazil* (0°, 52°W)	90
MacDonnell Ranges, *Australia* (24°S, 130°E)	130
Macedonia, *country in Europe* (42°N, 22°E)	99
Maceio (MAS ay OH), *Brazil* (10°S, 36°W)	89
Machala, *Ecuador* (3°S, 80°W)	90
Mackay, L., *Australia* (22°S, 129°E)	130
Mackenzie Bay, *Canada* (70°N, 138°W)	40
Mackenzie Mts., *Canada* (64°N, 130°W)	44
Mackenzie R., *Northwest Terr.* (65°N, 125°W)	40
Mackinac, Straits of, *Mich.* (46°N, 85°W)	63
Macomb (muh KOHM), *Ill.* (40°N, 91°W)	65
Macon (MAY kuhn), *Ga.* (33°N, 84°W)	69
MacRobertson Land, *region of Antarctica* (70°S, 60°E)	137
Madagascar, *country in Africa* (20°S, 45°E)	107
Madawaska R., *Ontario* (45°N, 76°W)	46-47
Madeira Falls (muh DEER uh), *waterfall in Brazil* (10°S, 65°W)	90
Madeira Is., *Atlantic O.* (33°N, 17°W)	114
Madeira R., *Brazil* (8°S, 64°W)	90
Madeleine Is. (MAD uh LAYN), *Gulf of Saint Lawrence* (47°N, 62°W)	47
Madison, *Ind.* (39°N, 86°W)	70
Madison, *Wis.* (43°N, 89°W)	63
Madison R., *Mont.* (45°N, 112°W)	61
Madisonville, *Ky.* (37°N, 88°W)	70
Madras, *India* (13°N, 80°E)	122
Madre Lagoon, *Mexico* (25°N, 98°W)	82
Madrid, *Spain* (40°N, 4°W)	96
Madurai (MAHD uh RY), *India* (10°N, 78°E)	122
Maebashi (MAH yuh BAHSH ee), *Japan* (36°N, 139°E)	125
Mafeking (MAF uh king), *South Africa* (26°S, 26°E)	109
Mafia (MAHF ee uh), *island in Indian O.* (8°S, 40°E)	110
Magadan, *Russia* (60°N, 151°E)	101
Magdalena R., *Colombia* (7°N, 75°W)	90
Magdeburg, *Germany* (52°N, 12°E)	99
Magellan, Strait of, *South America* (53°S, 70°W)	88
Magpie R., *Quebec* (50°N, 65°W)	47
Maiduguri (my DOO guh ree), *Nigeria* (12°N, 13°E)	108
Main R. (MYN), *Germany* (50°N, 5°E)	99
Maine, *state in U.S.* (45°N, 70°W)	73
Maitland, *Australia* (33°S, 152°E)	133
Maji, *Ethiopia* (6°N, 36°E)	107
Makassar Strait, *Borneo and Celebes* (3°S, 117°E)	130
Makgadikgadi Pans, *dry lakes in Botswana* (21°S, 25°E)	106
Makindu, *Kenya* (2°S, 38°E)	110

Name (Pronunciation), *Description* (Lat., Long.)	Page
Makran, *region of Asia* (26°N, 62°E)	115
Makurdi (mah KOOR dee), *Nigeria* (8°N, 9°E)	108
Malabar Coast, *India* (14°N, 74°E)	122
Malabo, *Eq. Guinea* (4°N, 9°E)	108
Malacca, Strait of, *Sumatra and Malay Pen.* (4°N, 100°E)	119
Malaga, *Spain* (37°N, 4°W)	114
Malakal, *Sudan* (10°N, 32°E)	107
Malang (muh LAHNG), *Indonesia* (8°S, 113°E)	131
Malaren, L., *Sweden* (59°N, 17°W)	107
Malawi, *country in Africa* (13°S, 34°E)	107
Malay Pen., *Asia* (5°N, 101°E)	123
Malaysia, *country of Asia* (3°N, 102°E)	123
Maldives, *country in Indian O.* (3°N, 74°E)	122
Male (MAH lay), *Maldives* (4°N, 74°E)	120
Malheur L. (mal HOOR), *Oreg.* (43°N, 119°W)	60
Mali (MAH lee), *country in Africa* (16°N, 2°W)	107
Malindi (muh LIHN dee), *Kenya* (3°S, 40°E)	110
Malmo, *Sweden* (56°N, 13°E)	96
Malpelo I., *Pacific O.* (4°N, 81°W)	90
Malta, *country in Europe* (36°N, 15°E)	99
Malta, *Mont.* (48°N, 108°W)	61
Maltese Is., *Mediterranean Sea* (36°N, 15°E)	99
Malugarasi R., *Tanzania* (5°S, 30°E)	110
Mammoth Cave N. P., *Ky.* (37°N, 86°W)	70
Mamore R. (MAHM uh RAY), *Bolivia* (14°S, 65°W)	88
Man, *Côte d'Ivoire* (7°N, 8°W)	108
Man, Isle of, *poss. of United Kingdom* (54°N, 5°W)	98
Manado, *Indonesia* (1°N, 125°E)	131
Managua, *Nicaragua* (12°N, 86°W)	85
Managua, L., *Nicaragua* (12°N, 86°W)	83
Manama, *Bahrain* (26°N, 51°E)	115
Manassas (muh NAS uhs), *Va.* (39°N, 77°W)	71
Manaus, *Brazil* (3°S, 60°W)	90
Manchester, *Conn.* (42°N, 72°W)	73
Manchester, *England* (53°N, 2°W)	98
Manchester, *Ky.* (37°N, 84°W)	70
Manchester, *N.H.* (43°N, 71°W)	73
Manchurian Plain, *China* (45°N, 125°E)	124
Mandalay, *Burma* (22°N, 96°E)	123
Mandan, *N. Dak.* (47°N, 101°W)	62
Mandara Mts. (mahn DAH ruh), *Nigeria* (10°N, 14°E)	108
Mangalore (MANG guh LAWR), *India* (13°N, 75°E)	122
Manhattan, *Kans.* (39°N, 97°W)	64
Manicouagan L. (MAN uh KWAHG uhn), *Quebec* (52°N, 68°W)	47
Manicouagan R., *Quebec* (51°N, 68°W)	47
Manila, *Philippines* (14°N, 121°E)	121
Manistee R. (MAN uh STEE), *Mich.* (44°N, 86°W)	63
Manitoba, *prov. in Canada* (57°N, 95°W)	45
Manitoba, L., *Canada* (51°N, 98°W)	45
Manitou Is. (MAN uh TOO), *L. Michigan* (45°N, 86°W)	63
Manitoulin I. (MAN uh TOO luhn), *L. Huron* (46°N, 83°W)	46
Manitowoc (MAN uht uh WAHK), *Wis.* (44°N, 88°W)	63
Maniwaki (MAN uh WAW kee), *Quebec* (46°N, 76°W)	47
Manizales (MAN uh ZAHL uhs), *Colombia* (5°N, 76°W)	90
Mankato (man KAY toh), *Minn.* (44°N, 94°W)	62
Mannar, Gulf of (muh NAHR), *Asia* (8°N, 79°E)	122
Mannheim, *Germany* (49°N, 9°E)	99
Manokwari, *Indonesia* (1°S, 134°E)	131
Manouane, L. (mah NOO uhn), *Quebec* (51°N, 71°W)	47
Mansel I., *Hudson Bay* (62°N, 80°W)	41
Mansfield, *Ohio* (41°N, 83°W)	71
Mansfield, *Pa.* (42°N, 77°W)	72
Mansfield, Mt., *Vt.* (45°N, 73°W)	73
Manyara, L. (muhn YAHR uh), *Tanzania* (3°S, 36°E)	110
Maoke Mts. (MOW kay), *New Guinea* (4°S, 139°E)	130
Maple Creek, *Saskatchewan* (50°N, 109°W)	45
Maputo, *Mozambique* (26°S, 33°E)	107
Mar del Plata, *Argentina* (38°S, 58°W)	89

Name (Pronunciation), *Description* (Lat., Long.)	Page
Maracaibo, (MAR uh KY boh), *Venezuela* (11°N, 72°W)	90
Maracaibo, L., *Venezuela* (10°N, 72°W)	90
Marajo I., *Brazil* (1°S, 49°W)	88
Maranon R., *Peru* (5°S, 75°W)	90
Marathon, *Ontario* (49°N, 86°W)	46
Marcy, Mt., *N.Y.* (44°N, 74°W)	72
Margarita, *island in Caribbean Sea* (11°N, 64°W)	90
Margherita, mt. *in Zaire* (0°, 30°E)	110
Maribor, *Slovenia* (47°N, 16°E)	99
Marie Byrd Land, *region of Antarctica* (78°S, 120°W)	137
Marietta, *Ga.* (34°N, 85°W)	68
Marietta, *Ohio* (39°N, 82°W)	71
Marion, *Ind.* (41°N, 86°W)	70
Marion, *Ohio* (41°N, 83°W)	70
Marion, *Va.* (37°N, 82°W)	71
Marion, L., *S.C.* (33°N, 80°W)	69
Markham, *Ontario* (44°N, 79°W)	46
Marmara, Sea of (MAHR muhr uh), *Black and Mediterranean Seas* (41°N, 28°E)	95
Marne R. (MAHRN), *France* (48°N, 4°E)	98
Maroa (mah ROH ah), *Venezuela* (3°N, 68°W)	90
Maroua (muh ROO uh), *Cameroon* (11°N, 14°E)	108
Marquette, *Mich.* (47°N, 87°W)	65
Marrakech, *Morocco* (32°N, 8°W)	114
Marseille (mahr SAY), *France* (43°N, 5°E)	98
Marshall, *Minn.* (44°N, 96°W)	62
Marshall, *Tex.* (33°N, 94°W)	67
Marshall Islands, *country in Pacific O.* (10°N, 165°E)	135
Marshalltown, *Iowa* (42°N, 93°W)	65
Marshfield, *Wis.* (45°N, 90°W)	63
Martha's Vineyard, *Mass.* (41°N, 71°W)	73
Martin, L., *Ala.* (34°N, 86°W)	68
Martinique (mahr tuh NEEK), *overseas state of France* (15°N, 61°W)	85
Martinsburg, *W. Va.* (39°N, 78°W)	71
Martinsville, *Va.* (37°N, 80°W)	71
Maryland, *state in U.S.* (39°N, 77°W)	71
Marysville, *Kans.* (40°N, 97°W)	64
Maryville, *Tenn.* (36°N, 84°W)	70
Marzuq, *Libya* (26°N, 14°E)	114
Masai Steppe (mah SY), *Tanzania* (5°S, 37°E)	110
Masaka, *Uganda* (0°, 32°E)	110
Masan, *South Korea* (35°N, 129°E)	125
Mascarene Is. (MAS kuh REEN), *Indian O.* (21°S, 57°E)	106
Maseru (MAZ uh ROO), *Lesotho* (29°S, 27°E)	107
Masirah (muh SIHR uh), *island in Arabian Sea* (21°N, 59°E)	115
Mason City, *Iowa* (43°N, 93°W)	65
Massachusetts, *state in U.S.* (42°N, 72°W)	73
Massachusetts Bay, *Mass.* (42°N, 71°W)	73
Masset, *British Columbia* (54°N, 132°W)	44
Massif Central, *mt. region in France* (45°N, 3°E)	98
Massillon, *Ohio* (41°N, 82°W)	71
Matagami, *Quebec* (50°N, 78°W)	46
Matagorda Bay (MAT uh GAWRD uh), *Gulf of Mexico* (29°N, 96°W)	67
Matamoras, *Mexico* (26°N, 97°W)	84
Matandu R., *Tanzania* (9°S, 39°E)	110
Matane (muh TAN), *Quebec* (49°N, 68°W)	47
Mato Grosso Plateau, *Brazil* (13°S, 58°W)	88
Matsu (MAHT soo), *Japan* (35°N, 133°E)	125
Mattagami R. (muh TAG uh mee), *Ontario* (48°N, 81°W)	46
Mattoon, *Ill.* (39°N, 88°W)	65
Maturin (MAHT uh REEN), *Venezuela* (10°N, 63°W)	90
Maui (MOW ee), *island in Pacific O.* (21°N, 156°W)	57
Maumee R. (maw MEE), *U.S.* (41°N, 84°W)	70
Mauna Kea (MOW nuh KEE uh), *mt. in Hawaii* (20°N, 156°W)	57
Mauna Loa, *mt. in Hawaii* (19°N, 155°W)	57
Mauritania, *country in Africa* (20°N, 10°W)	107
Mauritius, *country in Indian O.* (20°S, 57°E)	107
May, Cape, *N.J.* (39°N, 75°W)	72

Name (Pronunciation), *Description* (Lat., Long.)	Page
Mayfield, *Ky.* (37°N, 89°W)	70
Mayotte, *island in Indian O.* (13°S, 45°E)	106
Maysville, *Ky.* (39°N, 84°W)	70
Mayumba (muh YOOM buh), *Gabon* (3°S, 11°E)	108
Mazar-e Sharif (muh ZAHR ee shuh REEF), *Afghanistan* (37°N, 67°E)	122
Mazatlan, *Mexico* (23°N, 106°W)	84
Mbabane (EM buh BAHN), *Swaziland* (26°S, 31°E)	107
Mbandaka (EM bahn DAHK uh), *Zaire* (0°, 18°E)	107
Mbeya (EM BAY uh), *Tanzania* (9°S, 33°E)	110
Mbuji-Mayi (em BOO jee MY ee), *Zaire* (6°S, 24°E)	106
McAllen, *Tex.* (26°N, 98°W)	66
McComb, *Miss.* (31°N, 90°W)	68
McConaughy, L., *Nebr.* (41°N, 102°W)	64
McCook, *Nebr.* (40°N, 101°W)	64
McFarlane R., *Saskatchewan* (59°N, 108°W)	45
McGrath, *Alaska* (63°N, 155°W)	57
McKenzie, *Tenn.* (36°N, 89°W)	70
McKenzie R., *Oreg.* (44°N, 122°W)	60
McKinley, Mt., *Alaska* (63°N, 151°W)	57
M'Clintock Channel, *Northwest Terr.* (72°N, 103°W)	40
M'Clure Strait, *Arctic O.* (75°N, 120°W)	40
McMillan, L., *N. Mex.* (33°N, 104°W)	59
McMinnville, *Tenn.* (36°N, 86°W)	70
Mdantsane, *South Africa* (33°S, 27°E)	109
Mead, L., *U.S.* (36°N, 114°W)	58
Meadow Lake, *Saskatchewan* (54°N, 108°W)	45
Mealy Mts., *Newfoundland* (53°N, 59°W)	47
Mecca, *Saudi Arabia* (21°N, 40°E)	115
Medan, *Indonesia* (4°N, 98°E)	121
Medellin, *Colombia* (6°N, 76°W)	90
Medford, *Oreg.* (42°N, 123°W)	60
Medicine Bow Mts., *Wyo.* (41°N, 106°W)	61
Medicine Hat, *Alberta* (50°N, 111°W)	45
Medina, *Saudi Arabia* (24°N, 40°E)	115
Mediterranean Sea, *Europe, Africa, and Asia* (38°N, 5°E)	114-115
Medora (mih DOHR uh), *N. Dak.* (47°N, 104°W)	62
Meerut (MAY ruht), *India* (29°N, 78°E)	122
Mega, *Ethiopia* (4°N, 38°E)	107
Mekambo, *Gabon* (1°N, 14°E)	108
Meknes, *Morocco* (34°N, 6°W)	114
Mekong, Mouths of the (MAY KAWNG), *delta in Vietnam* (10°N, 106°E)	123
Mekong R., *Asia* (17°N, 105°E)	118-119
Mekrou R. (MEHK roo), *Africa* (12°N, 2°E)	108
Melbourne (MEHL buhrn), *Australia* (38°S, 145°E)	133
Melbourne, *Fla.* (28°N, 81°W)	69
Melfort, *Saskatchewan* (53°N, 105°W)	45
Melilla (muh LEE uh), *terr. of Spain* (35°N, 3°W)	114
Melville I., *Arctic O.* (75°N, 110°W)	40
Melville I., *Australia* (11°S, 131°E)	130
Melville, L., *Newfoundland* (54°N, 59°W)	47
Melville Pen., *Northwest Terr.* (68°N, 84°W)	41
Memphis, *Tenn.* (35°N, 90°W)	70
Menasha, *Wis.* (44°N, 88°W)	63
Mendocino, Cape, *Calif.* (40°N, 124°W)	58
Mendoza, *Argentina* (33°S, 69°W)	89
Menihek Lakes, *Newfoundland* (54°N, 67°W)	47
Menominee Range (muh NAHM uh nee), *U.S.* (46°N, 89°W)	63
Mentawai Is., *Indonesia* (2°S, 100°E)	130
Mentor, *Ohio* (42°N, 81°W)	71
Meramec R. (MEHR uh MAK), *Mo.* (38°N, 91°W)	65
Merced (muhr SED), *Calif.* (37°N, 121°W)	58
Meredith, L., *Tex.* (36°N, 102°W)	66
Mergui Archipelago (MUHR GWEE), *Burma* (12°N, 97°E)	123
Merida (MER uh duh), *Mexico* (21°N, 90°W)	84
Meridian, *Miss.* (32°N, 89°W)	68
Merrillville, *Ind.* (42°N, 87°W)	70
Merrimack R., *N.H.* (43°N, 72°W)	73
Mesa (MAY suh), *Ariz.* (33°N, 112°W)	59
Mesa Verde N.P. (MAY suh VUR dee), *Colo.* (37°N, 108°W)	59
Mesabi Range (muh SAHB ee), *Minn.* (47°N, 93°W)	63

Name (Pronunciation), *Description* (Lat., Long.)	Page
Meshed, *Iran* (36°N, 60°E)	115
Mesopotamia (MEHS uh puh TAY mee uh), *region of Iraq* (32°N, 45°E)	115
Messina (muh SEE nuh), *Sicily* (38°N, 15°E)	99
Messina, Strait of, *Mediterranean Sea* (38°N, 16°E)	99
Methow R. (MET how), *Wash.* (48°N, 120°W)	60
Metz, *France* (49°N, 5°E)	98
Meuse R. (myooz), *France* (49°N, 5°E)	98
Mexicali, *Mexico* (33°N, 115°W)	84
Mexico, *country in North America* (24°N, 103°W)	84-85
Mexico, Gulf of, *Atlantic O.* (27°N, 90°W)	36
Mexico, Plateau of, *Mexico* (24°N, 103°W)	82
Mexico City, *Mexico* (19°N, 99°W)	84
Miami, *Fla.* (26°N, 80°W)	69
Miami Beach, *Fla.* (26°N, 80°W)	69
Miami R., *Ohio* (39°N, 85°W)	70
Michigan, *state in U.S.* (45°N, 85°W)	63
Michigan, L., *U.S.* (42°N, 87°W)	53
Michigan City, *Ind.* (42°N, 87°W)	70
Michipicoten I. (MIHSH uh puh KOHT uhn), *L. Superior* (48°N, 86°W)	46
Middelburg, *South Africa* (31°S, 25°E)	109
Middle Loup R. (LOOP), *Nebr.* (42°N, 100°W)	64
Middlesboro, *Ky.* (37°N, 84°W)	70
Middletown, *Ohio* (40°N, 84°W)	70
Midland, *Mich.* (44°N, 84°W)	63
Midland, *Tex.* (32°N, 102°W)	66
Miguel Aleman Res., *Mexico* (18°N, 97°W)	82
Milan, *Italy* (45°N, 9°E)	99
Mildura (mihl DOOR uh), *Australia* (34°S, 142°E)	133
Miles City, *Mont.* (46°N, 106°W)	61
Milford, *Del.* (39°N, 75°W)	71
Milford Res., *Kans.* (39°N, 97°W)	64
Milk R., *North America* (48°N, 109°W)	61
Mille Lacs L. (mil LAKS), *Minn.* (46°N, 94°W)	62
Millville, *N.J.* (39°N, 75°W)	72
Millwood L., *Ark.* (34°N 94°W)	67
Milwaukee, *Wis.* (43°N, 88°W)	63
Minas Basin (MY nuhs), *bay in Nova Scotia* (45°N, 64°W)	47
Minch, The, *strait in Hebrides Is.* (58°N, 6°W)	98
Mindanao (MIHN duh NAH oh), *island in Philippine Sea* (8°N, 126°E)	119
Mindoro (mihn DOHR oh), *island in South China Sea* (13°N, 121°E)	123
Mingan (MING guhn), *Quebec* (50°N, 64°W)	47
Mingan Archipelago Reserve, *Quebec* (50°N, 64°W)	47
Minneapolis, *Minn.* (45°N, 93°W)	62-63
Minnesota, *state in U.S.* (46°N, 95°W)	62-63
Minnesota R., *Minn.* (45°N, 95°W)	62
Minot (MY naht), *N. Dak.* (48°N, 101°W)	62
Minsk, *Belarus* (54°N, 28°E)	97
Miquelon (MIK uh LAHN), *island in Atlantic O.* (47°N, 56°W)	41
Miramichi R. (MIHR uh muh SHEE), *New Brunswick* (47°N, 66°W)	47
Mirim L., *South America* (33°S, 53°W)	88
Mishawaka, *Ind.* (42°N, 86°W)	70
Miskigum R., *Ohio* (40°N, 82°W)	71
Miskolc (MISH kohlts), *Hungary* (48°N, 21°E)	99
Missinaibi R. (MIS uh NY bee), *Ontario* (50°N, 83°W)	46
Mississagi R. (MIHS uh SAHG ee), *Ontario* (46°N, 83°W)	46
Mississauga, *Ontario* (44°N, 80°W)	46
Mississinewa L., *Ind.* (41°N, 86°W)	70
Mississippi, *state in U.S.* (32°N, 90°W)	68
Mississippi R., *U.S.* (32°N, 92°W)	53
Mississippi R. Delta, *La.* (29°N, 89°W)	67
Missoula, *Mont.* (47°N, 114°W)	61
Missouri, *state in U.S.* (38°N, 94°W)	65
Missouri City, *Tex.* (29°N, 96°W)	67
Missouri R., *U.S.* (42°N, 96°W)	52-53
Mistassibi R., *Quebec* (51°N, 72°W)	47
Mistassini, L., *Quebec* (51°N, 73°W)	47
Misuratah (MIS uh RAHT uh), *Libya* (32°N, 15°E)	114
Mitchell, *S. Dak.* (44°N, 98°W)	62
Mitchell, Mt., *N.C.* (36°N, 82°W)	71
Mittelland Canal, *Germany* (54°N, 11°E)	99
Miyazaki (mee AHZ AHK ee), *Japan* (32°N, 131°E)	125
Mlala Hills, *Tanzania* (7°S, 32°E)	110
Mmabatho (mah BAH toh), *South Africa* (26°S, 26°E)	109
Moab, *Utah* (39°N, 110°W)	59
Mobile, *Ala.* (31°N, 88°W)	68
Mobile Bay, *Ala.* (31°N, 87°W)	68
Mobridge, *S. Dak.* (46°N, 100°W)	62
Mocha (MOH kuh), *Yemen* (13°N, 43°E)	115
Modena (MAWD ee nuh), *Italy* (45°N, 11°E)	99
Modesto, *Calif.* (38°N, 121°W)	58
Moe (MOH ee), *Australia* (38°S, 146°E)	133
Mogadishu, *Somalia* (2°N, 45°E)	107
Mogollon Rim (MUHG ee OHN), *Ariz.* (34°N, 111°W)	59
Mohave, L. (muh HAHV ee), *U.S.* (33°N, 115°W)	58
Moisie R. (mwa ZEE), *Quebec* (52°N, 67°W)	47
Mojave Desert (muh HAH vee), *Calif.* (35°N, 117°W)	58
Mokpo (MAHK POH), *S. Korea* (35°N, 126°E)	125
Moldova, *country in Europe* (47°N, 28°E)	97
Moline (Ill.) (42°N, 90°W)	65
Molokai, *island in Pacific O.* (21°N, 157°W)	57
Molopo R. (muh LOH POH), *Africa* (27°S, 21°E)	109
Molucca Sea, *Indian O.* (1°S, 125°E)	130
Mombasa, *Kenya* (4°S, 40°E)	110
Mona Passage, *Caribbean Sea* (18°N, 68°W)	83
Monaco, *country in Europe* (44°N, 7°E)	98
Moncton (MUHNG tun), *New Brunswick* (46°N, 65°W)	47
Mongolia, *country in Asia* (46°N, 101°E)	120-121
Mono L. (MOH noh), *Calif.* (38°N, 119°W)	58
Monongahela R. (muh NAHN guh HEE luh), *U.S.* (40°N, 80°W)	72
Monroe, *La.* (32°N, 92°W)	67
Monroe, *N.C.* (35°N, 81°W)	71
Monroe L., *Ind.* (30°N, 86°W)	70
Monroeville, *Pa.* (40°N, 80°W)	72
Monrovia, *Liberia* (6°N, 11°W)	108
Montana, *state in U.S.* (47°N, 113°W)	60-61
Montauk Point (MAHN TAWK), *N.Y.* (41°N, 72°W)	73
Montego Bay, *Jamaica* (18°N, 78°W)	85
Montenegro (mahn tuh NEE groh), *republic of Yugoslavia* (43°N, 19°E)	99
Monterey, *Calif.* (37°N, 122°W)	58
Monterey Bay, *Calif.* (37°N, 122°W)	58
Monterrey, *Mexico* (26°N, 100°W)	84
Montes Claros, *Brazil* (17°S, 44°W)	89
Montevideo (MAHN tuh vih DAY oh), *Uruguay* (35°S, 56°W)	89
Montgomery, *Ala.* (32°N, 86°W)	68
Montmagny (MO mah NYEE), *Quebec* (47°N, 71°W)	47
Montpelier (mahnt PEEL yuhr), *Vt.* (44°N, 73°W)	73
Montpellier (MOHN pehl YUH), *France* (46°N, 4°E)	98
Montreal, *Quebec* (46°N, 73°W)	47
Montreal R., *Ontario* (47°N, 80°W)	46
Montserrat, *island in Caribbean Sea* (17°N, 62°W)	83
Mooranyah L., *Australia* (33°S, 144°E)	133
Moorhead (MOHR hed), *Minn.* (47°N, 97°W)	62
Moose Factory, *Ontario* (51°N, 81°W)	46
Moose Jaw, *Saskatchewan* (51°N, 106°W)	45
Moose L., *Manitoba* (54°N, 100°W)	45
Moose R., *Ontario* (51°N, 82°W)	46
Moosehead L., *Maine* (46°N, 70°W)	73
Moosonee, *Ontario* (51°N, 81°W)	46
Morava R., *Europe* (49°N, 18°E)	98
Moravia (muh RAY vee uh), *region of Czech Rep.* (49°N, 17°E)	99
Moray Firth, *bay in Scotland* (58°N, 4°W)	98
Moreau R. (MOHR oh), *S. Dak.* (45°N, 102°W)	62
Morehead, *Ky.* (38°N, 83°W)	70
Morehead City, *N.C.* (35°N, 77°W)	71
Morelia, *Mexico* (20°N, 101°W)	84
Morgantown, *W. Va.* (40°N, 80°W)	71
Morioka (MOHR ee OH kuh), *Japan* (40°N, 141°E)	125
Morocco, *country in Africa* (32°N, 7°W)	114
Morogoro (MOH roh GOH roh), *Tanzania* (7°S, 38°E)	110
Moroni, *Comoros* (11°S, 43°W)	107
Moscow, *Idaho* (47°N, 117°W)	60
Moscow, *Russia* (56°N, 38°E)	97
Moses L., *Wash.* (47°N, 119°W)	60
Moshi, *Tanzania* (3°S, 37°E)	110
Mosquito Coast, *Nicaragua* (13°N, 84°W)	83
Mosquito Gulf, *Caribbean Sea* (9°N, 81°W)	83
Mostar (MOH STAHR), *Bosnia and Herzegovina* (43°N, 18°E)	99
Mosul (moh SYOOL), *Iraq* (36°N, 43°E)	115
Mouila, *Gabon* (2°S, 11°E)	108
Moulmein (mool MAHN), *Burma* (16°N, 98°E)	123
Moultrie, L. (MOHL tree), *S.C.* (33°N, 80°W)	69
Moundou (MOON doo), *Chad* (7°N, 16°E)	106
Mount Desert I., *Atlantic O.* (44°N, 68°W)	73
Mount Gambier, *Australia* (38°S, 141°E)	133
Mount Isa, *Australia* (20°S, 139°E)	131
Mount Lofty Ranges, *Australia* (33°S, 139°E)	133
Mount Pleasant, *S.C.* (33°N, 80°W)	69
Mount Rainier N.P. (ruh NEER), *Wash.* (47°N, 122°W)	60
Mount Revelstoke N. P., *British Columbia* (51°N, 118°W)	44
Mount Vernon, *Ill.* (38°N, 89°W)	65
Moyale (moh YAHL ee), *Kenya* (3°N, 39°E)	110
Mozambique (MOH zuhm BEEK), *country in Africa* (18°S, 34°E)	107
Mozambique Channel, *Indian O.* (20°S, 40°E)	106
Mtwara (ehm TWAHR uh), *Tanzania* (10°S, 40°E)	110
Mulhouse (muh LOOZ), *France* (48°N, 7°E)	98
Multan (mool TAHN), *Pakistan* (30°N, 71°E)	122
Mun R. (MOON), *Thailand* (15°N, 102°E)	123
Muncho Lake, *British Columbia* (59°N, 126°W)	44
Muncie, *Ind.* (40°N, 86°W)	70
Munich, *Germany* (48°N, 12°E)	99
Munising (MYOO nuh SING), *Mich.* (46°N, 87°W)	63
Munster (MOON stuhr), *Germany* (52°N, 8°E)	99
Murcia (MUHR shuh), *Spain* (38°N, 1°W)	114
Murdo (MUHR doh), *S. Dak.* (44°N, 101°W)	62
Mures R. (MYOOR esh), *Europe* (46°N, 24°E)	99
Murfreesboro, *Tenn.* (36°N, 86°W)	70
Murmansk, *Russia* (69°N, 33°E)	97
Murray, L., *S.C.* (34°N, 81°W)	69
Murray Bridge, *Australia* (35°S, 139°E)	133
Murray R., *Australia* (34°S, 142°E)	133
Murray River Basin, *Australia* (34°S, 142°E)	133
Murrumbidgee R. (MUHR uhm BIJ ee), *Australia* (35°S, 145°E)	133
Muscat (muhs KAT), *Oman* (24°N, 59°E)	115
Musgrave Range, *Australia* (25°S, 130°E)	130
Muskegon (muhs KEE guhn), *Mich.* (43°N, 86°W)	63
Muskegon R., *Mich.* (43°N, 86°W)	63
Muskogee (muh SKOH gee), *Okla.* (36°N, 95°W)	67
Muskwa R., *British Columbia* (59°N, 123°W)	44
Musquaro, L., *Quebec* (51°N, 61°W)	47
Musselshell R., *Mont.* (46°N, 108°W)	61
Mutton Bay, *Quebec* (51°N, 59°W)	47
Mwanza, *Tanzania* (3°S, 33°E)	110
Mweru, L., *Africa* (9°S, 29°E)	106
Myanaung (MYAN AWNG), *Burma* (18°N, 95°E)	123
Myitkyina (MEE chee NOH), *Burma* (25°N, 97°E)	123
Myrtle Beach, *S.C.* (34°N, 79°W)	69
Mysore, *India* (12°N, 77°E)	122

N

Nacogdoches (nak uh DOH chuz), *Tex.* (32°N, 95°W)	67
Nagano (nah GAHN oh), *Japan* (37°N, 138°E)	125
Nagasaki (NAHG uh SAHK ee), *Japan* (33°N, 130°E)	125
Nagoya (nuh GOY uh), *Japan* (35°N, 137°E)	125
Nagpur, *India* (21°N, 79°E)	122
Nahanni N. P. (nah HAHN ee), *Northwest Terr.* (62°N, 126°W)	44

Name (Pronunciation), *Description* (Lat., Long.)	**Page**
Nairobi, *Kenya* (1°S, 37°E)	110
Najd, *region of Saudi Arabia* (25°N, 43°E)	115
Nakhon Ratchasima (NAH KAWN rah CHAH sih MAH), *Thailand* (15°N, 102°E)	123
Nakina, *Ontario* (50°N, 87°W)	46
Nakuru (nah KOOR oo), *Kenya* (0°, 36°E)	110
Nam Dinh (NAHM DEEN), *Vietnam* (20°N, 106°E)	123
Namib Desert, *Africa* (22°S, 14°E)	106
Namibia, *country in Africa* (20°S, 17°E)	107
Nampa, *Idaho* (44°N, 117°W)	60
Nampo, *North Korea* (39°N, 125°E)	125
Namtu (NAHM TOO), *Burma* (23°N, 97°E)	123
Nan Ling (NAHN LIHNG), *mts. in China* (25°N, 112°E)	124
Nanaimo (nuh NY moh), *British Columbia* (49°N, 124°W)	44
Nanchang (nahn chang), *China* (29°N, 116°E)	124
Nancy, *France* (49°N, 6°E)	98
Nanjing, *China* (32°N, 119°E)	124
Nanning (NAHN NING), *China* (23°N, 108°E)	124
Nantes (nants), *France* (47°N, 2°W)	98
Nantucket I., *Atlantic O.* (41°N, 70°W)	73
Nantucket Sound, *Mass.* (42°N, 70°W)	73
Nanyuki (nahn YOO kee), *Kenya* (0°, 37°E)	110
Naococane, L., *Quebec* (53°N, 71°W)	47
Napa, *Calif.* (38°N, 122°W)	58
Naperville, *Ill.* (42°N, 88°W)	65
Napier, *New Zealand* (39°S, 177°E)	131
Naples, *Fla.* (26°N, 82°W)	69
Naples, *Italy* (41°N, 14°E)	99
Napo R. (NAHP oh), *South America* (3°S, 73°W)	90
Naracoorte (na ra KOO tee), *Australia* (37°S, 141°E)	133
Narbonne, *France* (43°N, 3°E)	98
Narmada R., *India* (23°N, 74°E)	122
Narragansett Bay, *R.I.* (41°N, 71°W)	73
Narvik, *Norway* (68°N, 17°E)	96
Nashua (NASH uh wuh), *N.H.* (43°N, 71°W)	73
Nashville, *Tenn.* (36°N, 87°W)	70
Nasik, *India* (20°N, 74°E)	122
Naskaupi R., *Newfoundland* (54°N, 62°W)	47
Nass R., *British Columbia* (55°N, 129°W)	44
Nassau, *Bahamas* (25°N, 77°W)	85
Nasser, L., *Africa* (23°N, 33°E)	115
Natal (nuh TAHL), *Brazil* (6°S, 35°W)	89
Natal, *prov. of South Africa* (28°S, 31°E)	109
Natashquan R., *Canada* (52°N, 62°W)	47
Natchez (NACH ez), *Miss.* (32°N, 91°W)	68
Natchitoches (NAK uh TAHSH), *La.* (32°N, 93°W)	67
Natron, L. (NAY truhn), *Africa* (2°S, 36°E)	110
Natuna Is., *South China Sea* (4°N, 108°E)	123
Nauru, *country in Pacific O.* (1°S, 167°E)	135
N'Djamena (ehn JAHM uh nuh), *Chad* (12°N, 15°E)	107
Nebraska, *state in U.S.* (42°N, 100°W)	64-65
Nechako R., *British Columbia* (54°N, 125°W)	44
Neenah, *Wis.* (44°N, 89°W)	63
Negro R. (NAY groh), *Argentina* (39°S, 66°W)	88
Negro R., *South America* (1°S, 65°W)	90
Neisse R. (NEES), *Europe* (51°N, 15°E)	99
Nejanilini L., *Manitoba* (60°N, 98°W)	45
Nelson, *British Columbia* (50°N, 117°W)	44
Nelson, Cape, *Australia* (38°S, 142°E)	133
Nelson R., *Manitoba* (56°N, 97°W)	45
Nelspruit (NEHL SPROYT), *South Africa* (25°S, 31°E)	109
Neman R., *Belarus and Lithuania* (55°N, 23°E)	95
Nemuro (NEHM uh ROH), *Japan* (43°N, 145°E)	125
Nemuro Strait, *Japan* (44°N, 145°E)	125
Nen R., *China* (47°N, 124°E)	124
Neosho R. (nee OH shuh), *U.S.* (38°N, 95°W)	64-65
Nepal, *country in Asia* (28°N, 84°E)	122
Nesselrode, Mt., *North America* (59°N, 134°W)	44
Netherlands, *country in Europe* (52°N, 5°E)	90
Netherlands Antilles, *overseas part of Netherlands* (12°N, 69°W)	90
Neuse R. (NOOS), *N.C.* (35°N, 77°W)	71
Nevada, *state in U.S.* (39°N, 118°W)	58
New Albany, *Ind.* (38°N, 86°W)	70
New Amsterdam, *Guyana* (6°N, 58°W)	90

Name (Pronunciation), *Description* (Lat., Long.)	**Page**
New Bedford, *Mass.* (42°N, 71°W)	73
New Bern, *N.C.* (35°N, 77°W)	71
New Braunfels (BROWN fulz), *Tex.* (30°N, 98°W)	66
New Britain, *Conn.* (42°N, 73°W)	73
New Britain, *Papua New Guinea* (5°S, 152°E)	131
New Brunswick, *N.J.* (41°N, 74°W)	72
New Brunswick, *prov. in Canada* (46°N, 66°W)	47
New Caledonia, *poss. of France* (22°S, 166°E)	131
New Castle, *Pa.* (41°N, 80°W)	72
New Delhi (DEL ee), *India* (28°N, 77°E)	122
New Glasgow (GLAS goh), *Nova Scotia* (46°N, 63°W)	47
New Guinea, *island in Pacific O.* (5°S, 141°E)	130
New Hampshire, *state in U.S.* (44°N, 72°W)	73
New Haven, *Conn.* (41°N, 73°W)	73
New Iberia, *La.* (30°N, 92°W)	67
New Ireland, *island in Bismark Sea* (3°S, 152°E)	130
New Jersey, *state in U.S.* (40°N, 74°W)	72
New London, *Conn.* (41°N, 72°W)	73
New Madrid, *Mo.* (37°N, 90°W)	65
New Mexico, *state in U.S.* (35°N, 107°W)	59
New Orleans, *La.* (30°N, 90°W)	67
New Providence I., *Bahamas* (25°N, 77°W)	69
New R., *Va.* (37°N, 81°W)	71
New Siberian Is., *Russia* (75°N, 140°E)	100
New South Wales, *state in Australia* (31°S, 145°E)	133
New York, *state in U.S.* (43°N, 78°W)	72-73
New York, *N.Y.* (41°N, 74°W)	72
New Zealand, *country in Indian O.* (40°S, 175°E)	131
Newark, *Del.* (40°N, 76°W)	71
Newark, *N.J.* (41°N, 74°W)	72
Newark, *Ohio* (40°N, 82°W)	71
Newburgh, *N.Y.* (42°N, 74°W)	72
Newcastle, *Australia* (33°S, 152°E)	133
Newcastle, *New Brunswick* (47°N, 66°W)	47
Newcastle upon Tyne, *England* (55°N, 2°W)	98
Newfoundland, *island in Gulf of Saint Lawrence* (48°N, 56°W)	41
Newfoundland, *prov. in Canada* (53°N, 60°W)	43
Newport, *Oreg.* (45°N, 124°W)	60
Newport, *R.I.* (41°N, 71°W)	73
Newport News, *Va.* (37°N, 76°W)	71
Newton, *Kans.* (38°N, 97°W)	64
Nezpique R. (NEHZ peek), *La.* (30°N, 93°W)	67
Ngangerabeli Plain (eng GAHNG uhr uh BEHL ee), *Kenya* (2°S, 40°E)	110
Nguru Mts. (eng GOO roo), *Tanzania* (6°S, 38°E)	110
Nha Trang (NYA TRAHNG), *Vietnam* (12°N, 109°E)	123
Niagara Falls, *city in N.Y.* (43°N, 79°W)	72
Niagara Falls, *city in Ontario* (43°N, 79°W)	44
Niagara Falls, *waterfall in North America* (43°N, 79°W)	72
Niamey (nyah MAY), *Niger* (14°N, 2°E)	107
Niangua R. (ny ANG gwuh), *Mo.* (38°N, 93°W)	65
Nias, *island in Indian O.* (1°S, 99°E)	130
Nicaragua, *country in Central America* (13°N, 86°W)	85
Nicaragua, L., *Nicaragua* (11°N, 86°W)	83
Nice (NEES), *France* (44°N, 7°E)	98
Nichicun, L., *Quebec* (53°N, 71°W)	47
Nicobar Is. (NIHK uh BAHR), *Bay of Bengal* (9°N, 93°E)	122
Nicosia (NIHK uh SEE uh), *Cyprus* (35°N, 33°E)	115
Niger (NY juhr), *country in Africa* (17°N, 10°E)	107
Niger Delta, *Nigeria* (5°N, 6°E)	108
Niger R., *Africa* (12°N, 4°E)	108
Nigeria, *country in Africa* (10°N, 7°E)	108
Niigata (nee GAHT uh), *Japan* (37°N, 139°E)	125
Niihau (NEE HOW), *island in Pacific O.* (22°N, 160°W)	57
Nile R., *Africa* (38°N, 31°E)	106
Nimes (NEEM), *France* (44°N, 4°E)	98
Nimule (NEE moo LAY), *Sudan* (4°N, 32°E)	110
Ninnescah R. (NIN ehs kah), *Kans.* (37°N, 97°W)	64
Niobrara R., *U.S.* (42°N, 103°W)	64
Nipigon, *Ontario* (49°N, 88°W)	46
Nipigon, L., *Ontario* (50°N, 89°W)	46

Name (Pronunciation), *Description* (Lat., Long.)	**Page**
Nipissing, L., *Ontario* (47°N, 80°W)	46
Nis (NISH), *Yugoslavia* (43°N, 22°E)	99
Nizhniy Novgorod (NIZH nee NAHV guh RAHD), *Russia* (56°N, 43°E)	97
Nodaway R., *U.S.* (41°N, 95°W)	65
Nogales (noh GAL uhs), *Ariz.* (32°N, 111°W)	59
Nogales, *Mexico* (31°N, 111°W)	84
Nome, *Alaska* (65°N, 165°W)	57
Norfolk, *Nebr.* (42°N, 97°W)	64
Norfolk, *Va.* (37°N, 76°W)	85
Norfolk I., *Tasman Sea* (29°S, 168°E)	130
Norfolk L., *U.S.* (36°N, 92°W)	67
Norilsk, *Russia* (69°N, 88°E)	100
Normal, *Ill.* (41°N, 89°W)	65
Norman, *Okla.* (35°N, 97°W)	67
Norman, L., *N.C.* (36°N, 81°W)	71
Norman Wells, *Northwest Terr.* (65°N, 128°W)	42
Normandy, *region of France* (49°N, 0°)	98
Norrkoping (NAWR CHUHP ing), *Sweden* (59°N, 16°E)	96
North America, *continent*	7
North Battleford, *Saskatchewan* (53°N, 108°W)	45
North Bay, *Ontario* (46°N, 79°W)	46
North Canadian R., *U.S.* (36°N, 99°W)	52-53
North Cape, *New Zealand* (34°S, 174°E)	130
North Cape, *Norway* (71°N, 25°E)	95
North Carolina, *state in U.S.* (36°N, 82°W)	70-71
North Cascades N.P., *Wash.* (48°N, 121°W)	60
North Channel, *L. Huron* (46°N, 83°W)	46
North Channel, *Scotland and Northern Ireland* (55°N, 6°W)	98
North Charleston, *S.C.* (33°N, 80°W)	69
North China Plain, *China* (34°N, 115°E)	124
North Dakota, *state in U.S.* (47°N, 100°W)	62
North I., *New Zealand* (37°S, 175°E)	130
North Korea, *country in Asia* (40°N, 127°E)	125
North Little Rock, *Ark.* (35°N, 92°W)	67
North Loup R. (LOOP), *Nebr.* (42°N, 100°W)	64
North Mount Lofty Ranges, *Australia* (33°S, 139°E)	133
North Platte, *Nebr.* (41°N, 101°W)	64
North Platte R., *U.S.* (42°N, 104°W)	64
North Saskatchewan R., *Canada* (53°N, 110°W)	44-45
North Sea, *Europe* (57°N, 3°E)	94
North West Cape, *Australia* (22°S, 113°E)	130
North York, *Ontario* (44°N, 79°W)	46
Northampton, *Mass.* (42°N, 73°W)	73
Northern Dvina R. (duh vee NAH), *Russia* (64°N, 43°E)	95
Northern European Plain, *Europe* (52°N, 10°E)	94-95
Northern Indian L., *Manitoba* (57°N, 97°W)	45
Northern Ireland, *part of United Kingdom* (55°N, 7°W)	98
Northern Mariana Is., *commonwealth of U.S.* (17°N, 145°E)	134
Northern Terr., *Australia* (18°S, 133°E)	131
Northfield, *Minn.* (44°N, 93°W)	63
Northumberland Strait, *Gulf of Saint Lawrence* (46°N, 63°W)	47
Northwest Territories, *Canada* (67°N, 120°W)	42-43
Norton, *Kans.* (40°N, 100°W)	64
Norton Sound, *Alaska* (64°N, 165°W)	57
Norwalk, *Conn.* (41°N, 73°W)	73
Norway, *country in Europe* (60°N, 8°E)	96-97
Norwegian Sea, *Arctic and Atlantic Oceans* (64°N, 0°)	94
Norwich, *Conn.* (41°N, 72°W)	73
Norwich (NAWR ich), *England* (53°N, 1°E)	98
Notre Dame Mts. (NOH truh DAHM), *Quebec* (47°N, 70°W)	47
Nottaway R., *Quebec* (51°N, 78°W)	46
Nottingham, *England* (53°N, 1°W)	98
Nouakchott (nwahk SHAHT), *Mauritania* (18°N, 16°W)	107
Nova Iguacu (EE gwuh SOO), *Brazil* (23°S, 43°W)	89
Nova Scotia, *prov. in Canada* (44°N, 63°W)	47
Novaya Zemlya (noh vuh yuh ZEM lee uh), *islands in Kara Sea* (72°N, 55°E)	95
Novi Sad (NOH vee SAHD), *Yugoslavia* (45°N, 20°E)	99

Name (Pronunciation), *Description* (Lat., Long.)   Page

Novokuznetsk, *Russia* (54°N, 87°E)   100
Novorossiysk (NOHV uh ruh SEESK), *Russia* (45°N, 38°E)   100
Novosibirsk, *Russia* (55°N, 83°E)   100
Nowra, *Australia* (35°S, 151°E)   133
Nubian Desert, *Africa* (21°N, 33°E)   106
Nueces R. (noo AY suhs), *Tex.* (28°N, 99°W)   66
Nueltin L., *Canada* (60°N, 100°W)   45
Nuevo Laredo, *Mexico* (28°N, 100°W)   84
Nullarbor Plain, *Australia* (32°S, 125°E)   130
Nunivak I., *Alaska* (60°N, 166°W)   57
Nurnberg (NOORN behrg), *Germany* (49°N, 11°E)   99
Nyasa, L., *Africa* (13°S, 35°E)   106

O

Oahe, L., *U.S.* (45°N, 101°W)   62
Oahe Dam (oh WAH hee), *S. Dak.* (44°N, 100°W)   62
Oahu, *island in Pacific O.* (22°N, 158°W)   57
Oak Ridge, *Tenn.* (36°N, 84°W)   70
Oakland, *Calif.* (38°N, 122°W)   58
Oaxaca (wah HAH kah), *Mexico* (17°N, 97°W)   84
Ob Bay, *Russia* (67°N, 72°E)   100
Ob R., *Russia* (64°N, 67°E)   100
Oba, *Ontario* (49°N, 84°W)   46
Obregon (OH bruh GOHN), *Mexico* (28°N, 110°W)   84
Ocala (oh KAL uh), *Fla.* (29°N, 82°W)   69
Ocean City, *Md.* (38°N, 75°W)   71
Ocmulgee R. (ohk MUHL gee), *Ga.* (32°N, 84°W)   69
Oconee L. (oh KOH nee), *Ga.* (33°N, 83°W)   69
Oconee R., *Ga.* (33°N, 83°W)   69
Odense (OH thehn seh), *Denmark* (55°N, 10°E)   99
Oder R., *Europe* (53°N, 14°E)   99
Odessa (oh DES uh), *Russia* (46°N, 31°E)   97
Odessa, *Tex.* (32°N, 102°W)   66
Ogbomosho (AHG buh MOH shoh), *Nigeria* (8°N, 4°E)   108
Ogden, *Utah* (41°N, 112°W)   59
Ogdensburg, *N.Y.* (45°N, 76°W)   72
Ogeechee R. (oh GEE chee), *Ga.* (32°, 81°W)   69
Ogoki Res. (oh GOH kee), *Ontario* (51°N, 88°W)   46
Ogoki R., *Ontario* (52°N, 86°W)   46
Ogooue R. (oh guh WAY), *Gabon* (1°S, 10°E)   108
Ohio, *state in U.S.* (40°N, 83°W)   70-71
Ohio R., *U.S.* (40°N, 81°W)   70-71
Oil City, *Pa.* (41°N, 80°W)   72
Oise R. (WAHZ), *France* (49°N, 2°E)   98
Oita (oh ih TAH), *Japan* (33°N, 132°E)   125
Ojos del Salado (oh hohz dehl suh LAHD oh), *mt. in South America* (27°S, 69°W)   88
Oka R., *Russia* (55°N, 41°E)   95
Oka-Don Plain, *Russia* (54°N, 43°E)   95
Okanagan L. (oh kuh NAHG uhn), *British Columbia* (50°N, 120°W)   44
Okanogan, *Wash.* (48°N, 120°W)   60
Okanogan, R., *North America* (49°N, 120°W)   60
Okayama (oh kuh YAHM uh), *Japan* (35°N, 134°E)   125
Okeechobee, L., *Fla.* (27°N, 81°W)   69
Okefenokee Swamp (OH kuh fuh NOH kee), *Ga.* (31°N, 82°W)   69
Okhotsk, Sea of, *Asia* (55°N, 150°E)   119
Oki Is., *Sea of Japan* (36°N, 133°E)   125
Okinawa, *island in East China Sea* (26°N, 128°E)   119
Oklahoma, *state in U.S.* (35°N, 99°W)   66-67
Oklahoma City, *Okla.* (35°N, 98°W)   67
Oland (UHR LAND), *island in Baltic Sea* (57°N, 17°E)   99
Olathe (oh LAY thuh), *Kans.* (39°N, 95°W)   65
Old Crow, *Yukon Terr.* (67°N, 140°W)   42
Old Hickory L., *Tenn.* (36°N, 87°W)   70
Olduvai Gorge (OHL duh vy), *Tanzania* (3°S, 35°E)   110
Olean (OH lee AN), *N.Y.* (42°N, 78°W)   72
Olenek R., *Russia* (68°N, 110°E)   119
Olifants R., *Africa* (24°S, 31°E)   109
Olifants R., *South Africa* (32°S, 19°E)   109

Olt R. (AWLT), *Romania* (45°N, 24°E)   99
Olympia, *Wash.* (47°N, 123°W)   60
Olympic Mts., *Wash.* (48°N, 124°W)   60
Olympic N.P., *Wash.* (48°N, 124°W)   60
Olympus, Mt., *Greece* (40°N, 22°E)   99
Olympus, Mt., *Wash.* (48°N, 124°W)   52
Omaha, *Nebr.* (41°N, 96°W)   64
Oman, *country in Asia* (20°N, 56°E)   115
Oman, Gulf of, *Arabian Sea* (25°N, 59°E)   115
Omdurman, *Sudan* (16°N, 32°E)   107
Omineca Mts. (oh mih NEHK uh), *British Columbia* (57°N, 126°W)   44
Omsk, *Russia* (55°N, 73°E)   100
Onega, L., *Russia* (62°N, 35°E)   95
Onega R., *Russia* (64°N, 39°E)   95
O'Neill, *Nebr.* (42°N, 99°W)   64
Oneonta, *N.Y.* (42°N, 75°W)   72
Onitsha (oh NIHCH uh), *Nigeria* (6°N, 7°E)   108
Ontario, *Calif.* (34°N, 118°W)   58
Ontario, *Oreg.* (44°N, 117°W)   60
Ontario, *prov. in Canada* (50°N, 90°W)   46-47
Ontario, L., *North America* (44°N, 77°W)   72
Ootsa L., *British Columbia* (54°N, 126°W)   44
Opinaca R. (oh PIHN uh KAW), *Quebec* (52°N, 78°W)   46-47
Opiscoteo L. (oh PISK oh TEE oh), *Quebec* (53°N, 68°W)   47
Oradea (aw RAHD yah), *Romania* (47°N, 22°E)   99
Oraibi (oh RY bee), *Ariz.* (36°N, 110°W)   59
Oran, *Algeria* (36°N, 1°W)   114
Orange, *Australia* (34°S, 149°E)   133
Orange Free State, *prov. of South Africa* (28°S, 25°E)   109
Orange R., *Africa* (28°S, 18°E)   109
Orangeburg, *S.C.* (33°N, 81°W)   69
Ore Mts., *Europe* (51°N, 13°E)   99
Oregon, *state in U.S.* (44°N, 123°W)   60
Orel, *Russia* (53°N, 36°E)   97
Orem, *Utah* (40°N, 112°W)   59
Orenburg, *Russia* (52°N, 55°E)   97
Orinoco R., *South America* (8°N, 66°W)   90
Orizaba, *mt. in Mexico* (19°N, 97°W)   82
Orkney Is., *Atlantic O.* (59°N, 3°W)   98
Orlando, *Fla.* (29°N, 81°W)   69
Orleans, *France* (48°N, 2°E)   98
Ormond Beach, *Fla.* (29°N, 81°W)   69
Osage R. (oh SAYJ), *U.S.* (38°N, 94°W)   65
Osaka, *Japan* (35°N, 136°E)   125
Osceola (ah see OH luh), *Iowa* (41°N, 94°W)   65
Oshawa, *Ontario* (44°N, 79°W)   46
Osijek (OH see YEK), *Croatia* (46°N, 19°E)   99
Oslo, *Norway* (60°N, 11°E)   96
Ossa, Mt., *Tasmania* (42°S, 146°E)   130
Ostrava (AW struh vuh), *Czech Republic* (50°N, 18°E)   99
Ostrowiec (aw STRAW vyets), *Poland* (51°N, 21°E)   99
Osumi Is. (OH suh MEE), *East China Sea* (30°N, 131°E)   125
Osumi Strait, *Philippine Sea* (31°N, 131°E)   125
Oswego (ah SWEE goh), *N.Y.* (43°N, 76°W)   72
Oti R., *Africa* (10°N, 0°)   108
Otish Mts., *Quebec* (52°N, 70°W)   47
Otoskwin R., *Ontario* (52°N, 89°W)   46
Otranto, Strait of, *Mediterranean Sea* (40°N, 19°E)   99
Ottawa, *Canada* (45°N, 76°W)   47
Ottawa R., *Canada* (46°N, 78°W)   46-47
Ottumwa (uh TUHM wuh), *Iowa* (41°N, 92°W)   65
Otway, Cape, *Australia* (39°S, 144°E)   133
Ouachita, L. (WAHSH uh TAW), *Ark.* (35°N, 93°W)   67
Ouachita Mts., *U.S.* (35°N, 95°W)   67
Ouachita R., *Ark.* (33°N, 93°W)   67
Ouagadougou (wah guh DOO goo), *Burkina Faso* (12°N, 2°W)   108
Ouargla (WAHR gluh), *Algeria* (33°N, 5°E)   114
Oudtshoorn (OHTS HAWRN), *South Africa* (34°S, 22°E)   109
Oueme R. (WEHM uh), *Benin* (9°N, 3°E)   108

Oujda (ooj DAH), *Morocco* (35°N, 2°W)   114
Oulu (OW loo), *Finland* (65°N, 26°E)   97
Outardes R. (oo TAHRD), *Quebec* (51°N, 69°W)   47
Outer Hebrides, *island group in Atlantic O.* (58°N, 7°W)   98
Ouyen, *Australia* (35°S, 142°E)   133
Overland Park, *Kans.* (39°N, 95°W)   65
Owasco L. (oh WAHS koh), *N.Y.* (43°N, 77°W)   72
Owen Sound, *Ontario* (44°N, 81°W)   46
Owens L., *Calif.* (36°N, 118°W)   58
Owensboro, *Ky.* (38°N, 87°W)   70
Owyhee Mts. (oh WY ee), *Idaho* (43°N, 117°W)   60
Owyhee R., *Oreg.* (43°N, 118°W)   60
Oxford, *England* (52°N, 1°W)   98
Oxford, *Miss.* (34°N, 90°W)   68
Oxford, *Ohio* (39°N, 85°W)   70
Oxnard, *Calif.* (34°N, 119°W)   58
Ozark Plateau, *U.S.* (37°N, 94°W)   65
Ozarks, L. of the, *Mo.* (38°N, 93°W)   65

P

Paarl (PAHRL), *South Africa* (34°S, 19°E)   109
Pacific Ocean   7
Pacific Range, *mts. in British Columbia* (51°N, 126°W)   44
Pacific Rim N.P., *British Columbia* (49°N, 126°W)   44
Padang (PAHD AHNG), *Indonesia* (1°S, 100°E)   121
Padre I., *Tex.* (27°N, 97°W)   67
Padua (PAD yoo uh), *Italy* (45°N, 12°E)   99
Paducah (puh DOO kuh), *Ky.* (37°N, 89°W)   70
Pahala (puh HAH luh), *Hawaii* (19°N, 155°W)   57
Pailolo Channel (py LOH LOH), *Hawaii* (21°N, 157°W)   57
Painted Desert, *Ariz.* (36°N, 111°W)   59
Paita (pah EET uh), *Peru* (5°S, 82°W)   90
Pakistan, *country in Asia* (30°N, 70°E)   122
Palatka, *Fla.* (30°N, 82°W)   69
Palau (pah LOW), *adm. by U.S.* (8°N, 135°E)   134
Palawan, *island in Sulu Sea* (10°N, 119°E)   119
Palembang, *Indonesia* (3°S, 105°E)   131
Palermo, *Sicily* (38°N, 13°E)   99
Palk Strait (PAWK), *Asia* (10°N, 80°E)   122
Palm Springs, *Calif.* (34°N, 117°W)   58
Palma, *Balearic Is.* (40°N, 3°E)   114
Palmas, Cape, *Africa* (4°N, 8°W)   108
Palmer I., *Antarctica* (72°S, 63°W)   137
Pamir Mts. (puh MIHR), *Asia* (38°N, 73°E)   100
Pamlico Sound, *N.C.* (35°N, 76°W)   71
Pampa, *Tex.* (36°N, 101°W)   66
Pampas, *plain in Argentina* (34°S, 62°W)   88
Pamunkey R. (puh MUHNG kee), *Va.* (38°N, 77°W)   71
Panama, *country in Central America* (8°N, 82°W)   85
Panama, Gulf of, *Pacific O.* (10°N, 80°W)   83
Panama, Isthmus of, *North America* (10°N, 80°W)   83
Panama City, *Fla.* (30°N, 86°W)   68
Panama City, *Panama* (9°N, 80°W)   85
Pantelleria Is. (pan TEHL uh REE uh), *Mediterranean Sea* (37°N, 12°E)   99
Panuco R. (PAHN uh koh), *Mexico* (22°N, 99°W)   82
Papua, Gulf of, *Coral Sea* (9°S, 145°E)   130
Papua New Guinea, *country in Pacific O.* (5°S, 143°E)   131
Paracel Is. (PAR uh SEHL), *South China Sea* (17°N, 112°E)   123
Paraguay, *country in South America* (23°S, 58°W)   89
Paraguay R., *South America* (19°S, 57°W)   88
Paramaribo, *Surinam* (6°N, 55°W)   90
Parana R., *South America* (23°S, 54°W)   88
Parent, *Quebec* (48°N, 75°W)   47
Paricutin Volcano (puh REE kuh TEEN), *mt. in Mexico* (19°N, 102°W)   82
Parinas, Point (puh REEN yuhs), *Peru* (5°S, 81°W)   90
Paris, *France* (49°N, 2°E)   98
Paris Basin, *region of France* (49°N, 2°E)   98
Park Falls, *Wis.* (46°N, 90°W)   63
Park Range, *Colo.* (40°N, 107°W)   59

Name (Pronunciation), *Description* (Lat., Long.)	Page
Parker Dam, *U.S.* (34°N, 114°W)	58
Parkersburg, *W. Va.* (39°N, 82°W)	71
Parma, *Italy* (45°N, 10°E)	99
Parma, *Ohio* (41°N, 82°W)	71
Parnaiba R. (PAHR nuh EE buh), *Brazil* (7°S, 45°W)	89
Parronatta, *Australia* (34°S, 151°E)	133
Parry Sound, *Ontario* (45°N, 80°W)	46
Pas, The (PAH), *Manitoba* (54°N, 101°W)	45
Pasadena, *Calif.* (34°N, 118°W)	58
Pasadena, *Tex.* (30°N, 95°W)	67
Pascagoula R. (PAS kuh GOO luh), *Miss.* (31°N, 89°W)	68
Pasco, *Wash.* (46°N, 119°W)	60
Pasto, *Colombia* (1°N, 77°W)	90
Patagonia, *plateau in Argentina* (48°S, 71°W)	88
Paterson, *N.J.* (41°N, 74°W)	72
Pathfinder Res., *Wyo.* (42°N, 107°W)	61
Patman, L., *Tex.* (33°N, 95°W)	67
Patna, *India* (26°N, 85°E)	122
Patos Lagoon, *Brazil* (31°S, 51°W)	88
Patras, *Greece* (38°N, 22°E)	99
Patuxent R., *Md.* (39°N, 77°W)	71
Pau (POH), *France* (43°N, 0°)	98
Paulo Afonso Falls, *waterfall in Brazil* (9°S, 38°W)	88
Pawtucket, *R.I.* (42°N, 71°W)	73
Payette R., *Idaho* (44°N, 116°W)	60
Pea R., *Ala.* (31°N, 86°W)	68
Peace River, *city in Alberta* (56°N, 117°W)	44
Peace R., *Alberta* (57°N, 117°W)	44-45
Peace R., *Fla.* (27°N, 82°W)	69
Pearl Harbor, *Oahu, Hawaii* (21°N, 158°W)	57
Pearl R., *Miss.* (32°N, 90°W)	68
Pec (PEHCH), *Yugoslavia* (43°N, 20°E)	99
Pechora Basin, *Russia* (67°N, 56°E)	95
Pechora R., *Russia* (67°N, 53°E)	95
Pecos (PAY kuhs), *Tex.* (31°N, 104°W)	66
Pecos R., *U.S.* (31°N, 103°W)	52
Pecs (PAYCH), *Hungary* (46°N, 18°E)	99
Pee Dee R., *U.S.* (34°N, 79°W)	53
Pegu, *Burma* (17°N, 97°E)	123
Peipus, L., *Russia* (58°N, 28°E)	95
Pelee, Mt. (puh LAY, mawn), *Martinique* (15°N, 61°W)	83
Pelly Bay, *Northwest Terr.* (69°N, 90°W)	43
Pelly Crossing, *Yukon Terr.* (63°N, 137°W)	42
Pelly Mts. (PEHL ee), *Yukon Terr.* (62°N, 134°W)	44
Pelly R., *Yukon Terr.* (62°N, 132°W)	44
Peloponnesus (PEHL uh puh NEE suhs), *peninsula in Greece* (37°N, 22°E)	99
Pemadumcook L., *Maine* (46°N, 69°W)	73
Pematangsiantar, *Indonesia* (3°N, 99°E)	123
Pemba, *island in Indian O.* (5°S, 40°E)	
Pembina (PEHM buh nuh), *N. Dak.* (49°N, 97°W)	62
Pembina R., *North America* (49°N, 97°W)	62
Pembroke, *Ontario* (46°N, 77°W)	46
Pemigewasset R. (PEHM ih juh WAHS uht), *N.H.* (43°N, 72°W)	73
Pend Oreille, L. (PAHN duh RAY), *Idaho* (48°N, 116°W)	60
Pend Oreille R., *U.S.* (48°N, 117°W)	60
Pendleton, *Oreg.* (46°N, 119°W)	60
Pennines (PEH NYNZ), *mts. in England* (54°N, 2°W)	98
Pennsylvania, *state in U.S.* (41°N, 79°W)	72
Penobscot Bay, *Maine* (44°N, 69°W)	73
Penobscot R., *Maine* (45°N, 69°W)	73
Penrith, *Australia* (33°S, 151°E)	133
Pensacola, *Fla.* (31°N, 87°W)	68
Penticton, *British Columbia* (50°N, 120°W)	44
Penza, *Russia* (53°N, 45°E)	100
Peoria, *Ill.* (41°N, 90°W)	65
Peribonca R. (PEHR uh BAWNG kuh), *Quebec* (51°N, 71°W)	47
Perm, *Russia* (58°N, 57°E)	100
Perpignan (PEHR pee NYAHN), *France* (43°N, 3°E)	98
Perry L., *Kans.* (39°N, 96°W)	65
Persian Gulf, *Arabian Sea* (28°N, 51°E)	115
Perth, *Australia* (31°S, 116°E)	131

Name (Pronunciation), *Description* (Lat., Long.)	Page
Perth Amboy, *N.J.* (41°N, 74°W)	72
Peru, *country in South America* (8°S, 75°W)	89
Perugia (puh ROO juh), *Italy* (43°N, 12°E)	99
Peshawar (puh SHAH wuhr), *Pakistan* (34°N, 27°E)	122
Peter Pond L., *Saskatchewan* (56°N, 109°W)	45
Peterborough, *Australia* (33°S, 139°E)	133
Peterborough, *Ontario* (44°N, 78°W)	46
Petersburg, *Va.* (37°N, 78°W)	71
Petitsikapau L. (PEHT ee SIHK uh POW), *Newfoundland* (55°N, 67°W)	47
Petrified Forest N. P., *Ariz.* (35°N, 110°W)	59
Petropavlovsk-Kamchatskiy, *Russia* (53°N, 159°E)	101
Phenix City (FEE niks), *Ala.* (32°N, 85°W)	68
Philadelphia, *Miss.* (33°N, 89°W)	68
Philadelphia, *Pa.* (40°N, 75°W)	72
Philippine Sea, *Pacific O.* (15°N, 135°E)	119
Philippines, *country in Asia* (13°N, 123°E)	121
Phnom Penh (nawm pehn), *Cambodia* (12°N, 105°E)	121
Phoenix (FEE niks), *Ariz.* (33°N, 112°W)	59
Pico Bolivar (PEE koh buh LEE vahr), *mt. in Venezuela* (9°N, 71°W)	90
Pico Duarte, *mt. in Dominican Republic* (19°N, 71°W)	83
Piedmont Plateau (PEED MAHNT), *U.S.* (35°N, 83°W)	53
Pierre, *S. Dak.* (45°N, 100°W)	62
Pietermaritzburg (PEET uhr MAR uhts BUHRG), *South Africa* (30°S, 30°E)	109
Pietersburg (PEET uhrz BURG), *South Africa* (24°S, 29°E)	109
Pigeon R., *North America* (48°N, 90°W)	46
Pikes Peak, *Colo.* (39°N, 105°W)	9
Pikeville, *Ky.* (37°N, 83°W)	70
Pinang, *Malaysia* (5°N, 100°E)	123
Pinatubo, Mt. (PIHN uh TOO boh), *Philippines* (15°N, 120°E)	119
Pindus Mts., *Greece* (40°N, 21°E)	99
Pine Barrens, *N.J.* (40°N, 75°W)	72
Pine Bluff, *Ark.* (34°N, 92°W)	67
Pine Creek Res., *Okla.* (34°N, 95°W)	67
Pine Ridge, *S. Dak.* (43°N, 102°W)	62
Pines, L. O' the, *Tex.* (33°N, 95°W)	67
Ping R., *Thailand* (17°N, 99°E)	123
Piraeus (py REE uhs), *Greece* (38°N, 24°E)	99
Pisa (PEE zuh), *Italy* (44°N, 10°E)	99
Pit R., *Calif.* (42°N, 122°W)	58
Pitt I., *Hecate Strait* (54°N, 130°W)	44
Pittsburg, *Kans.* (37°N, 95°W)	65
Pittsburgh, *Pa.* (40°N, 80°W)	72
Pittsfield, *Mass.* (42°N, 73°W)	73
Pitcairn I., *Pacific O.* (25°S, 130°W)	135
Piura, *Peru* (5°S, 81°W)	90
Plano (PLAY noh), *Tex.* (33°N, 97°W)	67
Platte R., *U.S.* (41°N, 99°W)	64
Plattsburgh (PLATS BURG), *N.Y.* (45°N, 74°W)	72-73
Playgreen L., *Manitoba* (54°N, 98°W)	45
Plenty, Bay of, *New Zealand* (36°S, 177°E)	130
Pletipi, L. (PLEHT uh pee), *Quebec* (52°N, 70°W)	47
Ploiesti (plaw YESHT), *Romania* (45°N, 26°E)	99
Plovdiv, *Bulgaria* (42°N, 25°E)	99
Plum, *Pa.* (40°N, 80°W)	72
Plymouth (PLIHM uhth), *England* (50°N, 4°W)	98
Plymouth, *Ind.* (41°N, 86°W)	70
Plymouth, *Mass.* (42°N, 71°W)	73
Plzen (PUHL ZEHN), *Czech Republic* (50°N, 13°E)	99
Po R., *Italy* (45°N, 12°E)	99
Pocatello (POH kuh TEHL oh), *Idaho* (43°N, 113°W)	61
Pocono Mts. (POH kuh NOH), *Pa.* (41°N, 75°W)	72
Podgorica, *Yugoslavia* (42°N, 19°E)	99
Point Pelee N.P. (PEE LAY), *Ontario* (42°N, 83°W)	46
Point Reyes (RAYZ), *Calif.* (38°N, 123°W)	58
Pointe des Monts, *cape in Quebec* (49°N, 67°W)	47
Pointe Louis-XIV, *Quebec* (55°N, 80°W)	46
Pointe-Noire (PWANT nuh WAHR), *Congo* (5°S, 12°E)	107
Poland, *country in Europe* (52°N, 20°E)	99

Name (Pronunciation), *Description* (Lat., Long.)	Page
Polar Plateau, *Antarctica* (85°S, 90°E)	137
Pomerania (PAHM uh RAY nee uh), *region of Poland* (54°N, 15°E)	99
Pomeroy (PAHM roy), *Ohio* (39°N, 82°W)	71
Pomme de Terre Res. (pohm dee TEHR), *Mo.* (38°N, 93°W)	65
Pomona Res. (puh MOHN uh), *Kans.* (39°N, 96°W)	65
Pompano Beach (PAHM puh noh), *Fla.* (26°N, 80°W)	69
Ponca City (PAHNG kuh), *Okla.* (37°N, 97°W)	67
Ponce (PAWN say), *Puerto Rico* (18°N, 67°W)	85
Pontchartrain, L., *La.* (30°N, 90°W)	67
Pontiac, *Ill.* (41°N, 89°W)	65
Pontiac, *Mich.* (43°N, 83°W)	63
Pontianak, *Indonesia* (0°, 109°E)	131
Pontic Mts., *Turkey* (41°N, 37°E)	115
Poopo, L., *Bolivia* (19°S, 67°W)	88
Poplar Bluff, *Mo.* (37°N, 90°W)	65
Popocatepetl Volcano (POH poh kuh TAY peh tuhl), *mt. in Mexico* (19°N, 99°W)	82
Porcupine R., *North America* (67°N, 145°W)	57
Port Adelaide, *Australia* (35°S, 138°E)	133
Port Angeles, *Wash.* (48°N, 124°W)	60
Port Arthur, *Tex.* (30°N, 94°W)	67
Port-Au-Prince, *Haiti* (19°N, 72°W)	85
Port Blair, *Andaman Is.* (12°N, 93°E)	123
Port Elizabeth, *South Africa* (34°S, 26°E)	109
Port Gentil (PAWR zhawng TEE), *Gabon* (1°S, 9°E)	108
Port Harcourt, *Nigeria* (5°N, 7°E)	108
Port Hardy, *British Columbia* (51°N, 127°W)	44
Port Hawkesbury (HAWKS BUHR ee), *Nova Scotia* (46°N, 61°W)	47
Port Hedland, *Australia* (20°S, 119°E)	131
Port Huron (HYOOR uhn), *Mich.* (43°N, 83°W)	63
Port-Louis, *Mauritius* (20°S, 58°E)	107
Port Moresby, *Papua New Guinea* (9°S, 147°E)	131
Port Nolloth, *South Africa* (29°S, 17°E)	109
Port of Spain, *Trinidad and Tobago* (11°N, 62°W)	85
Port Orange, *Fla.* (29°N, 81°W)	69
Port Phillip Bay, *Australia* (38°S, 145°E)	133
Port Pirie, *Australia* (33°S, 138°E)	133
Port Said (sah EED), *Egypt* (31°N, 32°E)	115
Port Saint Lucie, *Fla.* (27°N, 80°W)	69
Port Stephens, *Australia* (33°S, 152°E)	133
Port Sudan, *Sudan* (20°N, 37°E)	107
Port-Vila, *Vanuatu* (18°S, 169°E)	131
Portage, *Ind.* (42°N, 87°W)	70
Portage, *Mich.* (42°N, 86°W)	63
Portage la Prairie (PORT ihj luh PREH ree), *Manitoba* (50°N, 98°W)	45
Portland, *Australia* (38°S, 142°E)	133
Portland, *Maine* (44°N, 70°W)	73
Portland, *Oreg.* (46°N, 123°W)	60
Porto, *Portugal* (41°N, 9°W)	114
Porto Alegre, *Brazil* (30°S, 51°W)	89
Porto-Novo, *Benin* (6°N, 2°E)	108
Porto Velho, *Brazil* (9°S, 64°W)	90
Portsmouth (POHRT smuhth), *England* (51°N, 1°W)	98
Portsmouth, *N.H.* (43°N, 71°W)	73
Portsmouth, *Ohio* (39°N, 83°W)	70
Portsmouth, *Va.* (37°N, 76°W)	71
Portugal, *country in Europe* (37°N, 8°W)	114
Possum Kingdom L., *Tex.* (33°N, 99°W)	66
Pothole Res., *Wash.* (47°N, 119°W)	60
Potomac R., *U.S.* (38°N, 77°W)	71
Potosi, *Bolivia* (20°S, 66°W)	89
Potsdam, *Germany* (52°N, 13°E)	99
Potsdam, *N.Y.* (45°N, 75°W)	72
Poughkeepsie (puh KIHP see), *N.Y.* (42°N, 74°W)	72
Powder R., *U.S.* (45°N, 106°W)	61
Powder River Basin, *U.S.* (45°N, 106°W)	61
Powell, L., *U.S.* (37°N, 111°W)	59
Powell River, *city in British Columbia* (50°N, 125°W)	44
Poyang L., *China* (29°N, 116°E)	124
Poznan, *Poland* (52°N, 17°E)	99

Name (Pronunciation), *Description* (Lat., Long.)	Page

Prague, *Czech Republic* (50°N, 14°E) 99
Prairie Dog Town Fork, *r. in U.S.* (35°N, 101°W) 66
Prairie du Chien (PRER ee duh SHEEN), *Wis.* (43°N, 91°W) 63
Pratt, *Kans.* (38°N, 99°W) 64
Prescott, *Ariz.* (35°N, 113°W) 59
Presque Isle (preh SKYL), *Maine* (47°N, 68°W) 73
Pretoria, *South Africa* (25°S, 28°E) 109
Pribilof Is. (PRIB uh LAWF), *Bering Sea* (57°N, 170°W) 57
Price, *Utah* (40°N, 111°W) 59
Prieska (PREE skuh), *South Africa* (30°S, 23°E) 109
Primrose L., *Canada* (55°N, 110°W) 45
Prince Alberni, *British Columbia* (49°N, 125°W) 44
Prince Albert, *Saskatchewan* (53°N, 106°W) 45
Prince Albert N.P., *Saskatchewan* (54°N, 106°W) 45
Prince Edward Island, *prov. in Canada* (47°N, 63°W) 47
Prince Edward I. N.P., *Prince Edward Island* (46°N, 63°W) 47
Prince Edward Is., *Indian O.* (47°S, 38°E) 106
Prince George, *British Columbia* (54°N, 123°W) 44
Prince of Wales I., *Arctic O.* (73°N, 99°W) 40
Prince of Wales I., *Gulf of Alaska* (56°N, 133°W) 57
Prince Patrick I., *Arctic O.* (77°N, 120°W) 40
Prince Rupert, *British Columbia* (54°N, 130°W) 44
Prince William Sound, *Alaska* (61°N, 147°W) 57
Princess Royal I., *Hecate Strait* (53°N, 129°W) 44
Princeton, *Ind.* (38°N, 88°W) 70
Principe, *island in Gulf of Guinea* (2°N, 8°E) 108
Pripyat Marshes, *Europe* (53°N, 26°E) 95
Pripyat R., *Europe* (52°N, 28°E) 95
Pristina (PRISH tih NAH), *Yugoslavia* (43°N, 21°E) 99
Providence, *R.I.* (42°N, 71°W) 73
Provo, *Utah* (40°N, 112°W) 59
Prudhoe Bay, *Alaska* (70°N, 148°W) 57
Prut R., *Europe* (47°N, 28°E) 99
Przemysl (puh SHEHM ISH uhl), *Poland* (50°N, 23°E) 99
Pskov (puh SKAWF), *Russia* (58°N, 28°E) 97
Puebla, *Mexico* (19°N, 98°W) 84
Pueblo, *Colo.* (38°N, 105°W) 59
Puerto Montt, *Chile* (42°S, 73°W) 89
Puerto Rico, *commonwealth of U.S.* (18°N, 67°W) 85
Puerto Vallarta (PWAIR tuh vuh YAHR tuh), *Mexico* (19°N, 105°W) 84
Puget Sound (PYOO jeht), *Wash.* (48°N, 123°W) 60
Pukaskwa N. P., *Ontario* (48°N, 86°W) 46
Pullman, *Wash.* (47°N, 117°W) 60
Pune (POO nuh), *India* (19°N, 74°E) 122
Punta Arenas, *Chile* (53°S, 71°W) 89
Punta Gorda (PUHN tuh GAWR duh), *Fla.* (27°N, 82°W) 69
Purgatoire R. (PUHR guh TWAHR), *Colo.* (37°N, 104°W) 59
Purus R. (puh ROOS), *Brazil* (6°S, 65°W) 90
Pusan, *South Korea* (35°N, 129°E) 125
Putumayo R., *South America* (2°S, 74°W) 90
Pyongyang, *North Korea* (39°N, 126°E) 125
Pyramid L., *Nev.* (40°N, 119°W) 58
Pyrenees, *mt. range in Europe* (43°N, 0°) 98

Q

Qaidam Basin, *China* (37°N, 95°E) 124
Qandahar (KAN duh hahr), *Afghanistan* (32°N, 66°E) 120
Qatar (KAH tahr), *country in Asia* (25°N, 51°E) 115
Qattara Depression, *lowland of Egypt* (29°N, 27°E) 115
Qilian Shan, *mt. range in China* (39°N, 98°E) 124
Qingdao, *China* (36°N, 120°E) 124
Qinghai L. (zhing hy), *China* (37°N, 100°E) 124
Qiqihar, *China* (47°N, 124°E) 124
Qom (KOHM), *Iran* (34°N, 51°E) 115
Qu'Appelle R. (kwa PEHL), *Canada* (50°N, 102°W) 45
Quebec, *prov. in Canada* (50°N, 70°W) 46-47
Quebec, *Quebec* (47°N, 71°W) 47

Queen Adelaide Archipelago, *Chile* (52°S, 75°W) 88
Queen Bess, Mt., *British Columbia* (51°N, 123°W) 44
Queen Charlotte Is., *British Columbia* (53°N, 132°W) 44
Queen Charlotte Sound, *British Columbia* (51°N, 130°W) 44
Queen Charlotte Strait, *British Columbia* (51°N, 128°W) 44
Queen Elizabeth Is., *Arctic O.* (76°N, 100°W) 40-41
Queen Maud Gulf, *Northwest Terr.* (68°N, 100°W) 40
Queen Maud Land, *region of Antarctica* (73°S, 30°E) 137
Queensland, *state in Australia* (22°S, 145°E) 131
Quelimane (kehl uh MAHN uh), *Mozambique* (18°S, 37°E) 107
Quesnel (kuh NEHL), *British Columbia* (53°N, 122°W) 44
Quesnel L., *British Columbia* (53°N, 121°W) 44
Quetta, *Pakistan* (30°N, 67°E) 122
Quezon City (KAY sohn), *Philippines* (15°N, 121°E) 121
Qui Nhon (kwee NYAWN), *Vietnam* (13°N, 109°E) 123
Quinault R., *Wash.* (47°N, 124°W) 60
Quincy, *Ill.* (40°N, 91°W) 65
Quincy, *Mass.* (42°N, 71°W) 73
Quito (KEE toh), *Ecuador* (0°, 78°W) 90

R

Rabat, *Morocco* (34°N, 7°W) 114
Race, Cape, *Newfoundland* (47°N, 52°W) 41
Racine, *Wis.* (43°N, 88°W) 65
Radom, *Poland* (51°N, 21°E) 99
Raft R., *Idaho* (42°N, 113°W) 61
Rainier, Mt. (ruh NEER), *Wash.* (47°N, 122°W) 60
Rainy L., *North America* (49°N, 93°W) 63
Rainy R., *North America* (49°N, 94°W) 63
Raipur (RY POOR), *India* (21°N, 42°E) 122
Rajang R. (RAHJ ahng), *Malaysia* (3°N, 113°E) 123
Rajkot (RAHJ KOHT), *India* (22°N, 71°E) 122
Raleigh, *N.C.* (36°N, 79°W) 71
Ramsey L., *Ontario* (47°N, 82°W) 46
Ranchi, *India* (23°N, 85°E) 122
Rangeley L. (RAYNJ lee), *Maine* (45°N, 71°W) 73
Rangoon, *Burma* (17°N, 96°E) 123
Rapid City, *S. Dak.* (44°N, 103°W) 62
Rappahannock R., *Va.* (38°N, 77°W) 71
Raquette R. (RAK uht), *N.Y.* (44°N, 75°W) 72
Ras Dashen, *mt. in Ethiopia* (13°N, 38°E) 106
Rasht, *Iran* (37°N, 50°E) 115
Rathbun Res., *Iowa* (41°N, 93°W) 65
Raton, *N. Mex.* (37°N, 104°W) 59
Ratz, Mt., *British Columbia* (57°N, 132°W) 44
Rawalpindi (RAH wuhl PIHN dee), *Pakistan* (34°N, 72°E) 122
Rawlins, *Wyo.* (42°N, 107°W) 61
Reading (REHD ing), *Pa.* (40°N, 76°W) 72
Recife (reh SEE fuh), *Brazil* (8°S, 35°W) 89
Recife, Cape, *South Africa* (34°S, 25°E) 109
Red Bluff L., *U.S.* (32°N, 104°W) 59
Red Deer, *Alberta* (52°N, 114°W) 44
Red Deer R., *Canada* (51°N, 112°W) 44-45
Red L., *Minn.* (48°N, 95°W) 53
Red Lake R., *Minn.* (48°N, 96°W) 62
Red R., *Asia* (23°N, 105°E) 119
Red R., *North America* (50°N, 97°W) 53
Red R., *U.S.* (34°N, 99°W) 66-67
Red River Valley, *U.S.* (47°N, 97°W) 62
Red Sea, *Africa and Asia* (19°N, 40°E) 115
Redding, *Calif.* (42°N, 122°W) 58
Redwood N. P., *Calif.* (41°N, 124°W) 58
Regensberg, *Germany* (49°N, 12°E) 99
Reggio di Calabria (REHJ oh DEE kuh LAHB ree uh), *Italy* (38°N, 16°E) 99
Regina (ruh JY nuh), *Saskatchewan* (51°N, 105°W) 45
Reidsville, *N.C.* (36°N, 80°W) 71
Reims (REEMZ), *France* (49°N, 4°E) 98
Reindeer L., *Saskatchewan* (57°N, 102°W) 45
Rend L., *Ill.* (38°N, 89°W) 65

Renmark, *Australia* (34°S, 141°E) 133
Rennes (REHN), *France* (48°N, 1°W) 98
Reno, *Nev.* (40°N, 120°W) 58
Republican R., *U.S.* (40°N, 101°W) 64
Resistencia, *Argentina* (27°S, 59°W) 89
Resolute, *Northwest Terr.* (75°N, 95°W) 43
Restigouche R. (REHS tih GOOSH), *Canada* (48°N, 67°W) 47
Reunion, *overseas state of France* (21°S, 56°E) 107
Revelstoke, *British Columbia* (51°N, 118°W) 44
Revillagigedo Is. (rih VIHL uh guh GEED oh), *Pacific O.* (18°N, 111°W) 82
Rexburg, *Idaho* (44°N, 112°W) 61
Reykjavik (RAY kyuh VEEK), *Iceland* (64°N, 22°W) 96
Rhine R., *Europe* (52°N, 7°E) 99
Rhinelander, *Wis.* (46°N, 89°W) 63
Rhode Island, *state in U.S.* (42°N, 71°W) 73
Rhodes, *island in Mediterranean Sea* (36°N, 28°E) 99
Rhodope Mts. (RAHD uh pee), *Europe* (42°N, 25°E) 99
Rhone R., *Europe* (44°N, 4°E) 98
Rice Lake, *Wis.* (46°N, 92°W) 63
Richland, *Wash.* (46°N, 119°W) 60
Richlands, *Va.* (37°N, 82°W) 71
Richmond, *Ind.* (40°N, 85°W) 70
Richmond, *Va.* (38°N, 77°W) 71
Ridgecrest, *Calif.* (35°N, 118°W) 58
Riding Mt. N. P., *Manitoba* (51°N, 100°W) 45
Riga (REE guh), *Latvia* (57°N, 24°E) 97
Riga, Gulf of, *Baltic Sea* (58°N, 23°E) 99
Rigolet (RIHG uh LEHT), *Newfoundland* (54°N, 58°W) 47
Rijeka (ree YEHK uh), *Croatia* (45°N, 14°E) 99
Rimini, *Italy* (44°N, 13°E) 99
Rimouski (rim OO skee), *Quebec* (48°N, 69°W) 47
Rio Atrato (uh TRAHT oh), *r. in Colombia* (7°N, 77°W) 90
Rio Branco, *Brazil* (10°S, 68°W) 90
Rio Bravo del Norte (REE oh BRAHV oh dehl NORT ee), *r. in Mexico and U.S.*, (29°N, 108°W) 82
Rio de Janeiro (REE oh day zhuh NAIR oh), *Brazil* (23°S, 43°W) 89
Rio de la Plata, *r. in South America* (35°S, 57°W) 88
Rio Gallegos, *Argentina* (52°S, 69°W) 89
Rio Grande (REE oh GRAN day), *r. in U.S. and Mexico* (28°N, 100°W) 52-53
Rio Hondo, *r. in N. Mex.* (34°N, 104°W) 59
Rio Madre de Dios (MAHD ree DAHD ee OHS), *r. in South America* (12°S, 68°W) 90
Rio Muni (REE oh MOO nee), *region of Equitorial Guinea* (2°N, 10°E) 108
Rio Rancho, *N. Mex.* (35°N, 107°W) 59
Riverina, *Australia* (35°S, 146°E) 133
Riverside, *Calif.* (34°N, 117°W) 58
Riverton, *Wyo.* (43°N, 108°W) 61
Riviera (RIHV ee EHR uh), *region of Europe* (44°N, 7°E) 99
Riviere-du-Loup (ree vee EHR duh LOO), *Quebec* (48°N, 70°W) 47
Riyadh (ree AHD), *Saudi Arabia* (25°N, 47°E) 115
Roanoke, *Va.* (37°N, 80°W) 71
Roanoke Rapids L. (ROH uh NOHK), *U.S.* (37°N, 78°W) 71
Roanoke R., *U.S.* (36°N, 77°W) 71
Robson, Mt., *Canada* (53°N, 119°W) 44
Rochester, *Minn.* (44°N, 92°W) 63
Rochester, *N.H.* (43°N, 71°W) 73
Rochester, *N.Y.* (43°N, 78°W) 72
Rock Hill, *S.C.* (35°N, 81°W) 69
Rock Island, *Ill.* (41°N, 90°W) 65
Rock R., *U.S.* (42°N, 90°W) 65
Rock Springs, *Wyo.* (42°N, 109°W) 61
Rockall, *island in Atlantic O.* (58°N, 14°W) 96
Rockford, *Ill.* (42°N, 89°W) 65
Rockhampton, *Australia* (23°S, 151°E) 131
Rocklands Res., *Australia* (37°S, 142°E) 133
Rockville, *Md.* (39°N, 77°W) 71
Rocky Mount, *N.C.* (36°N, 78°W) 71
Rocky Mountain N.P., *Colo.* (40°N, 106°W) 59
Rocky Mts., *North America* (45°N, 111°W) 36

Name (Pronunciation), *Description* (Lat., Long.)	Page
Roebuck Bay, *Australia* (19°S, 120°E)	130
Rogue R. (ROHG), *Oreg.* (42°N, 123°W)	60
Rojo, Cape, *Mexico* (21°N, 97°W)	82
Rolla (RAHL uh), *Mo.* (38°N, 92°W)	65
Rolling Fork, *r. in Ky.* (38°N, 86°W)	70
Romaine R., *Quebec* (50°N, 64°W)	47
Romania, *country in Europe* (46°N, 25°E)	99
Rome, *Ga.* (34°N, 85°W)	68
Rome, *Italy* (42°N, 13°E)	99
Rome, *N.Y.* (43°N, 75°W)	72
Ronne Ice Shelf, *Antarctica* (78°S, 65°W)	137
Roraima, Mt., *South America* (5°N, 61°W)	90
Rosario, *Argentina* (33°S, 61°W)	89
Roseburg, *Oreg.* (43°N, 123°W)	60
Ross Barnett Res., *Miss.* (32°N, 90°W)	68
Ross Bay Junction, *Newfoundland* (53°N, 66°W)	47
Ross Ice Shelf, *Antarctica* (82°S, 180°)	137
Ross L., *Wash.* (49°N, 121°W)	60
Ross Sea, *Antarctica* (75°S, 180°)	137
Rossignol L., *Nova Scotia* (44°N, 65°W)	47
Rostock, *Germany* (54°N, 12°E)	99
Rostov-on-Don, *Russia* (47°N, 40°E)	97
Roswell, *Ga.* (34°N, 84°W)	69
Roswell, *N. Mex.* (33°N, 105°W)	59
Rotterdam, *Netherlands* (52°N, 4°E)	98
Rouen (roo AHN), *France* (49°N, 1°E)	98
Rough River Res., *Ky.* (38°N, 86°W)	70
Round Rock, *Tex.* (31°N, 98°W)	67
Rouyn-Noranda (ROO uhn nuh RAN duh), *Quebec* (48°N, 79°W)	46
Rub al Khali (ROOB al KAHL ee), *region of Saudi Arabia* (22°N, 53°E)	115
Rubeho Mts., *Tanzania* (7°S, 36°E)	110
Ruby Mts., *Nev.* (40°N, 116°W)	58
Rufiji R. (roo FEE jee), *Tanzania* (8°S, 37°E)	110
Rugen (ROO guhn), *island in Baltic Sea* (54°N, 14°E)	99
Ruiz, Mt. (roo EEZ), *Columbia* (5°N, 75°W)	90
Rukwa, L. (RUHK wuh), *Tanzania* (8°S, 32°E)	110
Rupert R., *Quebec* (51°N, 79°W)	46
Ruse (ROO say), *Bulgaria* (44°N, 26°E)	99
Rushmore, Mt., *S. Dak.* (44°N, 103°W)	62
Russell, *Manitoba* (51°N, 101°W)	45
Russia, *country in Europe and Asia* (60°N, 60°E)	100-101
Rutland, *Vt.* (44°N, 73°W)	73
Ruvuma R. (ruh VUH mah), *Africa* (11°S, 40°E)	110
Rwanda, *country in Africa* (2°S, 30°E)	110
Rybinsk Res., *Russia* (59°N, 38°E)	95
Ryukyu Is. (ree OO KYOO), *Pacific O.* (26°N, 128°E)	121

S

Name (Pronunciation), *Description* (Lat., Long.)	Page
Sabah (SAHB ah), *region of Malaysia* (5°N, 116°E)	123
Sabine L. (suh BEEN), *U.S.* (30°N, 94°W)	67
Sabine R., *U.S.* (32°N, 95°W)	67
Sable, Cape, *Fla.* (25°N, 81°W)	69
Sable, Cape, *Nova Scotia* (44°N, 65°W)	47
Sable I., *Atlantic O.* (43°N, 59°W)	41
Sacandaga Res. (SAK uhn DAI guh), *N.Y.* (43°N, 74°W)	72
Sachigo L., *Ontario* (54°N, 92°W)	46
Sachigo R., *Ontario* (55°N, 89°W)	46
Sachs Harbour, *Northwest Terr.* (72°N, 125°W)	42
Sacramento, *Calif.* (39°N, 122°W)	58
Sacramento Mts., *U.S.* (33°N, 106°W)	59
Sacramento R., *Calif.* (40°N, 122°W)	58
Sacramento Valley, *Calif.* (40°N, 122°W)	58
Sado (SAHD oh), *island in Sea of Japan* (38°N, 138°E)	125
Safi, *Morocco* (32°N, 9°W)	114
Sagar (SAHG uhr), *India* (24°N, 79°E)	122
Saginaw (SAG uh NAW), *Mich.* (44°N, 84°W)	63
Saginaw Bay, *Mich.* (44°N, 84°W)	63
Saguenay R. (SAG uh NAY), *Quebec* (48°N, 71°W)	47
Sahara, *desert in Africa* (24°N, 10°E)	114-115
Sahel, *region of Africa* (14°N, 10°E)	106
Saimaa, L. (SY MAH), *Finland* (61°N, 28°E)	95

Name (Pronunciation), *Description* (Lat., Long.)	Page
Saint-Augustin R. (sant OH goos TEEN), *Canada* (51°N, 59°W)	47
Saint Augustine, *Fla.* (30°N, 81°W)	69
Saint Catharines, *Ontario* (43°N, 79°W)	46
Saint Clair, L., *Ontario* (43°N, 83°W)	46
Saint Cloud, *Minn.* (46°N, 94°W)	62
Saint Croix R. (KROY), *North America* (45°N, 69°W)	73
Saint Croix R., *U.S.* (45°N, 93°W)	63
Saint Elias, Mt. (ee LY uhs), *North America* (60°N, 141°W)	57
Saint Elias Mts., *Yukon Terr.* (61°N, 138°W)	44
Saint Etienne (SAN tay TYEHN), *France* (45°N, 5°E)	98
Saint Francis R., *North America* (47°N, 69°W)	47
Saint George, *Utah* (37°N, 114°W)	58
Saint George's Channel, *Ireland and Wales* (52°N, 6°W)	98
Saint Helena, *island in Atlantic O.* (15°S, 5°W)	107
Saint Helena Bay (HEL uh nuh), *Atlantic O.* (33°S, 18°E)	109
Saint Helens, Mt., *Wash.* (46°N, 122°W)	60
St. Ignace I. (IHG nuhs), *L. Superior* (49°N, 88°W)	46
Saint Jean, L. (SAN ZHAHN), *Quebec* (49°N, 72°W)	47
Saint Joe R., *Idaho* (47°N, 116°W)	60
Saint John, *New Brunswick* (45°N, 66°W)	47
Saint John R., *Canada and U.S.* (47°N, 69°W)	47
Saint John's, *Newfoundland* (48°N, 53°W)	61
Saint Johns R., *Fla.* (30°N, 82°W)	69
Saint Johnsbury (JAHNZ BER ee), *Vt.* (44°N, 72°W)	73
Saint Joseph, *Mich.* (42°N, 87°W)	63
Saint Joseph, *Mo.* (40°N, 95°W)	65
Saint Joseph I., *L. Huron* (46°N, 84°W)	46
Saint Joseph, L., *Ontario* (52°N, 91°W)	46
Saint Joseph R., *U.S.* (41°N, 85°W)	63
Saint Kitts and Nevis (NEE vihs), *country in Caribbean Sea* (17°N, 63°W)	85
Saint Laurent (SAN luh RAHN), *Quebec* (46°N, 74°W)	47
Saint Lawrence, Gulf of, *Atlantic O.* (48°N, 62°W)	47
Saint Lawrence I., *Bering Sea* (63°N, 170°W)	45
Saint Lawrence Is. N. P., *Ontario* (44°N, 76°W)	47
Saint Lawrence R., *Canada and U.S.* (48°N, 70°W)	47
Saint Louis, *Mo.* (39°N, 90°W)	65
Saint-Louis (SANG loo EE), *Senegal* (16°N, 16°W)	108
Saint Louis R., *Minn.* (47°N, 93°W)	63
Saint Lucia, *country in Caribbean Sea* (14°N, 61°W)	85
Saint Malo (SAN muh LOH), *France* (49°N, 2°W)	98
Saint Malo, Gulf of, *France* (49°N, 3°W)	98
Saint Mary's R., *U.S.* (41°N, 85°W)	70
Saint Matthew I., *Bering Sea* (60°N, 172°W)	57
Saint Maurice R. (SAN moh REES), *Quebec* (48°N, 74°W)	47
Saint Paul, *Minn.* (45°N, 93°W)	63
Saint Paul I., *Indian O.* (39°S, 78°E)	9
Saint Peters, *Mo.* (39°N, 91°W)	65
Saint Petersburg, *Fla.* (28°N, 83°W)	69
Saint Petersburg, *Russia* (60°N, 30°E)	97
Saint Pierre, *island in Atlantic O.* (47°N, 56°W)	41
Saint Pierre and Miquelon (MIK uh LAHNG), *terr. of France* (47°N, 56°W)	43
Saint Vincent, Cape, *Portugal* (37°N, 9°W)	114
Saint Vincent and the Grenadines, *country in Caribbean Sea* (13°N, 62°W)	85
Sainte Foy, *Quebec* (47°N, 71°W)	47
Sainte Genevieve (sant JEHN uh veev), *Mo.* (38°N, 90°W)	65
Sainte-Marguerite R. (mahr GREET), *Quebec* (50°N, 67°W)	47
Sajama, Mt., *South America* (18°S, 69°W)	88
Sakai, *Japan* (35°N, 135°E)	125
Sakakawea, L., *N. Dak.* (48°N, 102°W)	62
Sakhalin I., *Russia* (50°N, 143°E)	119
Salado R., *Argentina* (26°S, 64°W)	88
Salado R., *Mexico* (27°N, 100°W)	84
Salalah, *Oman* (17°N, 54°E)	115
Salekhard, *Russia* (66°N, 67°E)	100

Name (Pronunciation), *Description* (Lat., Long.)	Page
Salem (SAYL uhm), *Oreg.* (45°N, 123°W)	60
Salem, Cape, *Mass.* (43°N, 71°W)	73
Salerno, *Italy* (41°N, 15°E)	99
Salina (suh LY nuh), *Kans.* (39°N, 98°W)	64
Salinas (suh LEE nuhs), *Calif.* (37°N, 122°W)	58
Salisbury (SAWLZ BEHR ee), *Australia* (35°S, 138°E)	133
Salisbury, *Md.* (38°N, 76°W)	71
Salisbury, *N.C.* (36°N, 81°W)	71
Salluit, *Northwest Terr.* (62°N, 75°W)	43
Salmon (SAM uhn), *Idaho* (45°N, 114°W)	61
Salmon Creek Res., *Idaho* (42°N, 115°W)	61
Salmon R., *Idaho* (46°N, 116°W)	60-61
Salmon R. Mts., *Idaho* (44°N, 115°W)	61
Salonika (suh LAWN ih kuh), *Greece* (41°N, 23°E)	99
Salt Basin, *Tex.* (32°N, 105°W)	66
Salt Fork, *r. in Tex.* (34°N, 102°W)	66
Salt Fork, *r. in U.S.* (35°N, 100°W)	66
Salt Lake City, *Utah* (41°N, 112°W)	59
Salt R., *Ariz.* (34°N, 112°W)	59
Salt R., *Ky.* (38°N, 86°W)	70
Salt R., *Mo.* (40°N, 92°W)	65
Salta, *Argentina* (25°S, 65°W)	89
Saltillo (sahl TEE yoh), *Mexico* (25°N, 101°W)	84
Salto, *Uruguay* (31°S, 58°W)	89
Salton Sea, *Calif.* (33°N, 116°W)	58
Saluda R. (suh LOOD uh), *S.C.* (34°N, 82°W)	69
Salvador, *Brazil* (13°S, 38°W)	89
Salween R. (sal WEEN), *Asia* (18°N, 97°E)	118-119
Salzburg, *Austria* (48°N, 13°E)	99
Sam Rayburn Res., *Tex.* (31°N, 94°W)	67
Samara, *Russia* (53°N, 50°E)	97
Samarkand, *Uzbekistan* (40°N, 67°E)	100
Samos (SAY MAHS), *island in Aegean Sea* (38°N, 27°E)	99
Samothrace (SAHM uh THRAHK ee), *i. in Aegean Sea* (40°N, 26°E)	99
Samsun (sahm SOON), *Turkey* (41°N, 36°E)	115
San Ambrosio Island, *Pacific O.* (26°S, 80°W)	88
San Andres I., *Caribbean Sea* (13°N, 82°W)	83
San Angelo (san AN juh loh), *Tex.* (31°N, 100°W)	66
San Antonio, *Tex.* (29°N, 98°W)	66
San Antonio, Cape, *Argentina* (37°S, 57°W)	88
San Antonio R., *Tex.* (29°N, 97°W)	67
San Bernardino, *Calif.* (34°N, 117°W)	58
San Blas, Cape, *Fla.* (30°N, 86°W)	68
San Carlos L. (KAHR luhs), *Ariz.* (33°N, 110°W)	59
San Clemente (kluh MENT ee), *island in Pacific O.* (33°N, 119°W)	58
San Cristobal, *Venezuela* (8°N, 72°W)	90
San Diego, *Calif.* (33°N, 117°W)	58
San Felix I., *Pacific O.* (26°S, 80°W)	88
San Fernando, *Venezuela* (4°N, 68°W)	90
San Francisco, *Calif.* (38°N, 123°W)	58
San Joaquin R., *Calif.* (38°N, 121°W)	58
San Joaquin Valley, *Calif.* (37°N, 121°W)	58
San Jorge, Gulf of, *Atlantic O.* (46°S, 67°W)	88
San Jose (SAN hoh ZAY), *Calif.* (37°N, 122°W)	58
San Jose, *Costa Rica* (10°N, 84°W)	85
San Jose I., *Mexico* (25°N, 111°W)	82
San Juan (san HWAHN), *Argentina* (32°S, 68°W)	89
San Juan, *Puerto Rico* (19°N, 66°W)	85
San Juan Is. (san WAHN), *Puget Sound and Strait of Georgia* (48°N, 123°W)	60
San Juan Mts., *U.S.* (38°N, 107°W)	59
San Juan R., *Nicaragua and Costa Rica* (11°N, 85°W)	83
San Juan R., *U.S.* (39°N, 108°W)	59
San Lucas, Cape, *Mexico* (23°N, 110°W)	82
San Luis, *Argentina* (33°S, 66°W)	89
San Luis Obispo (san LOO uh suh BIS poh), *Calif.* (35°N, 121°W)	58
San Luis Potosi, *Mexico* (22°N, 101°W)	84
San Marcos (san MAHR kuhs), *Tex.* (30°N, 98°W)	66
San Marino, *country in Europe* (44°N, 12°E)	99
San Mateo, (san muh TAY oh), *Calif.* (38°N, 122°W)	58

Name (Pronunciation), *Description* (Lat., Long.) **Page**

San Matias, Gulf of, *Atlantic O.* (42°S, 64°W) 88
San Miguel R. (san muh GEHL), *Colo.* (38°N, 108°W) 59
San Pedro R. (san PAY droh), *Ariz.* (33°N, 111°W) 59
San Pedro Sula, *Honduras* (15°N, 88°W) 84
San Rafael (SAN ruh FEHL), *Calif.* (38°N, 123°W) 58
San Salvador, *El Salvador* (14°N, 89°W) 84
San Salvador I., *Atlantic O.* (24°N, 75°W) 83
San Sebastian, *Spain* (43°N, 2°W) 98
Sanaa (sah NAH), *Yemen (Sana)* (15°N, 44°E) 115
Sanaga R., *Cameroon* (5°N, 12°E) 108
Sand Hills, *Nebr.* (42°N, 102°W) 64
Sandakan (san DAHK uhn), *Malaysia* (6°N, 118°E) 123
Sandspit, *British Columbia* (53°N, 132°W) 44
Sandusky, *Ohio* (41°N, 83°W) 70
Sandusky R., *Ohio* (41°N, 83°W) 70
Sandy City, *Utah* (40°N, 112°W) 59
Sanford, *Fla.* (29°N, 81°W) 69
Sanford, *Maine* (43°N, 69°W) 73
Sanford, *N.C.* (35°N, 79°W) 71
Sangamon R. (SANG guh muhn), *Ill.* (40°N, 90°W) 65
Sangre de Cristo Mts., *U.S.* (38°N, 106°W) 59
Santa Ana, *Calif.* (34°N, 118°W) 58
Santa Barbara, *Calif.* (35°N, 120°W) 58
Santa Barbara Channel, *Calif.* (34°N, 120°W) 58
Santa Catalina, *island in Pacific O.* (33°N, 118°W) 58
Santa Clarita, *Calif.* (34°N, 118°W) 58
Santa Cruz (sant uh KROOZ), *Bolivia* (18°S, 63°W) 89
Santa Cruz, *Calif.* (37°N, 122°W) 58
Santa Cruz, *Canary Is.* (28°N, 15°W) 114
Santa Fe, *N. Mex.* (36°N, 106°W) 59
Santa Margarita I., *Mexico* (24°N, 112°W) 82
Santa Maria, *Brazil* (30°S, 54°W) 89
Santa Maria, *Calif.* (35°N, 120°W) 58
Santa Maria, *Colombia* (11°N, 74°W) 90
Santa Rosa, *Calif.* (38°N, 123°W) 58
Santander, *Spain* (43°N, 4°W) 98
Santarem, *Brazil* (3°S, 55°W) 90
Sante Fe (SAN tuh FAY), *Argentina* (32°S, 61°W) 89
Santee R., *S.C.* (33°N, 80°W) 69
Santiago, *Chile* (34°S, 71°W) 89
Santiago de Cuba, *Cuba* (20°N, 76°W) 85
Santiago del Estero, *Argentina* (27°S, 64°W) 89
Santo Domingo, *Dominican Republic* (19°N, 70°W) 85
Santos, *Brazil* (24°S, 47°W) 89
Sao Francisco R. (SOWN frahn SEE skoo), *Brazil* (14°S, 44°W) 88
Sao Luis (SOWN loo EES), *Brazil* (3°S, 44°W) 89
Sao Paulo (SOWN POW loo), *Brazil* (24°S, 47°W) 89
Sao Tome (SOWN taw MEH), *island in Gulf of Guinea* (0°, 7°E) 108
Sao Tome, *Sao Tome & Principe* (0°, 7°E) 108
Sao Tome and Principe (PREEN see puh), *country in Gulf of Guinea*(1°N, 7°E) 108
Saone R. (SOHN), *France* (46°N, 5°E) 98
Sapporo, *Japan* (43°N, 141°E) 125
Saragossa, *Spain* (42°N, 1°W) 114
Sarajevo (SAHR uh YAY voh), *Bosnia and Herzegovina* (44°N, 18°E) 99
Saratoga Springs, *N.Y.* (43°N, 74°W) 72
Saratov, *Russia* (52°N, 46°E) 97
Sarawak (suh RAH wahk), *region of Malaysia* (2°N, 112°E) 123
Sardinia, *island in Mediterranean Sea* (40°N, 9°E) 99
Sargodha (suhr GOHD uh), *Pakistan* (32°N, 73°E) 122
Sarh, *Chad* (9°N, 18°E) 107
Sarnia, *Ontario* (43°N, 82°W) 46
Saskatchewan, *prov. in Canada* (54°N, 106°W) 45
Saskatchewan R. (SAS KACH uh WAHN), *Canada* (53°N, 104°W) 45
Saskatoon, *Saskatchewan* (52°N, 107°W) 45
Sassandra R. (suh SAN druh), *Côte d'Ivoire* (7°N, 7°W) 108
Sassari (SAHS uh ree), *Sardinia* (41°N, 9°E) 99
Satilla R., *Ga.* (31°N, 82°W) 69

Satu Mare (SAHT oo MAHR uh), *Romania* (48°N, 23°E) 99
Saudi Arabia, *country in Asia* (24°N, 44°E) 115
Sault Sainte Marie (SOO SAYNT muh REE), *Mich.* (46°N, 84°W) 63
Sault Sainte Marie, *Ontario* (47°N, 84°W) 46
Sava R., *Europe* (46°N, 15°E) 99
Savannah, *Ga.* (32°N, 81°W) 69
Savannah R., *U.S.* (33°N, 82°W) 69
Savannakhet (suh VAHN uh KEHT), *Laos* (17°N, 105°E) 123
Savu Sea, *Indian O.* (9°S, 122°E) 130
Sawatch Range, *Colo.* (39°N, 106°W) 59
Sayan Mts., *Asia* (53°N, 95°E) 118-119
Saylorville Res., *Iowa* (42°N, 94°W) 65
Scandinavia, *region of Europe* (61°N, 12°E) 94-95
Scarborough, *Ontario* (44°N, 79°W) 46
Schefferville (SHEF uhr VIL), *Quebec* (55°N, 67°W) 47
Schenectady (skuh NEK tuh dee), *N.Y.* (43°N, 74°W) 72
Schleswig (SHLEHS veeg), *Germany* (55°N, 10°E) 99
Schreiber, *Ontario* (49°N, 87°W) 46
Scioto R. (sy OHT uh), *Ohio* (40°N, 83°W) 70
Scotia Sea, *Atlantic O.* (55°S, 50°W) 137
Scotland, *part of United Kingdom* (57°N, 5°W) 98
Scottsbluff, *Nebr.* (42°N, 104°W) 64
Scottsdale, *Ariz.* (34°N, 112°W) 59
Scranton, *Pa.* (42°N, 76°W) 72
Sea Is., *Atlantic O.* (32°N, 81°W) 69
Seaford, *Del.* (39°N, 76°W) 71
Seal R., *Manitoba* (59°N, 95°W) 45
Seattle, *Wash.* (48°N, 122°W) 60
Sebago L. (suh BAY goh), *Maine* (44°N, 71°W) 73
Sebastian Vizcaino Bay, *Baja California* (28°N, 115°W) 82
Second Cataract, *waterfall in Sudan* (22°N, 31°E) 115
Sechelt, *British Columbia* (49°N, 123°W) 44
Sedalia (sih DAYL yuh), *Mo.* (39°N, 93°W) 65
Seine R. (sayn), *France* (49°N, 1°E) 98
Sekondi-Takoradi (sehk uhn DEE TAK uh RAHD ee), *Ghana* (5°N, 2°W) 108
Selenge R. (SEHL ung GAH), *Mongolia* (49°N, 102°E) 124
Selkirk, *Manitoba* (50°N, 97°W) 45
Selma, *Ala.* (32°N, 87°W) 68
Selvas (SEL vuhz), *forest region in Brazil* (5°S, 65°W) 90
Semarang (suh MAHR ANG), *Indonesia* (7°S, 110°E) 131
Semey, *Kazakhstan* (50°N, 80°E) 100
Seminoe Res., *Wyo.* (42°N, 107°W) 61
Seminole, L. (SEHM uh NOHL), *U.S.* (31°N, 85°W) 68
Sendai (sen DY), *Japan* (38°N, 141°E) 125
Seneca L. (SEN ih kuh), *N.Y.* (42°N, 77°W) 72
Senecaville Res., *Ohio* (40°N, 81°W) 71
Senegal, *country in Africa* (15°N, 15°W) 108
Senegal R., *Africa* (16°N, 14°W) 108
Senneterre (sehn TEHR), *Quebec* (48°N, 77°W) 46
Seoul (sohl), *South Korea* (38°N, 127°E) 125
Sept-Iles (set EEL), *Quebec* (50°N, 66°W) 47
Sequoia N. P., (sih KWOY uh), *Calif.* (36°N, 119°W) 58
Serasun Strait, *Malaysia* (2°N, 109°E) 123
Serbia, *republic of Yugoslavia* (44°N, 21°E) 99
Serengeti Plain (SEHR uhn GEHT ee), *Tanzania* (3°S, 35°E) 110
Sergino, *Russia* (63°N, 66°E) 100
Serrai (SEHR ray), *Greece* (41°N, 24°E) 99
Seul, L. (SOOL), *Ontario* (50°N, 93°W) 46
Sevastopol, *Ukraine* (44°N, 33°E) 97
Severn R., *Ontario* (55°N, 89°W) 46
Severnaya Zemlya, *islands in Arctic O.* (80°N, 95°E) 100
Sevier Bridge Res. (suh VIR), *Utah* (38°N, 112°W) 59
Sevier L., *Utah* (39°N, 113°W) 58-59
Sevier R., *Utah* (38°N, 112°W) 58-59
Seville, *Spain* (37°N, 6°W) 114
Seward, *Alaska* (60°N, 150°W) 57

Seward Pen. (SOO uhrd), *Alaska* (65°N, 165°W) 57
Seychelles (say SHEHL), *country in Indian O.* (5°S, 55°W) 107
Sfax, *Tunisia* (35°N, 11°E) 114
Shache, *China* (38°N, 77°E) 124
Shackleton Ice Shelf, *Antarctica* (65°S, 105°E) 137
Shanghai, *China* (31°N, 121°E) 124
Shannon R., *Ireland* (53°N, 9°W) 98
Shark Bay, *Australia* (25°S, 113°E) 130
Sharpe, L., *S. Dak.* (44°N, 100°W) 62
Shasta L., *Calif.* (41°N, 122°W) 58
Shasta, Mt., *Calif.* (42°N, 122°W) 58
Shatt al Jarid, *seasonal lake in Africa* (33°N, 9°E) 114
Shawnee, *Okla.* (35°N, 97°W) 67
Sheboygan, *Wis.* (44°N, 88°W) 63
Sheffield, *England* (53°N, 1°W) 98
Shelburne, *Nova Scotia* (44°N, 65°W) 47
Shelby, *N.C.* (35°N, 82°W) 71
Shelbyville, *Tenn.* (35°N, 86°W) 70
Shelbyville, L., *Ill.* (39°N, 89°W) 65
Shellharbour, *Australia* (35°S, 151°E) 133
Shenandoah N. P., *Va.* (39°N, 78°W) 71
Shenandoah R., *Va.* (39°N, 78°W) 71
Shenyang, *China* (42°N, 123°E) 124
Sherbrooke, *Nova Scotia* (45°N, 62°W) 47
Sherbrooke, *Quebec* (45°N, 72°W) 47
Sheridan, *Wyo.* (45°N, 107°W) 61
Sherman, *Tex.* (34°N, 97°W) 67
Shetak, L., *Minn.* (44°N, 96°W) 62
Shetland Is., *North Sea* (61°N, 2°W) 98
Sheyenne R. (shy EN), *N. Dak.* (48°N, 99°W) 62
Shiawassee R. (SHY uh WAWS ee), *Mich.* (43°N, 84°W) 63
Shijiazhuang (shihr jah wahng), *China* (38°N, 115°E) 124
Shikoku, *island in Sea of Japan* (34°N, 134°E) 125
Shinyanga (sheen YAHNG guh), *Tanzania* (4°S, 33°E) 110
Shiraz, *Iran* (30°N, 52°E) 115
Sholapur (SHOH luh POOR), *India* (18°N, 76°E) 122
Shreveport, *La.* (33°N, 94°W) 67
Sialkot (see AHL KOHT), *Pakistan* (33°N, 74°E) 122
Siberia, *Asian Russia* (65°N, 120°E) 118-119
Sibu (SEE boo), *Malaysia* (2°N, 112°E) 123
Sichuan Basin (sich oo ahn), *region of China* (30°N, 105°E) 124
Sicily, *island in Mediterranean Sea* (37°N, 14°E) 99
Sidi-Bel-Abbes (SEE dee BEHL uh BEHS), *Algeria* (35°N, 1°W) 114
Sidi Ifni, *Morocco* (29°N, 10°W) 114
Sidney, *Nebr.* (41°N, 103°W) 64
Sidra, Gulf of, *Mediterranean Sea* (32°N, 19°E) 114
Sierra Leone, *country in Africa* (8°N, 12°W) 108
Sierra Madre del Sur, *mt. range in Mexico* (27°N, 100°W) 82
Sierra Madre Occidental, *mt. range in Mexico* (28°N, 107°W) 82
Sierra Madre Oriental, *mt. range in Mexico* (28°N, 102°W) 82
Sierra Maestra, *mt. range in Cuba* (20°N, 77°W) 83
Sierra Nevada, *mt. range in U.S.* (38°N, 120°W) 58
Sierra Vista, *Ariz.* (32°N, 111°W) 59
Sikeston (SYK stuhn), *Mo.* (37°N, 90°W) 65
Sikote-Alin Mts. (SEE kuh TAY uh LEEN), *Russia* (44°N, 135°E) 119
Silver City, *N. Mex.* (33°N, 108°W) 59
Silver Spring, *Md.* (39°N, 77°W) 71
Silvies R. (SIHL veez), *Oreg.* (44°N, 119°W) 60
Simand, L., *Quebec* (48°N, 79°W) 46
Simcoe, L., *Ontario* (44°N, 79°W) 46
Simeulue (SEE muh LOO uh), *island in Indian O.* (3°N, 96°E) 123
Simpson Desert, *Australia* (26°S, 137°E) 130
Sinai Pen. (SY ny), *Asia* (29°N, 33°E) 115
Singapore, *country in Asia* (1°N, 104°E) 123
Sinuiju (SHIHN ee JOO), *North Korea* (40°N, 125°E) 125
Sioux City (soo), *Iowa* (43°N, 96°W) 108
Sioux Falls, *S. Dak.* (44°N, 97°W) 62
Sipiwesk L., *Manitoba* (55°N, 98°W) 45
Sisseton, *S. Dak.* (46°N, 97°W) 62

Name (Pronunciation), *Description* (Lat., Long.)	**Page**
Sitka, *Alaska* (57°N, 135°W)	57
Sivas (sih VAHS), *Turkey* (40°N, 37°E)	115
Siwah Oasis (SEE wuh), *Egypt* (31°N, 25°E)	115
Sixth Cataract, *waterfall in Sudan* (16°N, 33°E)	115
Sjaelland (SHEHL luhn), *island in Kattegat* (56°N, 12°E)	99
Skagerrak, *strait between Norway and Denmark* (57°N, 9°E)	98
Skagit R. (SKAJ uht), *Wash.* (48°N, 122°W)	60
Skagway, *Alaska* (60°N, 135°W)	57
Skaneateles L. (SKAN ee AT luhs), *N.Y.* (43°N, 76°W)	72
Skeena Mts., *British Columbia* (57°N, 130°W)	44
Skeena R., *British Columbia* (55°N, 128°W)	44
Skopje, *Macedonia* (42°N, 22°E)	99
Skunk R., *Iowa* (41°N, 91°W)	65
Slave Coast, *region of Africa* (6°N, 2°E)	108
Slave Lake, *Alberta* (55°N, 115°W)	44
Slave R., *Canada* (60°N, 111°W)	44-45
Sligo (SLY goh), *Ireland* (54°N, 8°W)	98
Slovakia, *country in Europe* (49°N, 19°E)	99
Slovenia, *country in Europe* (46°N, 15°E)	99
Smallwood Res., *Newfoundland* (54°N, 64°W)	47
Smith, *Alberta* (55°N, 114°W)	44
Smith Mountain L., *Va.* (37°N, 80°W)	71
Smithers, *British Columbia* (55°N, 127°W)	44
Smoky Hill R., *U.S.* (39°N, 100°W)	64
Smoky R., *Alberta* (54°N, 119°W)	44
Smolensk, *Russia* (55°N, 32°E)	100
Smyrna (SMUHR nuh), *Ga.* (34°N, 85°W)	68
Snake R., *U.S.* (47°N, 118°W)	60-61
Snake River Plain, *Idaho* (43°N, 114°W)	61
Snowbird L., *Northwest Terr.* (61°N, 104°W)	45
Socorro (suh KAW roh), *N. Mex.* (34°N, 107°W)	59
Socotra, *island in Arabian Sea* (12°N, 54°E)	115
Sofia, *Bulgaria* (43°N, 23°E)	99
Sogne Fiord (SAWNG nuh FYAWRD), *Norway* (61°N, 6°E)	98
Sohag, *Egypt* (27°N, 32°E)	115
Sokode (soh KOH day), *Togo* (9°N, 1°E)	108
Sokoto (SOH kuh TOH), *Nigeria* (13°N, 5°E)	108
Solomon Islands, *country in Pacific O.* (9°S, 160°E)	131
Solomon R., *Kans.* (39°N, 98°W)	64
Solomon Sea, *Pacific O.* (8°S, 154°E)	130
Somali Pen., *Somalia* (10°N, 50°E)	106
Somalia, *country in Africa* (5°N, 47°E)	107
Somerset, *Ky.* (37°N, 85°W)	70
Somerset I., *Arctic O.* (73°N, 93°W)	41
Sondags R., *South Africa* (33°S, 25°E)	109
Songhua R., *China* (46°N, 125°E)	124
Songkhla, *Thailand* (7°N, 101°E)	123
Sonoran Desert, *U.S. and Mexico* (33°N, 113°W)	58-59
Soroti (soh ROH tee), *Uganda* (2°N, 33°E)	110
Souris R. (SOOR uhs), *U.S. and Canada* (49°N, 102°W)	62
South Africa, *country in Africa* (30°S, 25°E)	109
South America, *continent*	7
South Australia, *state in Australia* (28°S, 133°E)	133
South Bend, *Ind.* (42°N, 86°W)	70
South Carolina, *state in U.S.* (34°N, 80°W)	69
South China Sea, *Asia* (15°N, 115°E)	119
South Dakota, *state in U.S.* (45°N, 100°W)	62
South Georgia, *island in Atlantic O.* (54°S, 37°W)	8
South Henik L., *Northwest Terr.* (62°N, 97°W)	45
South Hill, *Va.* (37°N, 78°W)	71
South I., *New Zealand* (45°S, 170°E)	130
South Korea, *country in Asia* (36°N, 128°E)	125
South Loup R. (LOOP), *Nebr.* (41°N, 100°W)	64
South Moresby N. P., *British Columbia* (52°N, 132°W)	44
South Orkney Is., *Atlantic O.* (60°S, 45°W)	137
South Pass, *Wyo.* (43°N, 109°W)	61
South Platte R., *U.S.* (41°N, 104°W)	59
South Saskatchewan R., *Canada* (51°N, 110°W)	44-45
South Shetland Is., *Atlantic O.* (62°S, 60°W)	137
South Sioux City (SOO), *Nebr.* (43°N, 96°W)	64
Southampton, *England* (51°N, 1°W)	98
Southampton I., *Hudson Bay* (64°N, 84°W)	41

Name (Pronunciation), *Description* (Lat., Long.)	**Page**
Southern Alps, *New Zealand* (45°S, 169°E)	130
Southern Indian L., *Manitoba* (57°N, 99°W)	45
Soweto, *South Africa* (26°S, 28°E)	109
Spain, *country in Europe* (40°N, 5°W)	114
Spanish R., *Ontario* (46°N, 82°W)	46
Spartanburg, *S.C.* (35°N, 82°W)	69
Spencer, *Iowa* (43°N, 95°W)	65
Spencer Gulf, *Indian O.* (35°S, 137°E)	133
Split, *Croatia* (43°N, 16°E)	99
Spokane (spoh KAN), *Wash.* (48°N, 117°W)	60
Spokane R., *Wash.* (48°N, 118°W)	60
Spoon R., *Ill.* (41°N, 90°W)	65
Sporades (SPAWR uh deez), *islands in Aegean Sea* (37°N, 27°E)	99
Sprague R. (SPRAHG), *Oreg.* (42°N, 122°W)	60
Spratly Is., *South China Sea* (9°N, 112°E)	123
Spree R. (SHPRAY), *Germany* (52°N, 14°E)	99
Spring Hill, *Fla.* (29°N, 83°W)	69
Springbok, *South Africa* (30°S, 18°E)	109
Springdale, *Ark.* (36°N, 94°W)	67
Springfield, *Ill.* (40°N, 90°W)	65
Springfield, *Mass.* (42°N, 73°W)	73
Springfield, *Mo.* (37°N, 93°W)	65
Springfield, *Ohio* (40°N, 84°W)	70
Springfield, *Oreg.* (44°N, 123°W)	60
Springfontein (SPRING fawn TAHN), *South Africa* (30°S, 26°E)	109
Sri Lanka, *country in Asia* (8°N, 81°E)	122
Srinagar, *India* (34°N, 75°E)	122
Stamford, *Conn.* (41°N, 74°W)	72-73
Stanley, *N. Dak.* (48°N, 102°W)	62
Stanovoy Mts. (STAN uh VOY), *Russia* (55°N, 125°E)	101
State College, *Pa.* (41°N, 78°W)	72
Statesville, *N.C.* (36°N, 81°W)	71
Staunton, *Va.* (38°N, 79°W)	71
Stavanger, *Norway* (59°N, 6°E)	96
Steamboat Springs, *Colo.* (40°N, 107°W)	59
Steens Mt., *Oreg.* (42°N, 119°W)	60
Steinbach (STYN BAK), *Manitoba* (50°N, 97°W)	45
Sterling, *Ill.* (42°N, 90°W)	65
Steubenville, *Ohio* (40°N, 81°W)	71
Stevens Point, *Wis.* (44°N, 90°W)	63
Stewart, *British Columbia* (56°N, 130°W)	44
Stewart I., *Pacific O.* (47°S, 168°E)	130
Stikine R. (stik EEN), *British Columbia* (58°N, 131°W)	44
Stillwater, *Okla.* (36°N, 97°W)	67
Stockholm, *Sweden* (59°N, 18°E)	96
Stockton, *Calif.* (38°N, 121°W)	58
Stockton L., *Mo.* (38°N, 94°W)	65
Stockton Plateau, *Tex.* (30°N, 102°W)	66
Stoke-on-Trent, *England* (53°N, 2°W)	98
Stone Mt., *Ga.* (34°N, 84°W)	69
Storm Lake, *Iowa* (43°N, 95°W)	65
Stornoway, *Scotland* (58°N, 6°W)	98
Strasbourg (STRAHS BOORG), *France* (49°N, 8°E)	98
Stratford-upon-Avon, *England* (52°N, 2°W)	98
Stuart L., *British Columbia* (55°N, 125°W)	44
Stuttgart, *Germany* (49°N, 9°E)	99
Subotica (SOO buh TEET suh), *Yugoslavia* (46°N, 20°E)	99
Sucre (SOO kray), *Bolivia* (19°S, 65°W)	89
Sudan, *country in Africa* (13°N, 30°E)	107
Sudbury, *Ontario* (37°N, 81°W)	46
Sudd, *region of Sudan* (8°N, 30°E)	106
Suez (soo EHZ), *Egypt* (30°N, 33°E)	115
Suez Canal, *Egypt* (31°N, 33°E)	115
Suffolk, *Va.* (37°N, 77°W)	71
Sukhona R., *Russia* (60°N, 43°E)	95
Sukkur (SOOK uhr), *Pakistan* (28°N, 69°E)	122
Sulaiman Range (SOOL eye MAHN), *Pakistan* (69°N, 30°E)	122
Sulphur R., *Tex.* (33°N, 95°W)	67
Sulu Sea, *Asia* (8°N, 120°E)	119
Sumatra, *island in Indian O.* (0°, 102°E)	119
Sumba, *island in Savu Sea* (9°S, 120°E)	130
Sumbawa (soom BAH wuh), *island in Flores Sea* (8°S, 117°E)	130
Summerside, *Prince Edward Island* (46°N, 64°W)	47

Name (Pronunciation), *Description* (Lat., Long.)	**Page**
Sumter, *S.C.* (34°N, 80°W)	69
Sunnyvale, *Calif.* (37°N, 122°W)	58
Superior, *Wis.* (47°N, 92°W)	63
Superior, L., *North America* (48°N, 88°W)	63
Surabaya, *Indonesia* (8°S, 113°E)	130
Surat (SOOR uht), *India* (21°N, 73°E)	122
Surat Thani (SOOR aht AN ee), *Thailand* (9°N, 99°E)	123
Suriname, *country in South America* (4°N, 56°E)	89
Surrey, *British Columbia* (49°N, 123°W)	44
Surtsey I. (SURT see), *Atlantic O.* (63°N, 21°W)	94
Susah, *Tunisia* (36°N, 11°E)	114
Susquehanna R., *U.S.* (40°N, 76°W)	72
Sutton L., *Ontario* (54°N, 85°W)	46
Suwanee R., *Fla.* (30°N, 83°W)	69
Suwon, *South Korea* (37°N, 127°E)	125
Suzhou (soo joh), *China* (31°N, 121°E)	124
Svalbard, *poss. of Norway* (77°N, 20°E)	11
Swan Hill, *Australia* (35°S, 144°E)	133
Swan Hills, *Alberta* (55°N, 116°W)	44
Swan River, *Manitoba* (52°N, 101°W)	45
Swanson Res., *Nebr.* (40°N, 101°W)	64
Swaziland, *country in Africa* (27°S, 32°E)	107
Sweden, *country in Europe* (60°N, 15°E)	96-97
Sweetwater R., *Wyo.* (42°N, 108°W)	61
Swift Current, *Saskatchewan* (50°N, 108°W)	45
Switzerland, *country in Europe* (47°N, 8°E)	99
Sydney, *Australia* (34°S, 151°E)	133
Sydney, *Nova Scotia* (46°N, 60°W)	47
Syktyvkar (sik tif KAHR), *Russia* (62°N, 51°E)	97
Syr Darya, *r. in Uzbekistan* (46°N, 65°E)	100
Syracuse, *N.Y.* (43°N, 76°W)	72
Syria, *country in Asia* (35°N, 38°E)	115
Syrian Desert, *Asia* (32°N, 39°E)	115
Szczecin (SHCHET SEEN), *Poland* (53°N, 15°E)	99
Szeged (SEG ed), *Hungary* (46°N, 20°E)	99

T

Name (Pronunciation), *Description* (Lat., Long.)	**Page**
Tabessa, *Algeria* (35°N, 8°E)	114
Table Rock L., *U.S.* (36°N, 93°W)	65
Tabora, *Tanzania* (5°S, 33°E)	110
Tabriz, *Iran* (38°N, 46°E)	115
Tabuk (tuh BOOK), *Saudi Arabia* (28°N, 37°E)	115
Tacoma, *Wash.* (47°N, 123°W)	60
Taconic Mts. (tuh KAHN ihk), *N.Y.* (42°N, 74°W)	72-73
Tadoussac (TAD uh SAK), *Quebec* (48°N, 70°W)	47
Tadule L., *Manitoba* (59°N, 98°W)	45
Taegu (TAG oo), *South Korea* (36°N, 129°E)	125
Taejon (tah JAWN), *South Korea* (36°N, 127°E)	125
Tagus R., *Europe* (40°N, 4°W)	114
Tahat, Mt., *Algeria* (24°N, 6°E)	114
Tahoe, L., *U.S.* (39°N, 120°W)	58
Taichung (TY CHOONG), *Taiwan* (24°N, 121°E)	124
Taipei (TY PAY), *Taiwan* (25°N, 122°E)	124
Taiwan, *country in Asia* (24°N, 121°E)	124
Taiyuan (TY yoo AHN), *China* (38°N, 112°E)	124
Tajikistan, *country in Asia* (38°N, 69°E)	100
Tajumulco (TAH hoo MOOL KOH), *mt. in Guatemala* (15°N, 92°W)	82
Takamatsu, *Japan* (34°N, 134°E)	125
Taklimakan Desert, *China* (38°N, 80°E)	124
Taku R., *North America* (59°N, 134°W)	44
Talara, *Peru* (5°S, 82°W)	90
Tallahassee, *Fla.* (31°N, 84°W)	69
Tallinn, *Estonia* (59°N, 25°E)	97
Tamanrasset, *Algeria* (23°N, 7°E)	114
Tambora, Mt. (TAHM buh ruh), *Indonesia* (8°S, 118°E)	130
Tamesi R., *Mexico* (23°N, 98°W)	82
Tampa, *Gulf of Mexico* (28°N, 82°W)	69
Tampa Bay, *Fla.* (28°N, 82°W)	69
Tampere (TAHM puh RAY), *Finland* (61°N, 24°E)	97
Tampico, *Mexico* (22°N, 98°W)	84
Tana, L., *Ethiopia* (12°N, 37°E)	115
Tana R., *Kenya* (0°, 40°E)	110
Tanana R. (TAN uh NAW), *Alaska* (65°N, 148°W)	57
Tanezrouft (TAH nehz ruhft), *region of Algeria* (24°N, 1°E)	114

Name (Pronunciation), *Description* (Lat., Long.)	Page
Tanga, *Tanzania* (5°S, 39°E)	110
Tanganyika, L., *Africa* (7°S, 30°E)	110
Tangier (tan JEER), *Morocco* (36°N, 6°W)	114
Tanimbar Is., *Arafura Sea* (8°S, 131°E)	130
Tanzania, *country in Africa* (5°S, 35°E)	110
Taos (TAH ohs), *N. Mex.* (36°N, 106°W)	59
Tapajos R., *Brazil* (6°S, 57°W)	90
Tar R., *N.C.* (36°N, 78°W)	71
Tarakan (TAHR uh KAHN), *Indonesia* (3°N, 118°E)	123
Taranto, *Italy* (40°N, 17°E)	99
Taranto, Gulf of, *Ionian Sea* (40°N, 17°E)	99
Tarim Basin, *China* (40°N, 85°E)	124
Tarim R., *China* (41°N, 81°E)	124
Tashkent, *Uzbekistan* (41°N, 69°E)	100
Tasman Sea, *Pacific O.* (30°S, 165°E)	133
Tasmania, *state in Australia* (42°S, 147°E)	131
Tatar Strait, *Sea of Japan and Sea of Okhotsk* (50°N, 142°E)	101
Taunton (TAWNT uhn), *Mass.* (42°N, 71°W)	73
Taurus Mts. (TAW ruhs), *Turkey* (37°N, 33°E)	115
Tawakoni, L., *Tex.* (33°N, 96°W)	67
Taylor, Mt., *N. Mex.* (35°N, 108°W)	59
Taylorville, *Ill.* (40°N, 89°W)	65
Taymyr Pen., *Russia* (75°N, 105°E)	100
Tayshet, *Russia* (56°N, 98°E)	100
Tbilisi (tuh BIHL uh see), *Georgia* (42°N, 45°E)	100
Tegucigalpa (tuh GOO see GAHL puh), *Honduras* (14°N, 87°W)	85
Tehachapi Mts. (tuh HACH uh pee) *Calif.* (35°N, 119°W)	58
Tehran, *Iran* (36°N, 51°E)	115
Tehuantepec, Gulf of (tuh WAHN tuh PEHK), *Pacific O.* (16°N, 95°W)	82
Tehuantepec, Isthmus of, *Mexico* (17°N, 95°W)	82
Tel Aviv, *Israel* (32°N, 35°E)	115
Teles Pires R. (TEL uh SPIR uhs), *Brazil* (7°S, 58°W)	90
Tema (TAY muh), *Ghana* (6°N, 0°)	108
Temagami, L., *Ontario* (47°N, 80°W)	46
Temiscaming (tuh MIHS kuh ming), *Quebec* (47°N, 79°W)	46
Tempe (tem PEE), *Ariz.* (33°N, 112°W)	59
Temple, *Tex.* (31°N, 97°W)	67
Temuco, *Chile* (39°S, 73°W)	89
Tennessee, *state in U.S.* (36°N, 88°W)	70-71
Tennessee R., *U.S.* (35°N, 87°W)	70
Tennessee Tombigbee Canal, *Miss.* (35°N, 88°W)	68
Tepic (tay PEEK), *Mexico* (22°N, 105°W)	84
Teresina, *Brazil* (5°S, 43°W)	89
Terminos Lagoon, *Bay of Campeche* (19°N, 92°W)	82
Terrace, *British Columbia* (55°N, 129°W)	44
Terre Haute (TER uh HOHT), *Ind.* (39°N, 87°W)	70
Terrebonne Bay (TEHR uh BAHN), *Gulf of Mexico* (29°N, 91°W)	67
Teslin R., *Canada* (61°N, 133°W)	44
Tessalit, *Mali* (21°N, 1°E)	107
Teton Range (TEE TAHN), *Wyo.* (44°N, 111°W)	61
Tetouan (tay TWAHN), *Morocco* (36°N, 6°W)	114
Texarkana, *Ark. and Tex.* (33°N, 94°W)	67
Texas, *state in U.S.* (32°N, 100°W)	66-67
Texas City, *Tex.* (29°N, 95°W)	67
Texoma, L., *U.S.* (34°N, 97°W)	67
Thailand (TY land), *country in Asia* (17°N, 100°E)	123
Thailand, Gulf of, *South China Sea* (10°N, 102°E)	123
Thames (tehmz), *r. in England* (51°N, 1°E)	98
Thames R., *Ontario* (43°N, 82°W)	46
Thane (TAHN uh), *India* (19°N, 73°E)	122
Thasos (THAY sahs), *island in Aegean Sea* (41°N, 25°E)	99
Thayetmyo, *Burma* (19°N, 95°E)	123
Theodore Roosevelt L., *Ariz.* (34°N, 111°W)	59
Theodore Roosevelt N.P., *N. Dak.* (47°N, 104°W)	62
Thermopolis (thuhr MAHP uh lus), *Wyo.* (44°N, 108°W)	61
Thief River Falls, *Minn.* (48°N, 96°W)	62
Thies (TY ehs), *Senegal* (15°N, 17°W)	108
Thika, *Kenya* (1°S, 37°E)	110
Thimphu (thim PYOO), *Bhutan* (28°N, 90°E)	122

Name (Pronunciation), *Description* (Lat., Long.)	Page
Third Cataract, *waterfall in Sudan* (20°N, 30°E)	115
Thohoyandou (tuh HOY AHN doo), *South Africa* (23°S, 30°E)	109
Thomasville, *Ga.* (31°N, 84°W)	69
Thompson, *Manitoba* (56°N, 98°W)	45
Thompson R., *British Columbia* (51°N, 121°W)	44
Thon Buri (tuhn BOO ree), *Thailand* (14°N, 100°E)	123
Thousand Is., *St. Lawrence R.* (44°N, 76°W)	72
Three Points, Cape, *Ghana* (5°N, 2°W)	108
Three Sisters, *mts. in Oreg.* (44°N, 122°W)	60
Thule (TOO lee), *Greenland* (78°N, 70°W)	37
Thunder Bay, *city in Ontario* (48°N, 89°W)	46
Tianjin, *China* (39°N, 117°E)	124
Tiber R., *Italy* (42°N, 12°E)	99
Tibesti Mts., *Africa* (22°N, 18°E)	106
Tibet, Plateau of, *China* (34°N, 90°E)	124
Tiburon I., *Gulf of California* (29°N, 112°W)	82
Tien Shan, *mt. range in Asia* (42°N, 78°E)	124
Tierra del Fuego (tih EH ruh dehl foo AY go), *archipelago of South America* (54°S, 70°W)	88
Tifton, *Ga.* (31°N, 84°W)	69
Tigris R., *Asia* (35°N, 43°E)	115
Tijuana (tee WHAN uh), *Mexico* (33°N, 117°W)	84
Tiksi, *Russia* (72°N, 129°E)	100
Tillamook, *Oreg.* (45°N, 124°W)	60
Tillery, L., *N.C.* (35°N, 80°W)	71
Timbuktu, *Mali* (17°N, 2°W)	107
Timisoara (TEE mish WAHR uh), *Romania* (46°N, 21°E)	99
Timmins, *Ontario* (48°N, 81°W)	46
Timor, *island in Timor Sea* (9°S, 125°E)	130
Timor Sea, *Indian O.* (11°S, 125°E)	130
Tims Ford L., *Tenn.* (35°N, 86°W)	70
Tippecanoe R., *Ind.* (41°N, 87°W)	70
Tirane (tee RAH nuh), *Albania* (41°N, 20°E)	99
Tisza R. (TIHS AW), *Hungary* (47°N, 20°E)	99
Titicaca, L., *South America* (16°S, 70°W)	88
Titusville (TY tuhs VIL), *Fla.* (29°N, 81°W)	69
Tobique R., *New Brunswick* (47°N, 68°W)	47
Tobolsk, *Russia* (58°N, 68°E)	100
Tobruk (TOH BROOK), *Libya* (32°N, 24°E)	115
Tocantins R. (TOH kuhn TEHNS), *Brazil* (10°S, 48°W)	88
Tofino (toh FEE noh), *British Columbia* (49°N, 126°W)	44
Togo, *country in Africa* (8°N, 1°E)	108
Tok, *Alaska* (6°N, 14°W)	57
Tokelau, *poss. of New Zealand* (8°S, 176°W)	135
Tokyo, *Japan* (36°N, 140°E)	125
Toledo, *Ohio* (42°N, 84°W)	70
Toledo Bend Res., *U.S.* (32°N, 94°W)	67
Toluca (tuh LOO kuh), *Mexico* (19°N, 100°W)	84
Tomah (TOH muh), *Wis.* (44°N, 90°W)	63
Tombigbee R., *U.S.* (32°N, 87°W)	68
Tomsk, *Russia* (56°N, 85°E)	100
Tonawanda, *N.Y.* (43°N, 79°W)	72
Tonga, *country in Pacific O.* (20°S, 175°W)	135
Tonkin, Gulf of, *South China Sea* (20°N, 108°E)	123
Tonle Sap (TAHN lay SAHP), *l. in Cambodia* (13°N, 104°E)	123
Tonopah (TOHN uh PAH), *Nev.* (38°N, 117°W)	58
Topeka, *Kans.* (39°N, 96°W)	64-65
Torngat Mts., *Canada* (59°N, 64°W)	41
Toronto, *Ontario* (44°N, 79°W)	46
Toronto Res., *Kans.* (38°N, 96°W)	64
Tororo, *Uganda* (1°N, 34°E)	110
Torrance, *Calif.* (34°N, 118°W)	58
Torrens, L., *Australia* (31°S, 138°E)	130
Torreon, *Mexico* (25°N, 103°W)	84
Torres Strait, *New Guinea and Australia* (10°S, 141°E)	130
Toubkal Mt. (TOOB kuhl), *Morocco* (31°N, 8°W)	114
Touggourt (too GOORT), *Algeria* (33°N, 6°E)	114
Toulon (too LOHN), *France* (43°N, 6°E)	98
Toulouse (too LOOZ), *France* (44°N, 1°E)	98
Tours (TOOR), *France* (47°N, 1°E)	98
Townsville, *Australia* (19°S, 147°E)	131
Towson, *Md.* (39°N, 77°W)	71
Toyama (toh YAHM uh), *Japan* (37°N, 137°E)	125

Name (Pronunciation), *Description* (Lat., Long.)	Page
Trail, *British Columbia* (49°N, 118°W)	44
Tralee (truh LEE), *Ireland* (52°N, 10°W)	98
Trans-Alaskan Pipeline, *Alaska* (67°N, 150°W)	57
Transvaal (trans VAHL), *prov. of South Africa* (25°S, 30°E)	109
Transvaal Basin, *South Africa* (23°S, 29°E)	109
Transylvanian Alps, *mt. range in Europe* (45°N, 23°E)	99
Traralgon (truh RAL guhn), *Australia* (38°S, 147°E)	133
Traverse, L., *Minn.* (46°N, 97°W)	62
Traverse City, *Mich.* (45°N, 86°W)	63
Travis, L., *Tex.* (30°N, 98°W)	66-67
Trenton, *N.J.* (40°N, 75°W)	72
Tres Marias Is., *Pacific O.* (21°N, 107°W)	82
Tres Marias Res., *Brazil* (18°S, 46°W)	82
Tres Puntas, Cape, *Argentina* (47°S, 66°W)	88
Trieste (tree EST), *Italy* (46°N, 14°E)	99
Trindade, *island in Atlantic O.* (21°S, 29°W)	88
Trinidad, *Colo.* (37°N, 104°W)	59
Trinidad and Tobago, *country in Caribbean Sea* (11°N, 62°W)	85
Trinity R., *Calif.* (41°N, 123°W)	58
Trinity R., *Tex.* (32°N, 96°W)	67
Tripoli, *Lebanon* (34°N, 36°E)	115
Tripoli, *Libya* (33°N, 13°E)	114
Tripolitania, *region of Libya* (32°N, 13°E)	114
Trivandrum (truh VAN druhm), *India* (8°N, 77°E)	122
Trois-Rivieres (TRWAH ree VYER), *Quebec* (46°N, 73°W)	47
Trombetas R. (trohm BAY tuhs), *Brazil* (2°N, 56°W)	90
Trondheim, *Norway* (64°N, 10°E)	96
Trondheims Fiord, *Norway* (64°N, 9°E)	94
Trout L., *Ontario* (51°N, 93°W)	46
Troy, *Ala.* (32°N, 86°W)	68
Troy, *N.Y.* (43°N, 74°W)	72
Truckee R., *U.S.* (39°N, 120°W)	58
Trujillo (troo HEE yoh), *Peru* (8°S, 79°W)	90
Truro, *Nova Scotia* (45°N, 63°W)	47
Tselinograd (seh LIHN uh GRAHD), *Kazakhstan* (51°N, 71°E)	100
Tsugaru Strait (soo GAH roo), *Japan* (42°N, 140°E)	125
Tsushima (soo SHEE muh), *island in Korea Strait* (34°N, 129°E)	125
Tuamoto Archipelago, *island group in Pacific O.* (20°S, 140°E)	132
Tucson (TOO sahn), *Arizona* (32°N, 111°W)	59
Tucuman (TOO koo MAHN), *Argentina* (27°S, 65°W)	89
Tucumcari (TOO kum KAHR ee), *N. Mex.* (35°N, 104°W)	59
Tug Fork, *r. in U.S.* (38°N, 82°W)	71
Tugela Falls, *South Africa* (29°S, 29°E)	109
Tugela R. (too GAH luh), *South Africa* (29°S, 31°E)	109
Tula, *Russia* (54°N, 38°E)	97
Tulcan (tool KAHN), *Ecuador* (1°N, 78°W)	90
Tullulah (tuh LOO luh), *La.* (32°N, 91°W)	67
Tulsa, *Okla.* (36°N, 96°W)	67
Tunduru (tuhn DOO roo), *Tanzania* (11°S, 37°E)	110
Tunis (TOO nihs), *Tunisia* (37°N, 10°E)	114
Tunisia, *country in Africa* (34°N, 10°E)	114
Tupelo (TOOP uh LOH), *Miss.* (34°N, 89°W)	68
Turan Lowland, *Kazakhstan* (43°N, 60°E)	118
Turin (TOO rihn), *Italy* (45°N, 8°E)	99
Turkana, L., *Africa* (4°N, 36°E)	110
Turkey, *country in Asia and Europe* (39°N, 35°E)	115
Turkey R., *Iowa* (43°N, 92°W)	65
Turkmenistan, *country in Asia* (40°N, 57°E)	100
Turks and Caicos Is., *Atlantic O.* (22°N, 72°W)	85
Turku, *Finland* (61°N, 22°E)	97
Turlock (TER, 37°N, 121°W)	58
Turpan Depression (toor pahn), *China* (42°N, 90°E)	124
Turtle Mts., *N. Dak.* (49°N, 100°W)	62
Tuscaloosa, *Ala.* (33°N, 87°W)	68
Tuttle Creek L., *Kans.* (39°N, 97°W)	64

Name (Pronunciation), *Description* (Lat., Long.)	**Page**
Tuvalu, *country in Pacific O.* (5°S, 174°E)	135
Tuz, L. (TOOZ), *Turkey* (39°N, 33°E)	115
Tver, *Russia* (57°N, 36°E)	100
Twin Falls, *Idaho* (43°N, 115°W)	61
Twin Falls, *Newfoundland* (54°N, 65°W)	47
Tyler, *Tex.* (32°N, 95°W)	67
Tyrrhenian Sea (tih REE nee uhn), *Mediterranean Sea* (39°N, 12°E)	99

U

Name (Pronunciation), *Description* (Lat., Long.)	**Page**
Uaupes (wow PEHS), *Brazil* (0°, 67°W)	90
Ubangi R., *Africa* (3°N, 23°E)	106
Uberaba, *Brazil* (20°S, 48°W)	89
Ucayali R. (OOK uh YAH lee), *Peru* (7°S, 75°W)	90
Udaipur (oo DY POOR), *India* (25°N, 74°E)	122
Ufa, *Russia* (55°N, 56°E)	97
Ugalla R. (oo GAH lah), *Tanzania* (6°S, 31°E)	110
Uganda, *country in Africa* (2°N, 32°E)	110
Uinta Mts.(yoo IHN tuh), *Utah* (41°N, 110°W)	59
Ujiji (oo JEE jee), *Tanzania* (5°S, 30°E)	110
Ujung Pandang, *Indonesia* (5°S, 119°E)	131
Ukiah (yoo KY uh), *Calif.* (39°N, 123°W)	58
Ukraine, *country in Europe* (49°N, 30°E)	97
Ulan Bator, *Mongolia* (48°N, 107°E)	121
Ulan Ude (oo LAHN oo DAY), *Russia* (52°N, 108°E)	124
Uliastay (OOL yoh STY), *Mongolia* (48°N, 97°E)	124
Ulm (OOLM), *Germany* (48°N, 10°E)	99
Ulsan (OOL SAHN), *South Korea* (36°N, 129°E)	125
Ulungur R. (oo loon gyoor), *Asia* (47°N, 85°E)	124
Umlazi (oom LAHZ ee), *South Africa* (30°S, 31°E)	109
Umnak I. (OOM NAK), *Bering Sea* (53°N, 169°W)	57
Umtata (oom TAH tuh), *South Africa* (32°S, 29°E)	109
Unalakleet (UHN uh LAK leet), *Alaska* (64°N, 161°W)	57
Unalaska I. (UHN uh LAS kuh), *Bering Sea* (54°N, 166°W)	57
Ungava Bay, *Hudson Strait* (60°N, 68°W)	41
Ungava Pen., *Quebec* (61°N, 75°W)	41
Unimak I. (YOO nuh MAK), *Bering Sea* (55°N, 164°W)	57
United Arab Emirates, *country in Asia* (24°N, 53°E)	115
United Kingdom, *country in Europe* (55°N, 3°W)	98
United States, *country in North America* (40°N, 100°W)	54-55
University City, *Mo.* (39°N, 90°W)	65
Unzen, Mt. (OON ZEN), *Japan* (33°N, 130°E)	125
Upington, *South Africa* (28°S, 21°E)	109
Upper Arlington, *Ohio* (40°N, 83°W)	70
Upper Arrow L., *British Columbia* (51°N, 118°W)	44
Upper Iowa R., *Iowa* (43°N, 92°W)	65
Upper Klamath L. (KLAM uth), *Oreg.* (42°N, 122°W)	60
Upper Pen., *Mich.* (46°N, 86°W)	63
Upper Red Lake, *Minn.* (48°N, 95°W)	62
Uppsala (UHP suh LAH), *Sweden* (60°N, 18°E)	96
Ural Mts., *Russia* (64°N, 59°E)	95
Ural R., *Europe and Asia* (48°N, 52°E)	95
Uralsk (yoo RALSK), *Kazakhstan* (51°N, 51°E)	97
Uranium City, *Saskatchewan* (60°N, 109°W)	45
Urawa (oo RAH wuh), *Japan* (36°N, 140°E)	125
Urbana (UHR BAN uh), *Ill.* (40°N, 88°W)	65
Urmia, L., *Iran* (38°N, 46°E)	115
Uruguay, *country in South America* (33°S, 56°W)	88
Uruguay R., *South America* (29°S, 57°W)	89
Urumqi, *China* (43°N, 88°E)	124
Usambara Mts. (oo suhm BAHR uh), *Tanzania* (5°S, 38°E)	110
Usangu Flats (oo SAHNG goo), *Tanzania* (8°S, 34°E)	110
Ushuaia (YOO SWAY yuh), *Argentina* (55°S, 68°W)	89
Ussuri R., *Russia* (46°N, 132°E)	101
Ust-Kut, *Russia* (57°N, 106°E)	100
Usumacinta R. (YOO suh muh SINT uh), *North America* (18°N, 92°W)	82
Utah, *state in U.S.* (39°N, 113°W)	58-59

Name (Pronunciation), *Description* (Lat., Long.)	**Page**
Utah L., *Utah* (40°N, 112°W)	59
Ute Res. (YOOT), *N. Mex.* (35°N, 103°W)	59
Utica (YOO tih kuh), *N.Y.* (43°N, 75°W)	72
Utikuma L., *Alberta* (56°N, 116°W)	44
Utrecht (YOO TREKT), *Netherlands* (52°N, 5°E)	98
Uwajima (oo wuh JEE muh), *Japan* (33°N, 133°E)	125
Uzbekistan, *country in Asia* (42°N, 63°E)	100

V

Name (Pronunciation), *Description* (Lat., Long.)	**Page**
Vaal R. (VAHL), *South Africa* (27°S, 27°E)	109
Vaasa (VAHS uh), *Finland* (63°N, 22°E)	97
Vacaville (VAK uh vil), *Calif.* (38°N, 122°W)	58
Vadodara, *India* (22°N, 73°E)	122
Vaduz (VAH doots), *Liechtenstein* (47°N, 10°E)	99
Vail, *Colo.* (40°N, 106°W)	59
Val-d'Or, *Quebec* (48°N, 78°W)	46
Valdes Pen., *Argentina* (43°S, 64°W)	88
Valdez, *Alaska* (61°N, 146°W)	57
Valdosta, *Ga.* (31°N, 83°W)	69
Valencia, *Spain* (39°N, 0°)	114
Valencia, *Venezuela* (10°N, 68°W)	90
Valentine, *Nebr.* (43°N, 101°W)	64
Vallejo (vuh LAY oh), *Calif.* (38°N, 122°W)	58
Valletta (vuh LEHT uh), *Malta* (36°N, 15°E)	99
Valley City, *N. Dak.* (47°N, 98°W)	62
Valley Forge, *Pa.* (40°N, 76°W)	72
Valparaiso, *Chile* (33°S, 72°W)	89
Van, L., *Turkey* (39°N, 43°E)	115
Vancouver, *British Columbia* (49°N, 123°W)	44
Vancouver, *Wash.* (46°N, 123°W)	60
Vancouver I., *British Columbia* (50°N, 127°W)	44
Vanderhoof, *British Columbia* (54°N, 124°W)	44
Vanern, L., *Sweden* (59°N, 13°E)	94
Vanuatu (VAH noo AH too), *country in Pacific O.* (19°S, 169°E)	131
Varanasi (vuh RAHN uh see), *India* (26°N, 83°E)	122
Vardar R., *Europe* (41°N, 22°E)	99
Vardo (VAHR DUHR), *Norway* (70°N, 31°E)	97
Varna, *Bulgaria* (43°N, 28°E)	99
Vatican City, *country in Europe* (42°N, 12°E)	99
Vattern, L., *Sweden* (58°N, 14°E)	94
Venezuela, *country in South America* (7°N, 65°W)	90
Venice, *Italy* (45°N, 12°E)	99
Ventura (ven TOOR uh), *Calif.* (34°N, 119°W)	58
Veracruz (VEHR uh KROOZ), *Mexico* (19°N, 96°W)	84
Verde, Cape, *Senegal* (14°N, 18°W)	108
Verde R., *Ariz.* (34°N, 112°W)	59
Verdigris R. (VUHR duh gruhs), *U.S.* (37°N, 96°W)	64-65
Verdun (vuhr DUHN), *France* (49°N, 5°E)	98
Vereeniging (fuh REEN ih KING), *South Africa* (27°S, 28°E)	109
Verkhoyansk (VEHR kuh YANSK), *Russia* (68°N, 133°E)	100
Verkhoyansk Range, *Russia* (70°N, 130°E)	101
Vermilion R., *Ill.* (41°N, 89°W)	65
Vermillion, *S. Dak.* (43°N, 97°W)	62
Vermillion R., *S. Dak.* (43°N, 97°W)	62
Vermont, *state in U.S.* (44°N, 73°W)	73
Vernon, *British Columbia* (50°N, 119°W)	44
Verona, *Italy* (45°N, 11°E)	99
Versailles (vehr SY uh), *France* (49°N, 2°E)	98
Vesuvius, Mt., *Italy* (41°N, 14°E)	99
Vichy (VISH ee), *France* (46°N, 3°E)	98
Vicksburg, *Miss.* (32°N, 91°W)	68
Victoria, *British Columbia* (48°N, 123°W)	44
Victoria, *Mexico* (24°N, 99°W)	84
Victoria, *Seychelles* (5°S, 56°E)	107
Victoria, *state in Australia* (37°S, 143°E)	133
Victoria, *Tex.* (29°N, 97°W)	67
Victoria Falls, *waterfall in Africa* (18°S, 26°E)	106
Victoria I., *Arctic O.* (74°N, 110°W)	40
Victoria, L., *Africa* (1°S, 33°E)	110
Victoria, L., *Australia* (34°S, 141°E)	133
Victoria Land, *region of Antarctica* (73°S, 160°W)	137
Victoria Nile, *r. in Uganda* (2°N, 31°E)	110

Name (Pronunciation), *Description* (Lat., Long.)	**Page**
Viedma, *Argentina* (41°S, 63°W)	89
Vienna, *Austria* (48°N, 16°E)	99
Vienne R. (vee EHN), *France* (47°N, 1°E)	98
Vientiane (vyehn TYAHN), *Laos* (18°N, 103°E)	123
Vietnam, *country in Asia* (17°N, 107°E)	123
Vijayawada (VIHJ uh yuh WAHD uh), *India* (17°N, 81°E)	122
Villahermosa (VEE yuh ehr MOH zuh), *Mexico* (18°N, 93°W)	84
Vilnius, *Lithuania* (55°N, 25°E)	100
Vincennes (vin SENZ), *Ind.* (39°N, 87°W)	70
Vineland, *N.J.* (39°N, 75°W)	72
Vinh, *Vietnam* (18°N, 106°E)	123
Vinson Massif, *mt. in Antarctica* (79°S, 86°W)	137
Virgin Is., *Caribbean Sea* (18°N, 65°W)	83
Virgin R., *U.S.* (37°N, 114°W)	58
Virginia, *state in U.S.* (37°N, 80°W)	70-71
Virginia Beach, *Va.* (37°N, 76°W)	71
Virginia City, *Nev.* (39°N, 120°W)	58
Visalia (vih SAYL yuh), *Calif.* (36°N, 119°W)	58
Visby (VIHS bee), *Sweden* (58°N, 18°E)	99
Viscount Melville Sound, *Northwest Terr.* (74°N, 110°W)	40
Vishakhapatnam (vih SHAHK uh PUHT nuhm), *India* (18°N, 83°E)	122
Vistula R., *Europe* (43°N, 19°E)	99
Vitoria, *Brazil* (20°S, 40°W)	89
Vladivostok, *Russia* (43°N, 132°E)	101
Voi (VOY), *Kenya* (3°S, 39°E)	110
Vojvodina (VOY vuh DEE nuh), *prov. of Serbia* (45°N, 20°E)	99
Volcano Is., *Pacific O.* (24°N, 141°E)	119
Volga R., *Russia* (48°N, 46°E)	95
Volga R. Delta, *Russia* (46°N, 48°E)	95
Volga Upland, *Russia* (52°N, 45°E)	95
Volgograd, *Russia* (49°N, 44°E)	97
Volgograd Res., *Russia* (50°N, 46°E)	95
Volos (VOH LAHS), *Greece* (39°N, 23°E)	99
Volta, L., *Ghana* (7°N, 0°)	108
Vorkuta, *Russia* (67°N, 64°E)	100
Voronezh (vuh RAWN ish), *Russia* (52°N, 39°E)	95
Voyageurs N.P., *Minn.* (49°N, 93°W)	63
Vyatka R., *Russia* (57°N, 50°E)	95

W

Name (Pronunciation), *Description* (Lat., Long.)	**Page**
Wabasca R., *Alberta* (57°N, 114°W)	44
Wabash R., *U.S.* (38°N, 88°W)	70
Waco (WAY koh), *Tex.* (32°N, 97°W)	67
Waconda L., *Kans.* (40°N, 98°W)	64
Waddington, Mt., *British Columbia* (51°N, 123°W)	44
Wagga Wagga, *Australia* (35°S, 147°E)	133
Wahpeton (WAW puh tuhn), *N. Dak.* (46°N, 97°W)	62
Wailuku, *Hawaii* (21°N, 156°W)	57
Wainwright (WAYN ryt), *Alberta* (53°N, 111°W)	45
Waipahu (wy PAH hoo), *Hawaii* (21°N, 158°W)	57
Wakayama (WAHK uh YAHM uh), *Japan* (34°N, 135°E)	125
Wakkanai (WAHK uh NY), *Japan* (45°N, 142°E)	125
Wales, *part of United Kingdom* (53°N, 4°W)	98
Walla Walla, *Wash.* (46°N, 118°W)	60
Wallis and Futuna, *poss. of France* (13°S, 176°W)	135
Wallkill R., *N.Y.* (41°N, 74°W)	72
Wallowa Mts. (wuh LOW uh), *Oreg.* (45°N, 117°W)	60
Walvis Bay, *terr. of South Africa* (23°S, 15°E)	109
Wangaratta, *Australia* (36°S, 146°E)	133
Wappapello L., *Mo.* (37°N, 90°W)	65
Wapsipinicon R. (WAHP suh PIN uh kuhn), *Iowa* (92°W, 43°N)	65
Warner Robins, *Ga.* (33°N, 84°W)	69
Warren, *Ark.* (34°N, 92°W)	67
Warren, *Mich.* (43°N, 83°W)	63
Warren, *Ohio* (41°N, 81°W)	71
Warren, *Pa.* (42°N, 79°W)	72
Warrnambool (WAWR nuhm BOOL), *Australia* (38°S, 142°E)	133
Warsaw, *Poland* (52°N, 21°E)	99
Warta R. (VAHRT uh), *Poland* (52°N, 17°E)	99

Name (Pronunciation), *Description* (Lat., Long.)	Page
Warwick, *R.I.* (42°N, 71°W)	73
Wasatch Range, *U.S.* (41°N, 111°W)	59
Wash, The, *bay in England* (53°N, 0°)	98
Washington, *state in U.S.* (47°N, 123°W)	60
Washington, D.C. (39°N, 77°W)	71
Washington, Mt., *N.H.* (44°N, 71°W)	73
Washington, *Pa.* (40°N, 80°W)	72
Waskaganish, *Quebec* (52°N, 79°W)	46
Waterbury, *Conn.* (42°N, 73°W)	73
Wateree L. (WAWT uh ree), *S.C.* (34°N, 81°W)	69
Waterford, *Ireland* (52°N, 7°W)	98
Waterloo, *Iowa* (43°N, 92°W)	65
Waterloo, *Ontario* (43°N, 81°W)	46
Waterton Lakes N. P., *Alberta* (49°N, 114°W)	44
Watertown, *N.Y.* (44°N, 76°W)	72
Watertown, *S. Dak.* (45°N, 97°W)	62
Waterville, *Maine* (45°N, 70°W)	73
Watseka (waht SEE kuh), *Ill.* (41°N, 88°W)	65
Watson Lake, *Yukon Terr.* (60°N, 129°W)	44
Watts Bar L., *Tenn.* (36°N, 85°W)	70
Waukegan (waw KEE guhn), *Ill.* (42°N, 88°W)	65
Wausau (WAW SAW), *Wis.* (45°N, 90°W)	63
Wauwatosa (WAW wuh TOH suh), *Wis.* (43°N, 88°W)	63
Waw, *Sudan* (8°N, 28°E)	107
Wawa, *Ontario* (48°N, 85°W)	46
Waycross, *Ga.* (31°N, 82°W)	69
Weddell Sea, *Antarctica* (70°S, 45°W)	137
Wei R. (way), *China* (35°N, 106°E)	124
Weirton (WIRT uhn), *W. Va.* (41°N, 81°W)	71
Weiss L., *Ala.* (34°N, 86°W)	68
Welch, *W. Va.* (37°N, 82°W)	71
Welkom (VEL kum), *South Africa* (28°S, 27°E)	109
Welland Canal, *Ontario* (43°N, 79°W)	46
Wellesley Is., *Australia* (16°S, 139°E)	130
Wellington, *New Zealand* (41°S, 175°E)	131
Wellington I., *Pacific O.* (49°S, 75°W)	88
Wemindji, *Quebec* (53°N, 79°W)	46
Wenatchee, *Wash.* (47°N, 120°W)	60
Wentworth, *Australia* (34°S, 142°E)	133
Wenzou (wuhn joh), *China* (28°N, 121°E)	124
West Allis, *Wis.* (43°N, 88°W)	63
West Bank, *terr. in Asia* (32°N, 35°E)	115
West Frisian Is., *North Sea* (53°N, 6°E)	98
West Grand L., *Maine* (45°N, 68°W)	73
West Indies, *island group in Caribbean Sea* (22°N, 78°W)	83
West Jordan, *Utah* (41°N, 112°W)	59
West Lafayette (LAHF ee ET), *Ind.* (40°N, 87°W)	70
West Memphis, *Ark.* (35°N, 90°W)	67
West Palm Beach, *Fla.* (27°N, 80°W)	69
West Plains, *Mo.* (37°N, 92°W)	65
West Siberian Plain, *Russia* (60°N, 75°E)	118
West Virginia, *state in U.S.* (39°N, 81°W)	70-71
Westbrook, *Maine* (44°N, 69°W)	73
Western Australia, *state in Australia* (25°S, 120°E)	131
Western Dvina R. (duh vee NAH), *Europe* (56°N, 26°E)	95
Western Ghats, *mt. range in India* (14°N, 75°E)	122
Western Sahara, *adm. by Morocco* (25°N, 13°W)	114
Western Samoa, *poss. of U.S.* (10°S, 172°W)	135
Westport, *New Zealand* (42°S, 172°E)	131
Wetar (WEH TAHR), *island in Banda Sea* (7°S, 126°E)	130
Wetaskiwin (wih TAS kuh WIHN), *Alberta* (53°N, 113°W)	44
Weyburn (WAY buhrn), *Saskatchewan* (50°N, 104°W)	45
Wheaton, *Md.* (39°N, 77°W)	71
Wheeler L., *Ala.* (35°N, 87°W)	68
Wheeler Pk., *Nev.* (39°N, 114°W)	58
Wheeler Pk., *N. Mex.* (37°N, 105°W)	59
Wheeling, *W. Va.* (40°N, 81°W)	71
White L., *La.* (30°N, 93°W)	67
White Mts., *N.H.* (44°N, 71°W)	73
White Nile, *r. in Africa* (14°N, 33°E)	106
White Plains, *N.Y.* (41°N, 74°W)	72
White R., *Ark.* (36°N, 92°W)	67
White R., *Ind.* (39°N, 87°W)	70

Name (Pronunciation), *Description* (Lat., Long.)	Page
White R., *S. Dak.* (43°N, 102°W)	62
White R., *U.S.* (40°N, 109°W)	59
White River, *Ontario* (49°N, 85°W)	46
White Sea, *Russia* (66°N, 40°E)	95
White Sulphur Springs, *Mont.* (47°N, 111°W)	61
White Sulphur Springs, *W. Va.* (38°N, 80°W)	71
White Volta R., *Africa* (13°N, 1°W)	108
Whitecourt, *Alberta* (54°N, 116°W)	44
Whitefish Bay, *L. Superior* (47°N, 85°W)	63
Whitehorse, *Yukon Terr.* (61°N, 135°W)	44
Whitewater R., *U.S.* (39°N, 85°W)	70
Whitney, L., *Tex.* (32°N, 97°W)	67
Whitney, Mt., *Calif.* (37°N, 118°W)	58
Whyalla, *Australia* (33°S, 138°E)	133
Wichita, *Kans.* (38°N, 97°W)	64
Wichita Falls, *Tex.* (34°N, 98°W)	66
Wichita Mts. (WIHCH uh TAW), *Okla.* (35°N, 99°W)	66
Wick, *Scotland* (58°N, 3°W)	98
Wicklow Mts., *Ireland* (53°N, 6°W)	98
Wiesbaden (VEES BAHD uhn), *Germany* (50°N, 8°E)	99
Wight, Isle of (WYT), *English Channel* (51°N, 1°W)	98
Wilkes-Barre (WIHLKS bair ee), *Pa.* (41°N, 76°W)	72
Wilkes Land, *region of Antarctica* (70°S, 120°E)	137
Willamette R., *Oreg.* (45°N, 123°W)	60
Willapa Bay (WIHL uh PAW), *Pacific O.* (47°N, 124°W)	60
William "Bill" Dannelly Res., *Ala.* (32°N, 87°W)	68
Williams Lake, *city in British Columbia* (52°N, 122°W)	44
Williamsburg, *Va.* (37°N, 75°W)	71
Williamsport, *Pa.* (41°N, 77°W)	72
Williston, *N. Dak.* (48°N, 104°W)	62
Williston L., *British Columbia* (56°N, 123°W)	44
Willmar, *Minn.* (45°N, 95°W)	62
Willow, *Alaska* (62°N, 150°W)	57
Willowlake R., *Northwest Terr.* (63°N, 123°W)	44
Wilmington, *Del.* (40°N, 76°W)	71
Wilmington, *N.C.* (34°N, 78°W)	71
Wilson, *N.C.* (36°N, 78°W)	71
Wilson L., *Ala.* (35°N, 88°W)	68
Wilson's Promontory, *Australia* (39°S, 147°E)	133
Winchester, *Ky.* (38°N, 84°W)	70
Winchester, *Va.* (39°N, 78°W)	71
Wind Cave N.P., *S. Dak.* (44°N, 103°W)	62
Wind R., *Wyo.* (43°N, 109°W)	61
Wind River Range, *Wyo.* (43°N, 110°W)	61
Windhoek (VINT HOOK), *Namibia* (23°S, 17°E)	107
Window Rock, *city in Ariz.* (35°N, 109°W)	59
Windsor, *Ontario* (42°N, 83°W)	46
Windward Is., *Caribbean Sea* (13°N, 62°W)	83
Windward Passage, *Caribbean Sea* (20°N, 74°W)	83
Winisk L., *Ontario* (53°N, 87°W)	46
Winisk R., *Ontario* (55°N, 85°W)	46
Winnebago, L., *Wis.* (44°N, 89°W)	63
Winnemucca, *Nev.* (41°N, 118°W)	58
Winnipeg, *Manitoba* (50°N, 97°W)	45
Winnipeg R., *Canada* (50°N, 96°W)	45
Winnipeg, L., *Manitoba* (53°N, 98°W)	45
Winnipegosis, L. (WIHN uh puh GOH suhs), *Manitoba* (52°N, 100°W)	45
Winnipesaukee, L. (WIHN uh puh SAW kee), *N.H.* (44°N, 71°W)	73
Winona, *Minn.* (44°N, 92°W)	63
Winston-Salem, *N.C.* (36°N, 80°W)	71
Winter Haven, *Fla.* (28°N, 82°W)	69
Wisconsin, *state in U.S.* (45°N, 90°W)	63
Wisconsin Dells, *Wis.* (44°N, 90°W)	63
Wisconsin R., *Wis.* (44°N, 90°W)	63
Wloclawek (vlawt SLAH vehk), *Poland* (53°N, 19°E)	99
Wolf Point, *Mont.* (48°N, 106°W)	61
Wollaston L. (WOOL uh stuhn), *city in Saskatchewan* (58°N, 103°W)	45
Wollongong, *Australia* (34°S, 151°E)	133
Wonsan (WUHN SAHN), *North Korea* (39°N, 127°E)	125
Wood Buffalo N. P., *Canada* (59°N, 114°W)	44-45
Woods, L. of the, *Minnesota and Ontario* (49°N, 95°W)	62

Name (Pronunciation), *Description* (Lat., Long.)	Page
Woodstock, *New Brunswick* (46°N, 68°W)	47
Woodward, *Okla.* (36°N, 99°W)	66
Woomera, *Australia* (31°S, 137°E)	131
Wooster, *Ohio* (41°N, 82°W)	71
Worcester (WOOS tuhr), *Mass.* (42°N, 72°W)	73
Worcester, *South Africa* (34°S, 19°E)	109
Worthington, *Minn.* (44°N, 96°W)	62
Wounded Knee, *S. Dak.* (43°N, 103°W)	62
Wrangel I., *Chukchi Sea* (71°N, 180°)	101
Wrangell Mts. (RANG guhl), *North America* (62°N, 142°W)	57
Wrangell–Saint Elias N. P. (ee LY uhs), *Alaska* (60°N, 141°W)	57
Wroclaw (VRAWTS lahf), *Poland* (51°N, 17°E)	99
Wu R. (woo), *China* (27°N, 107°E)	124
Wuhan, *China* (31°N, 114°E)	124
Wuxi (woo shee), *China* (32°N, 120°E)	124
Wuyi Shan (woo yih shahn), *mts. in China* (26°N, 116°E)	124
Wuzhou (woo joh), *China* (24°N, 111°E)	124
Wyoming, *Mich.* (43°N, 86°W)	63
Wyoming, *state in U.S.* (43°N, 109°W)	61
Wyoming Range, *Wyo.* (43°N, 110°W)	61
Wytheville (WITH VIL), *Va.* (37°N, 81°W)	71

X

Xanthi (ZAN thee), *Greece* (41°N, 25°E)	99
Xi Jiang R. (shee jee ahng), *China* (24°N, 107°E)	124
Xiamen (shee ah muhn), *China* (25°N, 118°E)	124
Xian (shyee an), *China* (34°N, 109°E)	124
Xiang R. (shee ang), *China* (27°N, 112°E)	124
Xingu R. (sheeng GYOO), *Brazil* (5°S, 53°W)	90
Xuzhou (shyoo joh), *China* (34°N, 117°E)	124

Y

Yablanovyy Mts. (YAHB luh nuh VEE), *Russia* (53°N, 115°E)	100-101
Yakima (YAK ih MAW), *Wash.* (47°N, 121°W)	60
Yakima R., *Wash.* (46°N, 120°W)	60
Yakutsk, *Russia* (62°N, 130°E)	100
Yalong R. (yah long), *China* (32°N, 101°E)	124
Yalta (YAWL tuh), *Ukraine* (45°N, 34°E)	100
Yalu R. (yah loo), *Asia* (41°N, 125°E)	125
Yamal Pen., *Russia* (70°N, 70°E)	118
Yamoussoukro (YAHM uh SOO kroh), *Côte d'Ivoire* (7°N, 5°W)	108
Yampa R., *Colo.* (40°N, 109°W)	59
Yamuna R. (YAH muh nuh), *India* (27°N, 78°E)	122
Yangtze R., *China* (31°N, 110°E)	124
Yankton (YANG tuhn), *S. Dak.* (43°N, 97°W)	62
Yaounde (yah oon DAY), *Cameroon* (4°N, 12°E)	108
Yaqui R. (YAH kee), *Mexico* (28°N, 110°W)	82
Yarmouth, *Nova Scotia* (44°N, 66°W)	47
Yaroslavl, *Russia* (58°N, 40°E)	97
Yathkyed L. (YATH ky EHD), *Northwest Terr.* (63°N, 98°W)	45
Yatta Plateau, *Kenya* (2°S, 38°E)	110
Yazoo City, *Miss.* (33°N, 90°W)	68
Yazoo R., *Miss.* (33°N, 89°W)	68
Yekaterinburg, *Russia* (57°N, 61°E)	100
Yellow Sea, *Asia* (36°N, 123°E)	125
Yellowknife, *Northwest Terr.* (62°N, 114°W)	44
Yellowstone L., *Wyo.* (44°N, 110°W)	61
Yellowstone N.P., *Wyo.* (45°N, 110°W)	61
Yellowstone R., *U.S.* (46°N, 109°W)	61
Yemen, *country in Asia* (16°N, 44°E)	115
Yenisey R., *Russia* (68°N, 86°E)	118-119
Yerevan, *Armenia* (40°N, 45°E)	100
Yichang (yee chang), *China* (31°N, 112°E)	124
Yoho N. P., *British Columbia* (51°N, 117°W)	44
Yokohama, *Japan* (36°N, 140°E)	125
Yonkers, *N.Y.* (41°N, 74°W)	72
York, *England* (54°N, 1°W)	98
York, *Pa.* (40°N, 77°W)	72
York, Cape, *Australia* (11°S, 142°E)	130
Yorke Pen., *Australia* (34°S, 138°E)	133
Yorkton, *Saskatchewan* (51°N, 102°W)	45
Yorktown, *Va.* (37°N, 75°W)	71

176 Index

Name (Pronunciation), Description (Lat., Long.)	Page
Yosemite Falls (yoh SEHM ih tee), Calif. (38°N, 120°W)	58
Yosemite N.P., Calif. (38°N, 120°W)	58
Youngstown, Ohio (41°N, 81°W)	71
Yu R. (yoo), China (24°N, 107°E)	124
Yuan R. (yoo ahn), China (28°N, 110°E)	124
Yuba City (YOO buh), Calif. (39°N, 122°W)	58
Yucatan Channel (YOO kuh TAHN), Mexico and Cuba (22°N, 84°W)	83
Yucatan Pen., Mexico (20°N, 90°W)	83
Yugoslavia, country in Europe (45°N, 20°E)	99
Yukon R., North America (64°N, 160°W)	57
Yukon Territory, Canada (63°N, 135°W)	42
Yuma, Ariz. (33°N, 115°W)	58
Yunnan Plateau (yoo NAHN), China (26°N, 103°E)	124

Z

Name (Pronunciation), Description (Lat., Long.)	Page
Zadar (ZAHD AHR), Croatia (44°N, 15°E)	99
Zagreb, Croatia (46°N, 16°E)	99
Zagros Mts., Asia (35°N, 47°E)	115
Zahedan (ZAH hih DAHN), Iran (30°N, 61°E)	115
Zaire (ZAH IHR), country in Africa (3°S, 24°E)	107
Zambezi R., Africa (16°S, 33°E)	106
Zambia, country in Africa (15°S, 25°E)	107
Zanesville, Ohio (40°N, 82°W)	71
Zanzibar, city in Tanzania (6°S, 39°E)	110
Zanzibar, island in Indian O. (6°S, 40°E)	110
Zaria (ZAHR ee uh), Nigeria (11°N, 8°E)	108
Zaysan, L., Kazakhstan (48°N, 84°E)	100
Zhangjiakou (JAHNG zhee ah KOH), China (41°N, 115°E)	124

Name (Pronunciation), Description (Lat., Long.)	Page
Zhangzhou (jahng joh), China (25°N, 118°E)	124
Zhengzhou (jung joh), China (35°N, 114°E)	124
Zhitomir (ZHEE TOH meer), Ukraine (50°N, 29°E)	99
Zibo (dzee bwo), China (37°N, 118°E)	124
Ziguinchor (ZEE GAN SHOHR), Senegal (13°N, 16°W)	108
Zimbabwe, country in Africa (20°S, 30°E)	107
Zinder, Niger (14°N, 9°E)	107
Zion N. P. (ZY uhn), Utah (37°N, 113°W)	58-59
Zouirat, Mauritania (23°N, 12°W)	114
Zuni R. (ZOO nee), U.S. (35°N, 110°W)	59
Zunyi, China (28°N, 107°E)	124
Zurich (ZOO rik), Switzerland (47°N, 9°E)	99